W9-BUT-435

The Grain Trade in the Old Northwest

This book is the 1965 award winner of the Agricultural History Society

The Grain Trade

UNIVERSITY OF ILLINOIS PRESS

BY JOHN G. CLARK

in the Old Northwest

URBANA AND LONDON, 1966

To my father and mother,
EMMETT S. AND ELIZABETH L. CLARK

ACKNOWLEDGMENT

In 1963 this study was submitted to the Graduate School, Leland Stanford, Junior, University, as a dissertation in partial fulfillment of the requirements for the degree of Doctor of Philosophy. This phase of the study was accomplished under the capable direction of Professor David M. Potter, in whose debt I stand. Appreciation must also be tendered Professor Don E. Fehrenbacher of Stanford for his critical reading of the manuscript and to Mr. William McKeeman, lately of Stanford, who introduced me to the world of computer science.

Since 1963, the work has been considerably revised and additional debts accumulated. I wish especially to thank Professor George L. Anderson of the University of Kansas for his perceptive reading of the manuscript and his encouragement. The University of Kansas, through its General Research Fund, contributed materially to the completion of a final draft. My wife, Lois E. Clark, has been absolutely necessary in preparing the manuscript in each of its drafts.

A portion of the study dealing with New Orleans appeared in *Agricultural History*, 38 (July, 1964).

The author is responsible for all errors of fact and opinion.

J. G. C.

Lawrence, Kansas
March 22, 1966

CONTENTS

LIST OF TABLES

INTRODUCTION

In 1783 the area south of the Great Lakes and east of the Mississippi River was ceded to the United States by Britain in the Treaty of Paris. Within the next three years, the states of Virginia, Massachusetts, New York, and Connecticut, which had extensive claims to parts of this territory lying north of the Ohio River, in turn ceded their lands to the Confederation government. In 1787 the Northwest Ordinance, providing for the government of the Northwest Territory, was adopted by the Congress of the Confederation. Settlement, however, proceeded rather slowly during the next decade.

Several obstacles to effective settlement were present. British garrisons remained in various northwestern strongholds after the Treaty of Paris and did not withdraw until the negotiation of Jay's

Treaty provided for British evacuation before June 1, 1796. Conflicting Indian claims to large parts of the Northwest also served to retard settlement and stimulated serious unrest among the various tribes—unrest which was exacerbated by the continued presence of British troops in the Northwest. After the disastrous defeat of General Arthur St. Clair's forces in 1791 and the virtual end of American military power in the Northwest, emigration was reduced to a mere trickle. No progress was made in meeting the challenge of Indian power until General Anthony Wayne's victory at the Battle of Fallen Timbers in 1794, in northwestern Ohio. The signing of the Treaty of Greenville gave the United States clear title to the land of the Northwest Territory and curbed the military threat of the Indians in Ohio. The Indian problem was not, however, completely resolved until 1813. Legislative enactments providing for the survey and sale of lands in the Territory followed in 1796. Thus, between 1783 and 1796 the East North Central states were opened for settlement, and in 1802 Congress passed the Ohio Enabling Act, admitting to the Union the first public land state.

The Northwest Territory, ultimately divided into the states of Ohio, Indiana, Illinois, Michigan, and Wisconsin, formed a land area of some 238,000 square miles, compared to the approximately 340,000 square miles of the original 13 states. The soil and climate of a large part of the area were admirably suited for the production of cereals and the raising of large numbers of livestock. Some regions, such as the wet lands of east central Illinois or the marshy lands east of Toledo along the Lake Erie shore, would require extensive drainage before cultivation was possible. Most of the land, particularly that along the numerous rivers of Ohio, Indiana, and Illinois—such as the Scioto, Wabash, and Illinois—was of great fertility. So rich were the bottoms of the Scioto River valley that one traveler observed in 1818 a dung heap, bigger than the barn it surrounded and of such little value that the farmer thought it would be cheaper to move the barn than to remove or use the manure.[1]

In most of the East North Central states, spring wheat was sown in April or May, while the latter month was preferred for planting corn. In northeastern Ohio, the northern two-thirds of

---

[1] Thomas Hulme, *Journal of a Tour in the Western Countries of America —September 30, 1818–August 8, 1819*, in William Cobbett, *A Year's Residence in America* (Boston, 1824), 224. Morris Birkbeck, *Letters from Illinois* (Philadelphia, 1818), 36, noted a similar occurrence attesting to the nuisance value of manure and the natural richness of the land.

Michigan, slightly more than the southern one-half of Wisconsin, and most of Illinois and Indiana, the growing season averages from 120 to 150 days. In the extreme north of Michigan and Wisconsin, the average is from 90 to 120 days. Southwestern Indiana and southern Illinois often have over 200 days without a killing frost. Harvest time arrived in the middle of July for wheat and rye and during the latter part of the month for oats. Corn was generally gathered in October, or left to stand in the fields, into which live-stock was often driven to feed off it. In many areas it was common for winter wheat to be sown between the rows of standing corn.[2] Soft winter wheats were the preferred crop for most of the North-west until the 1850's. At that time, farmers along the Illinois-Wisconsin border experienced much difficulty with winter wheat due to severe winters and were compelled to turn to spring wheat. In most of the Northwest the climate was suitable for winter wheat.

Throughout the entire antebellum period, the critical time for each farmer was the harvest period, which normally had to be completed within two weeks. It was at this crucial moment that most farmers were completely dependent upon their own labor and that of their families, for hired labor was scarce and expensive. Under these circumstances, it was more expedient for farmers, as soon as the repeated cropping of the lands resulted in falling yields of grain per acre, to "make a purchase of new land in the neighborhood or even to sell their cleared land, and proceed in quest of a new set-tlement, than to adopt a system of rotation of crops assisted by manure."[3] In spite of the sometimes overwhelming obstacles and the primitive conditions of agricultural techniques, the yields of the virgin lands were often immense—60 to 80 bushels of corn per acre and 20 to 30 bushels of wheat. And during the course of the period under review, 1815 to 1860, while the yield on older lands became less bountiful, new lands were put into cultivation which more than compensated for the declining fruitfulness of the old.

In 1796 C. F. Volney, a French visitor to the Ohio valley, stood on the bank of the Scioto River admiring corn reaching upwards of

---

[2] Daniel Drake, *Natural and Statistical View or Picture of Cincinnati and the Miami Country* (Cincinnati, 1815), 89-90; John Woods, *Two Years Residence in the Settlement on the English Prairie in the Illinois Country, United States* . . . (London, 1822), 220; William C. Howells, *Recollections of Life in Ohio from 1813 to 1840* (Cincinnati, 1895), 148-149.

[3] James Stuart, *Three Years in North America* (2 vols., 3rd ed., Edinburgh, 1833), I, 258.

12 feet and thought that at some future date the Northwest would be the Flanders of the United States for corn and cattle.[4] In due time this prophecy was realized, and the East North Central states became the granary of the United States and an important contributor to the grain trade of the Western World.

The relative importance of the East North Central states to the wheat production of the United States reached its peak in 1859, when the five states produced 79 million bushels, or 46 per cent of the nation's crop. In 1869, although wheat production rose by 40 million bushels, the Northwest's share of the total showed a slight decline to 44 per cent. The center of wheat production, reaching the East North Central states by 1860, then shifted to the trans-Mississippi West. By 1899 the trans-Mississippi West produced over 65 per cent of the nation's crop, and over 90 per cent a decade later.

Corn was more widely distributed than wheat during the nineteenth century. In the pre–Civil War years, the South produced more corn than the Northwest until the decade of the 1850's. In 1859 the five states under consideration produced 33 per cent of the corn harvested in the United States, and a decade later 36 per cent. Thereafter the proportion declined, and by 1899 the West North Central states produced 40 per cent of the country's corn.[5] But Illinois, Indiana, and Ohio still raised a significant portion of the crop.[6] It was this potential which Volney recognized while gazing at the Scioto cornfields.

In 1815 the obstacles to such a development in the Northwest seemed insuperable. Population, reaching 270,000 in 1810, was insufficient to provide much of a local market for grain. The only route to an outside market was the Ohio-Mississippi river system which provided an outlet only to Ohio, Indiana, and Illinois, and then only to those sections which were watered by streams tributary to the Ohio or Mississippi. Settlement first concentrated along these streams. Those farmers in close proximity to a navigable stream, none navigable at all times, were faced with the hazards of shipping via those waterways to the unpredictable grain market at

---

[4] C. F. Volney, *View of the Climate and Soil of the United States of America to Which Are Annexed Some Accounts of Florida, the French Colony on the Scioto, Certain Canadian Colonies, and the Savages or Natives* (London, 1804), 28-29.

[5] This includes the states of Minnesota, Iowa, Missouri, North and South Dakota, Nebraska, and Kansas.

[6] This discussion is based on the Federal Census, 1850-1900.

New Orleans or other equally uncertain markets along the lower Mississippi. Innumerable delays, caused by low water or slack markets; excessive cost in time, particularly in making the return trip prior to the advent of steamboats; the danger of spoilage ruining the barreled pork or flour; the constant threat of shipwreck—all made the trade highly speculative and perilous. Steamboats ameliorated these conditions, but not sufficiently to eliminate the inherent dangers of shipping over natural waterways. All of these practical limitations of the southern route had an important effect upon the commodities exported. For the most part, bulk cereals formed a negligible part of exports during the entire period. Grain was shipped in concentrated forms—flour, pork, lard, whiskey—which could better stand the cost of freight and were more easily handled. In the southern trade, derivatives of corn were most valuable and exported in larger quantities than flour.

In 1815 the Northwest did not utilize the Great Lakes route to eastern markets. Here the initial physical impediments to the development of such a trade appeared more insurmountable than in the river trade. The rivers emptying into the lakes were smaller and of less commercial utility than those flowing south from the watersheds of the Northwest. Moreover, as late as 1824 there was no route to the Atlantic coast cut through from the eastern end of the Great Lakes. As a result, the more northerly regions of Ohio, Indiana, and Illinois were settled less rapidly than regions in the Ohio basin. In 1815 Cleveland was struggling for existence, and the few other inhabited spots, such as Detroit and Prairie du Chien, were sustained by the fur trade. The Indian tribes, too, were an obstacle to the settlement of the northernmost regions of trans-Appalachia. Not until the Battle of the Thames in 1813 was the military threat of the Indians in the Northwest eliminated.

The consequences of all this were to place a severe limit on the ability of settlers in the Northwest to develop economically. The inhabitants were primarily farmers, whose prosperity depended upon agricultural development. But with markets so inaccessible, the incentive to increase production was lacking. The region was constrained to function on a subsistence level of agriculture. The grain trade down the Mississippi River was not an overly important auxiliary in view of the small surplus available for shipment. Moreover, not all of the inhabitants were able to use the route. The economy of the Northwest was essentially of a local or, at the most, of a regional nature. Henry Adams, in describing the state of the Republic in 1800, wrote that:

half a million people had crossed the Alleghanies and were struggling with difficulties all their own, in an isolation like that of Jutes or Angles in the fifth century. . . .

The valley of the Ohio had no more to do with that of the Hudson, the Susquehanna, the Potomac, the Roanoke, and the Santee, than the valley of the Danube with that of the Rhone, the Po, or the Elbe.

[N]ature was rather man's master than his servant, and the five million Americans struggling with the untamed continent seemed hardly more competent to their task than the beavers and buffalo which had for countless generations made bridges and roads of their own.[7]

This had quite as much applicability to the United States of 1815 as of 1800.

Within a generation, these conditions were to undergo a radical transformation, amounting in certain phases to changes of revolutionary proportions. Under the stimulus of the Erie Canal and the canal systems of Ohio, Indiana, and Illinois, the major focus of the grain trade shifted from the Ohio-Mississippi route to the Great Lakes. With markets accessible to larger areas of the East North Central states, agriculture emerged from its self-sufficient stage and became increasingly commercialized. The opening of the lake route to the East stimulated the trade in bulk wheat, necessitating constant improvements in the methods of handling and storing the grain. Large areas unable to avail themselves of canal transportation were shortly provided with even speedier, safer, and cheaper facilities. Railroads, penetrating the Northwest, enabled previously isolated regions to participate in the commerce of the country. In the 1850's railroads were of primary importance in transporting cereals from the centers of production to secondary markets such as Chicago, which owed its great growth to the railroad. At the eastern end of the lakes, railroads competed with the Erie Canal and St. Lawrence River routes to tidewater. During the decade of the 1840's, the grain trade of the East North Central states was transformed from an exchange of largely local consequences to one dependent upon intersectional communications and serving the needs of vast areas in the East and South. Simultaneously, an increasing quantity of grain from the East North Central states found its way to overseas markets, particularly to Great Britain. Between

---

[7] Henry Adams, *History of the United States of America During the Administration of Thomas Jefferson* (2 vols. in 1, New York, 1930), 5-8.

1850 and 1860 the invasion of the foreign grain market advanced more rapidly than at any period since 1800, both relatively and absolutely. But the predominant role of the grain trade of the Northwest resided in its ability to feed the nation. By 1860 the Northwest was the feeding power—the Flanders of the United States.

The Grain Trade of the
Old Northwest Before the
Transportation Revolution

In 1840, the first year in which over-all statistics of grain production in the United States are available, the East North Central states produced 31 per cent of the nation's wheat and 23 per cent of the corn. Ohio was the largest wheat-producing state and only Kentucky, Tennessee, and Virginia surpassed Ohio, Indiana, and Illinois in total corn production. The region had a population of just under 3 million, representing 17 per cent of the national total. One-half resided in Ohio, which was the third most populous state in the country in 1840. Though the population of the Northwest was relatively small, these states, excluding Wisconsin, produced almost twice as much wheat per capita as any other section.[1]

---

[1] *Compendium of the Sixth Census of the United States for 1840* (Washington, D.C., 1840), 78, 82, 86, 94, 102, 287-288, 323-324, 374-378 (hereafter cited as *[no.] Census, [year]*). The population of the East North Central states

In 1840 the Erie Canal had been open for 15 years. Its effect on the nation in general and the Northwest in particular was great, direct, and cumulative throughout the entire antebellum period. As the Ohio River had provided a natural avenue leading west over which thousands of immigrants could travel and settle the southern portions of Ohio, Indiana, and Illinois, so the Erie Canal furnished an all-water route to the northern portions of those states, and in addition much accelerated the peopling of Wisconsin and Michigan. During the first decade of its operation, the Erie Canal had its greatest effect in developing the south shore of Lake Erie. A rising population resulted in an expansion of production to meet the needs of the emigrants and an augmented demand for the importation of eastern manufactured goods. At the same time, the Erie Canal reduced considerably the cost of freighting goods both east and west.[2] Perhaps most important of all the ramifying consequences of the Erie was the stimulation and incentive it gave to Ohio in the late 1820's and 1830's, and Indiana and Illinois somewhat later, to undertake the construction of their own internal improvements joining interior areas to the Great Lakes. It was only when this was done that the Northwest, and particularly Ohio in the 1830's, could take full advantage of the connection opened up to the Atlantic coast.

A rising population and increased production should not be taken to mean, however, that the East North Central states, by the 1830's, were well moved into the role of serving as the dominant grain supplier of the United States. The Erie Canal and other avenues of trade, either by waterway or by rail, were ultimately to bring these states to a high degree of specialization in supplying grain for urban markets on the eastern seaboard and in Europe. This process of specialization, although visible in local areas within the Northwest by 1840, had not yet advanced very far. In fact, only a

grew rapidly, from 792,000 or 8 per cent of the national population in 1820, to 12 per cent of the population in 1830, and 17 per cent in 1840. Thereafter, to 1860, the population, though still increasing at a more rapid rate than the United States as a whole, rose at a reduced rate and formed 22 per cent of the total population in 1860.

[2] Freight rates between Buffalo and Albany were at once reduced 90 per cent. A hundredweight of goods via the Erie Canal could be transported from New York to Columbus, Ohio, for 35 per cent less cost than from Philadelphia, although the distance from the latter was much less. *Niles Weekly Register,* XXIX (December 24, 1825), 262 (hereafter cited as *NWR*). See also Isaac Lippincott, *Internal Trade of the United States, 1700-1860* (St. Louis, 1916), 116, 137-139.

few areas within the region, notably in Ohio, had made the transition from a basically subsistence to a predominantly commercial agriculture. Ohio alone, as Table 2 suggests, was in a position to furnish significant quantities of grain for export.

The conditions existing in most areas of the Northwest were such as to preclude a large grain trade. Population, outside of Ohio, was relatively small and insufficiently concentrated to allow large productivity or trade. Access to markets was limited to those areas adjacent to navigable streams, or the two major canals constructed by Ohio after 1825. Even within Ohio large areas of the state were too distant from the canals to make shipments economically feasible. River systems, then, were essential, and these were supplemented only by primitive and often unserviceable roads. By 1840 the conditions had been altered significantly only in Ohio to allow a grain trade of some substance to appear along the lakes and to allow the Ohio river trade to develop more fully.[3]

That transportation facilities were to be a key factor in the overall development of the United States was widely acknowledged by the 1820's. As early as 1810, Congressman Peter Buel Porter of New York, in a speech in the House, argued that the paramount evil from which the West suffered was the want of a market.[4] Western abundance, handicapped by the lack of a market at home and by the prohibitive expense and difficulty of getting the surplus to an Atlantic port, found its only outlet to the South through New Orleans. There was no doubt that the inadequacy of transportation, both in the East and even more in the West, would, if uncorrected, have a retarding effect on American development.

The old trails and traces into the interior had, with wear and usage, become roads, and as farmers settled and cleared their land along these routes branches shot out from the parent stem to the numerous embryo towns sprouting off the main road. These roads were, however, rarely functional for purposes of heavy commercial transportation. Rain turned a road into an impassable quagmire. Bridges over the innumerable streams and creeks intersecting the roads were few, poorly constructed, and just as likely to disappear with a freshet. With roads in such primitive condition Americans

---

[3] From 1820 to 1840 Ohio's population increased by almost 950,000. Of this, 582,000 were added between 1830 and 1840. This was the greatest increase which Ohio was to experience until 1900-1910.

[4] *Annals of Congress,* 11 Cong., 2 Sess. (1809-10), 1388.

in 1820, as in 1750, depended upon their streams and rivers to move themselves and most of their merchandise. And these streams held their own uncertainties: sudden freshets, rapids, snags, drought, sand bars, floating debris at all times imperiled both crew and vessel.[5]

As of 1820 the federal government had done little to meet the growing demand of the West for connections with the eastern seaboard or for local river improvements, except to provide the Cumberland Road, completed to Wheeling in 1818.[6] Most of the internal improvements projects that had been completed or started were privately inaugurated ventures which received occasional and minimal state support.

Land carriage was far too costly for the grain producer to send large quantities any great distance. Vast sums of money were expended upon turnpikes, but this was not the answer to the problem of the farmer. Robert Fulton wrote Albert Gallatin that it cost $1 to ship a barrel of flour to Philadelphia from a point 79 miles distant.[7] Wheat which sold at 50 cents a bushel in western New York cost from 75 cents to $1 a bushel to transport to New York City.[8] Flour in New York brought from two to four times the amount it sold for in Cincinnati or Pittsburgh. Farmers were totally dependent upon natural waterways as the means of transporting their sur-

---

[5] The literature of the Old Northwest is replete with caustic comments of travelers, both American and foreign, regarding the abominable conditions of American roads and the perils faced on navigable waterways. Among the best are F. A. Michaux, *Travels to the West of the Alleghany Mountains, in the States of Ohio, Kentucky, and Tennessee and Back to Charleston, by the Upper Carolines* (London, 1805), reprinted in Reuben G. Thwaites, ed., *Early Western Travels, 1748-1846* (32 vols., Cleveland, 1904), III; Estwick Evans, *A Pedestrious Tour of Four Thousand Miles Through the Western States and Territories During the Winter and Spring of 1818. Interspersed with Brief Reflections upon a Great Variety of Topics: Religious, Moral, Political, Sentimental &c. &c.* (Concord, N.H., 1819), reprinted in *ibid.*, VIII; James Flint, *Letters from America Containing Observations on the Climate and Agriculture of the Western States, the Manners of the People, the Prospects of Emigrants, &c. &c.* (Edinburgh, 1822), reprinted in *ibid.*, IX.

[6] The classic statement of American transportation needs is found in Albert Gallatin, "Report on Roads and Canals, Communicated to the Senate, April 6, 1808," *American State Papers*, 37, *Miscellaneous*, I, 724-921. Gallatin, in recommending that the central government expend some $20 million in developing a comprehensive and national transportation network, was mindful that private or state capital, without the active financial aid of the federal government, could not accomplish such a tremendous undertaking.

[7] *Ibid.*, 917-920.

[8] Porter speech in *Annals*, 11 Cong., 2 Sess., 1394.

plus to market. Moreover, transportation inadequacies compelled
farmers to produce what could best stand a protracted shipment or
could best be converted into a form inexpensive enough to ship.
Throughout the 1820's and 1830's, the West shipped south and received overland manufactured goods from the East while agitating
in seeming futility for the means to ship their produce directly to
the Atlantic seaboard.

Ohio's commerce during most of the antebellum period was to
a large degree based on her excellent river system, supplemented
by canals after the late 1820's. The more important of Ohio's interior rivers were tributary to the Ohio River, and of these, the Scioto,
the Muskingum, and the Miami were most significant. These south-
flowing streams were in general larger and more frequently navigable for greater distances than streams such as the Cuyahoga,
Maumee, or Sandusky, which emptied into Lake Erie. This meant
that even after the Erie Canal was opened, the area in Ohio which
could connect with the lake and canal system was far smaller than
the area which could still connect with the Ohio and Mississippi
system. It was in the valleys of the streams which provided these
connections that settlement first concentrated, attracted by the comparatively good navigability available and the wonderful fertility
of the deep, black, alluvial soil. Marvelous stories of the fertility of
the soil in these river valleys filtered through to the receptive ears
of restless Easterners.[9]

Ohio experienced its first population boom after 1815, but in
1830 most people were still concentrated in the southern half of the
state. In the fertile valleys of rivers flowing toward the Ohio, the
pioneer farmers, and even those that followed them, operated in a
largely noncommercial, family economy. There were few markets
even for those in the immediate vicinity of a navigable stream. One
settler, farming some 35 miles from the Ohio River, wrote that 50
cents a bushel at the river was a great price for wheat, but "as two
horses and a man were required for four days to make the journey,
in good weather . . . it was not to be expected that we could realize

---

[9] Other Ohio River tributaries included the Hockhocking, Little Miami,
and Big Beaver rivers. For a good contemporary account of Ohio, and especially
the Miami valley region, see Daniel Drake, *Natural and Statistical View or Picture of Cincinnati and the Miami Country* (Cincinnati, 1815). According to a
British traveler's description of corn in the Scioto valley in 1837, "Fields of
corn with the stalks rising to a height of 18 feet are common all over the valley,
and in some particular spots, it has been known to reach the . . . height of
25 feet." J. S. Buckingham, *America, Historical, Statistical, and Descriptive*
(3 vols., London, 1841), III, 373-374.

more than twenty-five cents in cash for it. But there was no sale
for it in cash. The minimal price for it in trade was usually thirty
cents . . . ." [10]

Although some grain was shipped, it was neither of sufficient
quantity nor was it produced solely for sale in a particular market
and cannot be considered strictly commercial agriculture. The situation was exacerbated for the farmer by a number of factors: the
limited technological knowledge at his disposal; the sheer physical
difficulties encountered in clearing and fencing his land, raising a
house, sowing and reaping a crop—the effective size of which, when
drought, disease, frost, or some other natural calamity did not inter-
fere, was determined by the quantity of labor brought to bear at
harvest time; and the limited and high price of hired labor. Under
such conditions the farmer was fortunate if he could exist from year
to year without plunging perilously into debt and its consequences
—mortgages and foreclosure.

Corn and wheat were the principal crops of Ohio. The former
grain, prepared in a score of different ways, was the principal food
of the earlier settlers. Although wheat was the more important cash
crop, corn was of greater general utility and the early farmers depended upon it more fully than wheat, both for their own suste-
nance and for that of their livestock. Many farmers cultivated corn
in sufficient quantities to allow them to sell all their wheat to millers
for eventual export. Rye, although popular as a food crop in the
pre-1830 period, was generally utilized in a distillery or used as
feed for livestock. For the latter purpose, however, corn was the
staple grain used. Barley was not cultivated to any great extent
except in the immediate vicinity of breweries.[11]

Corn, the most versatile crop, yielded between 60 and 100
bushels per acre in the verdant river bottoms of the Miami and

---

[10] William Cooper Howells, *Recollections of Life in Ohio from 1813 to
1840* (Cincinnati, 1895), 138. W. Faux, *Memorable Days in America: Being a
Journal of a Tour to the United States. Principally Undertaken to Ascertain, by
Positive Evidence, the Conditions and Probable Prospects of British Emigrants;
Including Accounts of Mr. Birkbeck's Settlement in the Illinois: And Intended
to Show Men and Things as They Are in America* (London, 1823), reprinted
in Thwaites, *Early Western Travels*, XI, 290-291, observed that farmers were
so short of capital as to be forced to sell as soon as possible after harvest, even
though prices were sure to be higher the following spring. Morris Birkbeck,
*Notes on a Journey in America from the Coast of Virginia to the Territory of
Illinois* . . . (Dublin, 1818), 141, commented in a similar vein about the pressures forcing farmers to sell low instead of holding their crop for a rise in prices.

[11] Drake, *Natural View of Cincinnati*, 54-56; Flint, *Letters from America*,
117; Michaux, *Travels to the West*, 190-191; W. A. Lloyd, J. I. Falconer, and

Scioto and could be marketed in bulk, or as meat, either in barrels or on the hoof, or as whiskey. During the period before 1840, most of the corn reached market in its concentrated forms.[12]

Cattle fattened on the lush grasses of the Scioto prairies were driven to market in Baltimore as early as 1804. The trade increased gradually until a drop in wheat prices at the close of the War of 1812 gave added impetus to the raising and feeding of livestock. Timothy Flint, while crossing the western ridges of the Alleghenies, encountered a drive of more than 1,000 cattle and swine from the Mad River country in Ohio.[13] This trade continued, though never reaching great proportions, until the railroads made it possible to ship livestock through from states west of Ohio, where they were raised more cheaply. But before this had occurred, the pork trade and hog raising had risen to a predominant position in the livestock industry of Ohio.[14]

C. E. Thorne, *The Agriculture of Ohio* (Wooster, Ohio, 1918), 54. Oats, barley, and rye were generally of local importance and entered but little into either domestic or foreign commerce. These grains were worth considerably less in proportion to their weight than wheat, or even corn. Oats, the most important, yielded about one-half as much weight per bushel as wheat or corn. Thus, it would cost twice as much to ship per bushel. There were but few instances before 1860 when transportation costs were so low as to allow the profitable shipment of oats any distance.

[12] Paul W. Gates, *The Farmer's Age: Agriculture 1815-1860* (New York, 1960), 48, maintains that the southern demand for corn early stimulated production in the Ohio valley, but Cincinnati's bulk corn exports were negligible until the late 1840's. Charles Cist, *Cincinnati in 1841: Its Early Annals and Future Prospects* (Cincinnati, 1841), 84; C. P. McClelland and C. C. Huntington, *History of the Ohio Canals. Their Construction, Cost, Use and Partial Abandonment* (Columbus, Ohio, 1905), Appendix J, 177.

[13] Timothy Flint, *Recollections of the Last Ten Years* (Boston, 1826), 9. William Renick, *Memoirs, Correspondence and Reminiscences* (Circleville, Ohio, 1880), 12, was one of the first to make the drive east. John Melish, *Travels in the United States of America, in the Years 1806 & 1807, and 1809, 1810, & 1811* . . . (2 vols., Philadelphia, 1812), II, 246, observed large numbers of livestock raised in Coshocton, 30 miles north of Zanesville, for the eastern market. He noted that cattle worth over $2,000 had been raised and sold off one 90-acre tract.

[14] The *Sangamo Journal*, September 17, 1841, in reporting a cattle drive from Peoria, through Springfield, for sale in Ohio, recalled that in the mid-1830's Ohio and Indiana cattle were arriving for sale in Illinois. During the intervening years, it had become cheaper to raise cattle in Illinois than in Ohio. Although most of Ohio's pork was exported in the barrel to the South, some hogs were driven to the Atlantic in the late 1830's and 1840's. James Hall, *Notes on the Western States: Containing Descriptive Sketches of Their Soil, Climate, Resources, and Scenery* (Philadelphia, 1838), 275, wrote of the passage of 69,000 hogs, mostly from Ohio, through Kentucky toward South Carolina. (The pork and whiskey industry will be dealt with in greater detail in Chapter VI.)

Before 1835 Ohio's exports were dependent upon river routes to the South, and the major market was New Orleans. It is difficult to reconstruct the size of Ohio's trade in the period prior to 1839 with anything approaching precision. Neither bulk wheat nor bulk corn was an important part of the trade. Both grains were converted into forms more easily transportable and worth more in proportion to their weight than the bulk grains. Wheat was exported as flour. Corn went mainly in what was known in the trade as provisions— pork, lard, hams and bacon, and other pork products—and as whiskey. In the early period flour was the most important single product, but provisions and whiskey together were probably of greater value after 1825.

After the War of 1812, the flour trade of Ohio with New Orleans became very precarious. Prices were quite low—25 cents per bushel in store goods being a high price for wheat.[15] Shipments of flour on the Ohio River seem to have remained at a fairly stable level, amounting to some 200,000 to 300,000 barrels between 1820 and 1830. Most of this, along with some 200,000 bushels of corn and oats, and perhaps 30,000 to 50,000 barrels of pork and 75,000 barrels of whiskey annually, were carried downstream on some 3,000 flatboats and 100 or so steamboats.[16] Most of Ohio's produce was shipped from Cincinnati, but large quantities also descended the Muskingum and Scioto rivers from centers like Zanesville, Circleville, and Chillicothe. Circleville was reported to have shipped over $100,000 worth of produce down the Scioto in 1822, and over 130 flatboats were reported descending the Miami in 1826, loaded with over 30,000 barrels of flour not included in Cincinnati's exports.[17]

---

[15] Renick, *Memoirs*, 11. Cincinnati flour in the late summer of 1820 was priced at $2.25, *NWR*, XXII (August 24, 1822), 406, while at Dayton flour was nominally priced at $2.50, wheat at 30 cents, and corn at 12 cents, *ibid.* (June 8, 1822), 239; and in 1824 corn at Cincinnati was 8 cents a bushel, *ibid.*, XXIII (October 23, 1824), 123.

[16] Frank H. Dixon, *A Traffic History of the Mississippi River System* (Washington, D.C., 1909), 17, estimates that flour comprised 25 per cent of the value of all the products descending the Mississippi. *Western Journal of Commerce*, II, 87, quoted in Isaac Lippincott, *A History of Manufactures in the Ohio Valley to the Year 1860* (Chicago, 1914), 87, for 1819; *NWR*, XX (June 9, 1821), 239, XXXIII (November 3, 1827), 150. There is no indication that steamboats had any pronounced effect on the quantities of produce descending the river, as by far the larger part of the surplus went downstream on flatboats.

[17] William F. Gephart, *Transportation and Industrial Development in the Middle West* (New York, 1909), 103; Benjamin Drake and E. D. Mansfield, *Cincinnati in 1826* (Cincinnati, 1827), 78.

Thus it is very difficult to use data on the river traffic as the basis for estimating the grain production in, or the grain trade of, Ohio or its parts. The problem is further complicated by the fact that some of the flour passing down the upper Ohio was from western Pennsylvania and western Virginia, while some of the export originating at Pittsburgh and Wheeling was of Ohio production.[18]

Concerning Cincinnati in 1820, an Englishman wrote that the town's great importance was readily apparent. "A large steam grist mill, three large steamboats on the stocks, and two more on the Kentucky side . . . attracted my attention. The beach is lined with keel boats, large arks for carrying produce, family boats, and rafts of lumber. On shore the utmost bustle prevails, with drays carrying imported goods, salt, iron, and timber, up to the town and in bringing pork, flour, &c. to be put aboard of boats for New Orleans." [19]

With a population of some 12,000 in 1824, which had increased to about 31,000 by 1848, Cincinnati had several large woolen and cotton factories, some glass and iron works, at least two breweries,

---

[18] Pittsburgh was a major distributing center for goods from the East until the Great Lakes route surpassed it. Even after Pennsylvania's system of canals was completed in 1840—14 years in the building—only insignificant quantities of western produce utilized this passage to reach the East. Wheeling and Pittsburgh were constant rivals for the eastern trade. Wheeling served as the western terminal of Baltimore, and Pittsburgh as the western end of Philadelphia's trade network. Thus, the two cities functioned within the general framework of commercial rivalry between Baltimore and Philadelphia. George W. Ogden, *Letters from the West, Comprising a Tour Through the Western Country and a Residence of Two Summers in the States of Ohio and Kentucky: Originally Written in Letters to a Brother*, reprinted in Thwaites, *Early Western Travels*, XIX, 27; Henry B. Fearon, *Sketches of America. A Narrative of a Journey of Five Thousand Miles Through the Eastern and Western States of America* . . . (2nd ed., London, 1818), 186-205; Richard C. Wade, *The Urban Frontier: The Rise of Western Cities, 1790-1830* (Cambridge, Mass., 1959), 166-169. J. Leander Bishop, *A History of American Manufactures from 1608 to 1860* . . . (2 vols., Philadelphia, 1864), II, 404, estimates that 280,000 barrels of flour were manufactured in 1836 at Pittsburgh.

[19] Flint, *Letters from America*, 149. The steam grist mill, Cincinnati's largest structure, was erected in 1812-14. It was 110 feet high and capable of producing 700 barrels of flour weekly. It burned in 1823 and was rebuilt by 1826 with decreased flour-manufacturing capacity, but with a distillery and fulling mill added. Drake and Mansfield, *Cincinnati in 1826*, 60. By 1828 Cincinnati reported well over 700 steamboat arrivals yearly. *NWR*, XXXIV (June 28, 1828), 284. By 1832 over 130 steamboats had been constructed at its shipyards. Patrick Shirreff, *A Tour Through North America Together with a Comprehensive View of the Canadas and United States as Adapted for Agricultural Emigration* (Edinburgh, 1835), 282-283.

and a few distilleries. Her pork industry was still in its infancy and was not to approach maturity until the 1830's.[20]

Until the mid-1820's flour was Cincinnati's most valuable export. Most of the flour shipped from the town was received already processed and was merely reshipped at the wharves. The export business was mainly derived from surplus produced and carried via wagons or the Miami River from surrounding counties. This tributary area expanded but little until the Whitewater Canal enabled Cincinnati to tap southeastern Ohio, and again in the middle 1840's when railroads made it possible to ship produce to Cincinnati from counties isolated from either the Miami or Scioto rivers.

In 1825, in response to a growing southern demand for provisions, exports of pork, lard, ham, and bacon exceeded those of flour in value. Annual flour exports fluctuated between 27,000 and 58,000 barrels between 1820 and 1828, with an export value of between $165,000 and $200,000. In 1830, with the Miami and Erie Canal completed to Dayton, exports of flour jumped to about 130,000 barrels, about the upper limit of flour exports until 1840. This did not represent a very impressive increase over a 20-year period, and the flour trade did not maintain its relative importance in Cincinnati's total export trade. Total exports increased from about $1,000,000 in 1826 to $4,000,000 in 1832 and $9,000,000 in 1839. Simultaneously, pork packing and other hog derivatives increased in importance. In 1825 the value of pork exports formed 30 per cent of Cincinnati's total exports, and in 1839 44 per cent. Pork leadership was maintained through 1860 with flour, grain, and whiskey next in value.[21]

One significant event in the story of Cincinnati's expanding commerce was the construction of the Miami and Erie Canal from Cincinnati to Dayton between 1825 and 1828, and extension north to Toledo in 1837. The canal was an important route by which Cin-

---

[20] Drake, *Natural View of Cincinnati*, 147; John Woods, *Two Years Residence in the Settlement on the English Prairie in the Illinois Country, United States* . . . (London, 1822), 99; James Hall, *The West: Its Commerce and Navigation* (Cincinnati, 1848), 266. Lloyd, Falconer, and Thorne, *Agriculture of Ohio*, 67, note that the Scioto country packed more pork in the early 1820's than Cincinnati.

[21] R. Carlyle Buley, *The Old Northwest. Pioneer Period. 1815-1840* (2 vols., Indianapolis, 1950), I, 527, for exports in the 1820's; Cist, *Cincinnati in 1841*, for exports in the 1830's; Drake and Mansfield, *Cincinnati in 1826*, 77; Thomas S. Berry, *Western Prices Before 1861. A Study of the Cincinnati Market* (Cambridge, Mass., 1943), 216-220, for the early hog trade.

cinnati received grain supplies. In June, 1828, just before the canal
reached Dayton, 67 miles to the north, Cincinnati received via the
canal 276 barrels of whiskey, 531 barrels of flour, 200 barrels of
corn, and assorted pork products—the first fruits of the extensive
program of internal improvements undertaken by Ohio in 1825.[22]

Receipts via the Miami Canal increased from 1828 to 1831 and
then leveled off for the remainder of the decade, while receipts at
Portsmouth, the southern terminal of the Ohio Canal, never did
reach a high level. In both ports very little bulk wheat was received, but mostly flour, pork, and whiskey. In fact, the total impact of the canals was much less dramatic in southern than in
northern Ohio.

In the south, no new market opportunities were created; conditions for shipment were somewhat improved by the canals and
freight rates to the Ohio River may have been lowered. Dayton, for
instance, at the confluence of the Miami and Mad rivers, had been
shipping southward on flatboats since 1800. In 1818, 1,700 barrels
of flour were exported to New Orleans. The opening of the Miami
Canal meant merely that the river was supplemented by a more
reliable parallel route that led directly to Cincinnati.[23] The effect
of the canals in southern Ohio was less striking because this region
was already rather fully settled and had developed a more mature
economy compared with that in the north. This development occurred largely as a consequence of the excellent river connections
existing in the south and due to the fact that the Ohio River itself
was a major avenue for immigrants. Moreover, a large number of
settlers entered the Northwest from points south of the Ohio River
like western Virginia and Kentucky.

In the northern region of Ohio, although the Erie Canal had
been opened since 1825, farmers in the interior were unable to utilize this potential route to the East until the early 1830's. At that
time the Ohio Canal was completed from Cleveland to Portsmouth.
Prior to this connection, the Erie Canal functioned primarily as a
route by which immigrants and eastern manufactured goods gained
entrance to the growing market in western New York and along the
Lake Erie shore. With the completion of the Ohio Canal in 1832,
farmers in the interior of Ohio were given access to Lake Erie and

---

[22] *NWR*, XXXIV (June 28, 1828), 284.
[23] *Hunt's Merchants' Magazine*, XXVI (May, 1852), 572-573 (hereafter
cited as *Hunt's*).

a new market in the East via the Erie Canal. Certain areas in central Ohio were able to utilize both northern and southern routes. Zanesville's traditional route was via the Muskingum River to the Ohio, and the Muskingum Improvement project facilitated the shipment of produce considerably, but Zanesville could and did ship to Dresden, on the Ohio Canal, and then to Cleveland.[24]

After 1835, points in central Ohio near the canals had a choice of alternate routes to market; south to the Ohio and New Orleans; south to the Ohio and then up-river to Pittsburgh and Philadelphia via the Pennsylvania system of canals and inclined planes; north on the Ohio Canal to Cleveland and Buffalo; or north to Cleveland, the Welland Canal, which opened a passage from Lake Erie to Lake Ontario, and thence to Lake Ontario ports or to Montreal. Of these routes, that to the south and that to Buffalo assumed the greatest importance. Produce south of a latitudinal line running through Columbus-Newark-Zanesville-Steubenville has generally been thought of as moving in a southerly direction. This division of Ohio into two more or less separate market structures is of little importance before 1835, when there was no traffic moving north to speak of, and was significantly modified by railroads in the 1850's. Moreover, even during the period after 1835 and before the railroads, much flour and wheat from south of this line flowed to Cleveland and other Lake Erie ports. It is true, however, that very little wheat went south while more corn, whiskey, and provisions took the southern route. The geographical division in Ohio is often extended westward to apply to the remainder of the Old Northwest, but it has less pertinence to Indiana, still less to Illinois, and none at all to Michigan and Wisconsin.[25]

The new transportation improvements of the 1830's and the completion of the Wabash and Erie Canal to Toledo in 1842 were of greatest benefit to Cleveland and Toledo and their tributary regions. The canals enabled both towns to reach far back into the

---

[24] The impact of the Ohio Canal, in terms of production and population, upon the Lake Erie shore and areas inland from Lake Erie will be taken up in greater detail in Chapter III.

[25] A. L. Kohlmeier, *The Old Northwest as the Keystone of the Arch of the American Federal Union. A Study in Commerce and Politics* (Bloomington, Ind., 1938), 19-20, makes much of this geographical split in Ohio's market system. Abraham H. Sadove, *Transport Improvement and the Appalachian Barrier. A Case Study in Economic Innovation* (Harvard University, unpublished doctoral dissertation, 1950), 142; Buley, *The Old Northwest*, I, 535.

interior of Ohio for farm produce while simultaneously expanding
the area in which manufactured goods were distributed.

Situated on the bend which the Cuyahoga River makes before
emptying into Lake Erie, Cleveland received her first canal boat in
July, 1827, laden with flour and whiskey from Portage Summit—
38 miles distant. From that moment, as Table 1 indicates, Cleveland's trade and over-all prosperity rose quickly while her population increased from under 2,000 in 1832 to over 9,000 in 1837.[26]
The figures in the table represent only Cleveland's canal receipts.
In addition, unknown quantities arrived via wagon and coasting
vessels. In 1836 exports were just slightly less than canal receipts.[27]
It is thus assumed that canal receipts were the equivalent of exports and that receipts via other means were probably small and
retained for local consumption. In terms of bushels of wheat (flour
converted to five bushels of wheat), Cleveland's receipts increased
by 2.5 million bushels, or just under 800 per cent, from 1830 to
1840. Corn was of little importance until the late 1840's and early

TABLE 1. ANNUAL RECEIPTS OF WHEAT, FLOUR, AND CORN AT CLEVELAND,
VIA CANAL, 1827-39 (IN THOUSANDS)

Year	Wheat (bu.)	Flour (bbl.)	Corn (bu.)
1827–29 ave.	–	7	–
1830	177	33	–
1831	288	58	–
1832	289	54	–
1833	387	98	75
1834	334	105	3
1835	387	132	53
1836	464	167	392
1837	549	204	280
1838	1,229	287	107
1839	1,516	265	82 [a]

[a] Includes oats.

Sources: Cist, *Cincinnati in 1841*, 299; McClelland and Huntington, *History of the Ohio Canals*, Appendix J, 175-176; Cleveland *Plain Dealer*, January 2, 1844.

---

[26] Julius P. B. MacCabe, *Directory. Cleveland and Ohio City. For the Years 1837-1838* (Cleveland, 1837). [Charles F. Hoffman], *A Winter in the West* (2 vols., New York, 1835), I, 84, observed that Cleveland's harbor had been much improved by running a pier from both sides of the Cuyahoga's mouth out into Lake Erie.

[27] MacCabe, *Cleveland Directory*, 58.

1850's. Pork receipts varied between 10,000 and 20,000 barrels through the 1830's, and whiskey was received in smaller quantities.

The stimulation that the Ohio Canal, in conjunction with the Welland and Erie canals, gave to parts of Ohio was great in terms of population growth, production, export, and import. Farmers in many sections of Ohio reaped great advantages from the completed canals, which were called into existence by the real need for improved transportation within the state. At the same time, Ohio expended large sums of money on road construction which aided farmers in getting their produce to the major canals, and later to the railroads. New energy was injected into the economy of counties traversed by the canals. Commercial centers such as Akron, Newark, and Massillon arose. The latter, laid out in 1826, was by 1840 one of the principal grain markets in the state.[28]

But, as a subsequent section will point out in greater detail, the benefits of canals were not diffused evenly throughout the state. The impact of the Ohio Canal seemed to intensify as the distance from Lake Erie increased, particularly in the upper and middle Muskingum River valley. Production increases along the shore of Lake Erie, in the Western Reserve, were considerably less substantial than in areas to the south. A like situation occurred with the completion of the Wabash and Erie Canal to Toledo. The Maumee River valley, although nearer to Toledo, developed much less rapidly than the country of the upper Wabash, through which the canal ran.

Ohio probably exported about 3.4 million bushels of wheat in 1835, compared to just under 2 million in 1830; and by 1839 shipments over the lakes alone were close to 3.5 million bushels, of which Cleveland contributed 80 per cent.[29] Cincinnati, Portsmouth, and other river ports contributed another 300,000 barrels of flour.

---

[28] Francis P. Weisenburger, *The Passing of the Frontier, 1825-1850* (Columbus, Ohio, 1941), 14, states that Massillon shipped over 280,000 bushels of wheat in 1836. Prices were also considerably higher at points on the canals like Massillon. *NWR*, XXXIX (February 19, 1831), 442, reported that wheat at Massillon was worth 18 cents more per bushel than on the Ohio River, and a similar differential was reported for 1839. Renick, *Memoirs*, 83, recalled that corn prices doubled at Newark when the canal reached that point. Land values were also greatly increased in areas contiguous to the canals.

[29] The rest was shipped primarily from Sandusky, Toledo, Huron, Milan, and Venice. This is in substantial agreement with the estimates of Kohlmeier, *Old Northwest as Keystone*, 33-34, of over 800,000 barrels of flour and 2 million bushels of wheat exported from Ohio in 1839.

Thus the great increase in Ohio's exports is directly attributable to the increasing production of wheat in the north central part of the state. The bulk of the corn, pork, and whiskey continued to flow southward by way of the Ohio and Mississippi rivers—also in increased quantities.[30] By the 1830's, then, Ohio was an active participant in the economic life of the nation.

Until the 1840's Ohio was for all practical purposes the only state participating in the grain trade of the Great Lakes. Indiana and Illinois, lacking transportation and population in the northern regions, did not develop a lake trade of considerable proportions until the 1840's. Illinois did not reach the stage of the lake trade which Ohio had attained in the 1840's until the following decade. Although Indiana may have made occasional and small grain shipments through Michigan City or Toledo, Indiana and Illinois traded primarily with the South. In both states, settlement concentrated in the southernmost sections along the Ohio River and progressed northward but slowly, clinging to river valleys such as the Wabash, Kaskaskia, and Illinois.[31] Certain sections of both states were settled relatively quickly and at a fairly steady rate, the period of slowest growth falling between 1810 and 1830. Thereafter, the population of Indiana increased by over 300,000 in each decade until the Civil War. Illinois evidenced a similar rate of growth until the decade preceding the war, when her population shot ahead of Indiana's for the first time.[32]

---

[30] Cincinnati, Portsmouth, and Cleveland contributed over 80 per cent of Ohio's export of provisions. Barreled pork exports at 43,000 in 1836 had tripled by 1839. Lard exports increased by six times, reaching 3.8 million pounds in 1839. Cincinnati furnished most of this. Cleveland *Plain Dealer*, March 12, 1845.

[31] The southern portions of each state were settled first despite the fact that the soil was inferior, lying in nonglaciated sections, the terrain was more rugged than areas to the north, and rainfall was often excessive. See Russell H. Anderson, "Advancing Across the Eastern Mississippi Valley," *Agricultural History*, XVII (April, 1943), 99, and Richard L. Power, *Planting Corn Belt Culture. The Impress of the Upland Southerner and Yankee in the Old Northwest* (Indianapolis, 1953), 37.

[32] The aggregate increase per decade from 1810 to 1860 was:

Year	Indiana	Illinois
1810–20	122,658	43,929
1820–30	195,853	102,334
1830–40	342,835	318,738
1840–50	302,550	375,287
1850–60	360,012	860,481

Bureau of the Census, *Historical Statistics of the United States. Colonial Times to 1957* (Washington, D.C., 1960), 12-13.

Indiana's population was estimated at 67,000 in 1815. By that time settlement had spread along the Ohio River and up the Whitewater River valley in the east, and in the west up the lower reaches of the Wabash. The area stretching north from the Ohio River between the Indiana-Ohio boundary and the Wabash was a vast forest, inhabited mostly by people engaged in subsistence farming and hunting. Along the Ohio River, although settlements were more frequently encountered than in the interior, the terrain remained in its primeval state for the most part.[33] By the 1830's the bulk of Indiana's population was still in the southern half of the state, with the major river valleys considerably more densely settled than in 1820. Farmers had moved into the second, third, and fourth tier of southern counties and along the banks of the East and West forks of the White River, the major tributary of the Wabash. The Whitewater valley in the east was most thickly settled. But in the valley of the upper Wabash few people had ventured to the north of Fountain, Tippecanoe, or Montgomery counties. In the north, along the Wabash and the Indiana-Ohio line, it would take the completion of the Wabash and Erie Canal from Toledo to Lafayette, Indiana, in 1843, to furnish a real stimulus to settlement.[34] In the center of the state, Indianapolis was then a town of but 2,000 waiting impatiently for reliable communications with the Ohio River.[35]

Between 1820 and 1840 Indiana lacked not only adequate transportation facilities but also markets and a sufficiently concentrated population engaged in pursuits other than farming to provide some kind of local demand for foodstuffs. From the beginning of settlement in Indiana less land and labor was devoted to wheat than to corn and hogs. Through most of the 1840's comparatively small quantities of Indiana's produce entered into commerce. It is probable that Indiana produced less than 1 million bushels of wheat

[33] Elias Pymn Fordham, *Personal Narrative of Travels in Virginia, Maryland, Pennsylvania, Ohio, Indiana, Kentucky; and of a Residence in the Illinois Territory: 1817-1818*, Frederic A. Ogg, ed. (Cleveland, 1906), 96; Birkbeck, *Notes on a Journey in America*, 99-106; Woods, *Two Years in Illinois*, 107-108.

[34] Henry W. Ellsworth, *Valley of the Upper Wabash, Indiana, with Hints on Its Agricultural Advantages* . . . (New York, 1838), 2-3; Logan Esarey, *A History of Indiana from Its Exploration to 1850* (Indianapolis, 1915), 277; Power, *Planting Corn Belt Culture*, 73-74. For good accounts of Indiana's internal improvements projects, see Logan Esarey, *Internal Improvements in Early Indiana* (Indianapolis, 1912), and Elbert J. Benton, *The Wabash Trade Route in the Development of the Old Northwest* (Baltimore, 1903).

[35] William Oliver, *Eight Months in Illinois, with Information to Immigrants* (Newcastle-upon-Tyne, 1843, Chicago, 1924), 205.

in the 1820's, and the expansion to some 4 million bushels in 1839, though impressive if stated in terms of percentage increase, still provided Indiana with but 5.9 bushels per capita—hardly enough to warrant large exports. But whatever the quantities of produce shipped from Indiana, corn in its infinite forms held the lead throughout the antebellum period.[36]

The grain trade of Indiana had its primary destination at New Orleans. The Wabash River was the major avenue to that market from the interior. Flatboats carried most of the produce, although in the 1820's steamboats began nosing their way up the Wabash. By 1826 regular trips were being made to Terre Haute, and Logansport was reached in 1830. Lafayette, however, was the effective head of steamboat navigation and reported 60 arrivals in the spring season of 1836.[37] But steamboats did little to stimulate increased agricultural production since they had no effect on demand nor could they furnish transportation to farmers any distance from the rivers. Flatboats were much more adaptable to the hazardous conditions faced by those navigating the interior streams of both Indiana and Ohio. It is likely that most of the produce floated down the Muskingum, Miami, White, and Wabash rivers was carried in flatboats. Probably more of this was eventually transferred to steamboats in Ohio, and at Cincinnati in particular, than in Indiana, which lacked a large Ohio River port like Cincinnati. Moreover, it was probably cheaper in the 1830's to ship produce via flatboat.

It is estimated that between 1,200 and 1,500 flatboats annually descended the Wabash River system during the 1830's.[38] Since the Wabash and its tributaries were virtually unnavigable except dur-

---

[36] As in most sparsely settled areas, it was a difficult and costly process to get grain ground into flour. There being no market or use for bulk wheat, and a scarcity of mills, farmers often had to travel a considerable distance to get a few sacks of wheat ground, imperfectly, into flour. Moreover, the tolls at the mill were fairly steep, ranging from one-quarter to one-sixth of the wheat and upwards of one-sixth for other grains. Wheat worth but 25 cents and corn but 8 cents could not stand the cost of carriage more than 15 to 20 miles, thus only those farmers fortunately situated near a mill on a navigable stream could engage in a rudimentary form of commerce. David Thomas, *Travels Through the Western Country in the Summer of 1816* (Auburn, N.Y., 1819), 233; *NWR*, XXIX (November 12, 1825), 165.

[37] Louis C. Hunter, *Steamboats on the Western Rivers. An Economic and Technological History* (Cambridge, Mass., 1949), 38-39; John Scott, *The Indiana Gazetteer or Topographical Dictionary* (1826) (Indianapolis, 1954), 107; Morris Birkbeck, *Letters From Illinois* (Philadelphia, 1818), 55-56.

[38] *NWR*, XL (May 21, 1831), 194.

ing fall and spring high water, the trade had to be carried on at precisely those periods. Much of Indiana's produce was shipped in the spring, each shipper trying to be among the first to reach a cash market for his surplus. The result was the "Wabash Glut." Great quantities of goods arrived at New Orleans at about the same time, rapidly sated the market, and depressed prices to a point where shipment was barely, if at all, profitable. Neither period of freshet lasted much longer than two months, the fall rise being followed by a freeze, and the spring by drought and low water. The same conditions faced farmers along the interior rivers of all the streams in the Northwest.

Flatboat landings were numerous along these major rivers and streams. In 1826, 152 flatboats laden with 250,000 bushels of corn, over 4,500 barrels of pork, 10,000 hams, and 2,500 cattle and hogs were reported passing Vincennes on the spring rise. Bloomfield, situated on the West Fork of the White River, Lawrenceburg, 20 miles below Cincinnati, and Salem, on the Big Blue Creek, were among Indiana river communities engaged in shipping grain, provisions, and other farm products via flatboat to southern markets.[39] Not until the late 1830's and the 1840's were the farmers in central and northern Indiana to have a choice of two markets, and until the railroads became effective carriers of grain, farmers in southern Indiana continued to rely upon the unstable and often glutted market at New Orleans. Some of the pressure was relieved as a result of the great expansion of cotton culture to the banks of the Mississippi in the 1820's and 1830's, which provided an expanded market above New Orleans. Virtually the same problems were being faced by Illinois at this time.

The populating of Illinois proceeded in a similar pattern and at about the same pace as that of Indiana until 1850. Some 50,000 inhabitants in 1818 increased to 157,000 in 1830 and 476,000 a decade later.[40] Population followed the river valleys into the interior and settled along the Mississippi and Ohio rivers on the west and south. In the 1820's there was little concentrated population along the middle or upper reaches of the Illinois River, but settlement

---

[39] *Ibid.*, XXVI (July 8, 1826), 338; Scott, *Indiana Gazetteer*, 50-51, 79-83, 101-102.

[40] Jedidiah Morse, *The American Universal Geography; or A View of the Present State of all the Kingdoms, States, and Colonies in the Known World* (2 vols., 7th ed., Charleston, S.C., 1819), I, 600; Frederick Gerhard, *Illinois as It Is; Its History, Geography, Statistics, Agriculture* (Chicago, 1857), 55.

had advanced to Calhoun County on the Mississippi and up the
Wabash to Crawford County.

Southern Illinois was heavily wooded, with prairie lands dip-
ping as far south as Williamson County. Emigrants avoided these
prairies if possible and kept to the timbered lands and the streams,
which were fringed with strips of woodland.[41] In general the prairie
lands were predominant in the east central counties. In both the
north and the south there were pockets of marsh and swamplands,
with the worst areas in the south. In the triangular area between
the confluence of the Illinois and Mississippi rivers the land was
heavily timbered. The same terrain prevailed in the northwest corner of the state.[42] The east central prairie counties, extending westward from the Indiana line, were the last to be settled, as population initially leapfrogged this region to the country south and west
of Lake Michigan.[43]

Prior to the 1830's agriculture in Illinois was in a crude state.
Corn rather than wheat was the staple crop, wheat being raised in
only a few counties. Mills were scarce, and those available utilizing
horses or oxen were of small capacity and produced flour of indif-
ferent quality. As late as 1842 grist mills were still inadequate, the
average toll for grinding ranging about one-sixth, which was a considerable price, with wheat under 50 cents per bushel. By 1830,
with the erection of mills in the southern part of Illinois, farmers
did expand their wheat production, often sowing winter wheat in
the standing cornfields in August or September.[44] Illinois wheat
producers suffered a succession of deficient wheat crops from 1821
to 1823 and from 1827 to 1829, so it is unlikely that Illinois could
afford to export much of its crop. Even with an expanded production during the 1830's, population had increased by three times and

[41] *Ibid.*, map; Ogden, *Letters from the West*, 56.

[42] Gerhard, *Illinois as It Is*, maps; Paul W. Gates, *The Illinois Central
Railroad and Its Colonization Work* (Cambridge, Mass., 1934), 9.

[43] The details of the settlement process can be found in *ibid.*; Arthur C.
Boggess, *The Settlement of Illinois, 1778-1830* (Chicago, 1908); Theodore L.
Carlson, *The Illinois Military Tract. A Study of Land Occupation, Utilization,
and Tenure* (Urbana, Ill., 1951); Judson F. Lee, *Transportation as a Factor in
the Development of Northern Illinois Previous to 1860* (Chicago, 1917); William V. Pooley, *The Settlement of Illinois from 1830 to 1850* (Madison, Wis.,
1908).

[44] Oliver, *Eight Months in Illinois*, 125. *Transactions of the Illinois State
Agricultural Society*, II (1856-57), 314-316, states that a steam mill was erected
at Belleville in 1830 which did something to stimulate production and the construction of new mills in St. Clair County.

market conditions had changed but little, so that Illinois exports probably did not exceed 500,000 bushels annually.[45]

Most of the state's exports consisted of provisions, bulk corn, and whiskey. The major arteries from the interior were the Kaskaskia and Illinois rivers in the west and the Wabash, Little Wabash, and Big Muddy in the east. As in Indiana, flatboats provided the means for shipping the bulk of the produce. Steamboats navigated the Illinois and Wabash with some success and even made an effort to sail smaller streams such as the Sangamon.[46] Steamboats probably had a greater impact in Illinois than in Indiana since, in addition to the Wabash River, produce flowed south on the Illinois to the Mississippi and also went overland to the Mississippi from counties bordering on the river. Most of the important shipping centers were located on the Illinois or Mississippi rivers.

In the 1820's most producers, preferring to ship directly to the South, by-passed such Ohio River towns as Kaskaskia, Shawneetown, or Cairo, and interior towns like Vandalia or Springfield found only a tenuous prosperity in supplying the needs of emigrants.[47] Springfield, on the Sangamon River, was the principal mart of a region in which considerable livestock was raised. In 1841, however, the town was excitedly awaiting the completion of a railroad from the Illinois River which would, it was confidently expected, ensure the future of Springfield as a great produce market.[48]

Below St. Louis, the Illinois shore was depicted as a backwater: "The total want of everything like the marks of civilization, excepting at wide intervals, and then a poor log hut, looking insignificant amid the mightiness of the silent forest. . . . There is a grandeur, but it is the grandeur of desolation." [49] There were no towns of any size or importance until Alton, 18 miles below the mouth of

---

[45] *Ibid.*, 316, says much of the wheat was destroyed by smut and the black weevil. Governor Thomas Ford, *A History of Illinois from Its Commencement as a State in 1818 to 1847*, Milo M. Quaife, ed. (2 vols., Chicago, 1943), I, 133-134.

[46] [Samuel A. Mitchell], *Illinois in 1837; a Sketch Descriptive of the Situation, Boundaries, Face of the Country* . . . (Philadelphia, 1837), 36.

[47] Lewis C. Beck, *A Gazetteer of the States of Illinois and Missouri Containing a General View of Each State* . . . (Albany, N.Y., 1823), 59-60.

[48] *Ibid.*, 66; Vandalia *Intelligencer*, October, 1825, quoted in *NWR*, XXIX (November 26, 1825), 208, XXXVI (July 4, 1829), 304; Mitchell, *Illinois in 1837*, 25-26; *Sangamo Journal*, October 8, 1841. Interior towns to the north like Decatur, Paris, Danville, and Bloomington were country hamlets through the 1830's.

[49] Oliver, *Eight Months in Illinois*, 50.

the Illinois. Alton served more as a depot for the St. Louis trade with the Illinois River than as a center which shipped directly to the South.[50]

The towns situated along the Illinois River were often of considerable importance as markets for the surrounding countryside. Naples enjoyed an extensive river trade, exporting over $1 million in farm produce in 1835, a year in which 302 steamboat arrivals and departures were recorded.[51] Beardstown, a few miles below the mouth of the Sangamon River, handled the Sangamon country surplus. By 1837 Beardstown was the leading pork-packing center in the state, slaughtering 15,000 hogs in 1836-37 and between 40,000 and 70,000 hogs annually in the 1840's.[52] Above Beardstown, Peoria and Peru were important river ports. By 1839 the five flour mills of Peoria were handling grain brought there from the surrounding counties.

The ports mentioned above were all dependent upon the southern route and southern markets for disposal of their produce. And

---

[50] Beck, *Gazetteer of Illinois and Missouri*, 87-88, 117, 149. Below St. Louis, Harrisonville, Monroe County, and Portland, Randolph County, were reported shipping produce south in 1823. St. Louis will be dealt with in greater detail in later pages. J. M. Peck, *A Gazetteer of Illinois in Three Parts . . .* (Jacksonville, Ill., 1834), 174; Mitchell, *Illinois in 1837*, 113-114.

[51] *Ibid.*, 125; Peck, *Gazetteer of Illinois*, 260.

[52] Mitchell, *Illinois in 1837*, 104, 115-116. Lee, *Transportation in Development of Northern Illinois*, 71-76, in noting 450 steamboat arrivals at Beardstown in 1836, attributes the prosperity of that place and the Illinois and Mississippi river counties in general to the coming of the steamboat. This is probably overstating the influence of an innovation which was important but not crucial to the development of the Northwest. Unlike the railroads, it opened no new lands to settlement although it expedited the process. The steamers, operating on natural waterways, were wholly at the mercy of unfavorable climatological conditions and limited in the routes that could be navigated. They served limited areas and provided no solution to the problem of the farmer located at any distance from a navigable river. They created no new markets for grain though they facilitated the development of established ones. It is true, however, that steamboats sped up the trade between ports, and particularly with New Orleans. Moreover, steamboats did make feasible a large up-river trade for New Orleans and reduced, by the quickness of a return journey, the arduousness and time lost in shipping from the Northwest to the South. The fact that new commercial centers appeared concurrently with the growth of the steamboat industry should not be taken to imply that the latter caused the former. These new centers would have been created without the steamboat, though perhaps in larger numbers with each serving a more limited area. Steamboats perhaps tended to concentrate the grain trade at fewer depots than would have been the case without them, but the grain trade would have still existed, as a grain surplus or deficiency depended upon forces and pressures totally independent of the absence or presence of the steamboat.

this was not developing rapidly enough, nor were freight rates declining quickly enough or prices rising sufficiently, to encourage any great expansion of grain production. If production did expand from 1820 to 1840, it was due largely to an influx of new farmers plowing up new lands rather than to an increase in yield or a conscious effort to produce a marketable surplus. As a correspondent from Lewiston, Illinois, in the Spoon River country, wrote to the New York *Tribune* in 1842: "We have all the necessaries of life in abundance, but we are pinched beyond all example for money. Even wheat does not bring it now. When the Illinois and Michigan Canal is completed, we shall have a market, but not till then." [53] The canal was not to be a panacea; but between it and the railroads which quickly followed, new markets were made accessible to producers in north and central Illinois. Then, in Illinois as in Indiana, under the impact of its major canal effort, and to an equal degree in Ohio, the southern market, with New Orleans as its focus, became less central to the grain trade of the Northwest. But this was a development of the future, and until then the northwestern states as a whole were more dependent upon the Mississippi River system than upon any alternative route to market.

The fact that markets were primarily in the South was not without effect on the amount of land and labor devoted to the cultivation of particular crops in the East North Central states and the use made of them after harvest.[54] The best market for corn and provisions existed in the South and, while there was little demand in that section for bulk wheat, flour was an important requirement. Flour was also in demand at New Orleans for export, both to overseas and Atlantic coast markets. Those few areas in the Northwest with access to the South concentrated on these products, and since corn was so extensively used it was the staple crop and continued to be so until a demand for bulk wheat was created by the opening of routes to Lake Erie and the East. At this time, as will be demonstrated in following sections, a geographical specialization in a particular grain developed in parts of Ohio, Indiana, and Illinois— as, for instance, the upper and middle Muskingum valley became the wheat belt of Ohio. Until that time, farmers in the Northwest produced enough grain to meet strictly local consumption needs, with any surplus shipped south if the produce could reach a south-

---

[53] New York *Tribune*, January 18, 1842.
[54] This question is dealt with in more detail in a later chapter.

flowing stream, and even such a fortunate location was no assurance that the effort would be rewarding. It was at this time that Cincinnati began to concentrate on pork packing—an industry completely dependent upon the corn crop of the immediate vicinity. In Indiana and Illinois, commercially less developed than Ohio, the grain trade was even more corn-oriented than in Ohio.

During the first 15 years of the period discussed above, roughly 1815 to 1830, transportation inadequacies inhibited the development of an extensive grain trade. With the coming of canals to Ohio during the late 1820's and 1830's, and later to the other states, accessibility to markets led to larger crops—crops more and more frequently grown to supply nonlocal needs. To the degree that this occurred in particular areas at various times, agriculture emerged from a subsistence to a commercial level.

From Table 2 it appears that, although the percentage increases were extraordinary in each of the five states, Ohio alone, under the stimulus of a far-reaching internal improvements program, was producing sufficiently large quantities to support an ex-

TABLE 2.[55] ESTIMATED TOTAL WHEAT PRODUCTION OF THE EAST NORTH CENTRAL STATES AND THE UNITED STATES FOR 1820, 1830, 1835, AND 1839 (IN THOUSANDS OF BUSHELS)

	1820	1830	1835	1839
Ohio	3,400	5,580	8,320	16,571
Indiana	578	1,570	2,600	4,049
Illinois	335	750	1,500	3,335
Michigan	50	125	1,014	2,157
Wisconsin	–	–	200	212
Totals	4,363	8,025	13,634	26,326
U.S. Production	29,000 to 35,000	40,000 to 45,000	–	84,823

[55] The estimates for Ohio are based on known export figures from various shipping centers, primarily Toledo, Sandusky, Cleveland, and Cincinnati, and on the assumption that after exports there remained a sufficiency of grain to supply at least four bushels of wheat per capita. For the remaining states the estimate is based largely on a four-bushel consumption per capita, in addition to the known fact that only small quantities of wheat were exported. Although these quantities are unknown, they would not change the production figures significantly. The East North Central states produced 31 per cent of the nation's wheat in 1839; 37 per cent in 1849; and 46 per cent in 1859. It is assumed that this ascending proportion can be applied to the period before 1839, and on this basis it is estimated that the East North Central states produced 15 per cent of

port trade of any significance. Between 1820 and 1830 Ohio's total exports, almost entirely to the South, ranged between 1 and 2 million bushels. Any increase throughout this decade is attributable to activity along the lake shore, as Cincinnati's shipments via river remained fairly level from 1820 to 1839. The real growth in the grain trade of Ohio came in the 1830's and especially in 1835-40. This advance followed directly in time the construction of Ohio's system of canals, which provided interior farmers passage to Lake Erie and an eastern market. In 1835 Ohio's shipments via the lakes surpassed her wheat and flour shipments to the South. Lake shipments probably exceeded 2 million bushels in 1835 and 3.5 million in 1839.

Wisconsin and Michigan were of no importance in the grain trade until the 1840's, although Michigan wheat and flour did begin to move east through Toledo around 1836. Indiana and Illinois produced little more wheat than that required to meet local demands and, as with the larger part of Ohio, were heavily dependent upon the market in the South and at New Orleans. Ohio dominated this trade as well as the growing trade based at the busy little ports on Lake Erie.

---

the nation's wheat in 1820 and 20 per cent in 1830. Using these proportions, total U.S. wheat production was some 29 million bushels in 1820. A slightly higher figure, 35 million bushels, was arrived at by adding total wheat and flour exports to a figure representing the wheat requirements of 8 million whites at 3.5 bushels per capita and 1.5 million slaves at 1 bushel per capita. Wheat consumption in the North was estimated, by contemporaries, at between 5 and 7 bushels per capita, while in the South it ranged from 2 to 4 bushels. Slaves received little if any wheat bread or wheat products and subsisted largely on corn and pork, as did large numbers of interior farmers in both the North and the South. For Ohio alone, in 1830, a figure arrived at by multiplying 4 bushels per capita by a population of 793,000 would yield 3 million bushels, leaving, according to the table, some 400,000 bushels for export, which is probably underestimating the quantity by a few hundred thousand bushels.

In 1840 the figure representing total U.S. production was arrived at by estimating the share of the Northwest to be 20 per cent. This resulted in a total of 40 million bushels. If exports are added to consumption requirements of the 1840 population, using the same per capita consumption as in 1830, 45 million bushels is the result.

The increase between 1830 and 1840, some 40 million bushels, is accounted for by the rapid expansion in wheat production in Ohio, and to a less extent in the other four states, and an increase of production in New York, Pennsylvania, and Virginia. Western New York and Pennsylvania made great strides in production as new lands were opened for settlement and profitable cultivation by such works as the Erie Canal and the Pennsylvania system of canals.

Sacks, Barrels, and Hogsheads: The Grain Trade of New Orleans Before 1840

CHAPTER II

New Orleans was the oldest market for northwestern grain and provisions—until the mid-1830's almost the only one, and until the late 1830's the principal one. In absolute terms the grain trade of New Orleans grew steadily during the antebellum period.[1] But in relative terms, the focal importance of New Orleans declined. The river system which gave New Orleans her first advantage later proved less satisfactory than other routes, and the ascendancy of New Orleans passed away. But it was controlling while it lasted,

[1] The general commerce of New Orleans expanded more rapidly than that in grain and provisions, reflecting the increasing interest of New Orleans in cotton and other southern staples. Between 1816 and 1839 the value of receipts from up-river sources rose from $8 million to $42 million. W. F. Switzler, "Report on the Internal Commerce of the United States," *House Executive Documents*, 50 Cong., 1 Sess., No. 6, Part 2 (1888), Serial 2552, 218-219, 377 (hereafter cited as Switzler, "Report on Internal Commerce").

and it is the purpose of this chapter to treat of the era of New Orleans' controlling ascendancy.

The grain trade of New Orleans grew from one of small proportions in the late eighteenth century to a fairly large traffic before the War of 1812, and to this trade the Northwest contributed a rising volume. For most of the period, from 1790 to 1815, the trade was sensitive to the wars in Europe. Markets in the West Indies, for instance, were alternately closed and reopened to American produce, depending upon the progress of the war and the strategies of England, France, and Spain as belligerents. During most of this period, the trade in grain, and commerce in general, was extremely precarious, but also quite lucrative if conducted successfully.

After the War of 1812, New Orleans entered into a prosperous era lasting four decades. During that time, and most noticeably in the 1850's, rival markets for the grain of the Northwest diverted increasing quantities of produce from the southern route through New Orleans. In the period 1820-40, however, New Orleans suffered but little from the encroachments of competing American markets and dominated the trade in foodstuffs of the Ohio valley and upper Mississippi.

Volney had written in 1797 that the chief focus of the "borderers of the great Kanhawah and the Ohio" was upon the Gulf of Mexico and the waters flowing into the same.[2] By this he meant the Mississippi, which was, between 1763 and 1803, a Spanish river in its lower courses just as the Gulf of Mexico became a Spanish lake with the cession of Florida to Spain by Britain in 1783. Early in the history of upper Louisiana, the great waterway had carried grain and flour downstream to New Orleans or settlements above that port, but until the 1790's the volume of traffic in grain passing down the Mississippi was relatively small. In the period subsequent to the American Revolution, western Americans realized, as Easterners were often loathe to do, that control or at least free navigation of the Mississippi was absolutely essential for the prosperity of the Ohio and Mississippi valleys.[3]

---

[2] C. F. Volney, *View of the Climate and Soil of the United States of America to Which Are Annexed Some Accounts of Florida, the French Colony on the Scioto, Certain Canadian Colonies, and the Savages or Natives* (London, 1804), 21.

[3] The two major works on the Mississippi problem are Arthur P. Whitaker's *The Spanish-American Frontier: 1783-1795. The Westward Movement and the Spanish Retreat in the Mississippi Valley* (Boston, 1927), and *The*

From 1784 to 1787 the Mississippi River was closed by Spain to all but Spanish ships. In 1788 it was reopened to Americans subject to a 15 per cent duty, computed and enforced so as not to be excessively burdensome. The Treaty of San Lorenzo in 1795 granted to Americans the free navigation of the river and a deposit at New Orleans or some other convenient spot. Traffic, however, remained small; only 5,400 barrels of flour arrived at New Orleans in 1794. But after 1795 the downstream trade increased, so that by 1800 goods worth over $1 million were received at New Orleans, mainly from Kentucky, Tennessee, western Pennsylvania, and Virginia. This trade had increased to $2.6 million in 1802 and over $5.3 million in 1807, mostly from Kentucky and Pennsylvania, with Ohio's shipments rising.[4]

The most important single item in the downstream traffic to New Orleans was flour. The great stimulus to this traffic was the establishment of the American deposit in April, 1798, and Spain's opening of Havana and other Spanish colonial ports to neutral shipping in the same year. By 1801 some 470 flatboats and keels were reported passing or embarking from Cincinnati carrying over 90,-000 barrels of flour. About the same quantity was reported passing Louisville the following year and at least 73,000 barrels in 1803. For the four years 1804-07, New Orleans received a total of 133,403 barrels, including at least 47,000 from Pittsburgh and points on the Monongahela River, which would represent a decline over the previous three years. Of this total, Ohio probably had not supplied over 5,000 barrels annually.

From 1804 to 1814 at least 226,000 barrels of flour cleared New Orleans for foreign ports. Of this total, 44.5 per cent went to the West Indies, mainly Cuba and the French islands; 30 per cent was

---

Mississippi Question, 1795-1803. A Study in Trade, Politics, and Diplomacy (New York, 1934).

[4] Whitaker, *The Spanish-American Frontier*, 68-69, 83-84, 95-102; Emory R. Johnson *et al.*, *History of Domestic and Foreign Commerce of the United States* (2 vols., Washington, D.C., 1915), I, 200-209. F. A. Michaux, *Travels to the West of the Alleghany Mountains, in the States of Ohio, Kentucky, and Tennessee and Back to Charleston, by the Upper Carolines* (London, 1805), reprinted in Reuben G. Thwaites, ed., *Early Western Travels, 1748-1846* (32 vols., Cleveland, 1904), III, 145, recorded that during the French Revolution the inhabitants of western Pennsylvania, as at Bedford some 180 miles from Philadelphia, found it to their advantage to ship their corn to New Orleans via Pittsburgh.

destined for Spain and Portugal; and 20 per cent for Central America and west Florida. This represents a definite decline from the period 1801-03. The decline is more marked if one considers the fact that fully 66,598 barrels, or 25 per cent of the 11-year total, were shipped to Spain and Portugal in the two years 1812-13. Moreover, the trade to markets other than the Iberian Peninsula was very unevenly distributed from year to year, and, while 133,403 barrels were shipped to other markets between 1804 and 1807, only 26,000 were shipped to them in the years 1808-11 and 1814. This shrinkage must also be set against the over-all increase in New Orleans receipts from inland sources, which reached $8 million in 1816.[5]

There is no doubt that the wars in Europe exerted a considerable influence on the grain trade at New Orleans. At times the trade was greatly hampered, particularly when Britain blockaded the West Indian possessions of France and Spain. But at times, as during the Peninsular Wars, a vast though temporary market was opened for American foodstuffs. From 1807 to 1812 American commerce was impeded by embargo and nonimportation legislation, and from 1812 to 1815 by war with England. In spite of these impediments there is no evidence that the major markets for American grain, particularly the West Indies, took smaller quantities of American foodstuffs in the period 1800-1812 than they received during the 1790's. It may be, however, that the trade from New Orleans was more severely restricted than that originating at other American seaports.

It is also possible that northwestern farmers, during certain of these years, shipped less produce to New Orleans, for instance in 1814, when the Ohio valley suffered a harvest failure. Or, if shipments of grain passing down the Mississippi suffered no diminution, fewer of them were reaching New Orleans. The latter may well be what happened, for it was reported that, in the winter of 1810-11, when New Orleans exports were very low, 197 flatboats and 14 keelboats passed the Falls at Louisville carrying 18,611 barrels of flour, 6,300 barrels of beef, and 6,000 barrels of pork and whiskey, along

---

[5] Charles Cist, *Cincinnati in 1841: Its Early Annals and Future Prospects* (Cincinnati, 1841), 188; W. Freeman Galpin, "The Grain Trade of New Orleans, 1804-1814," *Mississippi Valley Historical Review*, XIV (March, 1928), 498-500.

with livestock and lumber. New markets were arising on the lower
reaches of the Ohio and on the Mississippi above New Orleans.[6]
But whatever the reason—whether less grain was reaching New
Orleans or because the overseas demand was shrinking—the grain
trade of New Orleans would seem to have contracted from 1804 to
1814.[7]

With the return of peace in 1815, New Orleans entered upon
a 45-year period in which enormous progress was made along all
commercial lines. Throughout these years, New Orleans was the
leading export center in the nation in terms of dollar volume of
domestic exports, except for 1847 and a few years during the 1850's,
when New York's domestic exports exceeded those of the Crescent
City. Though the advance of New Orleans was extraordinary, with
receipts from up-river sources valued at $12.6 million in 1820 and
$185.2 million in 1860, and exports increasing from $7.2 million to
$107.5 million over this period, the advance did not proceed at an
even rate during the four and a half decades.

Stated in terms of dollar and percentage increase, the receipts
of New Orleans from sources up the Mississippi River increased by
$9 million, or 65 per cent, from 1820 to 1830; $28 million, or 90 per
cent, from 1830 to 1840; $47 million, or 65 per cent, in the following
decade; and $88 million, or 91 per cent, from 1850 to 1860. In other
words, the dollar volume increase was greater and the rate of
growth more rapid in the decade preceding the war than in the
prior 35 years.[8] The earlier period, then, from the Treaty of Ghent

---

[6] Galpin, "Grain Trade of New Orleans," 501-504; W. P. and Julia P.
Cutler, eds., *Life, Journals and Correspondence of Reverend Manasseh Cutler*
(2 vols., Cincinnati, 1888), II, 318-319; John Melish, *Travels in the United
States of America, in the Years 1806 & 1807, and 1809, 1810, & 1811* . . . (2
vols., Philadelphia, 1812), II, 153.

[7] Neither Galpin, "Grain Trade of New Orleans," Whitaker, *Mississippi
Question*, nor Johnson *et al.*, *Domestic and Foreign Commerce*, indicate sufficient awareness that the New Orleans grain trade entered into a decline from
1804 to 1814. Leland D. Baldwin, *The Keelboat Age on Western Waters* (Pittsburgh, 1941), 181-182, notes that flatboat and barge arrivals in New Orleans
declined from 1807 to 1814. Of the arrivals in 1805-07, Kentucky led as the
place of origin with 30 per cent of the total, Mississippi followed with 24 per
cent, and Pennsylvania was third with 17 per cent. Ohio followed Tennessee
and Virginia with but 7 per cent of the total.

[8] James Hall, *The West: Its Commerce and Navigation* (Cincinnati,
1848), 190, 216; E. W. Gould, *Fifty Years on the Mississippi; or Gould's History of River Navigation* (St. Louis, 1889), 214; Switzler, "Report on Internal
Commerce," 209-219. This section will deal with the period to 1840. New
Orleans' role in foreign trade will be covered in Chapter X.

until 1832, was one of only relatively moderate advance. The curve for receipts from up-river rises more sharply from 1832 to 1838; and, after a period of temporary instability and fluctuation caused by the depression of the late 1830's and early 1840's, these receipts rose steeply from 1843 to 1860. A similar trend is noticeable in the receipts of wheat flour and corn.[9]

If the grain trade at New Orleans advanced, even moderately, it was in spite of the facilities available for getting the produce to market. The inadequacies, both in transportation and finance, were so great at New Orleans that its acceptability as a market depended to a great degree upon the fact that for a long time it was the only one available to many farmers in the Northwest.

A number of factors impinged on the produce market which made it precarious at all times. For one thing, prices were often depressed because the market was glutted. One flatboat owner found the market so low, under $2 a barrel for flour, that he contracted with a steamboat to reship the flour back to the Louisville market. Another entrepreneur, with a vessel loaded with livestock, began his voyage in December, 1834. On Christmas Day the flatboat was pierced by a snag. The cattle and hogs were freed and, along with the crew, forced to swim ashore. By January 4 the boat had been repaired but the ice was too thick to risk proceeding further. Natchez was reached on January 23, where the steers were sold but no offers were received for the hogs or pork. New Orleans was sighted on February 1, but only after a sudden midnight storm had very nearly destroyed the vessel. The pork went for 4 cents a pound and the corn at 15 cents a bushel. Eleven dollars was received for the boat—hardly a remunerative voyage.[10]

Another hazard of the trade lay in the fact that treacherous conditions on the Mississippi and Ohio rivers had to be faced and overcome before arriving at a market which was treacherous in itself. From 1822 to 1827 the loss of property on the Ohio and Mississippi, by snags alone, including steamboats and flatboats and their cargoes, amounted to at least $1.3 million. The federal government

---

[9] Gould, *Fifty Years on the Mississippi*, 202-205; *De Bow's, the Commercial Review of the South and West*, VII (November, 1849), 415 (hereafter cited as *De Bow's Review*); Johnson *et al.*, *Domestic and Foreign Commerce*, I, 213-214.

[10] *NWR*, XXVI (July 8, 1826), 330; Milo M. Quaife, ed., *Growing Up with Southern Illinois, 1820 to 1861, from the Memoirs of Daniel Harmon Brush* (Chicago, 1944), 86-92.

finally instituted a regular service to remove impediments to navigation, with the result that losses were reduced to $381,000 in the period 1827-32 and dropped still lower until the service was discontinued, whereupon they again rose to serious proportions. It was reported that St. Louis alone, between 1839 and 1843, lost 183 steamboats, and in 1842 merchandise, produce, and steamboats valued at $1.4 million were reported destroyed.[11]

The market at New Orleans was partially conditioned by the favorable or unfavorable depth of the river, and this in turn was of prime importance in establishing freight rates and in determining the amount of cargo a boat could carry. The effects of low water were felt from one end of the Mississippi River system to the other.[12]

Low water generally occurred from June until the fall rise—usually in September, but often as late as October or November. Navigation then continued until a winter freeze, which terminated the shipping season. This normally occurred in December. Spring brought melting snows, swollen feeder streams, the melting of ice, and a pronounced rise in the river, often of flood proportions. It was on this spring rise that large quantities of produce were shipped. It has been maintained that in early days Ohio valley farmers "regularly" waited until the spring following harvest to grind and ship their wheat, partly because shipping was more plentiful and milling often cheaper, and partly because they hoped for a better price. But it appears that considerable quantities of produce moved downstream during the fall rise. The presumed regularity of spring shipments is also questionable, partly because it is doubtful that many could afford to retain possession of their crops until spring. In any event, by 1835 techniques of slack-water shipping and the use of canals to interior points facilitated the movement of a larger part of the crop during the harvest season.

---

[11] "The Annual Amount of Trade and Commerce on the Upper Mississippi River, 1844," *Senate Executive Documents*, 28 Cong., 1 Sess., No. 242 (1844), Serial 434, 32.

[12] Thomas S. Berry, *Western Prices Before 1861. A Study of the Cincinnati Market* (Cambridge, Mass., 1943), 45-49, 61-65, has concluded that freight rates from Cincinnati to New Orleans declined from 1815 to 1840, drifted slowly upward between 1843 and 1850, and assumed a definite upward movement after 1850. Rates from other points in the Northwest experienced a similar movement. Throughout the entire period, flatboat rates were less than steamboat with the smallest differential in the spring of the year, which normally brought advantageous river conditions for steamers.

If there happened to be low water during the two shipping seasons, this put an effective stop to most river trade. As the water receded, and the rains or thaw failed to materialize, boats of the larger class were first forced to lighten their cargoes and then suspend operations. In 1820 low water in September forced 18 steamboats to lie in at Shippingport and Portland, Kentucky.[13] Before the canal at Louisville was completed in 1828, low water had a particularly noticeable impact on trade from areas north of the Falls through to the lower Ohio and the Mississippi. Shippers were forced to bear the added expense of unloading north of the Falls, drayage around the rapids, and reloading on another vessel south of Louisville.[14] This, of course, was a temporary stimulus to Louisville's teamster industry.

Steamboats of the smaller class, and flatboats last of all, would be forced to take to shore if the stage of the river dropped lower. New Orleans in the fall of 1838 watched with alarm as low water made navigation on the Ohio difficult and finally impossible. The river was reported so low "that the fish have to swallow each other to make room." Through the early days of November, only the smallest vessels were able to proceed south with cargoes. The stock of flour on hand at New Orleans had dwindled to about 2,700 barrels when an exporting house purchased the lot and held it for $20 a barrel. The *Picayune* charged that speculators were intercepting flour above New Orleans and holding it in expectation of still higher prices. The speculation failed, however, as reports came through from the north that the river was rising. Flour prices declined to $15, then to $10, and to $8 by November 22; and, on November 23, the *Picayune* announced that ships were departing from Cincinnati laden with freight. A moral to the story which the *Picayune* did not ignore was the great necessity of energetic action in pushing rail-

---

[13] *NWR*, XIX (September 30, 1820), 79.

[14] James Flint, *Letters from America Containing Observations on the Climate and Agriculture of the Western States, the Manners of the People, the Prospects of Emigrants, &c. &c.* (Edinburgh, 1822), reprinted in Thwaites, *Early Western Travels*, IX, 286. Louisville, from early times, did a considerable freighting and pilotage business. In the 1800's there was a constant agitation for a canal around the Falls, but Louisville's inhabitants feared that such a passage might injure their community's status as entrepot in the north-south trade. B. Henry Meyer *et al.*, *History of Transportation in the United States Before 1860* (Washington, D.C., 1948), 280, estimates that Louisville received some $15,000 annually for piloting flatboats alone.

roads to the north so as to obviate the city's dependence on the river and to tap new markets.[15] High prices at New Orleans were matched by low quotations in Cincinnati during a less severe siege of low water in 1840. Produce accumulated at the wharves during March and April because many steamboats were unable to operate and the available shipping was inadequate, thus forcing freight rates up and flour down from $3.50 to $2.95 a barrel.[16]

Farmers, though just emerging from a subsistence agriculture, were debtors, with heavy demands being made on their limited supplies of cash. Their only resource was land and the crop that it produced. Hard cash was at a premium during most of the ante-bellum period; witness the practice of cut money. The farmers had payments to make on their land and various essential supplies to purchase, all of which necessitated the sale of crops as soon as possible after harvest, regardless of price in many instances. Economically, it was hardly feasible for most farmers to hold their crops until spring in anticipation of a better price.[17] This accounts for the heavy concentration of shipments in the fall months at both New Orleans and St. Louis.

Of 270,000 barrels of flour received at New Orleans from October, 1832, to September, 1833, 44 per cent arrived between November 1 and February 29, and 38 per cent from March through June. At St. Louis, in 1846, 40 per cent of the flatboats arrived in October, November, and December; while three years later 53 per cent of the wheat received at St. Louis arrived during the same three months.[18] This would indicate that a fairly large share of the autumn crop was marketed as soon as the harvest was complete. The heaviest spring receipts at New Orleans were pork products, as the packing season extended from freeze to thaw.

---

[15] *The Daily Picayune* (New Orleans), November 6-23, 1838.

[16] Cincinnati *Advertiser and Journal*, March 17, 1840.

[17] Governor Thomas Ford, *A History of Illinois from Its Commencement as a State in 1818 to 1847*, Milo M. Quaife, ed. (2 vols., Chicago, 1943), I, 138-141, and W. Faux, *Memorable Days in America: Being a Journal of a Tour to the United States. Principally Undertaken to Ascertain, by Positive Evidence, the Conditions and Probable Prospects of British Emigrants; Including Accounts of Mr. Birkbeck's Settlement in the Illinois: And Intended to Show Men and Things as They Are in America* (London, 1823), reprinted in Thwaites, *Early Western Travels*, XI, 236, were among numerous observers who commented on the tendency of farmers to sell low in the fall, either out of ignorance, habit, or necessity.

[18] James Hall, *Notes on the Western States: Containing Descriptive Sketches of Their Soil, Climate, Resources, and Scenery* (Philadelphia, 1838), 284; *Hunt's*, XVII (August, 1847), 169, XXIV (March, 1851), 301.

In the pioneer stages of the grain trade, many farmers had no way of marketing their crops except to take their own shipments of produce downstream and dispose of their goods personally at some market along the river or at New Orleans. Many of the 3,000 to 4,000 flatboats descending western rivers each year, of which 1,200 to 1,500 came from the Wabash and White rivers, were owned by the farmers whose produce was being transported.[19] Individuals or groups of farmers in the same neighborhood could knock together a flatboat and start out when the water was favorable. The journey often originated on streams which, under the best conditions, were unnavigable for steamboats, and terminated when the head of steamboat navigation was reached on a larger river. At this point, the goods were reloaded on steamboats for the journey to market. In some cases the farmer would continue with his produce to make the final sale, or he could designate an agent, often the steamboat captain, to perform this function in his name. But the farmer retained ownership of the produce until the sale was consummated.

Numerous farmers were unwilling or unable personally to engage in the marketing of their crops at any distance from home. The trip took them away from home for a long period of time; and, if the sale was in the spring, the farmer was forced to remain at home in order to prepare his ground for the new crops. Moreover, the farmer needed to get as quick a return as possible for his crops in order to be able to buy those goods which he was incapable of producing himself. Cash was scarce; markets, at best unstable, were difficult to reach; processing of the grain was also a burdensome and expensive requirement. In this set of circumstances, as population increased and towns sprang up, there appeared the country merchant, who collected the produce following the harvest and marketed it wherever the best profit was believed obtainable.[20]

The extensive trading activity of produce merchants in com-

---

[19] Henry B. Fearon, *Sketches of America. A Narrative of a Journey of Five Thousand Miles Through the Eastern and Western States of America . . .* (2nd ed., London, 1818), 199.

[20] Fred M. Jones, *Middlemen in the Domestic Trade of the United States, 1800-1860* (Urbana, Ill., 1937), 45-46, maintains that the produce trade of the country merchant, as part of his general barter business, was not practiced after 1850. However, the role of the merchant as middleman continued to exist in areas of Wisconsin and Michigan which were in the early stages of settlement. Moreover, the general practice of gathering produce at a local depot and consigning it to a commission merchant at a larger market was, in a more highly organized way, just what the early merchant had done.

munities emerging from a pioneer and noncommercial pattern of existence performed a signal service in the development of the area. This was an integral part of the developmental process itself, flourishing at different times and places, until the increasing sophistication of business organization and new modes of transportation and communication made it obsolete in its original form.[21]

The bartering of store goods for produce was, in many instances, the only way a merchant could dispose of his goods. In those days of great capital scarcity, cash sales were few, so that the storekeeper was more or less compelled to receive produce as payment for a past debt or in direct exchange for utensils, textiles, and other manufactured goods. And once the merchant had accepted produce, it had to be disposed of in order for him to cancel his own financial obligations.[22] A merchant might transport his goods to a major local market such as Cincinnati or St. Louis, sell it or consign it for shipment to New Orleans, or he might take it to New Orleans himself.

Such a venture ended profitably for one merchant. In the fall and winter of 1846, Daniel Brush, of Illinois, constructed two flatboats and purchased $3,500 worth of pork, wheat, and corn. When he reached St. Louis, purchasers were found for the boats and all the produce, and Brush cleared some $600. Not all ventures ended on so happy a note. Only six years previously, Brush had lost about $2,000 shipping a load of livestock to New Orleans.[23] Another merchant, who had accumulated produce during the winter of 1844, constructed large flatboats which were hauled down the Mississippi by steamboat. Poor markets were encountered at Memphis, Vicks-

---

[21] Lewis E. Atherton, *The Pioneer Merchant in Mid-America* (Columbia, Mo., 1939), 90-91, writes that the merchant was an integral part of the three-cornered trade relationship that characterized American economic life before the Civil War. The West relied on the East for merchandise and manufactured products. The South purchased foodstuffs from the West. Western credits established in the South were transferred to eastern merchants to pay for goods purchased there. Certain qualifications must be noted to this widely accepted construction. Much western produce was sent directly to the East, where a domestic market rivaling that of the South was forming in the 1830's. A considerable part of the produce that reached New Orleans was also destined for north Atlantic coast markets, so that New Orleans served merely as a place of transfer to ocean-going vessels. And last, a growing share of the manufactured goods that reached the South via the western rivers was the product of western manufacturers.

[22] Brush, *Growing Up with Southern Illinois*, 146-147.

[23] *Ibid.*, 113-114.

burg, and Natchez, and an overprovisioned market at New Orleans forced the owner to sell at a loss.[24]

Often the produce merchant engaged in a speculation in the trade in which goods were bought for cash to be sold later, hopefully, at a profit. In the fall of 1845, J. M. D. Burrows, in expectation of a heavy foreign demand based on rumors of an English crop deficiency, bought up large quantities of flour and grain. Then the Mexican War intervened and the English shortage proved less serious than reported. Burrows, who had bought flour at $4.00 to $4.50 a barrel, could find no purchasers in St. Louis, where the nominal price was $2.25. So he shipped his commodities to New York, via New Orleans, most of the flour souring in transit, and was forced to sell his flour at a little over a dollar a barrel. His wheat, for which he had paid 60 cents, sold at 25 cents a bushel.[25]

In time the barter business of country merchants stimulated the development of the forwarding and commission merchant business in the larger towns along the Mississippi and Ohio rivers. These organizations handled grain for both farmers and merchants, provided storage facilities, found the most efficient transportation, and made an effort to sell at the dearest market.[26] Houses dealing in the produce trade gradually adopted the policy of extending cash advances to country merchants with whom they had consistently dealt, which enabled the merchant in turn to offer increased credit facilities to the producer. During the 1830's and early 1840's the financial resources of New Orleans were adequate to help finance the movement of produce from the Ohio valley and upper Mississippi River. But with the development of giant grain markets, like Chicago and Milwaukee in the 1850's, and the accumulation of large amounts of capital in such centers, New Orleans no longer held the lead in providing the credit necessary to draw to itself the produce of the Old Northwest.

It should be clear, then, that the grain trade to New Orleans operated at times under rather grave liabilities. To a certain extent,

---

[24] J. W. Spencer and J. M. D. Burrows, *The Early Days of Rock Island and Davenport*, Milo M. Quaife, ed. (Chicago, 1942), 182-185.

[25] *Ibid.*, 186-188.

[26] Atherton, *Pioneer Merchant*, 99-100. Isaac Lippincott, *Internal Trade of the United States, 1700-1860* (St. Louis, 1916), 97, records that Pittsburgh merchants in 1819 advertised that they owned a warehouse and that goods consigned to them would be forwarded promptly to destination, subject to a charge of 2½ per cent.

these disadvantages were overcome by the stark fact that in the period following the War of 1812, New Orleans was the only large and central grain market which most farmers in the Northwest could reach. Fortunately for the Northwest, an important generalized demand developed in the Southwest, along the lower Mississippi River, which could be reached directly. This rising consumer market, which will be discussed below, may be one reason for the slightness of the increases in the grain trade at New Orleans between 1815 and 1835.

Over a period of 20 years, the rise in grain receipts at New Orleans, as shown in Table 3, does not assume striking proportions.

TABLE 3. AVERAGE ANNUAL RECEIPTS OF WHEAT FLOUR, CORN, PORK, AND WHISKEY AND AVERAGE ANNUAL DOLLAR RECEIPTS FROM UP-RIVER SOURCES AT NEW ORLEANS, by Five-Year Periods, 1820-40 (PRODUCE IN THOUSANDS, DOLLAR RECEIPTS IN MILLIONS)

Years	Flour (bbl.)	Corn (bu.)	Pork (bbl.)	Whiskey (bbl.)	Dollar Receipts
1820–24	111[a]	234[a]	11[a]	15[a]	$13.8
1825–29	142	468	33	30	20.9
1830–34	258	569	64	32	25.5
1835–39	316	1,734	119	39	41.6

[a] 1822-24.
Sources: see fn. 9.

For the space of a few years after 1815, produce receipts increased quite rapidly, with flour reaching 198,000 barrels in 1818 and 1819. Traffic down-river was heavy. In the year ending October 1, 1817, 1,500 flatboats and 500 barges loaded with produce descended the Mississippi. Pork and beef receipts doubled from 1815 to 1818 and the value of imports increased from $8.7 million in 1817 to $16.7 million in 1819. Of this, probably over 50 per cent came from the territory north of Mississippi.[27]

---

[27] Switzler, "Report on Internal Commerce," 191-192; Gould, *Fifty Years on the Mississippi*, 202-205; *De Bow's Review*, VII (November, 1849), 415. Johnson *et al.*, *Domestic and Foreign Commerce*, I, 213-214, attribute the increase in receipts from 1818 to 1819 to the steamboat, but as there were only six steamboats in operation in 1816 and probably under 50 in 1819, it seems probable that most of the receipts arrived via flatboat or barge. The two-way traffic between the Ohio valley and New Orleans had just been inaugurated, and steamboat tonnage did not surpass the tonnage of all other vessels until the early 1820's. Frank H. Dixon, *A Traffic History of the Mississippi River System* (Washington, D.C., 1909), 15, estimates that in 1826, 50 per cent of the freight on the Mississippi and Ohio rivers was carried by steamboat. But

This relatively rapid growth was nipped by the general downturn in business in 1819. The extremely high prices of cotton, wheat, tobacco, and sugar plunged sharply; land speculators, including many farmers, were forced to default on loans based on the flimsy credit of state banks which failed because they were overextended. Banks, which had multiplied rapidly after the war, failed in large numbers, carrying other businesses to the same fate. The business of the nation entered a period of depression.[28]

The basis of the earlier prosperity had been insubstantial, not only in a financial sense, with inflated land values, great speculation, and overextended banks and debtors, but in the sense that farm prices had risen largely as a result of two successive crop failures in Europe in 1816-18. Wheat flour exports for the United States reached a level in 1817 not surpassed until 1831 and not again until 1840.[29] The price of flour in Philadelphia, Boston, New York, and Baltimore ranged from $9.50 to $10.00 in 1817. Corn and wheat prices were similarly inflated. In the Northwest, wheat ranged from 75 cents to $1.00; corn from 50 to 80 cents; and flour from $5.75 to $10.00. By 1820 prices had suffered a serious decline as flour dropped to between $4.50 and $5.00 in the East and $1.00 at Pittsburgh.[30] The *Niles Weekly Register* recounted the sad tale of one individual who shipped 400 barrels of flour to New Orleans in the summer of 1820. The flour remained unsold until it spoiled and a

---

this would include all of the upstream freight and most of the downstream cotton, so it is problematical whether steamboats at any time between 1815 and 1860 carried more produce than flatboats.

[28] For a general account of the depression, see Paul W. Gates, *The Farmer's Age: Agriculture 1815-1860* (New York, 1960), 57; Earl S. Sparks, *History and Theory of Agricultural Credit in the United States* (New York, 1932), 253-254; R. Carlyle Buley, *The Old Northwest. Pioneer Period. 1815-1840* (2 vols., Indianapolis, 1950), I, 124-130.

[29] Charles H. Evans, "Exports, Domestic and Foreign, from the American Colonies to Great Britain, from 1697 to 1789, Inclusive. Exports, Domestic and Foreign, from the United States to All Countries, from 1789 to 1883, Inclusive," *House Miscellaneous Documents*, 48 Cong., 1 Sess., No. 49, Part 2 (1884), Serial 2236, Table 2, 20-23 (hereafter cited as Evans, "Exports, Domestic and Foreign").

[30] David Thomas, *Travels Through the Western Country in the Summer of 1816* (Auburn, N.Y., 1819), 103; Thomas Hulme, *Journal of a Tour in the Western Countries of America—September 30, 1818–August 8, 1819*, in William Cobbett, *A Year's Residence in America* (Boston, 1824), 226; M[athew] Carey, *A View of the Ruinous Consequences of a Dependence on Foreign Markets for the Sale of the Great Staples of This Nation, Flour, Cotton, and Tobacco* (Philadelphia, 1820), 22; George H. Thurston, *Pittsburgh as It Is; or, Facts and Figures, Exhibiting the Past and Present of Pittsburgh, Its Advantages, Resources, Manufactures, and Commerce* (Pittsburgh, 1857), 39.

final sale was made at $300. The *Register* commented sardonically: "If he had burnt his flour on the banks of the Ohio, instead of sending it to New Orleans, he might have saved money." [31]

For the next decade the grain trade remained relatively stable. Wheat flour prices remained low both in New Orleans and the Northwest while receipts at New Orleans rose but sluggishly. Corn was of little value in bulk, so that the general increase in corn receipts at New Orleans probably did not reflect a value of much more than $150,000 annually. Receipts of whiskey, pork, and beef were not much greater than those of 1810, nor did they increase at a rapid pace until the 1830's.[32] It seems apparent that grain receipts at New Orleans were not maintaining their relative importance in terms of the total value of up-river receipts. These data may also be indicative of the general inadequacy of New Orleans as a market for the surplus products of the Ohio valley. New Orleans was then but a small city, with a limited foreign demand for surplus grain products. The strictly local market utilized but a fraction of the produce available for export. And in this market, Kentucky, Indiana, Ohio, Illinois, Tennessee, and Missouri competed. Any temporary scarcity in the New Orleans market, as one observer wrote, "was soon supplied and most of the time it was completely glutted." [33]

It has already been suggested that, while the New Orleans market failed to expand rapidly, northwestern farmers did find a growing market in the lower Mississippi valley apart from New Orleans. Cotton farming reached the Mississippi soon after the war and, as the Southwest grew, northern grain farmers were provided with their first accessible domestic market. Northern produce began supplying this area shortly after the war. From the Ohio River, with the aid of the steamboat, produce could be carried up the Kentucky, Cumberland, or Tennessee rivers. The plantations, settlements, and growing river towns along the Mississippi could be reached directly by both steamer and flatboat.[34]

---

[31] *NWR*, XX (April 14, 1821), 97-98.

[32] Switzler, "Report on Internal Commerce," 195-196; Hall, *Notes on the Western States*; J. R. M'Culloch, *A Dictionary, Practical, Theoretical, and Historical, of Commerce and Commercial Navigation*, H. Vethake, ed. (2 vols., Philadelphia, 1852), II, 215-216.

[33] Ford, *A History of Illinois*, I, 136.

[34] R. B. Way, "The Commerce of the Lower Mississippi in the Period 1830-1860," Mississippi Valley Historical Association *Proceedings* (1918-19),

Memphis, Vicksburg, Natchez, eastern Arkansas, and northern Louisiana developed into considerable markets for northern produce, particularly corn and pork. Vicksburg was an important factor in the flatboat trade. In winter months "it was no uncommon thing to see . . . as many as four or five hundred 'broadhorns'" tied up at the landing.[35] Boats laden with corn, pork, peas, apples, whiskey, fowls, brooms, and other sundries would drift down the Ohio to the Mississippi, stopping at any settlement that looked promising. If the market was slow, the vessel would drift to the next town, and so on until the goods were sold and the boat then disposed of. Some goods were deposited at a Mississippi River port and transported considerable distances overland to interior markets such as Florence, Alabama, on the Tennessee River.[36]

The southern market was one which continued to expand and, unlike New Orleans, was not subject to external pressures and contracting demand. Cotton culture overran the rich bottomlands of Louisiana, Mississippi, Alabama, and parts of eastern Arkansas in the 1830's. With cotton came slaves and a concomitant rise in population which, whatever the price of cotton or sugar, had to be fed and did not produce enough grain or livestock to feed itself.

It is virtually impossible to determine the quantities and value of produce reaching southern markets other than New Orleans from sources in the Ohio valley.[37] The volume must have been at least equal to that recorded at New Orleans during the 1820's. In 1820 the number of boats of all kinds passing the Falls at Louisville was estimated at 2,400, carrying 200,000 barrels of flour, 160,000 bushels

---

60 (hereafter cited as MVHA *Proceedings*); Rudolph A. Clemen, "Waterways in Livestock and Meat Trade," *American Economic Review*, XVI (December, 1926), 640-652.

[35] H. S. Fulkerson, *Random Collections of Early Days in Mississippi* (Baton Rouge, La., 1885), 97.

[36] *Letters of William Pelham Written in 1825 and 1826*, reprinted in Harlow Lindley, ed., *Indiana as Seen by Early Travelers. A Collection of Reprints from Books of Travel, Letters and Diaries Prior to 1830* (Indianapolis, 1916), 361.

[37] This is a major objection to A. L. Kohlmeier, *The Old Northwest as the Keystone of the Arch of the American Federal Union. A Study in Commerce and Politics* (Bloomington, Ind., 1938), which documents with considerable accuracy the quantities of produce flowing through the "northeastern" gateway, but is forced to rely on an extrapolation from known St. Louis and Cincinnati exports and New Orleans receipts to estimate southern receipts. Thus, a large and unknown quantity of produce from obscure flatboat landings in Indiana, Illinois, and Ohio is unaccounted for. Unfortunately, this work can do little to improve upon the situation.

of corn and oats, 20,000 barrels of pork, and 9,000 tons of bacon and hams. In 1823, 300,000 barrels of flour passed the Falls. But New Orleans, in 1820, received only 150,000 of the 200,000 barrels of flour which had passed the Falls, and, in 1823, only 114,000 of the 300,000 barrels. The number of vessels arriving in New Orleans in 1821 was 902, including 287 steamboats and 441 flatboats.[38] The receipts represent approximately 50 per cent of the recorded shipments.

By the 1830's the proportion of western produce reaching the New Orleans market was probably still less. It was estimated that Mississippi was purchasing at least $2 million worth of northwestern produce in 1836.[39] At this time the entire surplus of the Ohio valley, including Kentucky and Pennsylvania, as well as the Northwest, and coal and manufactured products as well as agricultural commodities, was estimated at from $18 to $20 million. New Orleans receipts of flour, corn, and pork probably were not worth in excess of $3.5 million, or just 75 per cent more than the estimate for Mississippi alone.[40] Some vessels running down the Mississippi River and finding that New Orleans offered but little for their produce, continued to the Gulf, turned eastward, and made for Mobile, Alabama, thus competing with New Orleans' own extensive produce trade with that Gulf port. As early as 1823, numerous boats from "back of Virginia" were arriving at Mobile. In the middle and late 1830's a market for produce also opened up in the Republic of Texas, and for a time ports like Galveston were purchasing flour at $20 to $25 per barrel and corn at $1.50 to $2.00 a bushel.[41] The market in Texas, as well as those along the Gulf east of Mobile and south Atlantic ports, was generally supplied directly by New Orleans, although some vessels rigged for sea were being con-

---

[38] *NWR*, XX (June 9, 1821), 239, XXXIII (November 3, 1827), 150; Switzler, "Report on Internal Commerce," 377; *De Bow's Review*, VII (November, 1849), 415-416.

[39] United States Commissioner of Patents, *Annual Report on Agriculture, 1842* (Washington, D.C., 1843), 49 (hereafter cited as *Patent Report*, [year]).

[40] This estimate is based on New Orleans receipts of 2 million bushels of corn at 35 cents, 290,000 barrels of flour at $5, and 78,000 barrels of pork at $12. Prices in 1836 were rising, after a violent drop between 1833 and 1835, occasioned in part by the erratic financial condition of the country and exacerbated by President Jackson's campaign against the Bank of the United States. Prices were to drop again, as the decade ended with the United States in the midst of a depression.

[41] *NWR*, XXIV (March 8, 1823), 1; *The Daily Picayune*, September 25, 1838.

structed at places like Marietta, Delaware, Circleville, and Chillicothe in the 1820's, and, as they made their maiden voyages, might have touched at southern ports.[42] It is probable that something less than 50 per cent of the surplus products leaving the Old Northwest arrived at New Orleans during the 1820's, and that the proportion intercepted above that market grew steadily from 1830 until 1860. During years such as 1827, in which a severe drought damaged the corn crop in Georgia, Louisiana, Alabama, and Mississippi, the proportion of produce sold above New Orleans probably increased.[43] But in years of unusual foreign demand, particularly 1846-49, New Orleans receipts increased both relatively and absolutely.

Demand and prices in the New Orleans market were dependent upon a number of factors over which little control could be exercised, such as the almost static condition of the foreign market. Since this will be treated in subsequent pages, it will suffice to remark here that from 1815 to 1839 flour exports from the United States exceeded 1 million barrels in only six of those years: 1817-18, 1820-21, and 1830-31. Bulk wheat exports were insignificant—under 100,000 bushels in each year but 1818 and 1831—and the value of Indian corn and meal declined from $2.3 million in 1818 to $1 million in 1826, and to an annual average of $900,000 in 1835-39. Beef products as an export item declined in value from between $740,000 and $930,000 in 1822-25 to $372,000 in 1839, while pork products fluctuated between $1.2 million and $2.1 million during this period.[44] The foreign market for American grain was quite stagnant from 1820 to 1839. This fact alone does much to account for the relatively slow growth New Orleans experienced as a grain market.

---

[42] D. B. Warden, *Statistical, Political, and Historical Account of the United States of North America; from the Period of Their First Colonization to the Present Day* (3 vols., Edinburgh, 1819), II, 274. This was largely a revival of an industry which flourished between 1800 and 1807. Michaux, *Travels to the West*, 177, credits Marietta's citizens with being the first to conceive of exporting directly to the Caribbean Islands. The success attending the first voyages furnished the impetus which made shipbuilding an important industry at Pittsburgh, Cincinnati, Marietta, Wheeling, and other points. Extensive cordage works were located at Lexington, Kentucky. Many other towns engaged in the subsidiary industries connected with shipbuilding. See Baldwin, *Keelboat Age*, 159-174.

[43] *NWR*, XXXII (August 18, 1827), 402, XXXIII (October 6, 1827), 85.

[44] Evans, "Exports, Domestic and Foreign," 20-23; United States Treasury Department, *Commerce and Navigation. Annual Reports. 1821-39* (Washington, D.C., 1821-39). Until 1850 these reports are found in the published House and Senate documents, thereafter as separate volumes.

The New Orleans grain market was more active in terms of quantities handled from 1831 to 1839. Flour receipts rose to 361,000 barrels in 1831, dropped to 264,000 in 1837, and then rose to 436,-000 barrels in 1839. The large percentage improvement from 1830 to 1839, almost 225 per cent, represents an increase of only 300,000 barrels of flour. Cleveland, in 1839, was receiving 2.8 million bushels of wheat and flour (flour converted at five bushels to the barrel), or 87 per cent more than New Orleans. Buffalo, exploiting its position on the Erie Canal, handled almost 800,000 bushels in excess of New Orleans' receipts in 1838 and over 1 million bushels more in 1839. Flour inspections at New York City, fluctuating between a low of 216,000 barrels in 1819 and a high of 361,000 in 1824, rose rapidly as a result of the Erie Canal. Inspections in 1826, reaching 528,000 barrels, were 300 per cent greater than receipts at New Orleans; and inspections in 1830, amounting to 871,000 barrels, were 554 per cent greater. From 1833 to 1839, New York inspections remained just above the million-barrel mark, while New Orleans receipts increased. In 1839 New York was again receiving three times as much flour as New Orleans.[45] Thereafter, though the percentage difference declined, New York was considerably more important as a grain market than New Orleans, and after 1854 Chicago was also.

New Orleans made its greatest gain between 1820 and 1839 in the provisions trade. From the 1830's, barreled and bulk pork and lard exceeded flour and bulk corn in value. The increase was quite rapid, and was a reflection of the expansion of the corn-hog regime in the Ohio valley.

In 1822-26 New Orleans received an aggregate of 90,000 tons of barreled and bulk pork. By 1834 the receipts for that single year equaled 91,000 tons. At the same time receipts of lard had risen sharply from 35,000 hogsheads and barrels in 1825 to an annual average of 218,000 during the five years 1835-39. Receipts of bacon and bacon hams also increased, though much less rapidly than pork and lard, from 1828 to 1839.[46] During this period a barrel of pork was probably worth at least 50 per cent more than a barrel of flour. By 1837-38 the receipts of barreled pork alone were probably worth

---

[45] Hall, *Notes on the Western States*, 277; M'Culloch, *Dictionary*, I, 686, II, 215-216, 230; United States Treasury Department, *Statistics of the Foreign and Domestic Commerce of the United States* (Washington, D.C., 1864), 161.

[46] Switzler, "Report on Internal Commerce," 195-202, 216-218. To arrive at a common unit for pork, barrels were converted to pounds.

60 per cent of the total value of flour. To the total value of pork and pork products can be added the increase in bulk corn receipts, since pork was but another form of corn.

Even greater gains in pork and pork products were to be recorded at New Orleans in the following decade. The same is true for flour, for it was in the decade of the 1840's that New Orleans made its most impressive gains as a grain center. But in spite of this, the progress of New Orleans in developing her grain trade was less substantial than in the northern emporiums of Cleveland, Toledo, Chicago, and Milwaukee. In fact, New Orleans did relatively little in a systematic way to develop her produce business.[47] If it actually grew, it was more as a response to external forces to which New Orleans reacted by virtue of her strategic location. And whatever growth was experienced in the grain and produce business was completely overshadowed by the dominance the cotton trade exerted on the minds of her citizens. The grain trade brought some prosperity to New Orleans because of her geographic position. In the North, cities like Cleveland and Toledo flourished because the favorable aspects of their location were consciously exploited while disabilities were more or less systematically removed or ameliorated.

In spite of this, however, as late as 1856 and 1857, New Orleans handled over 7 million bushels of wheat and flour, but her role was of diminishing importance to the Northwest. Simultaneously, the Northwest was becoming increasingly less important to New Orleans. By this time the diversion of the grain trade of the Northwest to other outlets was already well under way.

---

[47] More will be said about the conditions under which the grain trade operated at New Orleans in Chapter VII.

The Rise of the Lake Erie Ports

CHAPTER III

Along the northern border of the United States, the Great Lakes provide a natural avenue of commerce between East and West. They had been exploited for purposes of trade since the French, during their occupancy of North America, ascended the St. Lawrence to Lake Ontario, crossed that lake to the southeast, made a portage at Niagara Falls, entered Lake Erie, and finally through a system of portages gained the Ohio River and asserted their authority over the whole Northwest. After a century of struggle initially between the French and the English, and then between the English and Americans, the control of the north shore of the lakes passed to England and the south shore to the United States. But during this time, the nature of the trade, which was mostly in furs, changed but little. Indeed, it did not experience any noticeable extension until the third and fourth decades of the nineteenth century. In those decades the Erie Canal was completed, permitting continuous navigation between the lakes and the port of New York. When this took place, immigrants began to pour into the regions in Ohio and Michigan fronting Lake Erie.

Before the mid-1830's the bulk of the trade along the lakes flowed from east to west. The Erie Canal was more important in providing a route for emigrants, their belongings, and eastern manufactured goods, than as an opening through which western goods could reach tidewater. Most of the northern sections of the Old Northwest were still in their infancy, with neither an established population nor a developed economy.[1] A major factor in the development of the region was the growth of the grain economy along the lakes and the rise of ports on the lakes to handle the grain trade. These ports were to develop at the places which were most accessible to the interior, largely at the mouths of streams. Thus Cleveland arose at the mouth of the Cuyahoga, Toledo at the mouth of the Maumee, and ports such as Milan and Sandusky at points where streams emptied into Lake Erie. Not all of these ambitious ports could succeed. Some would flourish while trade at others stagnated and eventually declined. Perhaps the most important criterion for success was the ability of such ports to improve their connections with the interior, thus expanding the area from which they drew the major articles of export and to which they sold goods imported from the East. The expansion of transportation facilities—first roads, then canals, and finally railroads—was essential for the economic growth of a lake port. Without such expansion, a port would eventually succumb to the more energetic policies of its competitors. Transportation was the key to the development of the grain trade of the lakes and to the growth of particular ports on the lakes.

After 1835 the lake trade expanded at an increasingly rapid tempo as eastern merchandise sought markets in the West and farm products were shipped from interior markets of Ohio to the East. The total lake trade rose steadily from $4 million in 1835 to $65.8

---

[1] In 1820 the northern one-third of Ohio contained only 11 per cent of the state's 581,000 inhabitants. Ten per cent were in the Western Reserve district. A decade later this region contained over 21 per cent of the population. In Indiana the northern 30 counties contained only 17 per cent of the population in 1839, over one-half living along the upper Wabash; in 1849, 26 per cent were in the north. Neither Michigan nor Wisconsin had 400,000 inhabitants in 1849, and the northwestern and lake shore counties of Illinois were settled but slowly until the 1840's.

million in 1831, while exports from the West formed 14 per cent of
the total in 1835. By 1846 the value of the lake trade was approaching $100 million.[2] Grain exports were probably worth about $13
million in 1841, or some 21 per cent of the total trade on the lakes.
This would be the equivalent of some 40 per cent of total western
shipments, and, if provisions and whiskey were added, in addition
to the unknown exports of ports like Venice and Ashtabula, the
foodstuffs trade would probably account for above 50 per cent of
the West's exports. During the early years of this expanding lake
trade, Ohio probably contributed over 80 per cent of the receipts
and exports, and although the proportion of the total trade based in
Ohio declined during the 1840's, it is likely that Ohio's lake trade
remained over one-half of the total until the 1850's, for as late as
1850 one-half of the 1.5 million people dependent on the lakes for
a market were located in Ohio.

A number of factors needed to be present along with an increase in population before a lake trade of great significance from
west to east could come into existence. Perhaps the most important
of these prerequisites was the development of an urban population
in the East dependent upon outside sources for its food supply.
Between 1820 and 1860 the population of New York, Philadelphia,
Baltimore, and Boston rose from 338,000 to 2 million, an increase of
over 500 per cent, while the population of the United States expanded by 225 per cent. The southern market along the lower Mississippi was too distant and expensive an outlet for the lake regions
to use. But the Atlantic coast could be reached by an all-water route
from a lake port such as Cleveland. And it was in the growing commercial and manufacturing centers of the East that western produce
found its domestic market and its outlet to world markets. During
the period 1825-45, routes from the lake shore to the East expanded
and multiplied, first with the Erie Canal, then the Welland Canal
connecting Lake Erie and Lake Ontario; and then in the early 1840's
the Western Railroad connected Albany with Boston and New England—the largest regional market for surplus foodstuffs in the
United States.

The existence of a route by which a market could be reached,

---

[2] "Report of the Chief Topographical Engineer, 1843," *House Executive
Documents*, 28 Cong., 1 Sess., No. 2 (1843), Serial 439, 160-161; "Report from
the Topographical Bureau in Relation to the Commerce, Navigation, and Means
of Defense of the Western Lakes and Rivers, 1847," *Senate Executive Documents*, 30 Cong., 1 Sess., No. 4 (1848), Serial 504, 42.

coupled with a swelling population in the lake shore counties, did not necessarily mean that a surplus would develop in the region sufficient to supply the needs of the lake ports and their markets. In fact, ports such as Cleveland and Toledo first tapped and were dependent upon the distant interior for their source of cereal products. The districts contiguous to these ports did not develop sufficiently to supply the demands for grain made on the lake ports by the East.

Since settlement and development in the eastern areas of the Northwest preceded the same process in the western, it was inevitable that the lake trade in grain should develop in various areas at a different pace and time. Table 4 indicates that Ohio's grain trade was of overwhelming quantitative importance for a period of years. The early predominance of the grain markets located on Lake Erie reflected this condition. The table also shows the steady and relatively rapid growth of the grain trade of Lake Michigan after 1845.

The most salient trend indicated in Table 4 is the pronounced rise in shipments and receipts between 1845 and 1847, caused entirely by an extraordinary foreign demand for American foodstuffs.[3] Perhaps most significant in terms of the Northwest was the manifest ability of the region to increase its total production sufficiently to meet this unusual demand. This had particular applicability to Ohio as the most settled and agriculturally diversified of the East North Central states. From 1840 to 1845, Ohio's Lake Erie markets had maintained a level of export so stable that one can reasonably assume that the areas feeding this trade were not increasing their production appreciably.[4] The relative position of Ohio in the lake trade had been declining at a constant rate due to increasing shipments from Michigan's ports on Lake Erie and Lake Michigan.

But between 1845 and 1847 Ohio was capable of doubling its

---

[3] U.S. exports of wheat and flour rose from 6.3 million bushels in 1845 to 26.3 million in 1847; corn from 840,000 bushels in 1845 to 16.3 million in 1847. Evans, "Exports, Domestic and Foreign," Table 2, 20-23.

[4] Ohio's share of the lake trade declined from 85 per cent of the total in 1840 to 62 per cent in 1845 and 51 per cent in 1846. The Cleveland *Plain Dealer*, January 15, 1845, maintained that Ohio's wheat crop had suffered a great decline from 1840 to 1844 despite an increase in acreage given over to wheat. The crops of 1842 and 1843 were reported to have suffered extensive damage from winter kill, rust, and drought, and the crop of 1844 was considered the lowest of the decade. This assessment is in close correspondence to the estimates in Table 4.

exports, which could be accomplished only by a corresponding increase in total production in the lake's feeder counties. Since the
rise in population in so brief a period could not have been large
enough to provide new farms commensurate with this increase, the

TABLE 4.[5] TOTAL ANNUAL EXPORTS OF WHEAT AND WHEAT FLOUR (REDUCED
TO BUSHELS) FROM ALL LAKE ERIE AND LAKE MICHIGAN PORTS, BY STATE, AND
TOTAL ANNUAL RECEIPTS AT BUFFALO AND OSWEGO, 1840-50 (IN THOUSANDS
OF BUSHELS)

Year	Buffalo-Oswego Receipts	Ohio	Michigan	Illinois	Wisconsin	Four-State Total
1840	4,987	5,834	984	10	–	6,828
1841	6,162	5,339	1,867	40	–	7,246
1842	6,199	5,263	1,566	582	–	7,411
1843	7,723	5,158	1,990	742	–	7,890
1844	8,003	5,965	2,234	923	–	9,122
1845	7,530	5,157	1,901	1,025	266	8,349
1846	14,600	7,402	4,650	1,600	584	14,336
1847	19,850	11,780	5,267	2,136	1,572	20,755
1848	14,868	7,900	3,500	2,386	2,132	15,918
1849	16,188	7,563	3,500	2,193	3,583	16,839
1850	14,569	7,855	4,770	1,339	1,596	15,560

growth in production can best be accounted for by a diversion of
effort from other agricultural pursuits to the production of wheat.
For a relatively constant population to double its wheat production
in the space of two years took an immense effort by farmers who
were considered skillful if they could reap two acres of wheat daily
during the harvest period of ten days to two weeks.[6] It is possible

---

[5] Ohio's lake exports are estimated from the known shipments of her
major markets—Cleveland, Sandusky, Toledo, Milan, and Huron. The totals for
Michigan for 1840-46 are based on the assumption that Detroit exported about
60 per cent of all of Michigan's grain, and those from 1847 to 1849 are based
on Michigan's estimated wheat production of between 4.7 and 4.9 million bushels from 1848 to 1850. Michigan Department of State, *Census and Statistics
of the State of Michigan, May, 1854* (Lansing, 1854), 389-393; *7 Census, 1850*,
904-905; *Patent Report, 1849*, 553. The figures for Illinois are represented by
exports from Chicago. Those for Wisconsin for 1847 and 1849 represent shipments from Milwaukee, Racine, and Kenosha (Southport). In 1845-46, 1848,
and 1850, Wisconsin's exports are Milwaukee's doubled since it appears that
Milwaukee exported about one-half of Wisconsin's total during the period 1845-
50. For Buffalo-Oswego, see Table 11.

[6] William Oliver, *Eight Months in Illinois, with Information to Immigrants*
(Newcastle-upon-Tyne, 1843, Chicago, 1924), 92. Leo Rogin, *The Introduction
of Farm Machinery in Its Relation to the Productivity of Labor in the Agricul-*

that the lake ports of Ohio, particularly Cleveland, drew a larger portion of their grain than normal from areas to the south, which usually sent their grain to markets on the Ohio River. Although total exports at Cincinnati show a large increase, equivalent to some 2.1 million bushels of wheat, between 1845 and 1847, Cincinnati's receipts of wheat and flour via the Miami Canal remained static from 1846 to 1850, and receipts at Portsmouth, on the Ohio Canal, did not attain significant proportions. Cincinnati was obtaining grain supplies, at least in part, from other areas than those served by the Miami Canal.[7]

In the period before 1860, the state of Michigan was oriented commercially to its limited frontage on Lake Erie rather than to its more extensive frontage on Lake Michigan. In terms of the over-all grain trade, Michigan lagged behind Ohio during the 1840's and Illinois and Wisconsin during the 1850's, all of which shipped part of their product by way of the Mississippi River system. In terms of the lake trade, however, Michigan, until the middle 1850's, was second only to Ohio, thus further confirming the dominant position of Lake Erie.

From Table 4 it is evident that Michigan's grain exports rose steadily through 1847 and leveled off until 1850. This was the result of a succession of poor crops. It was during the period 1840-47 that Michigan's relative importance in the total lake trade reached its peak. While Ohio markets, through 1847, were exporting more produce than the other four states combined, Michigan's share of the trade increased from 14 per cent in 1840 to 32 per cent in 1846.[8]

---

ture of the United States During the Nineteenth Century (Berkeley, Calif., 1931), 130, reckons one day of man labor as required to cradle, bind, and shock an acre of wheat, so that a family possessing a harvest force of three people could be expected to harvest little over 30 acres in a ten-day period.

[7] *Thirty-fourth Annual Report of the Cincinnati Chamber of Commerce and Merchants' Exchange . . . 1882* (Cincinnati, 1882), 155, 171. The Little Miami Railroad between Cincinnati-Xenia-Springfield-Columbus was completed in 1848 and offered some canal counties a parallel route to Cincinnati, as well as opening a new source area for that city. James Hall, *The West: Its Commerce and Navigation* (Cincinnati, 1848), 297. This partially accounts for Cincinnati's ability to increase exports of grain while not increasing grain receipts from the canal.

[8] During the early 1840's a considerable portion of Toledo's exports were derived from Michigan sources. It was estimated that from 1842 to 1846 Toledo received 87 per cent of wheat receipts and 75 per cent of flour from Michigan. *Hunt's*, XVI (February, 1847), 191. This means that Ohio's exports in Table 4 include that quantity of wheat raised in southeastern Michigan and marketed at Toledo.

After 1850 Michigan's grain trade suffered a relative decline which continued during the remainder of the decade. Michigan's lake trade was rapidly surpassed by both Illinois and Wisconsin, neither of which really hit stride until the 1850's, when Chicago and Milwaukee became the major grain entrepots in the Northwest.[9]

One student of the grain trade in the Old Northwest has estimated that the grain trade from that region doubled between 1839 and 1844, rising from some 6 million bushels of wheat in 1839 to about 12 million in 1844, of which in the latter year over 76 per cent went via the Great Lakes, compared to less than 60 per cent in 1839.[10] It appears that most of this increase (and it was probably about 75 per cent greater in 1844 than 1839 for the Northwest as a whole) was supplied by grain-exporting centers in states other than Ohio, since the latter's lake and river shipments remained stationary until 1846. But even while remaining at a stable level, Ohio grain markets supplied, from 1843 to 1845, between 62 and 65 per cent of total lake shipments, and Lake Erie as a whole furnished well over 60 per cent of the grain traffic as late as 1849, and over 80 per cent in the period prior to 1847. The lake trade is virtually synonymous with that of Lake Erie during most of the 1840's, and the centrality of this lake was associated with the rise of market centers like Cleveland, Sandusky, Toledo, Detroit, and a score of lesser known ports.

The grain markets on the lakes were engaged in a two-dimensional struggle. In the aggregate they formed part of a lake complex which used improved transportation facilities to tap regions farther from the lakes, thus competing with markets on the Ohio River for the grain of the intervening territory. And as individual markets they were, in many cases, rivals for the grain trade of the same areas. As noted, these separate markets developed or failed to develop according to their ability to tap and expand their hinterland.

----

[9] By 1860 Chicago was exporting almost twice as much wheat as the entire state of Michigan produced. (Illinois and Wisconsin will be treated in the following chapter on the Lake Michigan grain trade.)

Indiana's over-all position is impossible to determine. Her total grain trade exceeded Michigan's but was focused primarily on the South until the late 1840's, when indeterminable quantities began reaching Toledo and Chicago, as well as Michigan City, which was Indiana's major lake port. In subsequent pages attention will be directed to northern Indiana and its market outlets.

[10] A. L. Kohlmeier, *The Old Northwest as the Keystone of the Arch of the American Federal Union. A Study in Commerce and Politics* (Bloomington, Ind., 1938), 33-34, 52-53.

For most of these markets it was imperative to draw grain supplies from noncontiguous areas if a sustained growth was to be experienced. Both Cleveland and Toledo were compelled to tap the distant interior to procure grain, since neighboring counties supplied at a maximum 20 per cent of the grain entering the lake trade.[11]

The grain markets on Lake Erie, then, were obtaining their supplies from interior sources. The Ohio Canal put Cleveland in touch with the upper Muskingum valley. Turnpikes and railroads served Sandusky. The Wabash and Erie Canal allowed Toledo to draw supplies from the upper Wabash valley, while the Miami and Erie Canal brought to Toledo the surplus products of the Miami and Auglaize river counties. The Erie and Kalamazoo Railroad carried grain from southeastern Michigan to Toledo, and this development stimulated Detroit's efforts to exploit her interior.

CLEVELAND

During the period 1840-54, Cleveland was the major grain-forwarding center on the Great Lakes.[12] Cleveland's ascendancy was based upon its location at the mouth of the Cuyahoga River, the source of which was only a few miles distant from the northern reaches of the Tuscarawas River. This fact was a determinant in selecting the route of the Ohio Canal, which was completed in 1833, to provide a continuous waterway from Portsmouth to Lake Erie. By means of this canal, Cleveland was connected with neighboring counties and more distant counties in the Tuscarawas and upper Muskingum river valleys.

It has been maintained that the rise of the grain trade on the lakes was directly attributable to the surplus produced by the regions bordering on Lake Erie.[13] But an analysis of the data will show that, although Cleveland was the major port in the Western Reserve district of Ohio, it was not dependent upon this area for the bulk of its exports. Indeed, the six Western Reserve counties which were tributary to Cleveland produced a total of 972,000

---

[11] 6 *Census, 1840*, 275-276; Charles Cist, *Cincinnati in 1841: Its Early Annals and Future Prospects* (Cincinnati, 1841), 299.

[12] In 1855 Chicago's grain trade exceeded that of Cleveland and in 1858 Toledo's grain trade also surpassed Cleveland's for the first time. At this point Toledo became the major port on Lake Erie.

[13] Kohlmeier, *Old Northwest as Keystone*, 20; Emory R. Johnson *et al.*, *History of Domestic and Foreign Commerce of the United States* (2 vols., Washington, D.C., 1915), I, 230.

bushels of wheat in 1839, which, after feeding a population of 122,-569, left no more than 500,000 bushels as an exportable surplus. In 1840 Cleveland received and exported over 4.6 million bushels. The Western Reserve supplied even a smaller proportion of Cleveland's receipts in 1849.[14] The Reserve was not a major grain-growing area in the state, but was at this time developing a significant dairy and dairy products industry.[15]

Throughout the period 1835-55, Cleveland was dependent upon the Ohio Canal for the great bulk of her grain receipts. Well over 90 per cent of these, including pork and whiskey, arrived on the Ohio Canal. It was estimated that over 85 per cent of the wheat and flour shipped on the canal was destined for Cleveland in the years 1841-44.[16]

In terms of production, population, and consumption requirements, it has been established above that the Western Reserve district supplied Cleveland with less than 20 per cent of total wheat and flour receipts. The remainder, over 80 per cent of the receipts, came from counties south of the Western Reserve, and located in the Tuscarawas and upper Muskingum river valleys. Some writers have argued that the Ohio Canal and its western counterpart, the Miami Canal, while they did not benefit the southern portions of Ohio to any considerable degree, did not take away a significant amount of trade from the southern outlet and transfer it to the northern, but served as feeders to both routes.[17] But in terms of wheat alone, as Table 5 indicates, Cleveland receipts came from sources as far south as Roscoe, Coshocton, and Zanesville, areas which had, prior to the canals, shipped down the Muskingum to the Ohio River. This was a diversion of trade, although its proportions are unknown. But the question of diversion is not the central one. Emphasis should center on the fact that before canal connec-

---

[14] *6 Census, 1840,* 78, 275-276; *7 Census, 1850,* 817-818, 863-864; C. P. McClelland and C. C. Huntington, *History of the Ohio Canals. Their Construction, Cost, Use and Partial Abandonment* (Columbus, Ohio, 1905), Appendix J, 175-176. The counties involved are Cuyahoga, Geauga, Lake, Lorrain, Medina, Portage, and Summit.

[15] From 1839 to 1859 the Western Reserve raised between 20 and 25 per cent of the cattle in Ohio, of which some 45 to 50 per cent were dairy cattle.

[16] Cleveland *Plain Dealer,* March 12, 1845.

[17] Abraham H. Sadove, *Transport Improvement and the Appalachian Barrier. A Case Study in Economic Innovation* (Harvard University, unpublished doctoral dissertation, 1950), 155-177; Kohlmeier, *Old Northwest as Keystone,* 20.

tions were obtained for this area, there was very little trade of any kind. A grain trade of considerable proportions developed primarily because the canals gave the region an outlet to the north and Lake Erie. Cleveland derived the greatest benefit from this development.

TABLE 5. TOTAL WHEAT AND FLOUR SHIPPED ANNUALLY ON THE OHIO CANAL, ORIGIN OF TOTAL, AND PERCENTAGE OF CLEVELAND'S WHEAT RECEIPTS TO CANAL TOTAL, 1835-44 (IN THOUSANDS OF BUSHELS)

Year	Ohio Canal Total	Wheat from North of Roscoe	Wheat from South of Roscoe	Per Cent of Cleveland's Wheat Receipts to Total
1835	1,178	601	577	97
1836	1,467	837	629	88
1837	1,636	813	823	96
1838	2,738	1,345	1,392	97
1839	3,876	1,337	1,538	73
1840	4,853	2,705	2,147	95
1841	4,211	2,293	1,918	92
1842	3,868	2,059	1,808	88
1843	3,844	2,404	1,440	96
1844	3,621	2,404	1,220	96

Sources: *Hunt's*, VIII (March, 1843), 276, XII (May, 1845), 454; McClelland and Huntington, *History of the Ohio Canals*, Appendix J, 175-176.

Cleveland's area of supply covered virtually the entire northeastern quarter of Ohio, from Ashtabula and Trumbull counties in the extreme northeast to Coshocton, Knox, and Licking counties in central Ohio, between the upper Muskingum and upper Scioto river valleys. Several lateral or feeder canals connected the Ohio Canal with areas on either side and served to extend the territory from which Cleveland derived its cereals. The Beaver Canal from Akron to Mahoning County and a connection with the Pennsylvania canals was completed in 1839. The Walhonding Canal was constructed into Knox and Richmond counties. In 1846 the Sandy and Beaver Canal was completed from Bolivar on the Ohio Canal to a point in Columbiana County some 40 miles south of Pittsburgh.[18]

Numerous towns sprang up along the route of the Ohio Canal

---

[18] *NWR*, LV (October 6, 1838), 195; B. Henry Meyer et al., *History of Transportation in the United States Before 1860* (Washington, D.C., 1948), 288-289. The Beaver Canal, completed in 1846, was abandoned in 1852 due to the paralleling of the canal by the Pittsburgh, Fort Wayne, and Chicago Railroad.

and some, like Massillon, Akron, Roscoe, and Dover, became fairly important grain-forwarding centers for the surrounding countryside. This prosperity was intimately related to that of Cleveland and the Ohio Canal. In the 1850's, when Ohio was crisscrossed with competing railroad lines, the economies of these centers suffered great strains, from which most did not recover.

Akron was perhaps the most important of these towns and reacted with greater resiliency than most to the coming of the railroad. The Ohio Canal reached Akron in 1827. Five years later a spur canal from Pennsylvania was completed to Akron over which large quantities of wheat were shipped to Cleveland. All of the wheat that arrived at Cleveland from the south passed through the town. Considerable quantities of wheat were consigned through to New York from centers like Akron and Massillon and not offered for sale at Cleveland.[19] The grain trade of Akron grew to considerable dimensions in the 1840's, more or less mirroring market conditions in Cleveland. Much of the bulk wheat received at Akron, by wagon and canal, was manufactured into flour and shipped to Lake Erie.[20] The town forwarded some 376,000 barrels of flour to Cleveland in 1846 and 1847, and this consignment composed close to 30 per cent of Cleveland's receipts.[21] These figures are illustrative of the great dependence of Cleveland upon areas south of Akron for a grain supply.

Thirty miles south of Akron, the town of Massillon handled large quantities of bulk wheat, a portion of which was milled in Akron. Traffic at this canal depot was heavy; in one week in May, 1847, wagons hauled over 126,000 bushels of wheat to the town, and in that year 1.7 million bushels of wheat and flour cleared Massillon on the Ohio Canal.[22] In the early 1850's the grain trade at Massillon entered a decline as Cleveland's grain receipts via railroads cut

[19] Cleveland *Plain Dealer*, April 17, 1844.

[20] *Ibid.*, April 17, 1844, December 25, 1844. In 1843 and 1844 Akron manufactured 115,000 and 123,000 barrels of flour respectively. "Statistics of the Agriculture and Manufactures, Domestic Trade, Currency, and Banks of the United States," *Senate Documents*, 28 Cong., 2 Sess., Doc. 21 (1844), Serial 450, 231.

[21] Cleveland *Plain Dealer*, March 12, 1845; *Report to the President and Directors of the Ohio and Pennsylvania Rail-Road Company, 1848* (Philadelphia, 1849), 16; *Patent Report, 1847*, 622-627.

[22] *The Ohio Cultivator*, III (June 1, 1847), 84; "Statistics of the Agriculture and Manufactures . . . of the U.S." (1844), 334-339; *Patent Report, 1847*, 622-627.

heavily into canal traffic. By this time Massillon was located on the Ohio and Pennsylvania Railroad, and it may be assumed that some grain which had normally gone to Cleveland went east by rail.

Among other canal towns, Roscoe, Dresden, and Newark served as forwarding centers for Cleveland, although to a lesser degree than Massillon or Akron. Newark, located on the Licking River and connected by railroad to Sandusky, shipped over 200,000 bushels of wheat annually during the 1840's. Dresden, 15 miles north of Zanesville, was the terminus of the Muskingum Improvement project and received and forwarded grain on both the Ohio Canal and the Muskingum. Of 200,000 barrels of flour cleared from Dresden in 1846-57, 140,000 were received from the Muskingum Improvement while 180,000 barrels were shipped on the Ohio Canal—for the most part to the north. Roscoe shipped during the same two years 100,000 barrels of flour and 200,000 bushels of wheat.[23]

Next to Akron and Massillon, Dover, in Tuscarawas County, was the largest forwarding center on the Ohio Canal serving Cleveland. Located on the Tuscarawas River just above the mouth of Sugar Creek, the town shipped in the neighborhood of 54,000 barrels of flour and 410,000 bushels of wheat annually between 1843 and 1851.[24]

The quantities of wheat and flour shipped from the six towns of Newark, Dresden, Roscoe, Dover, Massillon, and Akron, if added together for the years 1846-47, closely approximate Cleveland's total receipts.[25] This affinity between receipts and shipments used conjointly with the known inability of Cleveland's immediate hinterland to supply over 20 per cent of Cleveland's receipts leads to the conclusion that Cleveland drew her grain from areas as distant as the middle Scioto and Muskingum valleys, probably as far south as McConnelsville on the Muskingum and Chillicothe on the Scioto. In the vicinity of these towns, the market was shared with Cleveland by the Ohio River terminals of Harmar and Portsmouth.

---

[23] *Ibid.*; "Statistics of the Agriculture and Manufactures . . . of the U.S." (1844), 334-339; *Lippincott's New and Complete Gazetteer of the United States* (Philadelphia, 1854), 330-331, 767.

[24] See fn. 23.

[25] For 1846 the six markets shipped 3.4 million bushels while Cleveland received 3.5 million, and in 1847 the latter received 5.8 million while the six towns forwarded the same quantity. "Statistics of the Agriculture and Manufactures . . . of the U.S." (1844), 334-339; McClelland and Huntington, *History of the Ohio Canals*, Appendix J, 175-176.

The same economic process which made Cleveland a collection center for the grain crops of a wide area of Ohio also made the town a vital staging and shipping center for grain surpluses and a distributing center for eastern manufactured articles seeking markets in the northern quarter of Ohio. In view of Cleveland's concentration upon the grain trade, it was natural that during the 1840's at least 50 per cent of the total value of Cleveland's exports should come from wheat and flour shipments.[26] If the figures should be modified to include exports of pork, pork products, and whiskey, this alteration would not change the relationship appreciably since shipments of those commodities were relatively small at that time.[27]

Exports of wheat flour and bulk wheat from 1840 to 1850 fluctuated rather sharply at some points in the decade; and, as Table 6 indicates, the grain trade did not grow appreciably over the ten-year period.

The ebb and flow in Cleveland's grain trade can be explained in various ways. In 1841 the decline in receipts and exports was accounted for by a partial failure in the wheat crop in southern Ohio which diverted shipments from Cleveland to the south to fill local consumption requirements.[28] The sharp drop in receipts in the fall of 1843 was blamed on poor prices, which caused farmers to hold back part of their crop, and impassable roads resulting from heavy rains after harvest.[29] A greatly expanded foreign demand was reflected in the marked rise in receipts and shipments from 1845 to

---

[26] The share of the grain trade in Cleveland's exports experienced a sharp diminution in the 1850's. In 1843, of a total export of $5.5 million, wheat and flour were valued at $2.9 million. In 1848 wheat and flour formed 57 per cent of an export of $6.7 million, but in 1851 wheat and flour made up only 32 per cent of $12.2 million worth of exports. Israel D. Andrews, "Reports on the Trade and Commerce of the British North American Colonies and upon the Trade of the Great Lakes and Rivers," *House Executive Documents*, 32 Cong., 2 Sess., Document 136 (1853), Serial 622, 168-169 (hereafter cited as Andrews, "Reports on Trade and Commerce"); *Hunt's*, XVI (April, 1847), 364.

[27] During the 1840's Cleveland probably exported about 10 per cent of Ohio's pork and whiskey. Receipts of pork at Cleveland fluctuated between 15,000 and 35,000 barrels during the decade, while Ohio's total exports were rising to over 300,000 barrels. Cleveland's whiskey trade did show an increase, with receipts rising from 14,000 barrels in 1843 to 29,000 in 1847 and 41,000 in 1848. At this time Ohio's total exports were approaching 200,000 barrels. Cleveland *Plain Dealer*, December 25, 1844; *Fisher's National Magazine and Industrial Record*, II (December, 1845), 615; *The Ohio Cultivator*, III (April 15, 1847), 58; *Patent Report, 1848*, 805.

[28] *NWR*, LXII (March 19, 1842), 85. Cincinnati's receipts also declined by some 50,000 barrels of flour. *Hunt's*, XII (May, 1845), 456.

[29] Cleveland *Plain Dealer*, January 1, 1844.

1846.[30] The trade returned quickly to former levels and failed to display any great energy until the early years of the 1850's, which were the peak years in Cleveland's grain trade before the Civil War.[31]

TABLE 6. ANNUAL RECEIPTS AND SHIPMENTS OF WHEAT, FLOUR, AND CORN AT CLEVELAND, 1840-49 (IN THOUSANDS)

Year	Receipts			Shipments		
	Wheat (bu.)	Flour (bbl.)	Corn (bu.)	Wheat (bu.)	Flour (bbl.)	Corn (bu.)
1840	2,155	505	96	2,000	500	–
1841	1,564	441	245	1,593	461	204
1842	1,312	493	219	–	–	–
1843	814	577	228	724	597	197
1844	977	495	264	931	521	216
1845	1,229	378	146	–	–	–
1846	1,598	342	558	1,672	368	527
1847	2,130	645	1,381	2,366	698	1,400
1848	1,585	418	651	1,267	473	690
1849	863	527	528	–	–	–

Sources: Receipts—McClelland and Huntington, *History of the Ohio Canals*, Appendix J, 175-176; *Hunt's*, XII (May, 1845), 454; *Patent Report, 1848*, 805. Shipments—Andrews, "Reports on Trade and Commerce," 168-169; "Report of the Chief Topographical Engineer, 1843," 158-159; *Hunt's*, VI (February, 1842), 190, X (March, 1844), 293, XVI (April, 1847), 364; *Fisher's National Magazine*, II (December, 1845), 615.

By far the greater part of Cleveland's grain exports traveled over the Lake Erie route to an eastern terminal, with Buffalo receiving the great bulk while Montreal and American ports on Lake Ontario shared the remainder.[32]

Cleveland began shipping produce to Montreal by way of the Welland Canal as early as 1831. By 1835 over $200,000 worth of

[30] In 1847, of 57 counties reporting wheat prices from 60 cents to $1 a bushel, 14 reported wheat above 86 cents. Nine of these were in the Western Reserve and three in the upper Muskingum—all within the area supplying Cleveland with grain. *Patent Report, 1848*, 528-531.

[31] In 1851-53 a total of 2.2 million barrels of flour and 8.2 million bushels of wheat were exported. Andrews, "Reports on Trade and Commerce," 168-169; *Hunt's*, XXIX (October, 1853), 512; Chicago *Daily Tribune*, March 27, 1854.

[32] Cleveland's lake tonnage increased from 1,029 in 1830 to 11,738 in 1844 and 38,238 in 1852. Cleveland *Plain Dealer*, January 2, 1844; *Lippincott's Gazetteer*, 250. The proportions carried by sail and steam are not known. In 1841 only 12,300 barrels of 461,000 shipped went via steamboat, but the use of steam probably increased through the remainder of the decade. *Hunt's*, VI (February, 1842), 190.

goods went to Canada. Freight rates at this time were cheaper by 25 cents a barrel of flour via the Welland Canal to Montreal than by the Erie Canal to New York.[33] For the most part, Cleveland wheat and flour sought Canadian ports because there it was given a preferred position in the foreign trade with England.[34] During the period 1841-44 about 20 per cent of Cleveland's grain exports went to Canada—mainly Montreal.[35] This trade was all but terminated by the repeal of the Corn Laws in 1845, for Canada was by then normally capable of supplying its own domestic market and there was no longer any advantage in going through a foreign port to reach the English market. Cleveland wheat passing the Welland Canal after 1845 sought markets such as Oswego and Rochester on Lake Ontario and Ogdensburg on the St. Lawrence. These, however, only supplemented the route normally followed through Buffalo to New York City.

During the 1840's Cleveland exported some 80 per cent of the grain leaving the Lake Erie ports of Ohio. The remainder was about equally divided between Milan-Huron, Sandusky, and Toledo, with villages like Vermilion, Venice, and Ashtabula shipping unknown, but negligible, quantities. Most of these towns failed to achieve more than limited and temporary success in their pursuit of commercial riches. The pretensions of Ashtabula were shattered when Trumbull and Mahoning counties, immediately to the south of Ashtabula, were penetrated by a canal which had Akron and Cleveland

---

[33] R. Carlyle Buley, *The Old Northwest. Pioneer Period. 1815-1840* (2 vols., Indianapolis, 1950), I, 538. In October, 1832, it cost one dollar per barrel of flour from Cleveland to Buffalo and another dollar in tolls and freight to Albany. Tolls were reduced by 16 cents a barrel in 1833, but it still cost around $2 a barrel from Cleveland to New York City. Rates would be higher in the spring and fall when demand upon lake shipping was at a peak. *The American Annual Register*, VII (1832-33), 315; *American Railroad Journal. Steam Navigation, Commerce, Mining, Manufactures*, XXVI (April 16, 1853), 242 (hereafter cited as *ARJ*). In April, 1844, flour was charged 92.5 cents from Cleveland to Buffalo, while charges from Buffalo to Albany had declined to 60 cents. *Ibid.*; Cleveland *Plain Dealer*, April 24, 1844. Canal tolls and freight were declining more rapidly than lake freight rates.

[34] American wheat ground into flour at a Canadian mill was taxed as Canadian flour in English markets. American flour replaced the Canadian product on the home market while the latter sought an overseas market.

[35] In 1841-44 produce shipments to Canada equaled just under $1 million annually. *Hunt's*, VI (February, 1842), 190; *Patent Report, 1842*, 54; Cleveland *Plain Dealer*, January 2, 1844, January 22, 1845; *Fisher's National Magazine*, II (March, 1846), 890.

as its major terminals. Cut off from its source of supply, Ashtabula by 1835 was no longer a factor in the grain trade. The pretensions of Milan-Huron and Sandusky, however, survived somewhat longer.

MILAN-HURON AND SANDUSKY

In 1840 the *Niles Weekly Register* made note of the departure from Huron, Ohio, of the schooners *Iowa* and *Helen Mar*, heavily laden with wheat and bound for upper Canada.[36] At this time Huron, at the mouth of the Huron River in Erie County, and Milan, eight miles south of Huron and on the same river, bade fair to become major shipping centers. Until 1845 exports from the Huron River exceeded both those at Sandusky, ten miles to the west, and at Toledo. As early as the 1830's, 30,000 to 40,000 bushels of grain reached Milan daily.[37] During the 1840's exports from this area rose rather steadily from some 400,000 bushels of wheat and flour in 1840 to 1.6 million in 1848. That their prosperity was almost wholly dependent on the grain trade is attested to by the fact that of a total export worth $538,000 in 1842, $457,000 came from produce; and in 1844, exports having risen to $825,000, grain shipments were valued at $624,000. The decline after 1847, when exports reached a value of $2.2 million, and when 1.6 million bushels of wheat were shipped, was precipitous. The next year grain exports plunged to some 700,000 bushels of wheat and flour, and in 1849 total exports were estimated at $639,000. Thereafter, the grain trade from this center was eclipsed by the growth of the neighboring port of Sandusky.[38]

The retrogression of Milan-Huron and the concomitant advance of Sandusky were not entirely fortuitous. At an early time, Sandusky displayed a laudable energy by improving upon its location at the head of Sandusky Bay. In the late 1820's a turnpike was pushed from Sandusky into Seneca, Crawford, and Marion counties.[39] The port began to show increased activity. The number of

[36] *NWR*, LVIII (April 11, 1840), 96.

[37] Harlan Hatcher, *Lake Erie* (Indianapolis, 1945), 227.

[38] *Hunt's*, VIII (May, 1843), 483, XII (February, 1845), 192, XXX (January, 1849), 97; *Patent Report, 1849*, 551, *1851*, 549-550. A similar fate overtook Venice, Ohio, three miles from Sandusky.

[39] W. A. Lloyd, J. I. Falconer, and C. E. Thorne, *The Agriculture of Ohio* (Wooster, Ohio, 1918), 30.

vessels entering the port rose from 355 in 1826 to 437 in 1828. Vast numbers of wagons were seen loading and unloading goods for distribution in the interior and for export.[40]

By 1835 Sandusky, with a population of over 4,000, entered a new stage in her commercial development. At that time a railroad, the Mad River and Lake Erie, was projected to run from Sandusky to Springfield to connect there with Cincinnati via the Little Miami Railroad. Construction on the northern section was begun in 1835. By 1845, 40 miles were in operation, and in 1846 the railroad reached Springfield.[41] During the period 1840-45, the grain trade of Sandusky did not rise appreciably. The value of grain exports remained between $600,000 and $650,000, while the quantities rose slightly from 500,000 bushels in 1840 to between 600,000 and 650,-000 in 1845. Similarly, the total value of all exports hovered between $800,000 and $850,000.[42] Thus, although the railroad came into operation as of 1845, it does not seem to have brought about any perceptible advance in Sandusky's economic life. In 1845, however, a second road was begun to Mansfield in Richland County, some 56 miles south of Lake Erie. This road was operating in 1846 when construction of an extension to Newark, on the Ohio Canal, was undertaken.[43]

The opening of the Mansfield road seems to have resulted in the immediate doubling of Sandusky's grain and flour receipts and an enormous growth in the hog trade. Hog arrivals rose from under 10,000 in 1844 to 105,000 in 1846. Wheat receipts jumped from 180,-000 bushels in 1844 to 934,000 in 1846, and flour from 36,000 to 52,000 barrels. In 1847 flour receipts had risen to 113,000 and wheat to 1.8 million bushels.[44] Part of this spectacular growth was due to production increases stimulated by an enlarged overseas demand, but much of this would have gone to other ports had it not been for the railroad to Mansfield. In 1846-47 the road deposited at Sandusky about one-third of her total receipts. This proportion seems

---

[40] *NWR*, XXXII (April 7, 1827), 112, XXXVI (April 14, 1829), 130.

[41] J. S. Buckingham, *America, Historical, Statistical, and Descriptive* (3 vols., London, 1841), III, 424-425; *Hunt's*, XXI (September, 1849), 240.

[42] *Ibid.*, VI (June, 1842), 572, VIII (May, 1843), 482-483, XII (February, 1844), 192; *Fisher's National Magazine*, II (March, 1846), 890. Pork products seem to have been worth from 10 to 20 per cent of the total value of agricultural exports.

[43] *Hunt's*, XIX (August, 1848), 216-217.

[44] Andrews, "Reports on Trade and Commerce," 177-179; *Hunt's*, XVI (April, 1847), 364.

to have declined during the 1850's while that carried by the Mad River and Lake Erie road increased.[45]

In 1848-49 Sandusky's grain trade continued to grow, except for a short decline, from high levels reached in 1847, and it surpassed the 1847 volume in 1851-52, when totals of 2.6 and 4 million bushels of wheat and flour were shipped. This latter figure was exceeded only by Cleveland and Toledo, the three ports being responsible for fully 80 per cent of Ohio's total wheat and flour exports. By 1854 the total value of exports from Sandusky had risen to over $11 million, or 14 times the value of 1845.[46]

Certain aspects of Sandusky's rise to commercial prominence deserve emphasis. The cardinal point is the impact—one which numerous communities were experiencing—that an energetic and consistently pursued program of improvements in transportation could have on the total economic development of a town. The railroads transformed Sandusky from a port of minor account to the second most important market on the Lake Erie shore of Ohio. These roads cut directly behind the ports of Milan-Huron, Venice, and Vermilion into the regions which previously had supplied them and then thrust south to intercept grain which normally traveled the canal route to Cleveland. The smaller ports quickly faded into relative commercial obscurity. Very shortly thereafter both Sandusky and Cleveland were to share an experience similar to Milan's, so far as the grain trade is concerned, when through railroads from the East appeared along the Lake Erie shore.

TOLEDO

West of Sandusky lay the Maumee valley, which was composed of three independent river systems: the Sandusky, Portage, and Maumee. Neither of the first two were of any commercial significance, while the Maumee served as a major artery of trade for Toledo. The source of the Maumee lay in Indiana and the river ran

---

[45] *Ibid.*, XIX (August, 1848), 216-217; *ARJ*, XXVI (June 26, 1853), 407; *Report to the Stock and Bond Holders of the Sandusky, Dayton and Cincinnati (Late Mad River and Lake Erie) Rail Road Company, 1860* (Sandusky, Ohio, 1860).

[46] "Improvement of the Navigation of the Northern and Northwestern Lakes, etc.," *House Reports*, 34 Cong., 1 Sess., No. 316 (1856), Serial 870, 6-7. In 1854 Cleveland's exports were three times greater than those of Sandusky. Toledo surpassed Sandusky as a grain market in 1851, but throughout most of the 1850's they were of roughly equal importance commercially.

in a northeasterly direction from Fort Wayne, Indiana, to a junction with the Auglaize River before emptying into Maumee Bay. The headwaters of the Maumee were in close proximity to the Wabash River, thus making it possible for canals to weld part of the upper Wabash into the Maumee River system.

The Maumee country was the last section of Ohio to be settled. As late as 1830, thousands of settlers turned north into Michigan or continued into Indiana rather than risk settling in the great Black Swamp, a marshy area some 40 miles wide and 120 miles long, stretching west from the Sandusky to the Maumee. This obstacle did much to retard the development of Toledo, on Maumee Bay, which experienced little growth through the late 1840's. The entire 19-county area had fewer than 190,000 inhabitants in 1849.[47]

In 1839 the entire Maumee valley produced 1 million bushels of wheat and the exportable surplus was probably around 500,000 bushels, or some 300,000 short of the exports recorded at Sandusky and Toledo for 1840. This disproportion increased until in 1849 Toledo and Sandusky exported over two times more wheat than was produced in the Maumee valley. As in the case of Cleveland, the immediate hinterland of these ports was unable to supply more than a minor part of the total exports.[48]

During the 1840's the key area to which Toledo looked for grain and produce was the southeastern corner of Michigan, particularly Lenawee, Monroe, and Washtenaw counties. The Erie and Kalamazoo Railroad, constructed from Toledo to Adrian and Lenawee counties in 1836, was the instrument by which Toledo exploited this region for its grain surpluses.[49] Over this road traveled the bulk of Toledo's grain receipts until the mid-1840's. In 1841 the Erie and Kalamazoo carried all but a small fraction of her total receipts. From 1842 to 1846 Toledo received an estimated 75 per cent of her flour and 87 per cent of her wheat from Michigan.[50] But in

---

[47] Francis P. Weisenburger, *The Passing of the Frontier, 1825-1850* (Columbus, Ohio, 1941), 7-8; *Hunt's*, XVII (November, 1847), 495; *6 Census, 1840*, 78; *7 Census, 1850*, 817-818.

[48] *Hunt's*, V (September, 1841), 215; *6 Census, 1840*, 275-276; *7 Census, 1850*, 863-864; Elbert J. Benton, *The Wabash Trade Route in the Development of the Old Northwest* (Baltimore, 1903), 104, fn. 55.

[49] *NWR*, LI (December 24, 1836), 272.

[50] *Hunt's*, XVI (February, 1847), 191; *ARJ*, XX (November 13, 1847), 728.

1845 the Wabash and Erie Canal, completed from Lafayette, Indiana, to Toledo in 1843, replaced the railroad as the primary carrier of grain supplies to Toledo.[51]

Two years after the Wabash and Erie reached Lafayette, the middle portion of the Miami and Erie Canal running north from Cincinnati was completed through Dayton to Defiance, where it made a junction with the Wabash and Erie Canal.[52] This opened the entire upper Miami valley to Toledo and, through the late 1840's, much of the wheat and flour arriving at Toledo originated in this area. Toledo, in the short space of nine years, had widened its market area from the original block of contiguous counties to an extensive area embracing southeastern Michigan, the northeastern quarter of Indiana, and the west central counties of Ohio's upper Miami River valley.

The connection of the Miami Canal with the Wabash and Erie Canal seems to have had a great impact. From 1839 to 1845 Michigan and sources along the upper Wabash supplied most of Toledo's grain. Receipts and exports remained stable, fluctuating between 350,000 and 400,000 bushels of wheat and flour annually. In 1845, however, there was a sharp movement upward, and over a million bushels were received and exported, along with close to a million bushels of corn.[53] The fall of 1847 brought a brisk business to the millers and grain merchants at Toledo and Maumee City. Wheat and flour prices were high and farmers transported wheat via wagon from a considerable distance.[54] Over 1.6 million bushels of flour and wheat and 1 million bushels of corn, valued at $2.3 million, were exported. From this time, Toledo's grain trade developed steadily, overtaking Sandusky in 1851 and Cleveland in the late

[51] George R. Baldwin, *Report Showing the Cost and Income of a Railroad as Surveyed from Toledo, Ohio, to Chicago, Illinois, Incorporated as the Buffalo and Mississippi Rail-Road* (Toledo, 1847), 62. Seventy-nine per cent of the produce arrived via canal in 1845.

[52] Arthur B. Hirsch, "The Construction of the Miami and Erie Canal," MVHA *Proceedings* (1919-20), 349; McClelland and Huntington, *History of the Ohio Canals*, 131.

[53] The volume of corn that entered commerce in bulk did not reach large proportions in the Lake Erie trade. In the 1850's well over one-half of the corn reaching Buffalo and Oswego originated at Chicago. Toledo led Lake Erie ports in corn shipments. United States Treasury Department, *Statistics of the Foreign and Domestic Commerce of the United States* (Washington, D.C., 1864).

[54] *Maumee River Times*, October 2, 1847.

1850's. By 1851, wheat, flour, and corn exports were valued at $3 million and by the following year at $6 million.[55]

Most of Toledo's grain shipments were consigned to Buffalo, with Rochester, Oswego, and Ogdensburg as alternate markets. In 1851, 90 per cent of the flour, 49 per cent of the wheat, and 66 per cent of the corn cleared from Toledo was marketed in Buffalo.[56] The remainder of the bulk wheat presumably went to eastern markets such as Rochester and Oswego, where considerably more wheat was ground than at Buffalo.[57]

The Toledo canals had as great an impact on the areas through which they passed as on Toledo itself. Their effect was more apparent in the counties of the upper Wabash and upper Miami than in the Maumee valley counties.[58] Cass county, Indiana, for example, largely dependent upon outside sources for flour in 1843, was reported shipping over 400,000 bushels of wheat and flour to Toledo in 1853.[59]

The seven Indiana counties of the upper Wabash (Group A in Table 7) served by the Wabash and Erie Canal made marked gains during the decade 1839-49. Population more than doubled. Wheat production rose by 260 per cent and corn by 190 per cent.[60] Analagous gains were made in the grain trade. Lafayette, Indiana, previously a dependency of New Orleans, shipped little wheat or flour prior to 1845, when 539,000 bushels of wheat and flour were shipped north on the canal along with 1,313 tons of pork and bacon. These shipments reflected the diversion of a trade which had previously been routed to the South. By 1849 some 600,000 bushels of

---

[55] *Patent Report, 1847*, 588-589; Andrews, "Reports on Trade and Commerce," 189-190; *Hunt's*, XXVIII (March, 1853), 477. The value of corn exports was approximately equal to that of bulk wheat and flour. Produce exports represented between 50 and 60 per cent of the total value of exports.

[56] Andrews, "Reports on Trade and Commerce," 108, 111, 133.

[57] In 1849 Toledo supplied 13 per cent of Oswego's wheat receipts, 3 per cent of flour, and 50 per cent of corn. *Patent Report, 1849*, 548; Toledo *Blade*, August 31, 1848.

[58] The wheat production of the Maumee valley increased by 100,000 bushels between 1839 and 1849, the total being hardly more than sufficient to supply local consumption requirements. *6 Census, 1840*, 275-276; *7 Census, 1850*, 863-864.

[59] Indiana State Board of Agriculture, *Third Annual Report, 1853* (Indianapolis, 1853), 63-64.

[60] *6 Census, 1840*, 82, 287-288; *7 Census, 1850*, 755-756, 791-792. The seven counties are Allen, Carroll, Cass, Huntington, Miami, Tippecanoe, and Wabash. Cass, Miami, and Wabash counties were dependent upon outside sources for their flour in 1839.

wheat and flour, 874,000 bushels of corn, and considerable quantities of pork, lard, and bacon passed over the canal from Lafayette.[61] In contrast to the improved position of Lafayette was the market isolation facing South Bend in St. Joseph County. While corn was

TABLE 7. PERCENTAGE OF TOTAL INDIANA WHEAT AND CORN PRODUCTION, POPULATION, AND POPULATION PER SQUARE MILE FOR EACH OF FOUR GROUPS OF NORTHERN INDIANA COUNTIES AND FOR NORTHERN INDIANA, 1839 AND 1849

1839	A	B	C	D	30 - County Total
Per cent Indiana wheat production	5.4	3.1	6.5	9.0[a]	24.0
Per cent Indiana corn production	5.0	5.3	2.0	2.0	14.3
Per cent Indiana population	5.0	3.7	6.1	2.2	17.0
Population per sq. mile	11.0	10.7	10.6	4.7	9.2
1849					
Per cent Indiana wheat production	13.0	7.0	14.0	8.0[a]	42.0
Per cent Indiana corn production	8.0	5.6	4.0	3.0	20.6
Per cent Indiana population	9.0	6.0	7.4	3.7	26.1[b]
Population per sq. mile	28.3	25.4	18.5	10.9	20.4

[a] In both 1839 and 1849 La Porte was the state's largest wheat-producing county, while St. Joseph, the eighth largest in 1839, was fifth in 1849.
[b] The total population of the 30 counties increased from 116,800 to 258,300. One-third of the increase occurred in Group A.
Sources: *6 Census, 1840*, 82, 287-288; *7 Census, 1850*, 755-756, 791-792.

worth 40 cents at Toledo in 1846, it was worth only 12 to 15 cents at South Bend, and could be disposed of only by carrying it by wagon to Michigan City—a 50-mile trip—or floating it down the

---

[61] Baldwin, *Report on a Railroad from Toledo to Chicago*, 64; [E. Chamberlain], *The Indiana Gazetteer or Topographical Dictionary of the State of Indiana* (Indianapolis, 1849), 400. Lafayette also served as a depot for counties not adjacent to the canal. Benton, *The Wabash Trade Route*, 101.

St. Joseph River to a small market at its mouth. Fifteen-cent corn could bear the expense of neither trip.[62]

The relative gains, attributable at least in part to the Wabash and Erie Canal, in four groups of counties in the northern third of Indiana, are summarized in terms of percentage growth in Table 7.[63]

For the entire northern area the growth was substantially greater than for Indiana as a whole from 1839 to 1849; but the rate of growth was not equal in the four groups. The counties along Lake Michigan, Group D, displayed the least over-all advance, and in wheat production this group lost ground, both absolutely and relatively, during a period when the remainder of the area showed real progress. The counties along the Wabash and Erie Canal, Group A, experienced the most accelerated growth rate. With a rapidly expanding population, the production of wheat per capita still rose from six bushels in 1839 to nine in 1849, resulting in a large surplus.[64] Group C, the counties located between the Michigan boundary and the counties along the Wabash Canal, experienced a growth in wheat production as pronounced as that of the Wabash group. The northern third of Indiana became the dominant wheat-producing section of the state, but did not exhibit a similar advance in corn. Indiana was predominantly a corn state, and the various areas shared more equitably in over-all corn productivity than was the case with wheat.[65]

But as far as Toledo was concerned, the general advance of the counties along the upper Wabash had the greatest pertinence, for it was this region that the Wabash Canal tapped directly, and the growth of the grain trade of the Wabash counties is coincidental with that of the market on Maumee Bay.

---

[62] Baldwin, *Report on a Railroad from Toledo to Chicago*, 101.

[63] Group A represents the counties adjacent to the Wabash Canal; Group B represents six counties south of and adjacent to Group A, including Adams, Clinton, Grant, Howard, Montgomery, and Wells; Group C represents ten counties lying north of the canal counties to the Michigan border, including De Kalb, Elkhart, Fulton, Koscuisko, La Grange, Marshall, Noble, Pulaski, Steuben, and Whitley. Group D represents the three counties touching Lake Michigan, Lake, La Porte, and Porter, and four counties contiguous with them, St. Joseph, Stark, Jasper, and Newton.

[64] The surplus in 1839 was probably not over 80,000 bushels, while in 1849 it was approaching 500,000.

[65] In 1849, 20 counties produced 40 per cent of the corn and each of 45 produced over 1 per cent of the total, with none over 3.4 per cent. Indiana's total crop rose from 28 million bushels of corn in 1839 to 53 million in 1849.

DETROIT

The city of Detroit served as a concentration and shipping center for produce grown in the interior of Michigan. During the late 1830's and early 1840's, Toledo and Detroit were competitors for the surplus of southeastern Michigan, but after 1845 Toledo developed its relationship with the upper Wabash valley, while depending less and less upon southeastern Michigan for grain supplies. At the same time, Detroit and Monroe, Michigan, a port fronting on Lake Erie, sought to monopolize the grain trade of this corner of the state and to extend the area with which they traded.

The Lower Peninsula of Michigan is surrounded by Lakes Erie, Huron, and Michigan. The waters of Erie touch the perimeter of the state only along the shores of Monroe County, but the Detroit River, issuing from Lake St. Clair, offered a navigable channel to that lake from whence settlement could spread into the east and south central prairies and oak openings. In 1830 the population had just reached 30,000, but in the next decade it advanced to 212,000, and to 398,000 in 1849. Settlement first spread into the southeastern corner of the state and then along the southern tier of counties from Lake Erie to Lake Michigan—then northward, virtually tier by tier.[66]

Michigan's soil was in general easily cultivated and not so stony as in New England. The settlers preferred the bur-oak openings for wheat, but looked askance at the sandy soil of the pine land. The large areas of heavily timbered land were judged unsuitable for wheat, both because of the difficulty of clearing the land and because of the thickness and adhesiveness of the porous soils. Much of the land was judged too cold for corn. The early farmers discovered, however, that the timbered lands produced excellent yields of hay and oats. The climate, though more severe than regions to the south, was influenced by the westerly winds coming off Lake Erie, which moderated the temperature and provided suitable rainfall for farming.[67] In general, Michigan farmers were less committed to wheat growing than farmers in northern Illinois and southern Wisconsin, which had an environment similar to Michigan's.

---

[66] George N. Fuller, *Economic and Social Beginnings of Michigan. A Study of the Settlement of the Lower Peninsula During the Territorial Period, 1805-1837* (Lansing, Mich., 1916), 199-200, 244; Almon E. Parkins, *The Historical Geography of Detroit* (Lansing, Mich., 1918), 174.

[67] Fuller, *Beginnings of Michigan*, 2, 18, 38-40; Robert Russell, *North America. Its Agriculture and Climate* . . . (Edinburgh, 1857), 98.

Despite the fact that wheat would never exert such a dominant influence in Michigan as in the states to the south and west, Michigan's wheat production did increase from 1837 to 1853. The crop rose from an estimated 1 million bushels in 1837 to over 4 million bushels during the years 1849-50, and to between 7 and 8 million from 1853 to 1860.[68] These quantities were insufficient for a large trade in grain, yet for a time, as noted in connection with Table 4, Michigan contributed over 30 per cent of the total wheat traffic on Lake Erie.

During the late 1830's, parts of Michigan imported grain while southeastern Michigan exported a surplus to Toledo. Grain exports to Michigan were from ports such as Cleveland and Sandusky. It is also probable that some of the grain received at Toledo from Michigan was shipped up through Lake St. Clair to the north central areas of the Lower Peninsula.[69] Rising steadily, Michigan's exports reached their upper limit in 1847, when an estimated 5.2 million bushels of wheat and flour, valued at about $5 million dollars, was sent to market.[70]

Almost 50 per cent of Michigan's wheat was raised in the southeastern counties of Oakland, Washtenaw, Jackson, Lenawee, Livingston, and Hillsdale, the first two alone producing 22.6 per cent of the state's crop in 1849.[71] The southernmost counties, Lenawee and Hillsdale, could ship directly to Toledo by rail or overland by wagon to the Wabash and Erie Canal, or via the Raisin River to Monroe. The more northern counties were generally dependent upon the Detroit market.

In the 1820's and 1830's Detroit was considerably more active as a receiving center for eastern merchandise, foodstuffs, and immigrants than as an exporting market. As early as 1816, a traveler in Pennsylvania passed numerous wagons transporting flour to Erie, Pennsylvania, for shipment to Detroit. A portion of this flour, and other products as well, was re-exported by Detroit to settlements

---

[68] 7 *Census, 1850*, 904-905; 8 *Census, 1860, Agriculture*, xxix-xxx; Michigan State Dept., *Census and Statistics, 1854*, 389-393, 379-383. Corn production increased at about the same rate and reached 12 million bushels in 1860.

[69] An article in *The Daily Picayune* (New Orleans), September 29, 1838, reported that Michigan had 1 million bushels of wheat ready for shipment to New York in 1838.

[70] *Hunt's*, XIX (July, 1848), 29.

[71] 7 *Census, 1850*, 904-905. In 1839 the same counties produced 46 per cent, with Oakland and Washtenaw producing 22 per cent. 6 *Census, 1840*, 323-324.

on Lake Huron and Lake Michigan. Detroit was a favored outlet
for wheat from Pennsylvania, New York, and Ohio, for prices were
generally high, the harbor was commodious, and storage facilities
were adequate; but the market was of a limited and temporary
nature.[72] By 1825 Detroit was being supplied by its own hinterland
—at this time producing enough grain to meet the needs of producers and new settlers, with any surplus being shipped north
rather than east.[73] Within the next decade vast numbers of emigrants reached Detroit and fanned out into Michigan and beyond.
About the same time wheat and flour from Detroit, Monroe, and
Lake Michigan ports began flowing east regularly and in rising
amounts.

Like Toledo, Detroit found the growth of her grain trade
contingent upon gaining access to interior grain-producing areas.
Toledo had developed both rail and canal; Detroit was to rely
largely on railroads. Toledo's early success with the Erie and Kalamazoo galvanized Detroit's efforts toward finishing a railroad to
Ypsilanti, 30 miles to the southwest. The road was completed in
1836, and as the Michigan Central was pushed on to Ann Arbor
by 1840, Kalamazoo by 1843, and Lake Michigan by 1849. During
the same period, Monroe, Detroit's competitor to the south, became
the eastern terminus of the Michigan Southern Railroad, completed
to Adrian in 1843 and to Hillsdale the next year.[74]

The grain trade of Detroit developed steadily from 1840 to
1847, when 614,000 barrels of flour were exported and total produce exports were valued at some $3.2 million. This level, reached
as a result of foreign demands on American food supplies, was not
maintained, nor was it equaled again until 1855.[75]

---

[72] David Thomas, *Travels Through the Western Country in the Summer
of 1816* (Auburn, N.Y., 1819), 36; Estwick Evans, *A Pedestrious Tour of Four
Thousand Miles Through the Western States and Territories During the Winter
and Spring of 1818. Interspersed with Brief Reflections upon a Great Variety
of Topics: Religious, Moral, Political, Sentimental, &c. &c.* (Concord, N.H.,
1819), reprinted in Reuben G. Thwaites, ed., *Early Western Travels, 1748-
1846* (32 vols., Cleveland, 1904), VIII, 194-195, 217-219; *NWR*, XX (June 16,
1821), 255.
[73] Detroit *Gazette*, December 13, 1825, quoted in Fuller, *Beginnings of
Michigan*, 220-221.
[74] *NWR*, LI (December 24, 1836), 272, LIV (July 1, 1843), 276, LVI
(August 31, 1844), 444; *Hunt's*, X (May, 1844), 478.
[75] *Ibid.*, XVI (February, 1847), 191, XVIII (January, 1848), 94-95,
XXXVI (November, 1856), 556-559; Cincinnati *Advertiser and Journal*, December 30, 1840; *NWR*, LIV (July 29, 1843), 345; *ARJ*, XIX (February 7,
1846), 85.

The grain traffic over the Michigan Central responded similarly. During the 1840's the road carried between 55 and 65 per cent of the flour received at Detroit. Between 1849 and 1860 the Central carried annually some 300,000 to 540,000 barrels of flour. A peak in the carriage of bulk wheat was attained in 1854, but no advance followed during the remainder of the decade. Gains in provisions traffic were also made before 1855, but were followed by a leveling off or an actual decline. The proportion of wheat and flour to the total freight carried by the Michigan Central also declined after 1849. This reflected the ability of the railroad to develop new categories of freight traffic. In 1849 freight charges derived from wheat and flour formed 53 per cent of the total; between 1858 and 1860, about 25 per cent.[76]

The above also reflects a comparatively static market structure at Detroit. The city served a region which was not overly committed to cereal production. Soon Michigan's wheat farmers, feeling the competition of cereals originating in the states of Illinois and Wisconsin, turned to other pursuits, much as the farmers of New England and New York had diversified their agriculture when faced with the competition of cheaper grain from newly opened lands in the West. This development was not yet completed in the 1850's and was temporarily halted in 1860 and 1861, when Detroit's grain exports rose rapidly to meet a new overseas demand.

What happened eventually to Detroit had already occurred at Monroe, casting the town into obscurity. As the eastern terminal of the Michigan Southern Railroad, Monroe had looked optimistically toward a bright future. In 1846 and 1847 over a million dollars' worth of wheat and flour were exported. But in the mid-1850's the Lake Shore Railroad made connections with the Michigan Southern via the line of the Erie and Kalamazoo.[77] One historian of Michigan sees the demise of Monroe as resulting from the withdrawal of the Michigan Southern's line of Lake Erie steamers.[78] Actually, this was not a causative but a reactive decision. Monroe's interior sources of supply were effectively cut off because it was no longer of any ad-

---

[76] Michigan Central Railroad Company, *Fourth Annual Report, 1850* (Boston, 1850), 28-29, *5 AR, 1851,* 32-33, *7 AR, 1853,* 17, *8 AR, 1854,* 28, 32, *9 AR, 1855,* 28, *10 AR, 1856,* 24, *11 AR, 1857,* 30, *12 AR, 1858,* 32, *14 AR, 1860,* 26, 30.

[77] *Hunt's,* XVI (February, 1847), 191; *Patent Report 1847,* 587.

[78] Parkins, *Detroit,* 191.

vantage to producers to ship their goods to Monroe for reshipment via steamboat when direct rail connections with Ohio or more eastern markets were available. A similar series of events had already set back such ports as Milan and Huron, and were impinging upon the markets at Cleveland and Sandusky.

Summary

Through the 1840's and into the 1850's, the grain trade of the Great Lakes was largely that of Lake Erie. It was conducted through the agency of a number of ports situated along the lake shores of Ohio and Michigan, and dependent upon grain supplies from the interior of those states and Indiana. These ports were engaged in receiving grain from surrounding areas and shipping it to markets, largely in the East, for consumption purposes. Each port, in order to accelerate the flow of grain through its hands, was constrained to improve its transportation connections with the interior.

This effort, in some cases, resulted in competition between lake ports and the river towns along the Ohio for the grain trade of the intermediate country. The Ohio Canal enabled Cleveland to extract supplies of grain from areas which had previously shipped via river to the South. The Wabash and Erie Canal performed a similar function for Toledo, diverting grain from the southern route via the Wabash River to Toledo and Lake Erie.

The extension of transportation networks was also accompanied by competition among the lake ports. At Detroit and Toledo, the early construction of the Erie and Kalamazoo Railroad from Toledo resulted in a rivalry over the grain surplus of southeastern Michigan. In another instance, involving Cleveland and Ashtabula, the construction of the Ohio Canal and its lateral branches enabled the former to penetrate the area from which the latter received its grain supplies, with such effect that the grain trade at Ashtabula virtually disappeared. A similar confrontation between Sandusky, Milan-Huron, and Venice worked to the advantage of Sandusky. The railroad from Sandusky to Mansfield was the decisive instrument. Thus, all along the shore of Lake Erie there was an economic battle for the agricultural surplus of a vast expanse of territory. Those cities prevailed which improved their connections with the interior.

The Rise of the
Lake Michigan Ports

CHAPTER IV

CONDITIONS OF THE LAKE MICHIGAN TRADE

While the trade of Lake Erie boomed, the region to the west remained a negligible factor in the trade during the 1840's. One student of American commercial development, in noting that by 1838 receipts of wheat and flour at Buffalo were greater than those at New Orleans, traced the origins of this trade to the growing importance of Toledo, Detroit, Cleveland, Chicago, Milwaukee, and others ports on the Great Lakes.[1] Care should be exercised, however, in attributing the grain trade to the Great Lakes region as a whole, for as late as 1840 the foodstuffs which were exported originated almost exclusively from Lake Erie ports.

---

[1] Emory R. Johnson *et al., History of Domestic and Foreign Commerce of the United States* (2 vols., Washington, D.C., 1915), I, 230.

The first cargo of grain from Lake Michigan, carried on the brig *John Kenzie* and consisting of 3,000 bushels of wheat, did not arrive at Buffalo until 1836.[2] In 1841, out of 1.2 million barrels of western flour carried by the Erie Canal to tidewater, only 50,000 to 100,000 barrels originated at Lake Michigan ports.[3] Lake Michigan's grain trade was but a small portion of the lake trade in general and remained so throughout the decade of the 1840's, although steadily rising. While it is true that the 150,000 people located in and around Chicago and Milwaukee, and dependent upon Lake Michigan for an outlet to market, were evolving a one-crop (wheat) system of agriculture comparable to the one-crop economy of parts of the South, it is not accurate to equate Lake Michigan's contribution to the grain trade with that of Lake Erie's. Lake Erie was the dominant market and trade area in the 1840's, as the lower Ohio valley and Mississippi valley had been dominant until the late 1830's.

The existing trade on Lake Michigan was shared, through most of the decade, by a number of lake shore markets which appeared to have equally bright prospects for future greatness. During the 1840's many of these ports were rivals for the grain surplus of the same area. And though the volume of trade at stake remained small, the lake shore centers which were later to loom so large began to develop their identity. There also developed for certain of these ports, besides the competition with other ports located on the lakes, a struggle with ports serving the southern route for the grain trade of the intervening country. In a way the story of the development of the trade on Lake Michigan parallels that on Lake Erie. In both cases two struggles were going on simultaneously: one between the lake ports, and the other between the lake route and the southern route to market. In the early part of the decade, the former competition was of greater moment to the contestants along Lake Michigan.

---

[2] James Croil, *Steam Navigation and Its Relation to the Commerce of Canada and the United States* (Toronto, 1898), 253-254.

[3] United States Treasury Department, *Statistics of the Foreign and Domestic Commerce of the United States* (Washington, D.C., 1864), 179-180; *The Cultivator*, VIII (February, 1841), 28. *Hunt's*, V (September, 1841), 215, puts the figure at 53,000, but St. Joseph, Michigan, and Michigan City shipped some 80,000 barrels of flour and 200,000 bushels of wheat in 1841. At least 700,000 barrels came from Lake Erie ports and the remainder from northwestern Pennsylvania, the Lake Erie shore of New York, and flour manufactured at Buffalo from western wheat.

Along the southeastern shore of Lake Michigan, St. Joseph, at the mouth of the St. Joseph River, and Michigan City, Indiana, some 45 miles to the south, were both of respectable size in the early period and handled produce from a large area. Until 1843 St. Joseph enjoyed a larger grain trade than Chicago, and as late as 1847 surpassed Milwaukee in receipts and shipments. Until 1846 the grain trade of Michigan City exceeded that centered at Milwaukee. Farther west, around the southern curve of Lake Michigan, was the bustling little town of Chicago, a market for both Michigan City and St. Joseph during the late 1830's. Both towns exported breadstuffs and provisions to Chicago, which was unable to obtain a sufficient supply of foodstuffs from neighboring areas. Up the lake shore to the north, Waukegan, Illinois, and Kenosha and Racine, Wisconsin, were competing with Chicago and Milwaukee for the grain surplus of the same interior areas. Until 1845 or 1846, Racine received more grain than Milwaukee, and during the period 1840-60 strove to maintain her position by pushing out plank roads into the interior and finally a railroad to the Mississippi River.

These ambitious markets were able to maintain their relative importance only if they persisted in their efforts to enlarge interior sources of supply and met with success. A market that failed to tap the growth potential of its interior first, by roads and canals, was soon confronted by the competition of other markets seeking to expand their trade in grain. Railroads added a new dimension to the competition, for with their introduction a grain entrepot a considerable distance away could gain access to the areas from which other markets drew their supplies. St. Joseph and Michigan City are cases in which the interaction of these factors resulted in a declining grain trade.

St. Joseph and Michigan City

St. Joseph enjoyed a natural route from the interior in the St. Joseph River, which rises in Hillsdale County and passes through Elkhart and South Bend, Indiana, before turning northwest to empty into Lake Michigan. In the 1840's small steamers were reported navigating the river as far east as Constantine.[4] For a

---

[4] *Lippincott's New and Complete Gazetteer of the United States* (Philadelphia, 1854), 1023.

time, St. Joseph was the only available market for the south-western corner of Michigan and a portion of Indiana.

In 1839 the town exported 42,000 barrels of flour, 52,000 bushels of wheat, and 4,000 barrels of whiskey, pork, and lard. Between 1840 and 1846 exports generally ranged between 450,000 and 550,000 bushels of wheat and flour and reached 829,000 in 1847.[5] The grain trade of southwestern Michigan concentrated at St. Joseph, but after 1847 the importance of the town as a wheat and flour market declined rapidly. By that time the Michigan Central Railroad was west of Kalamazoo and the Michigan Southern was not far behind. In 1849 the Central reached the lake at Michigan City, piercing the center of St. Joseph's area of supply. There was no longer any reason for farmers to haul grain to Lake Michigan when it could be transported directly to Detroit or Toledo at 66 cents per barrel and 19.8 cents per bushel of wheat. Both of these towns had better facilities for handling and reshipping the produce and both offered higher prices.[6]

Forty miles to the west of St. Joseph and across the lake from Chicago was Michigan City, Indiana's major lake port. An Indiana correspondent to a New York daily wrote of the great activity in the grain-buying business of the port in 1841. One firm, he wrote in September, 1841, "has already shipped this season 30,000 bushels of wheat, and it still continues to come in at an average of 2,000 bushels daily."[7] Teams hauling wheat were reported arriving from points some 125 miles away, and taking a return load of salt to make the trip profitable. Michigan City's area of supply extended as far south as Lafayette, east of South Bend, and included that part of the upper Wabash valley between Lafayette and Wabash.

From an export trade estimated at $15,000 in 1833, the value of Michigan City's exports grew to $210,000 in 1839 and $270,000 in 1840. Wheat exports rose from 97,000 bushels in 1839 to 200,000 in 1843, 425,000 in 1845, and 500,000 in 1847. The value of the

---

[5] *NWR*, LX (May 22, 1841), 191; James Hall, *The West: Its Commerce and Navigation* (Cincinnati, 1848), 235; *Hunt's*, VI (April, 1842), 342; George R. Baldwin, *Report Showing the Cost and Income of a Railroad as Surveyed from Toledo, Ohio, to Chicago, Illinois, Incorporated as the Buffalo and Mississippi Rail-Road* (Toledo, 1847), 56.

[6] *Hunt's*, XVIII (January, 1848), 94-95; Baldwin, *Report on a Railroad from Toledo to Chicago*, 58, quotes freight per bushel of wheat from St. Joseph to Buffalo at 43 cents and between 10 and 20 cents from Detroit, depending upon the season.

[7] New York *Tribune*, September 25, 1841.

export trade reached $370,000 the following year.[8] Noteworthy here is not growth but its abatement after 1840, particularly if compared with the activity at Chicago and Toledo. Chicago's export trade increased from a value roughly equal to Michigan City's in 1840-41 to a value 11 times greater in 1848. By 1852-53 the volume of grain exports at Michigan City was less than the level reached in the mid-1840's.[9]

Michigan City had commenced its career under optimum conditions. The county in which it was situated—La Porte—was the state's largest wheat producer in both 1839 and 1849. St. Joseph County was ranked eighth in 1839 and fifth in 1849. But in the six-county area from which it drew much of its produce, the growth was minimal from 1839 to 1849, in terms of wheat, corn, and population.[10] By 1843 the Wabash and Erie Canal, serving Toledo, penetrated the area along the upper Wabash, reaching Lafayette in 1843. By 1850 the Michigan Southern Railroad was completed through South Bend, Indiana, and passed a few miles south of Michigan City. Although the Michigan Central Railroad reached Michigan City in 1849, the town was no longer a factor to be considered in connection with the grain trade. Farmers previously sending grain to the port were able to use the two railroads or the canal to reach markets with facilities superior to those available at Michigan City. When the Michigan Central and Michigan Southern roads reached Chicago in the early 1850's, northwestern Indiana was added to the widening area utilizing the grain market at Chicago.

CHICAGO

When dealing with the startling rise of Chicago to eminence in the lake grain trade, it is rather easy to overlook the fact that until 1855 Chicago was but one of several large grain markets on the

[8] *De Bow's Review*, I (February, 1846), 158; Baldwin, *Report on a Railroad from Toledo to Chicago*, 51-52; *Patent Report, 1847*, 591; "Report of the Topographical Bureau, 1850," *Senate Executive Documents*, 31 Cong., 1 Sess., No. 48 (1851), Serial 558, 8.

[9] Andrews, "Reports on Trade and Commerce," 218; "Report of the Bureau of Topographical Engineers," *House Executive Documents*, 33 Cong., 1 Sess., No. 1 (1853), Serial 712, 163.

[10] Wheat increased from 367,000 bushels to 497,000, corn from 605,000 to 1,616,000, and population from 15,000 to 36,000. *6 Census, 1840*, 82, 287-288; *7 Census, 1850*, 755-756, 791-792.

lakes, and by no means the largest.[11] Chicago's gains between the years 1854 and 1856 were greater than those made in the entire previous history of the port, for it was only at this time that the conditions requisite for the fulfillment of Chicago's potential as a market were achieved. In the 1840's development had just begun.

In 1839 the hinterland of Chicago was sparsely settled. The region from Rock River to Chicago was described as a desolate waste and the region between Chicago and Springfield was virtually unsettled. The Rock River country contained only five people per square mile, fully one-third of the population living in Knox County. In the country along the upper Illinois River, there were few areas with over five inhabitants per square mile. Only 47,000 people resided in the great prairie region of east and south central Illinois. Most of the population was concentrated in the southern half of the state of Illinois, along the Mississippi, lower Illinois, Kaskaskia, and lower Wabash rivers.[12]

The development of the northern quarter of Illinois, which was settled more rapidly than east and south central Illinois, provided the early foundation for Chicago's commercial prosperity.[13] But it was upon the settlement of the prairie region to the south that Chicago's real growth depended. It was this very region that newcomers, for reasons real or fanciful, avoided until the middle 1850's.

As early as 1818 the author of a handbook for emigrants observed that "Americans, accustomed to a profusion of timber, for buildings, fences, and fuel, think [the prairies] unfit for the habitation of whites." [14] This attitude persisted into the 1850's, for, in spite of a modern student's judgment that "farm-making on the sodlands wrote its own chapter in ease of cultivation," contemporary assessments of the difficulties encountered in cultivating and settling prairie lands are numerous and, in some cases, convincing.[15]

---

[11] Toledo and Cleveland generally handled more grain than Chicago until 1855, and Milwaukee and Sandusky were about as large in the early 1850's. Chicago shipped the most corn as early as 1851.

[12] Milo M. Quaife, ed., *Growing Up with Southern Illinois, 1820 to 1861, from the Memoirs of Daniel Harmon Brush* (Chicago, 1944), 105; *6 Census, 1840*, 86.

[13] *7 Census, 1850*, 701-702.

[14] John Knight, *The Emigrant's Best Instructor, or The Most Recent and Important Information Respecting the United States of America* (2nd ed., London, 1818), 22.

[15] Richard L. Power, *Planting Corn Belt Culture. The Impress of the Upland Southerner and Yankee in the Old Northwest* (Indianapolis, 1953), 157-158.

Some of the objections stemmed from ignorance, such as the belief that because little timber grew on them, prairie lands were of low fertility, or the opinion that the prairies were more unhealthy than timbered lands. But many of the objections were based on experience. Timber was scarce. Water had to be dug for. The prairie sod was difficult to break and to cultivate initially. Some of the really flat lands required drainage before they could be extensively farmed. As one student has observed, cultivating the prairies required a larger and more constant outlay of capital than in the case of lands which were more heavily timbered and watered. Capital was something that few new settlers had in any abundance, nor was there any incentive to go heavily in debt in order to build a farm in a generally isolated region which lacked markets. Though the lack of timber did not indicate low fertility, it did require a heavy capital outlay to procure timber for fencing and buildings. Even after railroads had penetrated this region, timber was imported at high cost. Hedge or sod fences were unsatisfactory and barbed wire was a device of the future. Unless a landowner was fortunate in striking a plentiful supply of water, the digging of wells was an economic burden which farmers in the well-watered regions did not have to anticipate. And, though the land might have been of great fertility, most farmers were hampered by inadequacies of equipment and technological knowledge.[16] Emigrants for the most part bypassed the prairie country in the northward movement of population until the area was interlaced with railroads in the 1850's.

Some wheat was produced in all the settled regions of Illinois, but the wheat crop was centered along a line, often two or three counties wide, running from the mouth of the Illinois River to Will, Du Page, and Kane counties in the north. In 1839 the southern part of this belt led in production, but a decade later an expanded wheat-

---

[16] Patrick Shirreff, *A Tour Through North America Together with a Comprehensive View of the Canadas and United States as Adapted for Agricultural Emigration* (Edinburgh, 1835), 248-250; William Oliver, *Eight Months in Illinois, with Information to Immigrants* (Newcastle-upon-Tyne, 1843, Chicago, 1924), 245-246; *Transactions of the Wisconsin State Agricultural Society*, I, (1851), 243; Paul W. Gates, *The Farmer's Age: Agriculture 1815-1860* (New York, 1960), 180-188; R. Carlyle Buley, *The Old Northwest. Pioneer Period. 1815-1840* (2 vols., Indianapolis, 1950), I, 138-148; Clarence H. Danhoff, "The Fencing Problem in the Eighteen-Fifties," *Agricultural History*, XVIII (October, 1944), 170-173; Herbert A. Kellar, "The Reaper as a Factor in the Development of the Agriculture of Illinois, 1834-1865," *Illinois State Historical Society Transactions*, XXXIV (1927), 105-106.

growing area had arisen in the north, where 43.5 per cent of the state's crop was produced and where 14 of the top 20 wheat counties were located.

Chicago drew its grain supplies from this northern region, and the wheat-centered economy of the north, where over 20 bushels of wheat per capita were produced compared to 8 for the remainder of the state, was at once the cause and result of a growing Chicago market.[17] The augmentation of both production and commerce was a factor of improved transportation facilities, for before farmers would consistently produce a quantity of grain over and above that needed for home consumption, the latter itself increasing as emigrants arrived in larger numbers, they had to be assured of access to a market.

Chicago had derived limited quantities of grain since the late 1820's from roads like the Vincennes Trace leading to the Wabash country and the Princeton and Chicago state road to the southwest.[18] But "picturesque" though this Conestoga trade may have been, it could not have provided Chicago with very large quantities of grain or flour. For all practical purposes, Chicago remained fairly well insulated from all but its immediate interior until the 1840's. Between 1842 and 1848, the town's rising grain exports were largely derived from the contiguous counties.[19] In 1848 the Illinois and Michigan Canal was completed, expanding the area to the southwest from which Chicago drew grain supplies. In the middle and late 1850's, railroad development resulted in a further widening of Chicago's source area,

The scheme to connect Lake Michigan with the Illinois River via the south branch of the Chicago had been bruited about as early as 1819, when John C. Calhoun, as Secretary of War, advocated it as a military necessity. Nothing concrete occurred until Congress in 1827 granted Illinois alternate sections along each side of the pro-

---

[17] *6 Census, 1840*, 299-300; *7 Census, 1850*, 730-731. Counties close to the Mississippi shipped south via the river until the arrival of railroads from Chicago. Other counties farther to the east could utilize Kenosha, Wisconsin, and Waukegan, Illinois, as well as Chicago in the pre-railroad era.

[18] Bessie L. Pierce, *A History of Chicago* (2 vols., New York, 1937-40), I, 52-53, 97-99.

[19] Judson F. Lee, *Transportation as a Factor in the Development of Northern Illinois Previous to 1860* (Chicago, 1917), 23, states that by 1843 Chicago was receiving so much wheat that there were not enough vessels to carry it. This creates the impression of a great wheat traffic in the city when the grain exports were actually quite small—under 100,000 bushels in 1840-41.

posed route. Construction, however, was not initiated until 1836, and the canal was not completed until 1848. In the same year the Galena and Chicago Union Railroad carried the first wheat by rail to the Chicago waterfront. Thus, for the first eight years of the decade neither canals nor railroads exerted any considerable impact on the growth of Chicago as a grain market.[20] Thereafter the influence was overwhelming.[21]

In the first three years of the canal's operation (1848-50), the volume of wheat and corn carried was about equal—1.4 million bushels of wheat and 1.6 million of corn. During the decade of the 1850's, however, the proportion changed drastically, as five or six times as much corn was transported as wheat, while the quantities of oats carried were also generally larger than wheat.[22] This reflected the fact that the area along the middle and upper Illinois River was predominantly a corn-growing region. Wheat, on the other hand, was eventually to become one of the greatest articles of freight for the railroads in the 1850's. In the years 1848-50, the canal carried a rising share of the wheat received at Chicago—21 per cent in 1848, 25 per cent in 1849, and 36 per cent in 1850. However, this did not represent greater quantities. Chicago's receipts, as Table 8

---

[20] Until the 1850's the development of transportation facilities in Illinois lagged far behind that in Ohio, Indiana, and Michigan. In 1849 Illinois had 153 miles of canals and railroads in operation compared with Ohio's 1,086, Indiana's 300, and Michigan's 264. Illinois had one mile of rail or canal for every 355 square miles, while Michigan had one mile per 213 square miles, and Ohio had one mile per 37 square miles.

[21] Pierce, *History of Chicago*, I, 126-127; John H. Krenkel, *Illinois Internal Improvements, 1818-1848* (Cedar Rapids, Iowa, 1958), 42-46; and William V. Pooley, *The Settlement of Illinois from 1830 to 1850* (Madison, Wis., 1908), 478-484, all call attention to the stimulus given the grain trade by the food requirements of large numbers of canal laborers. This can be construed as influencing the Chicago market indirectly. The market created by the canal crews probably caused farmers in the immediate vicinity to grow enough extra grain to supply the new demands, and if the market was suddenly to contract, farmers would be forced to look elsewhere for an outlet. But this situation could have affected but a small percentage of the farmers in northern Illinois, and the loss of the canal market in 1841-42 could not, of itself, have freed enough grain to cause Chicago's exports to rise from 40,000 in 1841 to 587,000 in 1842. Chicago Board of Trade, *Nineteenth Annual Report of the Trade and Commerce of Chicago, 1876* (Chicago, 1877), 43. The explanation for this rise probably lies as much in faulty export figures for 1841 as in anything else. A full treatment of the role of the canal and railroads in Chicago's grain trade will come in later pages.

[22] *Fifth Annual Review of the Trade and Commerce . . . of Chicago, 1856* (Chicago, 1857), 31; John S. Wright, *Chicago: Past, Present, Future. Relations to the Great Interior, and to the Continent* (2nd ed., Chicago, 1870), 52-53.

indicates, declined from 1848 to 1850. The canal carried about 400,000 bushels in both 1848 and 1850. In 1849 the Chicago and Galena road carried less than 10 per cent of Chicago's wheat receipts, and in 1850 22 per cent. As late as 1850, then, wagons were the largest single source of Chicago's wheat receipts. But just two years later the railroad outstripped the combined traffic of canal and wagons. The Galena and the Michigan Central roads carried 55 per cent of the wheat received at Chicago in 1852. The proportion arriving via rail increased steadily as the decade progressed and new avenues of commerce penetrated the interior.[23]

In the early stages of this development in Chicago's grain trade, there were no striking increases recorded in the receipts or exports of wheat and flour that can be legitimately ascribed to the impact of either canal or railroad. The increase was consistent from 1842 to 1848; but, as is apparent from Table 8, the advance was greatest

TABLE 8. ANNUAL RECEIPTS OF WHEAT, FLOUR, AND CORN AT CHICAGO, 1842-52 (IN THOUSANDS)

Year	Wheat (bu.)	Flour (bbl.)	Corn (bu.)
1842	587[a]	3	88[b]
1843	689	11	–
1844	892	6	–
1845	957	14	–
1846	1,400	28	–
1847	1,974	33	106
1848	2,160	45	632
1849	1,936	51	703
1850	1,165	70	437
1851	748	57	3,336
1852	937	53	5,229

[a] The figures for 1842-49 are exports in all three commodities.
[b] The figures for 1842, 1850, and 1852 include corn, oats, barley, and rye.
Sources: Chicago Board of Trade, *19 AR, 1876*, 42-43; *Hunt's*, XXVI (April, 1851), 428-430.

before 1848—the year in which both the canal and the railroad came into Chicago. From 1848 to 1853 there is no advance at all, but a rather sharp diminution partially caused by a series of harvest failures in the early 1850's. Receipts and exports did not equal or exceed the quantities of 1848 until 1854. More important in explain-

[23] Chicago *Daily Tribune*, December 28, 1850; *5 AR, Commerce of Chicago, 1856*, 31.

ing this decline than either crop failures or the possible loss of trade
to rival markets is the fact that neither the canals nor the Chicago
and Galena Railroad facilitated the opening of new wheat-growing
lands. Both routes lay partially across areas which, as early as 1839,
were heavily committed to a wheat-growing economy. By 1849 the
commitment, particularly in the northern part of the state, had become more intense. Six northern tier counties produced 2 million
bushels of wheat—21 per cent of the state's crop. The canal touched
only Du Page along its southwestern border, and in 1849 the Galena
road had not reached Elgin, 42 miles northwest of Chicago. Wheat,
then, arrived at Chicago from previously established sources, although its shipment was expedited by the canal and, to a lesser degree, by the Galena road.

The effect of the canal upon the traffic in corn was quite different. This was a crop which, if shipped in bulk at all, had normally
gone south along the Illinois River to St. Louis and New Orleans.
An immediate increase in corn receipts followed the opening of the
canal. The increase was halted temporarily by a failure in the corn
crop in the lower Mississippi valley, and the resulting high prices
and great demand caused a diversion of corn traffic from Chicago
to the South, as well as a decrease in the quantities of corn fed to
livestock.[24] The upsurge in the corn trade during 1851-52, however,
was phenomenal, and for a time the value of the corn received and
shipped exceeded the value of other commodities received at or
shipped from Chicago.[25]

In 1851 the Illinois and Michigan Canal carried 90 per cent of
the corn and oats received at Chicago. While the share carried by
the canal declined in the following years, as late as 1860 it still

---

[24] *Hunt's*, XXVIII (May, 1853), 562; Chicago *Daily Tribune*, December
28, 1850. Receipts of corn at St. Louis increased by 1.1 million bushels from
1850 to 1851. St. Louis Merchants' Exchange, *Annual Statement of the Trade
and Commerce of St. Louis, 1878* (St. Louis, 1879), 52. Receipts at New
Orleans increased by about 200,000 bushels. 8 *Census, 1860, Agriculture,* clvi.
This suggests that most of the corn went directly to the stricken areas in the
South.

[25] In 1851 corn receipts were valued at $1.1 million while total grain ship-
ments equaled $1.6 million and continued, though in diminishing degree, to ex-
ceed the value of wheat and flour exports until 1855. The importance of corn is
even further accentuated if the commerce in pork and pork products is taken
into account. Andrews, "Reports on Trade and Commerce," 218; *Hunt's*, XXVI
(April, 1851), 428-430. It is not strictly accurate to maintain, as some students
of Chicago's grain trade do, that wheat dominated the produce trade of Chicago throughout 1840-60.

amounted to about one-third of total corn receipts.[26] Most of Chicago's corn came from upper Illinois River counties like Peoria which were able to use the canal. Some 90 per cent of the corn crop was raised in this region south of La Salle County. Over one-half of this was produced in the southernmost portion, to which Chicago did not gain access until the Chicago, Alton and St. Louis and the Chicago, Burlington and Quincy railroads penetrated the region in 1856-57.[27] Until that time this country shipped south, normally to St. Louis, while the counties north of this group were able to ship to both Chicago and St. Louis. It was in this section of the state that the two cities competed for the grain trade.

CHICAGO VERSUS ST. LOUIS

Among the various factors which a farmer in the middle Illinois River valley would weigh in making his decision to sell his surplus at St. Louis or Chicago, price and expenses such as transportation, storage costs, and drayage fees were probably the primary considerations. In general, prices were higher at both Chicago and St. Louis than at interior towns. This, of course, was an obvious requirement if there was to be any direct trade between source areas and ports.

During the years 1849-53 the average annual price at St. Louis was normally higher than at Chicago. The price difference varied from 61 cents per barrel more in 1851 to 19 cents per barrel more in 1853. In 1854 and 1855 flour was worth between $7.50 and $8.00 in both markets.[28] Against this, particularly when prices at these

---

[26] 5 AR, *Commerce of Chicago, 1856*, 31; Wright, *Chicago*, 52-53. By this time Illinois was interlaced with railroads, and the Rock Island road had been competing with the canal since 1854. In later years a large quantity of corn was used at Chicago to fatten hogs previous to the slaughter. But in the season of 1852-53 only 48,000 hogs were packed in Chicago, compared with 505,000 in 1861-62. *Hunt's*, XXVIII (May, 1853), 564; Chauncey M. Depew, ed., *One Hundred Years of American Commerce, 1795-1895* (2 vols., New York, 1895), II, 385.

[27] On the basis of contemporary yield estimates in Illinois of 15 bushels of wheat per acre and 40 bushels of corn, it appears that ten acres of corn were sown for every five of wheat in the Illinois valley, compared to four acres of corn for every seven of wheat in the north. The extent to which wheat was grown in standing corn is not known, but it seems to have been a rather common practice. 6 *Census, 1840*, 299-300; 7 *Census, 1850*, 730-731; J. M. Peck, *A Gazetteer of Illinois in Three Parts* . . . (Jacksonville, Ill., 1834), 30; Shirreff, *A Tour Through North America*, 248-249.

[28] *Hunt's*, XXX (April, 1854), 452, XXXII (June, 1855), 688.

ports were fairly close, must be set the costs of transport. In this aspect of the competition, Chicago could exert a greater influence than St. Louis, since the state of Illinois had the authority to regulate tolls on the canal, while St. Louis could do little to control freight rates on downstream traffic. Interested parties in Chicago believed that with a liberal reduction of tolls, Chicago could monopolize the trade of the Illinois River valley. The object was to make the Chicago market more attractive to shippers in the middle regions, more or less equidistant between the two ports.[29] By the end of the 1850's, Chicago was the dominant market in the Illinois valley, and it is probable that favorable freight rates to that town —both via canal and rail—contributed to its success.

In 1851, with flour worth about 61 cents more at St. Louis, receipts of wheat from the Illinois River increased at the Missouri port, while receipts declined at Chicago from 417,000 bushels in 1850 to 78,000 in 1851. This reflected a strong southern demand for grain arising from a crop failure in the lower Mississippi valley. By 1853 canal receipts had risen at Chicago to 340,000 bushels, while St. Louis receipts from the Illinois River had declined somewhat. In 1855, with wheat quoted at Chicago from $1.35 to $1.70 per bushel, canal receipts surpassed 1 million bushels. Receipts at St. Louis had also increased between 1852 and 1855, but the Illinois River furnished a diminished portion of this volume.[30]

Prices or freight rates, however, were not the only determinants involved. At some time before the price of grain at Chicago reached parity with that at St. Louis, the market at Chicago became the favored destination for grain in the middle Illinois River valley. This was due to a number of significant advantages which Chicago possessed to a greater degree than St. Louis. For one, Chicago's facilities for receiving and forwarding grain were superior to those at St. Louis. Grain shipments at St. Louis could not be handled in bulk, but only in sacks and barrels, which made shipping more expensive for the farmer. Moreover, storage facilities at St. Louis were wholly inadequate, and the existing warehouses were far removed from the wharves, necessitating extra drayage charges from

---

[29] Chicago *Daily Tribune*, December 28, 1850.

[30] *Hunt's*, XXVI (April, 1852), 429, XXX (April, 1854), 453; 5 AR, *Commerce of Chicago, 1856*, 31; Frederick Gerhard, *Illinois as It Is; Its History, Geography, Statistics, Agriculture* (Chicago, 1857), 393; St. Louis Merchants' Exchange, *Trade and Commerce, 1878*, 50-52.

boat to warehouse and back. Losses from poor handling were heavy, and much unloaded produce was left on the levee, so damp weather could result in heavy losses of grain and flour. St. Louis was also at the mercy of the river. Although Chicago's port was frozen in three or four months of the year, shipping could operate during the remaining months more consistently than at St. Louis, where much of the traffic was concentrated in two yearly periods of high water lasting from four to six weeks.[31]

The movement of great quantities of grain via canal and railroads into Chicago necessitated the erection of large elevators. Chicago's first steam elevator was built in 1848, and by 1855 the storage capacity of the town was 750,000 bushels. The entire storage capacity at St. Louis could not match, in 1860, that of two elevators erected on Illinois Central property at Chicago in 1858. These elevators could receive and ship 1.4 million bushels of grain every ten days.[32] Elevators such as these, and one with a capacity of 800,-000 bushels erected by the Chicago, Burlington and Quincy Railroad in 1860 and located on the waterfront, made the cost of storing and transferring grain cheaper at Chicago than St. Louis. The grain was also less liable to damage at the Lake Michigan port.[33]

The rapid expansion of the grain trade and facilities for handling the grain also required the development of new techniques of inspection, grading, and storage. Prior to this expansion the grain was handled in small lots, with the grain of a particular shipper retaining its identity by being stored separately from the grain of other dealers. The grain was also purchased by sample, because the quality of the grain had to be determined on the spot by the pur-

---

[31] Switzler, "Report on Internal Commerce," 62; Wyatt W. Belcher, *The Economic Rivalry Between St. Louis and Chicago, 1850-1880* (New York, 1947), 102. Lake commerce generally opened in mid-April and closed in mid-December. Occasionally navigation on the Erie Canal was delayed until May by the continued blocking of the Buffalo harbor by ice, as in 1831 and 1835. In 1842 an early freeze-up on the Erie Canal during the first week in December caught a large quantity of grain short of its destination. *Hunt's,* III (July, 1840), 90; *NWR,* LXIII (December 10, 1842), 240.

[32] Wright, *Chicago,* 157; Illinois Central Railway, *Report to the Shareholders, June, 1858* (London, 1858), 24. As a contrast, it is interesting to note the completion in 1963 of a grain elevator at the port of Montreal with a capacity of 5.5 million bushels of grain capable of unloading a giant grain-carrying laker carrying 1 million bushels in less than a day.

[33] Belcher, *Economic Rivalry Between St. Louis and Chicago,* 103; *Report of the Directors of the Chicago, Burlington & Quincy Railroad Company, 1861* (Chicago, 1861), 11.

chaser or his agent. Purchasing without prior inspection was risky, as some farmers and merchants were not above mixing grains of different quality. The old system became unworkable in the 1850's, and a method of inspection and storage by grade was developed. Wheat of the same quality was stored together, generally in the elevator of the shipping agency if the grain arrived by rail, or in a privately owned elevator if it arrived by wagon or canal. The grain was transferred from these buildings to the lake vessels for transportation to the East. The shipper did not retain possession of the same lot of grain originally purchased but was issued a receipt by the elevator for the specified amount of grain of a certain grade stored in the facility. The owner of the grain could then dispose of his grain by simply selling the receipts or by making other arrangements to ship to some other place an amount of grain equivalent to the quantity stipulated on the receipts. This development greatly facilitated the handling of grain and also resulted in an increase of direct purchases by eastern dealers.[34] In earlier days, little Chicago wheat was marketed directly in the East, largely because of the necessity of local purchasing by sample. The grain was handled by commission and produce merchants located in Chicago, who purchased it either on their own account or on contract from eastern dealers. Small quantities were also bought by owners and operators of lake vessels in order to ensure cargoes for their trips to the East.[35]

Chicago's growing financial resources, both cause and result of her expanding commerce, were deeply involved in the produce business throughout the period 1842-60. Some idea of the extent to which Chicago's prosperity was derived from the grain trade is conveyed by comparing the value of grain exports to the total value of

[34] Peter T. Dondlinger, *The Book of Wheat. An Economic History and Practical Manual of the Wheat Industry* (New York, 1908), 222; James E. Boyle, *Speculation and the Chicago Board of Trade* (New York, 1921), 41. The increase in storage facilities and the evolution of standard grading procedures at Chicago spurred the development of futures trading. In the late 1840's much of the grain purchased at Chicago was on a "to arrive" basis. Farmers prior to harvest would contract to sell grain at a specified price "to arrive" at a future date—at first within a few days, then weeks, months, or upwards of a crop season away. The quantities so handled by any one dealer were generally small through the 1850's, but in the aggregate of considerable volume. See *ibid.*, 51-54, and Arthur G. Peterson, "Futures Trading with Particular Reference to Agricultural Commodities," *Agricultural History*, VII (April, 1933), 72.

[35] Pierce, *History of Chicago*, I, 130-131; Thomas D. Odle, "The American Grain Trade of the Great Lakes, 1825-1873," *Inland Seas*, IX (Spring, 1953), 53-54.

exports. In 1848-49 grain exports contributed over 50 per cent of the total value. Thereafter the share of the grain trade declined in terms of percentage contribution, but increased greatly in dollar volume. In 1858 grain exports were valued at $11 million and meat products at $6 million. In 1860 exports of grain and meat products were valued at $21.7 million out of total exports worth $72.7 million.[36] The grain trade was also the major source of freight revenues of the railroads during the initial period of growth, and the railroads contributed immeasurably to Chicago's rise. The yearly increments in the number and tonnage of shipping calling at the port of Chicago are also partly attributable to the activity of the grain trade.[37] But the greater part of the general advance was a development of the middle and late 1850's.

CHICAGO VERSUS MILWAUKEE

During the late 1840's and early 1850's, Chicago shared the honors with Milwaukee as Lake Michigan's largest grain entrepot. Which of these two cities was to gain the ascendancy in the lake trade was a question unresolved until 1855 or 1856.

Chicago and Milwaukee were in direct competition for the grain surplus of a large strip of territory along the Illinois-Wisconsin boundary. In the 1850's this grain competition was to become a three-cornered affair as railroads based at Chicago, Milwaukee, and Racine reached the Mississippi River, where they could intercept the surplus produce of Iowa and Minnesota, normally earmarked for St. Louis.[38] In the period before 1854 or 1855, Chicago and Milwaukee competed for the surplus of a much smaller region, the northernmost tier of Illinois counties and the southernmost tier in Wisconsin. In this struggle both Chicago and Milwaukee were faced

---

[36] 7 *AR, Commerce of Chicago, 1858,* 36; Chicago Board of Trade, *19 AR, 1876,* 42-43.

[37] Arrivals in 1844 numbered 1,243 with an aggregate tonnage of 459,910. By 1854, 5,021 arrivals were reported with a total tonnage of 1,092,644. Three years later arrivals had increased to 7,557 and total tonnage to 1.7 million. Pierce, *History of Chicago,* I, 77; 7 *AR, Commerce of Chicago, 1858,* 36.

[38] In the post–Civil War years, the St. Paul–Minneapolis market developed to the extent that it competed on an equal basis with the Lake Michigan ports for the surplus produce of Minnesota, Wisconsin, and Iowa. Lake Superior then became a factor in the Great Lakes traffic in grain and Minneapolis the flour center of the United States. See Charles B. Kuhlman, *The Development of the Flour-Milling Industry in the United States with Special Reference to the Industry in Minneapolis* (Boston and New York, 1929).

with competition from Racine and Kenosha, Wisconsin. The competition focused upon the trade in wheat and flour, for neither the Wisconsin nor Illinois counties in question raised large quantities of corn (see Table 22).

In the late 1830's and early 1840's, the grain trade at Milwaukee was limited primarily to imports and to small shipments along the lake shore of Wisconsin to settlements not producing sufficient food supplies. During the late 1830's southeastern Wisconsin began to receive large numbers of immigrants, and by 1839 46 per cent of the population resided in the southeastern corner of the state.[39] These new settlers were soon engaged in wheat farming (wheat being the principal cash crop), which furnished the supplies upon which the grain trade of Milwaukee and other Wisconsin cities was based.

Grain growing was soon heavily concentrated in the southeast, where the soil was superior to that in the nonglaciated lands of the so-called Driftless area in the southwest. In 1839, 76 per cent of the state's wheat was produced in the southeastern counties of Walworth, Racine, Milwaukee, Rock, and Jefferson, while the southwestern corner including Iowa, Green, Grant, and Crawford counties produced only 18 per cent. In the next decade, total wheat production made a substantial advance, reaching 4.2 million bushels compared with the 212,000 reported ten years earlier. The crop remained concentrated in the east; Rock and Walworth counties alone produced 33.4 per cent of the total crop. By 1849 east central Wisconsin was a major factor in the wheat economy of the state, and the third and fourth tiers of counties between Lakes Horicon and Winnebago produced over 20 per cent of the crop.[40] As early as 1851 a Fond du Lac County farmer noted that immigrants and lumber camps, which had thus far exhausted the surplus of the area, would be insufficient markets as the wheat crop grew. An eastern market would then be necessary.[41]

Farming conditions in Wisconsin in the 1840's and 1850's represent in microcosm the problems and obstacles faced by farmers

[39] *6 Census, 1840,* 102.

[40] *Ibid.,* 347-348; *7 Census, 1850,* 931. Wisconsin farmers were heavily dependent upon wheat as a cash crop, producing 14.2 bushels per capita compared to 8.7 for the East North Central states as a group and 4.3 for the United States. Rock and Walworth counties each produced over 37 bushels of wheat per capita. *Ibid.*

[41] *Transactions Wisconsin Agricultural Society,* I (1851), 167.

throughout the Old Northwest during the frontier period, but in the case of Wisconsin, and Michigan also, the duration of the pioneer stage was measurably telescoped if compared to Ohio. While farmers in the middle Muskingum and Scioto river valleys waited two decades for an outlet to the north, three decades for a sizable eastern market, and some 40 years for a steady and large foreign demand, farmers in Wisconsin had only to get their crops to the lake in order to avail themselves of the growing marketing opportunities of the late 1840's and 1850's. By the late 1850's railroads crossed the state, providing speedy access to markets at Racine, Milwaukee, and Chicago. In 1851 wheat grown in Columbia County was without a means to market other than teams, and the price would not bear the cost of transportation.[42] By 1854 the Milwaukee and Mississippi Railroad reached Madison, 25 miles south of Columbia's southern border, and by 1847 the La Crosse and Milwaukee Railroad bisected the county.

The problems and risks were still there, however. Money was scarce and the expenses of opening a new farm often exceeded a settler's ability to pay. This meant either borrowing money, limiting the acreage to be developed, or both. In either event, the acreage planted was generally limited by the high price and short supply of labor at harvest time. Breaking up the land was an expensive proposition, often costing several times the original cost. Estimates ranged from $2.00 to $3.00 an acre in Illinois to $3.50 in Wisconsin.[43] For a few years, at least, farming was generally conducted at a subsistence level. Enough was raised to supply the wants of the farmer's family, and perhaps allow for an exchange of grain for store goods between the farmer and country merchant.

A serious problem faced by early Wisconsin farmers was the repeated failure of their winter wheat crops. In the early 1850's a series of winter wheat failures seems to have resulted in a sharp decline in wheat receipts at Milwaukee and Racine, and Chicago as well. Numerous farmers complained of winter kill, and it was difficult to convince them to turn to spring wheat, which was not widely grown in the United States until the late 1850's. Soft white winter wheats were preferred by millers and consumers, for aesthetic reasons rather than for nutritional value. Farming experts,

---

[42] *Ibid.*, 134.

[43] Gerhard, *Illinois As It Is*, 311; Milo M. Quaife, ed., *An English Settler in Pioneer Wisconsin. The Letters of Edwin Bottomley, 1842-1850* (Madison, Wis., 1918), 69.

theoretical and practical, united in advising deep plowing, thorough harrowing or rolling, drainage of surplus water, and early sowing with a drill during the last of August or first week of September.[44] While the above suggestions, if applied, would have mitigated the losses in the winter wheat crop, the crucial factor was climate. Winter conditions in Wisconsin were ordinarily too severe to allow the successful cultivation of winter wheat. By the late 1850's southern Wisconsin and northern Illinois farmers had discovered this irremediable obstacle and turned to spring wheat.[45]

It is not possible to do more than suggest the consequences which this trial and failure of winter wheat had on the Wisconsin grain trade. It did not prevent Wisconsin farmers from producing a marketable surplus of grain in the early 1840's. Nor did it appear to have any effect on the expansion of the grain trade at Wisconsin's ports during the late 1840's.

Milwaukee shipped its first wheat—4,000 bushels to Canada—in 1841. Grain began arriving at Milwaukee in fairly large quantities in 1845, when the lack of storage facilities prompted the erection of a grain elevator.[46] It appears likely that until the mid-1840's Racine shipped more grain than Milwaukee. Both ports then displayed marked progress up to 1850.[47] By 1847 Milwaukee, Kenosha (Southport), and Racine were shipping some 1.3 million bushels of wheat and 40,000 barrels of flour. Milwaukee shipped all but 15 per cent of the flour and 44 per cent of the wheat. Racine's total

---

[44] *Patent Report, 1858*, 284; *Transactions Wisconsin Agricultural Society*, I (1851), 106; Solon Robinson, ed., *Facts for Farmers; also for the Family Circle* . . . (2 vols., New York, 1865), II, 698.

[45] Farmers gave up winter wheat reluctantly for a number of reasons. Prices and yields were generally higher for winter than spring wheat. The former, planted in the fall, was ready for harvest earlier than spring wheat and thus extended the harvest period but did not compete for labor with the spring crops. Moreover, the milling of hard spring wheats was a more difficult process than that required for soft winter varieties, and many millers were not equipped to cope with this before 1860. C. R. Ball *et al.*, "Wheat Production and Marketing," *United States Department of Agriculture Yearbook, 1921* (Washington, D.C., 1922), 100-101; John Storck and Walter D. Teague, *Flour for Man's Bread. A History of Milling* (Minneapolis, 1952), 188; Kuhlman, *Development of the Flour-Milling Industry*, 77, 88; Bottomley, *Letters*, 156-157; 7 AR, Commerce of Chicago, 1858, 4.

[46] E. D. Holton, "Commercial History of Milwaukee," *Collections of the State Historical Society of Wisconsin*, IV (1857-58), 254-261.

[47] Racine was reported to have shipped 40,000 bushels of wheat in 1842. NWR, LXV (December 23, 1843), 272. NWR, LVIII (June 13, 1840), 240, reported the arrival of the steamboat *Great Western* at Buffalo with some flour manufactured at Perkin's Mills in Racine.

exports in that year were valued at $496,000 and Milwaukee's at $750,000. Racine's exports increased to a value of $631,000 in 1849 while Milwaukee's rose to $2.1 million, of which $1.9 million represented wheat and flour exports. In that year Milwaukee exported 1.1 million bushels of wheat and 137,000 barrels of flour. At this time Chicago's wheat and flour exports exceeded those of Milwaukee by only 350,000 bushels of wheat and flour, and until 1850 Milwaukee's flour-milling industry was considerably larger than Chicago's.[48]

Between 1850 and 1853 there was a material falling off in the grain trade of Wisconsin's ports. Milwaukee's exports dipped to about 800,000 bushels of wheat and flour in 1850 and 550,000 in 1851. Racine's wheat shipments declined to 280,000 bushels from over 500,000 in 1847, and the total value of exports at Racine fell to $580,000 and were lower still in 1851.[49] As noted earlier, Chicago's receipts and exports of wheat were in a decline at this time as well. Receipts at both Chicago and Milwaukee decreased by some 60 per cent from 1849 to 1851. Both were seeking surplus grain from the same area. A series of crop failures in that area would thus force the contraction of both markets, and Racine as well, which was located in the very region disputed over by Milwaukee and Chicago. The country in question at this time was still largely engaged in the cultivation of winter wheat, which suffered extensively during the winters of 1850-52. This failure was essentially a local one, not region-wide, as shown by the fact that known receipts at eastern terminals and New Orleans did not respond in like manner during this period.[50]

---

[48] *Patent Report, 1847*, 593-594; "Report of the Topographical Bureau, 1850," 8; *Transactions Wisconsin Agricultural Society*, I (1851), 205; Milwaukee Chamber of Commerce, *Fifth Annual Report for the Year 1862* (Milwaukee, 1863), 20.

[49] *Ibid.*; *Transactions Wisconsin Agricultural Society*, I (1851), 205; Chicago *Daily Tribune*, January 20, 1853.

[50] A factor contributing to the over-all recession in the grain trade was the general lessening of foreign demand since the great years of 1847-48. Buffalo's receipts fell from 15.7 million bushels of wheat and flour in 1847 to 10.7 million bushels in 1848, which was about the volume reached in 1846. In 1851 receipts were 300,000 bushels less than 1848. Treasury Dept., *Statistics of Foreign and Domestic Commerce*, 161. Receipts at Oswego rose during the entire period from 1847 to 1852. *Patent Report, 1849*, 548; Andrews, "Reports on Trade and Commerce," 77; *ARJ*, XXVII (January 21, 1854), 43. Receipts of flour at New Orleans displayed erratic ups and downs from 1847 to 1852, but receipts in 1852-53 were considerably larger than those in 1851. 8 *Census, 1860, Agriculture*, clvi.

Milwaukee, Chicago, and Racine had recovered much of the lost ground by 1854, and through the remainder of the decade they experienced consistent advances in the grain trade. Railroads played an instrumental role in the revival of trade at each city. The Racine and Mississippi Railroad, completed to Savanna, Illinois, in 1857, supplied Racine with large amounts of grain. Racine's receipts of wheat and flour increased from 924,000 bushels in 1858 to 1.6 million in 1861,[51] though this was only 10 per cent of Milwaukee's receipts and 6 per cent of Chicago's. A large proportion of the grain carried over the Racine and Mississippi road was diverted from Racine to both Chicago and Milwaukee. These towns had not been inactive in pushing their railroad connections west and northwest to points on the Mississippi River.

The La Crosse and Milwaukee and the Milwaukee and Prairie du Chien lines, both completed by the late 1850's, put Milwaukee in touch with the Mississippi. The Chicago, St. Paul and Fond du Lac Railroad intersected the Racine and Mississippi at Clinton, Wisconsin. The Chicago and Fond du Lac line carried 562,000 bushels of wheat and flour to Chicago in 1857.[52] This was produce raised only 65 miles west of Racine. From Janesville, a few miles north of Clinton, produce could also take the Milwaukee and Prairie du Chien route to Lake Michigan. By 1861 the Chicago and Fond du Lac was diverting over one-half of the flour originating on the Racine and Mississippi and some two-thirds of the pork and livestock.[53] Racine's source area, extending to the Mississippi in 1857, had shrunk by 1861 to two or three counties, and this was shared with other cities. Thereafter, Racine's grain traffic was entirely obscured by the struggle between Milwaukee and Chicago, and the energetic newcomer on the scene, Minneapolis, for the control of the grain trade west and southwest of Lake Michigan and in the trans-Mississippi region.

SUMMARY

The grain trade originating from the ports on Lake Michigan advanced from one of minor proportions in 1840 to one of some

---

[51] *7 AR, Commerce of Chicago, 1858,* 17; *Third Annual Report to the Trustees in Possession of the Racine and Mississippi Railroad, May, 1862* (Racine, Wis., 1862).

[52] *6 AR, Commerce of Chicago, 1857,* 34-35.

[53] Racine and Mississippi Railroad, *3 AR, 1862; Transactions Wisconsin Agricultural Society,* IV-VII (1854-57), 333.

significance at the end of the decade, although it continued to be smaller than that of Lake Erie until the middle and late 1850's. The steady progress in the Lake Michigan region was a consequence of rapid expansion in wheat and corn production in the areas using the lake as a route to market. This was made possible, or economically desirable from the producer's point of view, by the extension of transportation facilities from lake ports into the interior, tapping sections which previously were unable to reach the lake with their commodities.

In 1840 the grain trade was centered at a number of different ports, each with a seemingly equal potential for future development. Some failed and others succeeded in their quest for commercial power and economic prosperity. The question as to which ports were to achieve this station was fairly well decided during the 1840's. The minor towns fell into their places as minor towns, leaving Chicago and Milwaukee to contest for the bulk of the trade. This outcome was, in large part, the result of the energetic transportation policies pursued by the cities which were ultimately successful. The construction of the Michigan Southern and the Michigan Central from Toledo and Detroit cut off St. Joseph and Michigan City from the areas from which they had previously obtained grain. The ambitious ports between Milwaukee and Chicago—Kenosha, Racine, Waukegan—were squeezed out of the wheat belt lying along the Illinois-Wisconsin border by the superior facilities and complex rail networks thrust out from the two larger towns.

Chicago was engaged in an economic struggle on two fronts —with Milwaukee and with St. Louis—and her success was not apparent before 1854 or 1855. Through the agency of the Illinois and Michigan Canal, and later railroads such as the Chicago, Alton and St. Louis and the Rock Island, Chicago made a bid to dominate the grain trade of the Illinois River valley. By means of these roads, plus the Galena and the Chicago, Burlington and Quincy—all terminating at the Mississippi River—Chicago diverted from St. Louis grain shipped from the upper reaches of the river. The Milwaukee and Prairie du Chien and the La Crosse and Milwaukee railroads served to divert grain from the railroads of both St. Louis and Chicago. In the 1840's this complicated economic struggle was just being joined. By 1850 the rivalry had been narrowed to the principal contestants, but the final outcome was still in doubt.

The Rise of the
Eastern Receiving Centers
on the Great Lakes

CHAPTER V

However fierce the contest between the youthful commercial centers of the West in their efforts to engross the grain trade of a wide expanse of territory, the grain still flowed over the lakes and down the rivers and along the rails. From the standpoint of the history of Cleveland and Toledo or Chicago and Milwaukee, the history of the grain trade on the lakes is a story of rivalry and of shifting fortunes, but from the standpoint of the lake trade as a whole, it is also a story of how a steadily rising volume of grain called into being a number of important receiving centers such as Buffalo and Oswego at the eastern end of the lakes. The role assumed by these terminals was dependent only upon the total quantities leaving the Northwest, not upon the fact that Chicago at some point surpassed Milwaukee as a grain center.[1]

[1] In the rivalry between Chicago and St. Louis, or Cleveland and Cincin-

The competition between the eastern terminals to receive the grain surplus of the Northwest was as severe as that between the exporting centers. This economic struggle was intensified because it was often a phase of a still greater contest centered on the Atlantic coast between New York, Philadelphia, Boston, and Baltimore. Each of the seaboard cities sought to secure a larger share of the trade with the West, and to that end constructed canals and railroads to the West. In addition to competition between markets, there was also rivalry between different transportation systems operating from the same market.

The early phase of this struggle was initiated with the construction and completion of the Erie Canal from Albany to Buffalo between 1818 and 1825. This successful flank attack on the Appalachian barrier proved of enormous benefit, first of all to New York City and the regions through which the Erie Canal passed. In the mid-1830's the advantages of this route were exploited by the Northwest, which began shipping increasing quantities of grain via the canal to tidewater. This gave incentive to the other Atlantic coast ports, for if they were to remain competitive it was imperative that they counter New York's move by constructing their own transportation systems to the West. Philadelphia, by means of a system of canals and inclined planes, and Baltimore, with the Chesapeake and Ohio Canal, attempted to reach and tap the Ohio valley. Neither the Pennsylvania network, completed to Pittsburgh in 1834, nor Baltimore's canal effort, finished in 1850, proved to be as successful as the Erie Canal. Baltimore, moreover, undertook the construction of the Baltimore and Ohio Railroad in the very year, 1828, that construction was begun on her canal. Thus a new weapon was introduced in the commercial war.

Before Baltimore's project achieved its goal, other eastern cities entered the race to the West via rail. Boston pushed a railroad through to Albany in 1842, seeking to divert some of the traffic normally using the Hudson River route to New York, as well as to attain direct connections with the Great Lakes. New York countered this move, first with the Hudson River Railroad from New York to Albany where it connected with the various short lines to

---

nati, the eastern terminals did have interest. In the 1850's, when railroad connections between St. Louis and Cincinnati and the East diverted traffic from New Orleans, it did not result in increased receipts at lake terminals, for the produce went directly to the eastern seaboard or into the South.

Buffalo,[2] and second with the New York and Erie Railroad, begun in 1840 and completed to Dunkirk, on Lake Erie, in 1851. To the south, in 1852, the Pensylvania Railroad connected Philadelphia with Pittsburgh, and a year later the Baltimore and Ohio entered Wheeling, 35 years after the Cumberland Road arrived at the same spot. In the cases of these last two rail routes, there was competition not only with each other, but with the Pennsylvania canals and the Chesapeake and Ohio Canal. In New York the rivalry between transportation systems involved the two cross-state railroads and the Erie Canal. The New York and Erie road created a rival for Buffalo when it reached Dunkirk. All this, however, occurred in the 1850's. Until that time the Erie Canal and Buffalo dominated the grain traffic of the Great Lakes.

When the Northwest first entered upon a grain trade of large dimensions on the lakes, Buffalo was only one of several receiving centers at the eastern end seeking to increase its traffic in western grain. In 1829 the Welland Canal, paralleling the Niagara River a few miles to the west of it, opened Lake Ontario to the shipping of Lake Erie so that grain could pass the Welland to enter the markets at Rochester and Oswego or continue across Lake Ontario to the St. Lawrence River. On this river the produce could go to Montreal or Ogdensburg, New York. At various times one or several of these ports offered inducements to shippers which Buffalo could not match, but which were not enough to shake the town's preeminent position in the lake trade.

During the period 1825-53 the grain traffic of the Erie Canal grew to enormous proportions. In 1849 the United States produced 100.5 million bushels of wheat, some 37 per cent of which was raised in the East North Central states. The Erie Canal carried, in 1850, 22.6 million bushels of wheat and flour to tidewater, or 55 per cent of the total produced in the East North Central states, and 25 per cent of the national total.[3] The over-all growth, though

---

[2] These eight lines were eventually consolidated into the New York Central Railroad in 1853, and included the Mohawk and Hudson, Utica and Schenectady, Syracuse and Utica, Auburn and Syracuse, Auburn and Rochester, the Towanda, Attica and Buffalo, and the Buffalo and Niagara railroads. *ARJ*, XXVI (June 4, 1853), 354.

[3] The Erie Canal carried 14 per cent of total U.S. wheat production in 1839, and 20 per cent in 1860. *8 Census, 1860, Agriculture*, cxlvi; United States Treasury Department, *Statistics of the Foreign and Domestic Commerce of the United States* (Washington, D.C., 1864), 179-180.

large, was not attained at a steady rate of increase; nor were the sources of grain to remain constant.

There were periods, as in the initial stages of the trade, in which impressive percentage increases did not reflect much tangible growth but were the result of gains over previously low quantities. There were periods, such as between 1840 and 1844, of quiescence and decline. And there were stages in which weighty percentage gains were recorded over a volume which was already quite large. Such was the case during the years 1845-47.

Navigation on the middle section of the Erie Canal, from the Seneca River to Rome, commenced in 1820, and during the remainder of the season some 266,000 bushels of wheat and flour passed through Rome. None of this, of course, originated in the Northwest. Five years later, with the canal completed along its entire route, over 1.6 million bushels of wheat and flour were carried to the East. Almost from the beginning the canal carried more flour than New Orleans received from the Mississippi valley. The quantity of wheat and flour passing over the canal rose to 6 million bushels in 1833 and just under 7 million the subsequent year.[4]

Much the larger share of this grain was produced in western New York. The Ohio wheatlands did not supply significant quantities of grain to eastern markets until 1833-35, when, as observed in a previous chapter, Ohio's system of canals to Lake Erie became operational. Cleveland's exports for 1833 and 1834 totaled 1.7 million bushels of wheat and flour. Even if all of this had traversed the canal, it would have formed but 8 per cent of the two-year total carried over that route.[5] Between 1835 and 1840 the quantities of grain originating in the Northwest rose steadily in proportion to the grain of eastern origin carried by the Erie, until by 1841 over one-half of the grain traffic of the canal was supplied by the West and over 70 per cent of that by Ohio.[6] In 1840 some 40 per cent of the canal's grain traffic originated at Buffalo and Oswego,

[4] *ARJ*, IV (January 10, 1835), 2. The quantity of corn and other grains for 1833 and 1834 totaled 723,000 bushels.
[5] *Hunt's*, VIII (March, 1843), 276. Through the 1830's Cleveland probably contributed about 80 per cent of Ohio's total exports. The exports of the other states over the lakes were under 1 million bushels as late as 1840. See above, pp. 53-58.
[6] The difference between col. 2, Table 10, if to it is added the grain reaching the canal via places like Rochester and Tonawanda, and later by rail, and col. 3, Table 10, can be taken as approximating the quantity of grain of eastern production using the Erie Canal.

while one year later over 50 per cent was furnished by those ports.[7]

During the next five years, 1841-45, there was a notable slackening in the growth of the grain trade at the eastern end of the Great Lakes. Receipts at Buffalo and Oswego rose and fell during those five years, ending in 1845 at a level only 22 per cent greater than 1841. Lake shipments from the Northwest increased by only 15 per cent. The total volume of wheat and flour arriving at tidewater, however, registered a significant rise of 55 per cent during the period. Most of this is attributable to an increase in the grain trade of west central and central New York. This contraction in the growth rate was basically due to the leveling off of grain production in Ohio, as Table 4 suggests, and only a moderate increase in exports from Michigan. Although grain from as far west as Chicago and Wisconsin was reported arriving at Buffalo in 1839 and 1840, receipts from those sources remained small until after 1845.[8] However, even the moderate increase in receipts at Buffalo was due to the slowly expanding grain trade of states west of Ohio.

The slow growth rate experienced in both the eastern and western sectors of the Great Lakes suggests that the problem of an unmarketable surplus was not troubling northwestern farmers at this time. In Ohio the great era of canal construction had closed and railroads were still in their infancy. Grain production had expanded greatly from 1835 to 1839 to meet the demands of eastern markets now accessible from the interior of Ohio. The consumption demands of the East were being satisfactorily filled by 1841, and resulted in a leveling downward of grain production in Ohio and an upward adjustment of production in western New York.[9] Under

---

[7] The trend is similar in terms of total tonnage carried by the canal. In 1836 the West sent 54,219 tons while New York contributed 364,906 tons. By 1853, of 1.8 million tons carried to the Hudson River, 1.2 million were from the West. From 1851 to 1860, the source of 74.5 per cent of the total tonnage delivered at the Hudson was west of Buffalo. *Hunt's*, LXII (January, 1860), 30; Noble E. Whitford, *History of the Canal Systems of the State of New York, Together with Brief Histories of the Canals of the United States and Canada* (2 vols., Albany, 1906), I, Table 4, 910.

[8] Cincinnati *Advertiser and Journal*, June 18, 1840; Treasury Dept., *Statistics of Foreign and Domestic Commerce*, 161. The inclusion of corn in the above discussion would not change the results. See Table 11.

[9] In western New York, wheat production had declined in the years after 1835 due to the increasing flow of grain from the West. New York's farmers could not produce wheat as cheaply as Ohio's. The initial contraction of production was probably more than market conditions called for. By the early 1840's, New York farmers were again producing fairly large quantities of wheat for the coast market.

these circumstances, and with a foreign demand that was not rising from 1840 to 1845, it is probable that the quantity of grain sent to market from both Ohio and western New York was harvested from an acreage that remained fairly constant during the period, so that variations in the amounts of grain reaching market were the result of either good or bad crop conditions.

All of the northwestern states felt the impact of the eastern demand for grain, but none were as well prepared to meet it as Ohio. Aside from Ohio, and perhaps Michigan, none of these states had, by 1845, developed a transportation system adequate to its needs. To be sure, canals and railroads were in the making, but their cumulative effect was not appreciable as yet. Indiana was served by only the Wabash and Erie Canal in 1843, and the Illinois and Michigan Canal was not completed until 1848. Indiana had constructed 270 miles of canal and railroad as of 1845; Illinois had less than 150; and Wisconsin would not construct any until the 1850's. Table 9 reveals the disparity in transportation between the

TABLE 9. NUMBER OF SQUARE MILES OF AREA AND NUMBER OF PERSONS FOR EACH MILE OF RAILROAD IN THE EAST NORTH CENTRAL STATES, 1840, 1845, AND 1849

	1840		1845		1849	
State	Sq. Mi./ Mi. RR.	Pop./ Mi. RR.	Sq. Mi./ Mi. RR.	Pop./ Mi. RR.	Sq. Mi./ Mi. RR.	Pop./ Mi. RR.
Ohio	51	1,940	46	2,212	37	2,079
Michigan	485	1,861	252	1,364	213	1,505
Indiana	198	4,034	125	3,099	112	3,192
Illinois	2,092	18,314	435	5,093	355	5,565
Wisconsin	–	–	–	–	2,696[a]	15,256

[a] Figures are for 1850.
Sources: *ARJ*, XIX (January 3, 1846), 8, XXVI (January 1, 1853), 1; *Hunt's*, XXV (September, 1851), 380-382.

states in the Northwest at certain intervals during the 1840's. Although much was accomplished between 1840 and 1850, the five states had only 1,303 miles of railroad in 1840, 72 per cent of which was located in Ohio and Michigan.[10]

---

[10] *Hunt's*, XXV (September, 1851), 380-382. The number of square miles of area to one mile in railroad does not reveal the true picture in Michigan since so much of the northern portion of the Lower Peninsula and almost the entire Upper Peninsula were unpopulated. The extent to which Michigan roads served the settled portion of the state, compared to the performance in other states, is best illustrated by referring to miles per capita.

Moreover, while Ohio had passed out of the frontier stage and was fairly well settled by the 1840's, especially in those areas from which a grain surplus was derived, the other states were, in varying degrees, still in the process of settlement, and as a result large parts of them were barely self-sufficient in foodstuffs. Inadequate transportation, heavy increments to the population, and a none too dynamic market situation meant subsistence agriculture for many, with the surplus of one section going to feed the population of another. What remained went into the commerce of the lakes or the rivers. Farmers working within the limits of a subsistence economy had not the time, ability, need, or incentive to develop a system of agriculture sufficiently flexible to enable them to respond rationally to a given market situation. As much land was sown as a man and his family could clear, and if the available labor was not adequate to the needs of the harvest season, the ripened corn was allowed to rot or provide standing provender for livestock. In contrast to Ohio, in the areas of Michigan, Illinois, and Wisconsin which contributed small quantities of grain to the lake trade in this period, wheat reigned supreme as the cash crop and was produced to full capacity. Thus in the following period, 1846-53, when shortages in Europe resulted in sudden and enormous demands upon the productive capacity of the United States, the farmers in wheat belts west of Ohio did not respond as effectively in terms of increased production as did those in the upper river valleys of Ohio.

Overseas exports of wheat and flour doubled from 1845 to 1846 and doubled again in 1847. The increase of 20 million bushels from 1845 to 1847, as large as total exports between 1843 and 1845, was the consequence of major crop failures in England and Ireland. These markets received some 21 million bushels of wheat and flour in 1846-47 from the United States. Even at this, the United States supplied only 39 per cent of total British wheat and flour imports during the two peak years of American exports.[11]

---

[11] *Ibid.*, XLI (December, 1859), 739; Ezra C. Seaman, *Essays on the Progress of Nations, in Civilization, Productive Industry, Wealth, and Population* (New York, 1852), 222. Although British imports continued at similar high levels during the next four years, 1848-51, the United States contributed only from 9 to 17 per cent of total receipts. Traditional markets such as France, Prussia, and Russia furnished the remainder, and the United States lapsed into its traditional role as a supplementary source of supply to be used only in the event that preferred sources were unable to supply the required quantities.

The extent to which the producers served by the Erie Canal supplied the grain necessary to meet this demand is suggested by the high correspondence between receipts at Buffalo and Oswego, total production in the East North Central states, and total shipments by the Erie Canal system as shown in Table 10. Receipts at

TABLE 10. TOTAL RECEIPTS OF WHEAT AND FLOUR AT BUFFALO AND OSWEGO, AND AT TIDEWATER VIA THE ERIE CANAL; TOTAL WHEAT AND FLOUR EXPORTS OF THE EAST NORTH CENTRAL STATES BY LAKE; AND TOTAL WHEAT AND FLOUR EXPORTS OF THE UNITED STATES, 1840-53 (IN THOUSANDS OF BUSHELS)

Year	Buffalo-Oswego Total Receipts	Total Receipts at Tidewater via Canal	East North Central Total Lake Exports	U.S. Total Exports
1840	4,987	12,293	6,828	11,208
1841	6,162	10,060	7,246	8,397
1842	6,199	9,818	7,411	7,236
1843	7,723	12,022	7,890	4,519
1844	8,003	13,635	9,122	7,751
1845	7,530	15,830	8,349	6,300
1846	11,600	21,214	14,336	13,061
1847	19,850	28,038	20,755	26,312
1848	14,868	21,885	15,918	12,631
1849	16,188	21,087	16,839	12,067
1850	14,569	22,622	15,560	7,536
1851	16,639	23,119	16,298	12,038
1852	19,934	24,075[a]	22,505	16,691
1853	16,608	24,751	19,602	18,494

[a] The figures for 1852-53 are corrected since it appeared that the original quantities—30,829 and 34,183—had been arrived at by adding bulk wheat twice for each year.
Sources: col. 1, same as Table 11; col. 2, Treasury Dept., *Statistics of Foreign and Domestic Commerce*, 179-180; col. 3, same as Table 4; col. 4, Evans, "Exports, Domestic and Foreign," Table 2, 20-23.

Buffalo and Oswego increased by 12.3 million bushels and total receipts at tidewater by the same amount from 1845 to 1847. Exports via the lakes from the Northwest displayed a similar gain. To complete the correlation, exports of wheat and flour from New York City increased by 11.2 million bushels from 1845 to 1847. The fact that the United States supplied only 39 per cent of England's grain requirements during a period when the latter's primary sources were unable to meet her needs is testimony to the fact that American productivity had been pushed to its full capacity in expanding to the extent that it did.

The data on Table 10 also point to the conclusion that the Northwest assumed a preponderant role in supplying the abnormally high quantities of produce transported to English ports. The Northwest sent 21 million bushels via the Great Lakes alone in 1847, of which Buffalo and Oswego received 20 million. Before reaching tidewater, this quantity had risen to 28 million bushels by the addition of some 8 million bushels of New York grain. Most of this reached New York, where 14 million bushels were exported.[12] If all the wheat shipped from upstate New York to New York City were exported, it would still have required some 6 million bushels of western grain to equal total exports, since New York receipts from other sources were negligible. During the same year, 1847, New Orleans exported 6 million bushels of wheat and flour, the bulk of which was of northwestern origin.[13] If New Orleans' exports are added to the exports of northwestern wheat from New York, at the least 6 million bushels, the northwestern states can be credited with supplying, at a minimum, some 12 million bushels, or 46 per cent of total exports.[14] This proportion would have required extraordinary effort from a region containing but 19.5 per cent of the nation's population in 1849 while harvesting in that year 37.4 per cent of the country's wheat.[15] Table 4 shows that Ohio and Michigan were largely responsible for the gains in production in the East North Central states at this time.

During the period 1840-53, the domestic trade developed much more rapidly than the foreign trade in grain. While the total volume of grain reaching tidewater over the Erie Canal increased

---

[12] *Hunt's*, XLIII (November, 1860), 613. Some of the grain was diverted to Boston via the Western Railroad. In 1846 Boston received 658,000 barrels of flour from New York City, Albany, New Orleans, and the Western Railroad. Total receipts in 1846 reached 846,000 barrels, of which Boston generally re-exported some 10 to 15 per cent. *Ibid.*, XXI (November, 1849), 539.

[13] *De Bow's Review*, VI (December, 1848), 437-438. Some 80 per cent of New Orleans, total exports went to destinations designated as foreign (not including Cuba).

[14] A certain quantity of northwestern grain reached eastern markets via north central routes such as Pennsylvania's line of canals or were carried via wagon to the western end of Baltimore's railroad. Pittsburgh, for instance, shipped 298,000 barrels of flour via canal in 1847, presumably to Philadelphia. *Lippincott's New and Complete Gazetteer of the United States* (Philadelphia, 1854), 930.

[15] *7 Census, 1850*, lxxxii-lxxxvii. Corn exports in 1847 reached 16 million bushels, or double the quantity exported from 1833 to 1846. Evans, "Exports, Domestic and Foreign," Table 2, 20-21. The Northwest, however, probably contributed less than 25 per cent of the total. See Table 11.

by approximately 100 per cent, and that originating in the Northwest, represented by receipts at Buffalo and Oswego, rose by 190 per cent, the foreign trade increased by 70 per cent. But in 1846 and 1847 the foreign demand was of enormous importance in raising the levels of production and the volume of traffic over the lakes (see Table 10).

From 1847 to 1850 there was a general decline in the lake trade from the levels reached in 1847. The foreign trade fell much more sharply than the total trade on the Great Lakes, confirming the importance of the domestic demand for grain. Then, in 1850, there occurred another rise in the foreign demand for American foodstuffs, to which the East North Central states responded by an increase in the volume of grain shipped. The increase in domestic production, as in 1847, was primarily due to advances in production in Ohio and, to a lesser extent, in Michigan. At this time wheat-growing areas in Illinois and Wisconsin were suffering from a succession of winter wheat failures, while other lands, soon to produce enormous quantities of grain, were just being settled and penetrated by railroads.[16]

After 1853 the statistics of canal traffic, particularly of grain received at tidewater via the Erie Canal, lose their utility as an index both of the volume of the lake trade and of the function served by eastern receiving terminals. Railroads took an increasing share of the former canal traffic in items such as flour and provisions. Receipts at Buffalo and Oswego mounted, but the quantity of grain reaching the Hudson by way of the Erie Canal declined from 1854 to 1859. Railroad competition along the main line of the canal to Buffalo, as well as its major feeder from Oswego, cut deeply into the grain traffic of the canal. The decline in flour shipments from Buffalo over the canal from 1851 to 1853 was a direct result of increased shipments via railroad. In 1852 the Buffalo and Rochester Railroad carried 75,000 barrels of flour from Buffalo, and by 1856, out of flour receipts at Buffalo totaling 1.2 million barrels, only 76,000 were shipped eastward over the Erie Canal. Most of the bulk wheat continued to use the water route, but the railroads achieved a virtual monopoly of the flour traffic. At Os-

---

[16] Aggregate wheat and flour exports from Cleveland and Toledo increased from 5.1 million bushels in 1850 to 10.9 million in 1853, while Sandusky's rose by 2 million bushels from 1850 to 1852. Exports from Chicago and Milwaukee had declined from 1850 to 1852.

wego, by 1854, over one-half of the flour was carried by rail.[17]

Although Buffalo dominated the grain trade at the eastern end of the lakes, at various times one or several of the other lake markets—Ogdensburg, Oswego, Montreal, Dunkirk, Suspension Bridge—had advantages which Buffalo lacked. In the 1830's some western wheat passed the Welland Canal for Rochester. This grain was manufactured into flour, some of which was re-exported to Montreal. There it was used to supply local food requirements, thus replacing Canadian flour, which could then be exported at lower duties than American for the British market.[18] At the same time, freight rates from western ports through the Welland Canal to Oswego and thence to the Erie Canal were cheaper than rates via Buffalo over the entire length of the Erie Canal. The canal commissioners were sensitive to this inequality and reduced through rates on the main line for flour from 55 cents per barrel in 1830-32 to 39 cents in 1833 and to 35 cents in 1834.[19]

The Welland Canal route never assumed the importance that its early proponents had anticipated. The credit resources available at Canadian ports could not begin to compete with those available at Buffalo. Moreover, until 1843 ships of 300 tons and upward were unable to pass through the canal.[20] Most of the grain that did pass was destined for Oswego, the second largest lake port. In 1840-41 a total of 380,000 barrels of flour and 2 million bushels of wheat were shipped through the Welland Canal, of which Oswego and Rochester received at least one-half. In 1845 and 1846 some 7.3 million bushels of wheat and flour passed through the Welland Canal. Five million bushels of this were re-

---

[17] *Hunt's,* XXVIII (March, 1853), 310-311, XXXVII (December, 1857), 698, XL (May, 1859), 547.

[18] R. Carlyle Buley, *The Old Northwest. Pioneer Period. 1815-1840* (2 vols., Indianapolis, 1950), I, 538, maintains that this trade reached considerable proportions, but the actual figures controvert this position. In 1831, which was the peak year in the wheat and flour trade during the 1830's, Canada received only 40,000 barrels of flour from all American sources and negligible quantities of bulk wheat. D. G. Creighton, *The Commercial Empire of the St. Lawrence, 1760-1850* (Toronto, 1937), 250-251.

[19] The average rate per barrel declined from 98 cents in 1830 to 34 cents in 1858. Most of this was due to a reduction in tolls, which declined by 58 per cent from 1830 to 1852, while freight charges were reduced from an average of 43 cents per barrel in 1830 to 30 cents in 1852, or a reduction of 30 per cent. *ARJ,* XXVI (April 16, 1853), 242; *Hunt's,* XLII (January, 1860), 118.

[20] Hugh G. J. Aitken, *The Welland Canal Company. A Study in Canadian Enterprise* (Cambridge, Mass., 1954), 66-67.

ceived at Oswego. During the same two years Rochester shipped 1.7 million barrels of flour on the Erie Canal. The wheat required for this was derived in part from Lake Ontario's shipping as well as from the canal, from railroads, and from teams.[21]

On Lake Erie, Dunkirk served as the western terminal of the New York and Erie Railroad and intercepted some of the grain before it reached Buffalo or the Welland Canal. This trade never rivaled that of Buffalo or Oswego but it did divert considerable quantities of flour from the more easterly lake markets. Moreover, during the early stages of the railroads' growth, the grain trade of Dunkirk furnished the Erie with a considerable share of its total eastbound freight, most of which was concentrated in the winter months, when navigation of the canal had ceased.[22] During the period 1856-58, Dunkirk received about 350,000 barrels of flour annually but never more than 180,000 bushels of wheat. Flour receipts rose to 432,000 in 1859, 534,000 the next year, and 736,000 in 1861. During this latter year, Buffalo received 2.1 million barrels of flour and 27 million bushels of wheat, and Oswego 235,000 barrels of flour and 11 million bushels of wheat.[23] Dunkirk, then, had become a considerable depot for flour and received virtually no bulk wheat, as railroads could not carry bulk grain as cheaply as

[21] *Patent Report, 1842*, 54, *1847*, 582; *ARJ*, XVI (July, 1843), 296, XX (September 18, 1847), 598, XXIV (January 25, 1851), 63. Some of the grain passing the Welland Canal was Canadian, as was some of the grain which Oswego received. A portion of the grain which did not go to an American port on Lake Ontario, or to an American port on the St. Lawrence, was received at Montreal. Before the 1840's the trade between the lake ports on the American side and Canada was small. In 1839, 1840, and 1841, the American-Canadian trade was quite active, due to an augmented English demand and the fact that American wheat manufactured into flour at a Canadian mill was subject to the same duties in British markets as was Canadian flour. After 1841 American exports to Canada fell off partly as a result of British and Canadian legislation which placed duties on American wheat and flour that entered Canada. The repeal of the Corn Laws in 1846 eliminated the advantages of shipping through Canada to reach the English market, and the trade with Canada fell to very low levels until the latter half of the 1850's. During the period 1856-62, Montreal's receipts of wheat and flour formed about 10 per cent of all the grain shipped on the Great Lakes, some of which was of Canadian origin. Treasury Dept., *Statistics of Foreign and Domestic Commerce*, 177-178.

[22] *Report of the Directors of the New York and Erie Railroad Company, 1853* (New York, 1853), 100. Flour formed over one-third of the total tonnage carried eastward in 1853, livestock formed about 15 per cent, and provisions about 30 per cent.

[23] *Hunt's*, XXXVIII (March, 1858), 356; Treasury Dept., *Statistics of Foreign and Domestic Commerce*, 177-178.

the canal, nor did they have the necessary facilities for handling vast quantities of it.[24]

Buffalo's other major competitors were all located on Lake Ontario, or, as in the case of Ogdensburg and Montreal, on the St. Lawrence River. A portion of the trade passing to Lake Ontario was received again by the Erie Canal at Rochester or over the Oswego feeder canal, but a considerable amount passed down to Ogdensburg, where, by 1851, railroad connections existed with nearly all of the interior roads of New England. Ogdensburg served the home consumption market of New England and her prosperity was based entirely on her position as a major railhead. From flour imports of 5,000 barrels in 1847, receipts at Ogdensburg rose to 158,600 in 1850 and 375,000 by 1851.[25] In that year a line of 12 propeller-driven vessels was opened by the Northern Railroad between Ogdensburg and Chicago.[26] Through the 1850's, Ogdensburg generally received and shipped slightly more flour and considerably more bulk wheat than Dunkirk. After 1855 Ogdensburg's grain trade remained fairly static until 1861-62, when the grain trade over the lakes experienced a marked growth as a result of British demands for American wheat. While Ogdensburg at no time attained the stature of Oswego as a grain market, the latter port handling three to four times more grain, the St. Lawrence port did enjoy important advantages. For one thing, she possessed fairly adequate storage facilities—estimated at 800,000 bushels; and for another, she served a market area, including northern New York and northern New England, which was not reached by the Erie Canal or other competing routes.

In December, 1828, Oswego was joined to the Erie Canal at Syracuse by a lateral canal of some 38 miles. Two years later the

---

[24] *ARJ*, XXVI (February 12, 1853), 99.

[25] *Hunt's*, XXVIII (May, 1853), 562. In 1853 Buffalo interests complained that Ogdensburg was receiving much Michigan flour because of low freight rates and because of the alleged preference in New England for Michigan's flour. *Ibid.*, XXX (March, 1854), 301. In 1851 Chicago shipped 21,000 bushels of wheat and flour and 26,000 bushels of corn to Ogdensburg. In 1858 Ogdensburg received 71,000 barrels of flour, 135,000 bushels of wheat, and 494,000 bushels of corn from Chicago. The flour and wheat formed some 25 per cent of total receipts at Ogdensburg, and Chicago corn about 70 per cent. *Ibid.*, XXVI (April, 1852), 428-430; *Seventh Annual Review of the Trade and Commerce . . . of Chicago, 1858* (Chicago, 1859), 9.

[26] *The American Annual Register*, II-IV (1827-29), 33; *NWR*, XXXIX (November 27, 1830), 218.

schooner *Winnebago*, out of Cleveland, passed the Welland Canal with a cargo of wheat destined for Oswego.[27] In 1834 Oswego received a total of 461,000 bushels of wheat via the lakes and a sufficient quantity from local sources to allow her to ship 112,000 barrels of flour via canal. The following year Oswego's wheat receipts totaled 625,000 bushels from lake sources, and flour exports reached 138,000 barrels.[28] Through the succeeding seven years, 1836-42, receipts at Oswego remained virtually unchanged.[29]

The Oswego River provided an excellent source of power to the town, and the manufacture of flour soon became the major industry. By 1840 Oswego had about one-half the milling capacity of Rochester.[30] Grain-laden vessels could run alongside the mills and unload wheat while canal boats received flour from the other side. Oswego was less fortunately situated with regard to a local supply of grain than Rochester and consequently depended upon lake receipts to a greater degree than the Genesee town. Most of Oswego's grain was derived from the East North Central states, which, for the two years 1850-51, supplied Oswego with larger quantities of bulk wheat than they sent to Buffalo.

Canada was of some importance to Oswego as a source of bulk wheat and also flour to be re-exported to domestic markets. In the 1830's and 1840's Oswego received about one-sixth of her bulk wheat from Canadian producers and normally about 60 per cent of flour receipts. Oswego's flour receipts declined after 1853 but Canada still supplied over 50 per cent of total imports. Bulk wheat receipts increased during the 1850's, but the proportion originating in Canada declined steadily, until in 1858 it was only 9 per cent of total receipts. About one-fourth of the Canadian grain came from Toronto.[31] In connection with this, it should be noted

---

[27] *ARJ*, V (February 13, 1836), 85-86, (April, 1837), 254-255.

[28] *Hunt's*, XXII (June, 1850), 624-625. In 1835 Oswego shipped 48.5 per cent of the total wheat and flour received at tidewater over the Erie Canal. In 1837 Oswego contributed 16.2 per cent of the total and only 10 per cent in 1842. Thus, in 1842 Buffalo was responsible for 90 per cent of the canal's grain traffic.

[29] Charles B. Kuhlman, *The Development of the Flour-Milling Industry in the United States with Special Reference to the Industry in Minneapolis* (Boston and New York, 1929), 62.

[30] *ARJ*, V (February 13, 1836), 85-86; *Patent Report, 1849*, 582.

[31] *ARJ*, XXV (January 31, 1852), 73; *Hunt's*, XXX (June, 1854), 747, XXXVII (July, 1857), 39, XXXVIII (March, 1858), 355, (April, 1858), 467, XL (May, 1859), 548.

that flour receipts were of less value and volume in relation to bulk wheat imports at Oswego than at Buffalo, which did not develop an extensive milling industry.

The economic growth of Oswego was derived from her milling industry and an out-bound commerce with a wider range of market outlets than Buffalo possessed. Grain from Oswego could take any one of several routes to various seaboard markets. Oswego forwarded flour across Lake Ontario to Cape Vincent, at the head of the St. Lawrence, where it was transferred to the Rome and Watertown Railroad and often carried back to the canal or to one of the railroads from the East. Greater quantities of flour continued down the St. Lawrence, where a portion was unloaded at Ogdensburg for shipment into New England, and the remainder went on down the river to Montreal and Quebec. But the major route followed was to the East, until the late 1840's by way of Oswego's branch canal and thence over the main line of the Erie. After this time flour began to travel the iron rails in increasing quantities. The Syracuse and Oswego line connected with the canal and also with the short lines which were eventually consolidated into the New York Central, thus giving Oswego access to both Boston's Western Railroad at Albany and connections with New York City.

Until 1854 the canal carried virtually all of Oswego's bulk wheat exports and about 80 per cent of flour shipments. Thereafter, while the Erie continued to transport most of the grain, including corn totaling 2 to 3 million bushels yearly after 1857, some 45 to 55 per cent of the flour was forwarded via rail. Five to 10 per cent went down the St. Lawrence and the remainder traveled the canal.[32]

The origins of Oswego's grain receipts had also undergone a change during the 1850's. During the early 1840's most of the grain and flour of American production came from Ohio and in the latter half of the decade from Ohio and Michigan. In 1850 Toledo exported five times as much wheat and flour to Oswego as did Chicago. In 1858, 76 per cent of the corn and 47 per cent of the wheat and flour came from Illinois.[33] A similar development had occurred at the Buffalo market during this period. Illinois furnished 60 per cent of Buffalo's wheat and flour receipts by 1857, in con-

---

[32] *Ibid.*, XXXVII (July, 1857), 43, XXXVIII (May, 1858), 608.

[33] *Patent Report, 1849,* 582; Chicago *Daily Tribune,* December 28, 1850; *Hunt's,* XL (May, 1859), 548. Indiana supplied 20 per cent of the corn and 15 per cent of the wheat and flour. Wisconsin provided 18 per cent of the latter and Ohio only 8 per cent.

trast to 6 per cent in 1851, while Wisconsin supplied over 10 per cent in 1857 and 18 per cent a year later.[34]

Oswego grew steadily as a grain market from 1845 to 1853, as Table 11 indicates, and after a temporary relapse in 1854 it con-

TABLE 11. Total Annual Receipts of Wheat, Flour, and Corn at Buffalo and Oswego, 1840-53 (in thousands)

Year	Buffalo			Oswego		
	Wheat (bu.)	Flour (bbl.)	Corn (bu.)	Wheat (bu.)	Flour (bbl.)	Corn (bu.)
1840	1,005	597	71	765	46	–
1841	1,635	730	217ª	–	35	–
1842	1,555	734	460	–	42	–
1843	1,827	918	225	–	62	–
1844	2,178	915	146	–	–	–
1845	1,771	747	77	120	379ᵇ	9
1846	4,744	1,375	1,455	2,567	80	354
1847	6,489	1,857	2,862	3,287	153	914
1848	4,520	1,249	2,298	3,643	90	373
1849	4,044	1,207	3,322	3,614	318	383
1850	3,681	1,103	2,593	8,847	303	426
1851	4,167	1,258	5,989	4,232	390	1,252
1852	5,550	1,300	5,137	6,525	272	–
1853	5,420	976	8,066	4,354	391	–

ª Buffalo 1841-45 figures include other grains.
ᵇ Oswego 1845 exports.
Sources: Treasury Dept., *Statistics of Foreign and Domestic Commerce*, 161, quoting from Buffalo Board of Trade, *Annual Report, 1862*; *Hunt's*, V (September, 1841), 287, XVI (February, 1847), 364; *ARJ*, XVI (July, 1843), 293; *Patent Report, 1847*, 582, *1849*, 548; Andrews, "Reports on Trade and Commerce," 77.

tinued its course of expansion to the Civil War. But it could never quite match Buffalo's performance either in the grain trade or in commerce in general. Occasionally handling more grain than Buffalo before 1840, Oswego never approached the volume of Buffalo's grain trade thereafter. Oswego, in 1852, received some 65 per cent of the quantity of wheat and flour received by Buffalo. After 1853 Buffalo's grain trade increased at a more rapid pace than Oswego's, until in 1860 Buffalo's receipts of wheat, flour, and corn were twice those of Oswego.

Buffalo at an early period engrossed a major share of the lake

[34] Andrews, "Reports on Trade and Commerce," 108, 111, 133; *Hunt's*, XL (May, 1859), 600-601.

grain trade. A village isolated from the main stream of commercial activity in 1816, Buffalo by the late 1820's maintained a growing fleet of lake vessels which carried increasing quantities of goods and people to and from her wharves. Each spring and fall scores of grain-laden vessels entered the harbor to unload and pick up a return cargo of merchandise and immigrants. In September, 1842, 100,000 bushels of wheat reached Buffalo in 40 boats in the space of 24 hours, and exactly a year later, a 48-hour period witnessed the arrival of over 70 vessels laden with over 230,000 bushels of wheat and flour and large amounts of provisions.[35]

In 1852 grain receipts at Buffalo were valued at $15.4 million.[36] A decade earlier, Ohio and Michigan shipped almost 70 per cent of the wheat and flour received at Buffalo, while Buffalo received 76 per cent of all the wheat and flour shipped by the Northwest over the Great Lakes. In 1853, 52 per cent of the wheat and flour and most of the corn still came to Buffalo.[37] The wonder-working ingredient in this spurt of activity was the Erie Canal. The town immediately became an entrepot for merchandise and immigrants moving to the West, and, to a less extent, for produce from the West moving eastward.

During the years prior to the completion of Ohio's river-to-lake network of canals, Buffalo's grain trade experienced a slow growth. Receipts from the West were estimated to be between 360,000 and 700,000 bushels of wheat and flour in 1830.[38] In either case, the amount was considerably less than that passing over the canal to Albany. In 1833-34 Buffalo's shipments of wheat and flour totaled 1 million bushels, while 13 million bushels passed Utica over the Erie Canal.[39] Not until about 1835 did the grain trade of Buffalo begin to develop significantly.

---

[35] *NWR*, LXV (September 30, 1843), 80; David Thomas, *Travels Through the Western Country in the Summer of 1816* (Auburn, N.Y., 1819), 17; Duke Karl-Bernhard, *Travels Through North America, During the Years 1825 and 1826* (2 vols. in 1, Philadelphia, 1828), 74.

[36] In 1846 the total value of all imports via the lakes was $18.4 million. Grain formed 82 per cent of the total value in that year compared to 32 per cent in 1851 and 34 per cent in 1852. *Patent Report, 1852*, 422-424; *Hunt's*, XVI (June, 1847), 599.

[37] See sources for Table 11.

[38] *American Annual Register*, V (1829-30), 536. John Storck and Walter D. Teague, *Flour for Man's Bread. A History of Milling* (Minneapolis, 1952), 180, use the lower figure, while Buley, *The Old Northwest*, I, 537, quoting from the Cleveland *Herald*, February 2, 1831, cites the higher figure.

[39] *Hunt's*, XXIV (April, 1851), 451; *ARJ*, IV (January 10, 1835), 2.

Buffalo's preeminence, based on its position as western terminal of the canal, was not due entirely to this geographical situation. The canal, after all, could only float the barges loaded and placed on its water by men, and the harbor could furnish shelter only to those craft entering its mouth. There had to be some compelling reason for grain producers and dealers in the West to seek out the canal as a route. Grain going overseas did not necessarily go by the Erie Canal; it could go to New Orleans. But the volume of overseas shipments was static. Meanwhile, a growing domestic market on the Atlantic coast could be reached most directly by the Erie or the Welland canals. For a number of reasons, the Erie gained ascendancy over the Welland in the rivalry for western produce.

One advantage which Buffalo possessed at an early date was its superior business connections with markets farther to the east, especially New York. In the early days of the grain trade, the practice developed of making money advances to western millers, merchants, and, to a lesser extent, producers themselves. Often a produce dealer at some point of consumption would make arrangements with a forwarding house at Buffalo for the purchase of grain. Then the forwarding house, either with its own resources or with the aid of the financial resources of the eastern purchaser, could extend an advance for the purchase of grain to a third agent at the point of production. This last agent could, in turn, offer a similar advance to the farmer, merchant, or miller on the spot. Often the merchant or miller was the last agent in the line.[40]

Commission houses at Buffalo acted not only as agents for dealers in the east or for millers at a flour-manufacturing center such as Rochester, but also purchased grain on their own account or received grain on consignment.[41] They, in turn, would forward the grain, if on consignment or purchased outright, and if the final purchaser was yet undesignated, to a commission house or appointed agent in the East for final sale. Often this procedure was carried a step further should the eastern dealer ship the produce on consignment to a commission house in Liverpool or Rio de Janeiro for sale on the foreign market. If at each step the grain remained consigned to the agent, the ownership remained with the

---

[40] *Hunt's,* XVI (March, 1847), 271; Thomas D. Odle, "The American Grain Trade of the Great Lakes, 1825-1873," *Inland Seas,* IX (Spring, 1953), 54-56.

[41] *NWR,* XLVIII (May 30, 1840), 208.

farmer, or, as was more likely, with the merchant or miller who originally purchased the crop. Each step required the payment of a commission or fee, so it was to the advantage of the western dealer or producer to make a final sale as early in the sequence as possible. This entire procedure was attended by considerable risk and speculation, which was assumed by both the consignee and consignor.

Through the 1840's, produce dealers at Buffalo, as well as at Oswego and other grain centers, made only small outright purchases of grain. The general practice was to handle grain on a consignment basis. This was due primarily to the relative slowness of communication and transportation. At Buffalo, during this period, most of the grain was purchased by local millers, who bought the grain at the point of production in Ohio and had it shipped to their mills.[42] For a dealer at Buffalo to transact a final sale at Buffalo or in the West was to assume a great financial risk in a period when price fluctuations were often rapid and news of a rise or fall in price was slow in arriving. When a dealer did make a final purchase, it was generally to engage in a speculation and was based on the belief and hope that the market was rising. A rapid fall in the market often forced dealers to the wall.[43]

Improvements in transportation and communications, particularly the railroads and telegraph, effected a remarkable change in the marketing of grain. The telegraph put western markets in close touch with price changes in eastern centers, and the railroads facilitated delivery so that a favorable price change could be exploited. As a result, larger purchases of grain were made in markets such as Chicago and Buffalo. With the aid of telegraphic communication, a dealer in New York could also purchase directly at the point of production. The degree of risk, though still large, was lessened, and the long line of individuals making advances to other individuals further along the line was reduced. More important, as the time required for a shipment of grain to arrive at its destination was reduced, so too was the time in which a purchaser was overextended by an advance.[44] These improvements became operative in a full sense only after the Civil War, and largely in

[42] Treasury Dept., *Statistics of Foreign and Domestic Commerce*, 161.
[43] *Hunt's*, XV (July, 1846), 88.
[44] *Ibid.*, XVI (March, 1847), 269-272; Odle, "Grain Trade of the Great Lakes," 108.

regard to the purchase of flour. Wheat still traveled the lake route to market. But in the middle 1850's it was still safer than it had been previously to purchase bulk wheat directly, because of the speed with which price information reached western dealers and because of the implementation in the West of advanced grading, handling, and storing techniques.

Buffalo's superior financial resources and connections with the Atlantic coast, as well as an earlier emergence as a grain center than Oswego, gave her decisive advantages over her Lake Ontario competitor. Buffalo's commercial men consolidated and formalized business arrangements with their western counterparts before Oswego was really launched in the grain trade. Although it was estimated to cost 25 cents more per barrel of flour from Chicago to Albany by way of Buffalo than by way of the Welland Canal and Oswego, Buffalo's other advantages apparently more than canceled the unfavorable freight differential.[45]

Before the Welland Canal was enlarged in 1843, the amount of shipping centered at Buffalo or regularly plying the lakes between Buffalo and a western port was much larger than at Oswego. The enlargement of the Welland Canal enabled Oswego to increase its shipping capacity, but not sufficiently to rival Buffalo. Buffalo not only registered some two and a half times the number of arrivals that Oswego did in 1852, but the total tonnage of arrivals was six times greater at Buffalo.[46] This superiority stemmed from the greater assurance vessels had of securing a return cargo at Buffalo, due to the large amounts of eastern goods shipped over the Erie Canal to the West. Buffalo was thus capable of supplying more shipping when needed to move the grain in the spring and fall and also vessels of greater capacity than Oswego.

---

[45] Hugh S. Tremenheere, *Notes on Public Subjects, Made During a Tour in the United States and in Canada* (London, 1852), Appendix B, 159-160; Buley, *The Old Northwest*, I, 538; Bessie L. Pierce, *A History of Chicago* (2 vols., New York, 1937-40), I, 89. Rates from Chicago to Buffalo were from 2 to 3 cents cheaper than to Oswego during the summer and from 5 to 8 cents cheaper during busy seasons because, as the discussion that follows points out, more shipping was available to Buffalo. From 1854 to 1858 rates declined markedly to Buffalo. In October and November, 1854, rates ranged from 9 to 20 cents per bushel of wheat. Charges dropped during the next three years and in 1858 were between 4 and 6 cents per bushel. Spring rates dropped similarly. 7 *AR, Commerce of Chicago, 1858*, 37.

[46] *Lippincott's Gazetteer*, 157, 871. The total tonnage of Oswego arrivals in 1835 was 153,000. By 1851 the Canadian arrivals alone were 667,000. *ARJ*, V (February 13, 1836), 86; Andrews, "Reports on Trade and Commerce," 265.

Before the mid-1840's, shippers at both Buffalo and Oswego incurred a heavy expense in having grain unloaded from lake vessels and then reloaded into canal boats manually. This often caused bottlenecks during the seasons of heavy receipts. The brig *Osceola* from Chicago with 1,600 bushels required seven days to transfer its grain to canal boats. Poor weather often shut down operations completely. The average unloading speed seems to have been from two to three days per 5,000 bushels. But in 1843 the construction of a grain elevator at Buffalo, equipped with a special elevator to unload grain from a ship, so expedited matters that about 1,000 bushels an hour could be transferred. By 1860 one such elevator could unload, weigh, and transfer to another vessel some 7,000 bushels per hour. In 1860 Buffalo had storage facilities for about 6 million bushels of grain.[47]

Buffalo's predominance in the lake trade, then, rested in part on her strategic location at the western end of the Erie Canal. This more or less fortuitous factor of geographical situation was also shared with Buffalo by Chicago and New Orleans. Both lake ports developed excellent financial and technical facilities, for handling grain and attracting the grain trade to them, while New Orleans did little to draw grain supplies from the Ohio valley. The lake ports thus enabled the area tributary to the lakes to ship and market grain advantageously. This encouraged the growth of the grain economy in the area naturally oriented to the lakes, and also led to the lake ports' tapping areas which were indeterminately oriented.

The traffic over the Ohio and Mississippi rivers had great functional vitality, tied in as it was with the cotton economy of the Southwest, and this trade continued. But more and more New Orleans lost its place as the main market center for the economy

---

[47] Walter Havighurst, *The Long Ships Passing. The Story of the Great Lakes* (New York, 1942), 81; Harlan Hatcher, *Lake Erie* (Indianapolis, 1945), 228-230; James Croil, *Steam Navigation and Its Relation to the Commerce of Canada and the United States* (Toronto, 1898), 254. Storck and Teague, *Flour for Man's Bread*, 155-160, 180, maintain that this innovation permitted a tremendous growth of the grain trade of the Great Lakes and that it immediately effected a reversal in the proportions of bulk wheat and flour arriving at Buffalo. However, the growth of the grain trade on the lakes increased at a rate which was independent of the application of such an improvement. It may have resulted in an increase of receipts at Buffalo, but even this cannot be documented with any authority. Moreover, flour receipts continued to exceed wheat until 1853.

of the East North Central states.[48] More and more the grain trade of the Northwest with the generalized southern market overshadowed that commerce between New Orleans and the Northwest. During the 1840's the grain trade at New Orleans underwent a growth similar to that of Buffalo, but at the same time the southern port experienced the first premonitions of lake and rail competition. These developments eventually transformed New Orleans into a regional market serving the plantation economy.

Along the lakes, in the meantime, the primary orientation for the major part of the domestic trade had been definitely fixed, at least for wheat products, on a series of routes that bound the East North Central states to the Atlantic seaboard.

---

[48] Provisions receipts at New Orleans greatly exceeded those at Buffalo, probably on the average of about two to one in total value in the mid-1850's. But this represented a substantial gain for Buffalo, while the value of pork and pork products receipts at New Orleans showed little increase after 1852. Switzler, "Report on Internal Commerce," 195-210, 216-217.

The River Complex:
The Foodstuffs Trade of the
Upper Ohio Valley, 1840-50

CHAPTER VI

DISTINCTIVE FEATURES OF THE RIVER TRADE

The rise of the lake trade ultimately developed certain areas that were dependent exclusively upon it, but, from an over-all viewpoint, it did not supersede the trade which moved along the Ohio and Mississippi rivers, either to New Orleans or to other southern outlets. For a time there were two major trade complexes —the lake complex and the river complex. Both continued to grow and both simultaneously played a major part in the grain economy of the East North Central states.

Both lake and river routes experienced an enormous upswing in traffic during the 1840's. The lake trade, worth about $4 million in 1835, reached over $39 million in 1840. By 1851 the value was considerably more than $300 million. The total value of commerce on the Ohio and Mississippi rivers rose from an estimated $120 million in 1840 to $200 million in 1844. In 1846 the figure had climbed to $296 million and just three years later to $381 million.[1] The New Orleans and the general southern demand for northwestern produce grew at an exceptional rate during the 1840's. The advance at New Orleans was stimulated, to a degree, by the same forces which caused an amplification of the grain traffic on the Great Lakes, particularly the foreign demand for grain in the late 1840's. But New Orleans also benefited from a further extension and augmentation of the southern market for grain and provisions during the 1840's and 1850's.[2] Though these two complexes of trade were comparable in their volume and importance, they were unlike one another in many of their essential features.

One feature, already discussed to some extent, is that the river system not only used the natural arteries of the Ohio and Mississippi to reach its distant markets, but it also used natural waterways to tap the production areas where grain was collected. Unlike the lake trade, that of the rivers was decades old by the 1840's. Its conduct was relatively free from the obstacles which had required surmounting before a lake trade of any proportions could develop. The major rivers flowed south. The large tributaries of Indiana, the Whitewater and Wabash, the latter serving Illinois also, and the large interior streams of Ohio, the Muskingum, Scioto, and Miami rivers, rose in the northern sections of each state, and traversed some two-thirds of the whole distance from the lakes to the Ohio River. The major tributaries, including the Illinois River, were in turn fed by smaller streams such as the Little Miami and

---

[1] "Report from the Topographical Bureau in Relation to the Commerce, Navigation, and Means of Defense of the Western Lakes and Rivers, 1847," *Senate Executive Documents*, 30 Cong., 1 Sess., No. 4 (1848), Serial 504, 42; Switzler, "Report on Internal Commerce," 204. These figures include trade both up- and downstream. In 1846 the value of exports originating in the Northwest and including Kentucky and Missouri was estimated at $190 million. James Hall, *The West: Its Commerce and Navigation* (Cincinnati, 1848), 194; St. Louis *Old School Democrat*, February 29, 1844; Andrews, "Reports on Trade and Commerce," 248.

[2] The grain and provisions trade composed but a part of New Orleans' commerce. During the 1840's the value of cotton, sugar, and tobacco receipts normally formed between 65 and 80 per cent of total receipts. In 1849, the peak year for grain and provisions receipts at New Orleans, provisions receipts were valued at $15.3 million and grain at $14.3 million. Together they made up 36 per cent of the total value of receipts. *Hunt's*, XXIII (December, 1850), 659; Andrews, "Reports on Trade and Commerce," 756-757; *Patent Report, 1852*, 425.

Little Wabash rivers, all of which were normally navigable, at least for flatboats, for eight to ten weeks yearly.

The lake traffic, on the other hand, used feeder canals which often made use of the water of the streams entering the Great Lakes. These streams were much shorter and less navigable than the south-flowing rivers. The feeder canals had a double effect: to open undeveloped areas and to shift to the lakes the orientation of areas which had previously traded with the South. This development was well under way in Ohio and Indiana during the 1840's through the agency of the Ohio and the Wabash and Erie canals, and had its beginnings in Illinois when the Illinois and Michigan Canal was completed in 1848.[3]

Another distinction between the two trade complexes concerns the greater concentration on the lakes both in shipping and receiving and in the watercourses used. The nature of the lake trade was such that it resulted in a more intense centralization of that trade at a few major commercial centers. Unlike the lake trade, certain of the tributary river systems of the Ohio functioned fairly independently of, or at least were not dominated by, a major market at their mouth. The producers of the Muskingum, Scioto, Hocking, Wabash, and Kaskaskia river valleys were not tributary to a single market to the extent that farmers situated along the Maumee, Sandusky, or Cuyahoga river valleys, or the upper sections of the Muskingum and Scioto, were to Toledo, Sandusky, and Cleveland. Each farmer producing for the southern market could personally transport and sell his own produce at New Orleans. But the farmer of Wayne or Stark counties, Ohio, could not flatboat to Buffalo, nor could he build a lake-going vessel to carry his cargo. He had

---

[3] A. L. Kohlmeier, *The Old Northwest as the Keystone of the Arch of the American Federal Union. A Study in Commerce and Politics* (Bloomington, Ind., 1938), 37-38, writes that the northern part of the Ohio valley and the region "immediately to the south of the Great Lakes" had shown the most rapid increase in population, production, and import and export. Thus "it is clear," he continues, "that the southern part of the Old Northwest was not advancing economically in proportion to its population as fast in this period [1835-39] as the northern part." The section in Chapter III dealing with the Western Reserve and Maumee valley sections of Ohio suggests that Kohlmeier's generalization is not quite accurate, at least in regard to the "region immediately to the south of the Great Lakes," for neither of the above areas exhibited the growth that sections to the south did. Moreover, it would have been rather unusual if the preliminary impact of a new development in transportation had not resulted in a larger percentage growth in an area which started from a low base compared to an area with a higher base and a more developed economy.

no choice but to deposit his crops at a central market and let some-one else handle the transportation and often the final sale.[4]

The grain trade on the rivers, more decentralized at the start than the lake trade, was even more diffused as to destination. Over 90 per cent of the grain entering the lake trade reached Buffalo or Oswego. Probably not over 50 per cent of the produce carried on the rivers reached New Orleans.

Cincinnati and St. Louis were the major produce markets along the rivers and both served a fairly extensive region. Cincinnati's original source area was extended first by the Miami and Erie Canal, completed to the junction with the Wabash and Erie Canal in 1845, which opened to it the surplus of the middle Miami River valley, then by the Whitewater Canal from southeastern Indiana, completed in 1845, and finally by the Little Miami Railroad, opened to Xenia, Ohio, in 1845, and lengthened in the years thereafter. But much of the trade originating from areas up-river from Cincinnati was conducted without reference to that port.[5] Between Wheeling and Cincinnati, the major river towns were all engaged in the ship-ment of produce.

St. Louis served a great expanse of territory both east and west of the Mississippi River. Through the 1840's the primary sources of supply were the upper Mississippi River and the lower and middle Illinois River valley, the latter being dominated by Chicago at its northern end and St. Louis at its southern end. St. Louis began losing much of its trade from the East in the late 1840's and 1850's. At first the Illinois and Michigan Canal diverted traffic in the Illi-nois valley from St. Louis to Chicago. Then the railroads reaching

---

[4] The diffusion of the southern produce trade is obscured because of data limitations on the one hand and, paradoxically, by an abundance of data on the other. Such ports as Cincinnati, St. Louis, and New Orleans compiled fairly accurate and complete commercial statistics during the 1840's and 1850's. But ports even as large as Louisville and Pittsburgh, Marietta, Steubenville, Madison, Jeffersonville, and a host of smaller ports, to say nothing of innumerable flatboat landings along the major and minor streams, left at best only occasional refer-ences to their commercial activities. This gap is generally covered over in the narrative by focusing attention on the markets for which information is most complete, thus the tendency to analyze the trade between the Northwest and the South in terms of receipts at New Orleans and shipments from Cincinnati and St. Louis.

[5] In 1847 Portsmouth and Harmar shipped some 201,000 barrels of flour while Cincinnati exported only 276,000—100,000 of which were received via the Miami Canal. *Patent Report, 1847*, 622-628; *Thirty-fourth Annual Report of the Cincinnati Chamber of Commerce and Merchants' Exchange . . . 1882* (Cincinnati, 1882), 155.

out from Racine, Chicago, and Milwaukee to the Mississippi River intercepted produce that normally went to St. Louis. In spite of this, the grain trade of the Missouri town underwent a great expansion beginning in the late 1840's, as grain-producing areas west of the Mississippi replaced those from the East in the St. Louis market. The advance at St. Louis was of such a scale that the grain receipts at New Orleans in the 1850's did not reflect the steady loss of Cincinnati supplies which occurred after 1855.

The two other major markets on the western rivers were Pittsburgh and Louisville. The latter market was served by its own interior as well as areas adjacent to the Kentucky River. Part of its supplies were obtained from southern Indiana, although it had to compete for this trade with the towns of New Albany and Jeffersonville. The most important export from Louisville was tobacco, but there was an exchange of produce and provisions of a limited scope.[6] The grain trade never developed into one of large proportions. In the 1850's it appears that between 150,000 and 250,000 barrels of flour were received annually along with from 200,000 to 300,000 bushels of wheat and about the same quantity of corn. In the 1850's there were five or six flour mills operating, and some quantities of grain and flour were being received and shipped by the Louisville and Nashville Railroad.[7] Louisville's role in the grain trade was considerably smaller than that of Cincinnati or St. Louis, but her trade did serve to swell that of the river.[8]

Pittsburgh's grain trade also served to enlarge the volume of river traffic, although the grain trade itself was completely overshadowed by the growth of the iron and coal industries and manufacturing in general. As a grain-exporting market, Pittsburgh faced

---

[6] R. B. Way, "The Commerce of the Lower Mississippi in the Period 1830-1860," MVHA *Proceedings* (1918-19), 58.

[7] Isaac Lippincott, *A History of Manufactures in the Ohio Valley to the Year 1860* (Chicago, 1914), 162; "Report of the Bureau of Topographical Engineers, 1855," *Senate Executive Documents*, 34 Cong., 1 Sess., No. 1 (1855), Serial 811, 360; *ibid.*, 1856, *House Executive Documents*, 35 Cong., 1 Sess., No. 2 (1856), Serial 943, 337; *Hunt's*, XXXIII (July, 1855), 128, XLIII (October, 1860), 500-501; Frank H. Dixon, *A Traffic History of the Mississippi River System* (Washington, D.C., 1909), 34.

[8] Paul B. Trescott, "The Louisville and Portland Canal Company, 1825-1874," *Mississippi Valley Historical Review*, XLIV (March, 1958), 694, concludes in regard to the canal that its economic impact was slight and that any economic savings achieved by avoiding transhipment were wiped out by high tolls. The canal was soon too small to handle the larger steamers so that it was necessary either to use smaller vessels or incur the added expense of transferring loads.

two directions when Pennsylvania's internal improvements system
was completed from the East to the Ohio River in 1833. Wheat
and flour continued to use the river to reach New Orleans and
eventually the East Coast.[9] Most of the flour exported went by way
of the Pennsylvania or Susquehanna canals to either Philadelphia
or Baltimore. From 1841 to 1852 some 100,000 to 200,000 barrels of
flour annually moved east by canal.[10] It is unlikely that much produce was freighted to New Orleans after the Pennsylvania Railroad reached Pittsburgh in 1852. Nor does it appear that the manufacture of flour received any notable impetus from the railroad,
since flour valued at $828,000 was manufactured in 1857 compared
with $845,000 in 1846.[11]

Another feature distinguishing the lake trade from that of the
river was the dissimilarity in the composition of the trades. The
lake system served primarily a wheat economy, while the river system served mainly a corn economy. One student estimates that over
95 per cent of bulk wheat exports traveled the lake route through
the 1840's, while over 95 per cent of the corn and its derivatives
passed down the rivers. Flour went in both directions in large
quantities, but by 1849 over one-half of it was shipped via the
northeastern route, while from 1844 to 1860 the South received
about 30 per cent.[12]

---

[9] As early as 1836 Pittsburgh's rolling mills manufactured over $4 million
worth of goods. In 1856, while flour worth $845,000 was manufactured at Pitts-
burgh, the lumber business was valued at $3.2 million, and coal exports were
estimated at $4.6 million. George H. Thurston, *Pittsburgh as It Is; or, Facts and
Figures, Exhibiting the Past and Present of Pittsburgh, Its Advantages, Resources, Manufactures, and Commerce* (Pittsburgh, 1857), 60-63, 87-96;
Hunt's, XXX (June, 1854), 689.

[10] *De Bow's Review,* I (January, 1846), 78, XVI (April, 1854), 414;
Lippincott's New and Complete Gazetteer of the United States (Philadelphia,
1854), 930. The year 1843 was reported to be the first in which Baltimore received western flour in any quantity via the Susquehanna and Tidewater Canal,
which connected with Pennsylvania's system at Columbia. St. Louis *Old School
Democrat,* September 4, 1843.

[11] Thurston, *Pittsburgh as It Is,* 159-160. In 1853-54 Philadelphia re-
ceived about 350,000 barrels of flour from Pittsburgh via the Pennsylvania road.
In both 1859 and 1860, 320,000 barrels were received from Pittsburgh, but
some of this was received at Pittsburgh from the surrounding countryside. *ARJ,*
XXVII (May 6, 1854), 278; *Hunt's,* XXXII (February, 1855), 243; Andrews,
"Reports on Trade and Commerce," 138-139.

[12] Kohlmeier, *Old Northwest as Keystone,* 33-34, 52-53, 82-83, 116-118,
146-151. The distinction made here is accurate in its general emphasis although
the percentage figures representing destination are probably high for bulk
wheat and possibly corn. New Orleans alone in 1845-46 and 1856-57 received
bulk wheat equal to between 15 and 20 per cent of total lake shipments, while

The river trade consisted largely of corn, pork, and whiskey —none of which the deep South or Southwest produced in sufficient quantities to satisfy home requirements. The South also failed to produce a sufficient amount of wheat, so flour imports were necessarily heavy.

In the South the per capita production of wheat declined from 3.75 bushels in 1839 to 3.06 in 1849, and then rose to 3.68 in 1859.[13] However, the increase in the last decade was largely a result of production gains made in Virginia and Maryland. Six of the remaining eight states produced under 2.5 bushels per capita in 1859, as they had in 1849 and 1839. Alabama, Mississippi, Louisiana, and Florida each produced less than 1.5 bushels per capita in 1860, while Georgia and Texas produced just under 2.5.

The South had a special need for corn and, though producing a considerable corn crop, did not increase its production sufficiently from 1839 to 1859 to attain self-sufficiency.[14] The plantations of the South, whether cotton or sugar, did not normally produce enough foodstuffs to feed its labor force, which subsisted largely on corn and pork. The extent of the deficiency in corn can be estimated if it is assumed that each individual and hog in the South consumed 13 bushels of corn annually.[15] This is a minimum

---

Chicago's corn receipts were considerably higher than those recorded at New Orleans. The utilization of percentage comparisons between the northern and southern trade is severely limited by the great, but unknown, quantities of produce that arrived at the South from obscure shipping points in the Northwest.

[13] 6 *Census, 1840*, 275-276; 7 *Census, 1850*, 863-864; 8 *Census, 1860, Agriculture*, 184-185.

[14] The corn crop for Virginia, Maryland, North and South Carolina, Georgia, Alabama, Mississippi, Florida, Louisiana, and Texas rose from 143 million bushels in 1839 to 226 million in 1859, while in the East North Central states production rose from 87 million bushels to 280 million. 6 *Census, 1840*, 358-359; 8 *Census, 1860, Agriculture*, 184-185.

[15] Lewis C. Gray, *History of Agriculture in the Southern United States to 1860* (2 vols., New York, 1941), I, 560; Ulrich B. Phillips, *American Negro Slavery. A Survey of the Supply, Employment and Control of Negro Labor as Determined by the Plantation Regime* (New York, 1929), 265-266, 279; and Kenneth M. Stampp, *The Peculiar Institution. Slavery in the Ante-Bellum South* (New York, 1956), 282, agree that the majority of slaves consumed from 12 to 15 bushels of corn and from 150 to 200 pounds of pork and bacon yearly. It is probable that whites consumed at least this much of both foods. In pork the lower figure would be about the equivalent of one dressed hog, weighing 200 pounds originally on the hoof. *De Bow's Review*, VI (August, 1848), 146, and *Patent Report, 1847*, 528-530, agree that a 200-pound hog dressed down to about 140 pounds of pork and bacon. Hog producers generally considered it necessary to feed between 15 and 26 bushels to each hog to prepare it for slaughter. Henry W. Ellsworth, *Valley of the Upper Wabash, Indiana, with Hints on Its Agricultural Advantages* . . . (New York, 1838), 39-40; Theodore L. Carlson,

requirement since individuals probably consumed more than this amount in the course of a year.

The South needed 195 million bushels of corn to feed 4.8 million people and 10.2 million swine in 1849. But the South produced only 144 million bushels, thus leaving a deficit of almost 50 million bushels of corn, or its equivalent in corn meal, provisions, and whiskey.[16] Imports from the East North Central states plus Kentucky and Tennessee largely made up this deficit.

Thus, while there was a relatively large southern demand for flour, there was a huge requirement for corn. The relative size of the market for each grain exerted a strong influence on the crops produced by farmers seeking a market in the South. An increasing specialization developed in the areas tributary to the lakes and to the rivers. The more southerly parts of the river valleys feeding the Ohio and Mississippi were far more likely to concentrate on corn than were the more northerly sections.

CORN OR WHEAT: THE ONSET OF SPECIALIZATION

It was never, of course, so clear-cut a question as corn or wheat. Virtually all sections of the Northwest produced at least some of both. But it was a question of the relative amounts of land and labor which would be invested in a particular crop. By the 1830's certain areas of Ohio were specializing in corn or the feeding of livestock while others gave particular attention to wheat.

In the Muskingum River valley, for instance, corn predominated in the south and south central areas and wheat in the central and northern counties. The wheat counties of the Muskingum, in addition to the three Ohio River counties of Columbiana, Jefferson, and Belmont, and Fairfield County in the Hocking River valley, produced over 50 per cent of Ohio's wheat crop in both 1839 and 1849. This was the wheat belt of Ohio through 1850.[17] This was also the region from which Cleveland obtained most of its wheat and flour.

The Illinois Military Tract. A Study of Land Occupation, Utilization and Tenure (Urbana, Ill., 1951), 123. But, of course, not all hogs were being primed simultaneously.

[16] This estimate does not include that part of the corn crop which was utilized in whiskey manufacture or in the feeding of livestock other than swine. The deficit for each state was: Georgia, 9.7 million bushels; North and South Carolina, 7.1; Louisiana and Florida, 5.6; Mississippi and Alabama, 13.1; and Texas, 5.7. *7 Census, 1850,* lxxxii-lxxxvii.

[17] *6 Census, 1840,* 275-276; *7 Census, 1850,* 863-864.

The corn and hog belt of Ohio extended from Fairfield and Licking counties in the east through the middle Scioto River valley to the counties of the south and south central Miami River valley. This 17-county area produced 51 per cent of the corn crop in 1839 and 44 per cent in 1849. Both river valleys were also engaged in extensive livestock raising: the Miami valley concentrated on hogs and the Scioto on cattle. Over 30 per cent of the hogs in Ohio were raised in the above 17-county area. In both valleys the basis of the livestock industry was the immense corn crop. Ohio produced 10.1 bushels of corn per head of livestock in 1839, 14.7 in 1849, and 17.6 in 1859, while the Scioto valley's corn-livestock ratios for the same three years were 15.1, 27.0, and 25.0.[18]

Most of the wheat in the Scioto and Miami valleys was produced in the large corn-raising counties, and the proportion of wheat to corn diminished in each valley from south to north in 1839. This reflects the less settled conditions of the upper counties at this time. The wheat grown in the southern portions of the Miami and Scioto valleys utilized the river route to the South. Between 1839 and 1849 the wheat crop in Ohio declined from 16.5 million bushels to 14.4 million bushels. The greatest falling off was traced to the southern part. In 1849 the Scioto valley produced only 6.7 per cent of the state's crop compared to 12.2 in 1839. Only Adams, Highland, Pickaway, Morrow, and Hardin counties produced over four bushels per capita, while seven counties produced less than three.[19]

The meaning of this decline was subject to some dispute among contemporaries. Certain observers attributed the drop in wheat production at least in part to the numerous crop failures of the 1840's caused by attacks by the Hessian fly and wheat rust, as well as the "natural deterioration of the soil." These factors were said to have caused yields of wheat to decline even though the

---

[18] As a contrast, the Western Reserve raised more cattle, particularly dairy cattle, than the Scioto valley, yet had a corn-livestock ratio from one-third to one-half that of the Scioto valley. *6 Census, 1840,* 275-276; *7 Census, 1850,* 863-864; *8 Census, 1860, Agriculture,* 113-117. The cattle-feeding business of the Scioto valley reached its peak between 1840 and 1850. In the following decade hog raising predominated. *Ibid.*; William Renick, *Memoirs, Correspondence and Reminiscences* (Circleville, Ohio, 1880), 115.

[19] *The Ohio Cultivator,* I (January 1, 1845), 6; *The Cultivator,* III, Series 2 (January, 1846), 21. The seven counties were Scioto, Pike, Madison, Franklin, Delaware, Union, and Marion. This probably required them to import wheat for home consumption.

number of acres sown to wheat increased.[20] Others pointed to a greater concentration on hogs and corn. During this period corn production in the Scioto valley doubled, so that it is highly probable that the short wheat crop of 1849 is partially explained by a decrease in wheat acreage and a corresponding increase in corn acreage and production.[21]

The Miami valley share of Ohio's wheat crop increased from 1839 to 1849 while production remained stable. Within the valley there was a slight movement northward of the center of wheat production during the ten years. The proportion of the valley's wheat crop produced in the six northern counties increased from 17 to 35 per cent. The completion of a canal from the junction of the Miami and Erie and Wabash and Erie canals to Toledo in 1842 supplies part of the explanation for the crop shift.[22] These counties previously had access only to Cincinnati. The northward extension of the Miami Canal opened up the large wheat market at Toledo to the middle Miami valley. Toledo also was the major corn entrepot on Lake Erie. However, Cincinnati was the dominant market of the Miami valley, and the centrality of corn and hogs in this area was reflected in the composition of Cincinnati's foodstuffs traffic.

CINCINNATI AS A FOCUS OF THE RIVER TRADE

In 1847 a Cincinnati newspaper claimed that there was dependent upon the town "a circuit of country including in . . . Ohio,

---

[20] *The Ohio Cultivator*, I (January 1, 1845), 5, estimated that 2 million acres were sown to wheat in 1845. *Ibid.* (May 15, 1845), 75, traced wheat failures in 1843-44 to the Hessian fly and rust. The poor crop of 1847 was similarly explained. *Ibid.*, IV (March 15, 1848), 42.

[21] Table 5 indicates that Cleveland normally received above 85 per cent of total wheat and flour shipments on the Ohio Canal. Some of this grain came from as far south as Chillicothe and McConnelsville. Only in the years 1841-42 did Portsmouth, the southern terminal of the Ohio Canal, receive as much as 10 per cent of the total canal shipments. In 1846 Portsmouth received 38,700 barrels of flour while Chillicothe, Circleville, Columbus, and Carroll shipped 54,000. In 1847 the above four towns shipped 115,000 barrels via canal while the terminal port received only 71,000. At least a portion of the difference between shipments and receipts went to the north and probably to Cleveland. Cleveland *Plain Dealer*, January 15, 1845; *Hunt's*, XII (May, 1845), 454; *Patent Report, 1847*, 622-627.

[22] These counties included Darke, Miami, Clarke, Shelby, Logan, and Champaign. In 1846-47, 2.4 million bushels of wheat and flour passed the junction of the Miami and Wabash canals, along with 2.1 million bushels of corn. Of this, at least 20 per cent of the wheat and flour and 10 per cent of the corn was cleared from Dayton and Piqua. *Patent Report, 1847*, 624-628.

twenty-nine counties—running north to Shelby; twenty-one counties of Indiana, on the eastern side; twenty-six counties of northeastern Kentucky, and eleven counties of western Virginia." [23] That this immense area was tributary to Cincinnati in the sense that Cincinnati's publicists interpreted the term is incorrect. Parts of the areas mentioned had commercial dealings with Cincinnati at one time or another, some more than others, and not all simultaneously.

Cincinnati was primarily dependent upon the Miami River system for her supplies, which reached her via the Miami Canal. But here her domain suffered encroachment during the mid-1840's by Toledo, the northern terminal of the canal.

Cincinnati reached out toward eastern Indiana with the Whitewater Canal, which was completed through Wayne County, Indiana, to the National Road in 1845, though Cincinnati received her first goods over it two years earlier. This canal served to direct much of eastern Indiana's surplus to Cincinnati for a few years. But by 1850 a railroad from Indianapolis to Madison on the Ohio River was competing with the waterway, as Madison was competing with Cincinnati, and a few years later the Indianapolis and Cincinnati Railroad was diverting freight from the canal. The Whitewater Canal served Cincinnati during the 1850's, and as late as 1856 reports indicated that there was a ready market for grain at the mills located along its route.[24]

Numerous plank roads connected Cincinnati with the interior of Ohio. These turnpikes generally served as feeder routes for the Miami and Whitewater canals and later for the railroads. Considerable quantities of provisions reached Cincinnati by wagon over these plank roads, as the canals were generally iced in during the packing season. It was not uncommon for over 200 wagons to pass through Hamilton, Ohio, daily during the winter months on their way to Cincinnati.[25]

The most ambitious project undertaken by Cincinnati to expand her source and market area was the Little Miami Railroad. Construction of a line to connect at Springfield with the Mad River

[23] Cincinnati *Chronicle*, 1847, quoted in *De Bow's Review*, III (June, 1847), 583.

[24] *Hunt's*, XXX (February, 1854), 257-258; Indiana State Board of Agriculture, *Fifth Annual Report, 1856* (Indianapolis, 1856), 204. The canal was abandoned in the 1860's.

[25] Charles Cist, *Cincinnati in 1841: Its Early Annals and Future Prospects* (Cincinnati, 1841), 81-83.

and Lake Erie road from Sandusky was begun in 1837. The business recession of the late 1830's and early 1840's prevented rapid progress. In 1841 only 35 miles had been graded. But by 1845 the road was open to Xenia and the connection with the Mad River line was made the next year.[26] The route provided Cincinnati with most of the agricultural supplies upon which the grain trade was based. In the decade of the 1850's the superiority of the railroad was to work a profound alteration in both the volume of exports of grain and provisions and the direction which such shipments took to market.

TABLE 12. ANNUAL RECEIPTS OF FLOUR, WHEAT, AND OTHER GRAIN; ANNUAL RECEIPTS OF FLOUR VIA THE MIAMI CANAL; AND ANNUAL FLOUR EXPORTS AT CINCINNATI, 1845-59 (IN THOUSANDS)

Year	Flour Receipts (bbl.)	Canal Flour Receipts (bbl.)	Wheat Receipts (bu.)	Other Grain Receipts (bu.)	Flour Exports (bbl.)
1845	202	122	487	46 [a]	151
1846	–	118	434	340	195
1847	548	209	591	1,445	582
1848	152	92	571	746	201
1849	448	105	385	640	267
1850	232	111	323	1,002	299
1851	482	317	389	809	391
1852	511	185	377	952	408
1853	447	146	344	1,268	313
1854	429	85	408	1,490	333
1855	342	61	437	1,583	199
1856	547	77	1,069	1,785	509
1857	485	82	738	2,703	417
1858	633	110	1,212	2,154	609
1859	588	73	1,274	2,236	562

[a] Corn only.
Source: Cincinnati Chamber of Commerce, *34 AR, 1882*, 162-171.

The grain trade of Cincinnati did not display marked activity during the 1830's and there was no perceptible upturn at the start of the new decade. In March, 1840, flour was at $3.00 a barrel, which prompted speculators to buy freely in anticipation of a rise in price. In April flour dropped to $2.90, wheat was at 60 cents, and corn could find no buyers at 20 cents. Flour receipts averaged

[26] *Ibid.*, 79-80; Hall, *The West*, 297.

124,000 barrels a year for the five years 1840-44. Wheat remained at about 60 cents and corn between 20 and 30 cents a bushel.[27] Thereafter, as Table 12 shows, Cincinnati's grain receipts increased, although with considerable fluctuation through the late 1850's. The initial rise in 1845 and 1847 was a direct result of an increased foreign demand, which caused a similar upswing in all American grain markets.

While Cincinnati's flour receipts rose during the 15 years 1845-59, the proportion carried on the canal diminished from some 40 to 60 per cent of total receipts between 1845 and 1851 to 15 per cent in 1857-60. From 1840 to 1844 Dayton alone supplied 55 per cent of Cincinnati's total flour reecipts. But during the remaining years of the decade, Dayton's total contribution fell to 25 per cent. In addition to Dayton, Middletown and Hamilton were receiving centers which fed Cincinnati. The aggregate flour shipments of the three towns account for all of Cincinnati's receipts via canal in 1846-47.[28]

The remainder of Cincinnati's flour receipts arrived via wagon from mills in the vicinity, from the Whitewater Canal, from the upper Ohio River, and beginning in 1845 from the Little Miami Railroad. In 1845-46 the railroad reported that more freight was available than it could handle. In November, 1846, 50,000 bushels of grain and flour were stored at Springfield and Xenia waiting for transportation to Cincinnati. In 1845, its first year of operation, the road carried 25,000 barrels of flour, 300 tons of pork and bulk meat, 100,000 bushels of grain, and 20,000 barrels of whiskey to Cincinnati. The following year the road carried 81,000 barrels of flour, 33,000 barrels of whiskey, and 12,000 barrels of beef, pork, and lard, in addition to live hogs and grain.[29] During the following four years, 1847-50, Cincinnati received 23 per cent of its total flour receipts and 15 per cent of its grain from the Little Miami road. The canal and railroad together supplied 60 per cent of Cincinnati's flour during the above four years.[30]

---

[27] Cincinnati *Advertiser and Journal,* March 24, April 23, 1840; Ohio Commissioner of Statistics, *Seventh Annual Report to the Governor, 1863* (Columbus, 1863), 25; *Hunt's,* XII (May, 1845), 456.

[28] *Hunt's,* XII (May, 1845), 456; *Patent Report, 1847,* 624-628; *Hunt's,* XXVI (May, 1852), 575.

[29] *ARJ,* XIX (November 28, 1846), 776, XX (January 9, 1847), 28.

[30] *Hunt's,* XXIV (March, 1851), 383. The quantities of produce arriving over the Whitewater Canal are not known. Wayne County, through which the

Rising prices, receipts, and shipments typified the last years of the 1840's in the Cincinnati market, as elsewhere.[31] From 60 cents a bushel in the early 1840's, the price of wheat rose to 90 cents and $1.00 in 1845 and 1847, while corn rose from 20 cents to 33 and 37 cents in 1850. Flour, $3.00 a barrel in 1840, was up to $4.12 in September, 1847, and $5.08 three months later. This was the most prosperous year of the decade for Cincinnati's grain trade. Grain exports in that year were valued at $3.2 million and were not exceeded in value again until 1856. But the grain trade formed only 6 per cent of the value of Cincinnati's total exports, which reached an estimated $55.7 million in that year.[32] A considerable share of total exports, however, represented goods which arrived at Cincinnati for re-export and distribution to interior markets both north and south. These goods were, in the main, of eastern manufacture. If only domestic exports are considered, that is, those goods manufactured at or undergoing some transformation at Cincinnati prior to export, then the significance of the grain trade becomes more manifest. In 1847 the share of the grain trade in the purely domestic exports of Cincinnati was approximately 30 per cent.[33] Even at this, the major domestic industry was not the trade in grain but that in provisions. It was from this commerce that Cincinnati earned the sobriquet "Porkopolis" of the West.

In 1861 it was estimated that 323 million pounds of pork entered into the commerce of the United States, of which 50 per cent

---

canal passed, was reported shipping some $400,000 worth of flour, pork, and beef to Cincinnati in the late 1840's. Nearby Henry County was also heavily engaged in the provisions trade, preparing some 32,000 head of livestock for market in 1848. [E. Chamberlain], *The Indiana Gazetteer or Topographical Dictionary of the State of Indiana* (Indianapolis, 1849), 249, 429.

[31] The correspondence in the movement of flour receipts at Cincinnati and New Orleans is almost absolute. From 1845 to 1860 annual flour receipts rose and fell together in 12 of the 16 years. In 1851 and 1854 the deviation was slight. In 1846 receipts rose sharply at New Orleans while remaining stable at Cincinnati and in 1857 receipts dropped at Cincinnati while rising at New Orleans.

[32] Ohio Commissioner of Statistics, *7 AR, 1863*, 25; *Hunt's*, XXIII (October, 1850), 343; Hall, *The West*, 326-328.

[33] In 1847 some $44 million of Cincinnati's total exports were designated as sundry merchandise and manufactures while receipts in this obscure category were valued at $49 million. It is assumed that the difference between receipts and exports formed a part of Cincinnati's local retail and wholesale commerce. The difference between the total value of exports and exports in the above category, some $12 million, is further assumed to be of local origin and manufacture.

was consumed in the East or exported.[34] The hub of this vast trade was located in the Ohio valley, with Cincinnati as the dominant packing city in the United States. In the late 1830's and early 1840's, Cincinnati's annual pack formed some 30 per cent of the total packed in the West. This proportion declined in the late 1840's and during the 1850's as packing in Indiana and Illinois increased. But even as late as 1860, Cincinnati packed about 18.5 per cent of the total.[35]

Cincinnati's packing industry was well established by 1830. During the packing season of 1826-27, 40,000 hogs were packed, of which 30,000 were slaughtered in the town and the remainder brought in dressed via wagons. In 1840 packing was Cincinnati's major industry. An estimated 48 packers produced some $3 million worth of provisions. In 1850 manufactures of provisions reached a value assessed at $5.9 million. This had increased to $10.2 million by 1860.[36]

Corn was the raw material which sustained this industry. Cincinnati's commerce throughout this period, as well as the general prosperity of the West, was contingent to a high degree upon the success of the corn crop. It is probable that about one-half of a

[34] *Patent Report, 1861,* 264. At a minimum this would require the slaughter of 1.6 million hogs. This estimate does not include the pork and bacon consumed at the place of slaughter; through the 1860's farmers continued to slaughter their own hogs, retaining what was required for home consumption and shipping the rest to market for packing. Neither does it include swine driven to distant points of consumption for slaughter and packing. As early as 1810 some 40,000 head of swine were driven from Ohio to the East. Jedidiah Morse, *The American Universal Geography; or A View of the Present State of all the Kingdoms, States, and Colonies in the Known World* (2 vols., 7th ed., Charleston, S.C., 1819), I, 623. In 1835-36 some 128,000 hogs were reported passing over the Cumberland Road, some from Ohio and Indiana. *NWR,* LI (January 3, 1837), 304. Charles T. Leavitt, "Transportation and the Livestock Industry of the Middle West to 1860," *Agricultural History,* VIII (January, 1934), 29, estimates that 220,000 live hogs moved east and south in 1842 and 350,000 in 1850. With the coming of extensive railroad facilities this figure increased to 740,000 by 1860. The live-hog trade was more important with the East than the South. As noted in Chapter III, Sandusky received 105,000 swine in 1851. In the same year Cleveland exported 80,000 live hogs. Andrews, "Reports on Trade and Commerce," 168.

[35] In addition to the states listed in Table 13, the West includes Tennessee, Kentucky, Iowa, and Missouri. Tennessee and Kentucky, from 1852 to 1858, packed an average of 368,000 hogs annually. Iowa and Missouri packed about 250,000 yearly from 1854 to 1859.

[36] Benjamin Drake and E. D. Mansfield, *Cincinnati in 1826* (Cincinnati, 1827), 78. The industry concentrated on a small stream called Deer Creek, subsequently nicknamed "Bloody Run." *ARJ,* V (January 21, 1837), 45; Cist, *Cincinnati in 1841,* 56; Andrews, "Reports on Internal Commerce," 710-711; *De Bow's Review,* XXIX (December, 1860), 782.

corn crop went to fatten hogs and cattle or into the manufacture of whiskey, with the remainder consumed locally or exported.[37] A scarcity of fodder during the winter of 1842-43 in the Scioto valley, caused by a short corn crop the previous fall, resulted in large hog losses from starvation. A scarcity of corn or high corn prices in the region surrounding Cincinnati generally resulted in a short pack.[38]

TABLE 13. ESTIMATED ANNUAL AVERAGE HOG PACK FOR FIVE-YEAR PERIODS, 1845-59, IN THE WEST, OHIO, CINCINNATI, INDIANA, ILLINOIS, AND CHICAGO (IN THOUSANDS OF HOGS)

Five-Year Period	West	Ohio	Cincinnati	Indiana	Illinois	Chicago
1845–49	1,048 [a]	508	332	224 [a]	150 [a]	–
1850–54	1,675	575	377	487	290	–
1855–59	2,178	584	406	428	461	76

[a] Average of 1845-46, 1848-49.

Sources: *Patent Report, 1848*, 638-639, *1849*, 459, *1851*, 566-568; *Hunt's*, XXXVI (June, 1857), 730, XXXVIII (May, 1858), 640; *De Bow's Review*, VI (August, 1848), 145, XII (January, 1852), 67-68, XV (August, 1853), 194, XVI (May, 1854), 539, XX (April, 1856), 517, XXIII (November, 1857), 489; *ARJ*, XXXII (February 12, 1859), 98; Cincinnati *Enquirer*, February 1, 1853; Cist, *Cincinnati Miscellany*, II, 331; Chauncey M. Depew, ed., *One Hundred Years of American Commerce, 1795-1895* (2 vols., New York, 1895), II, 384; *Seventh Annual Review of the Trade and Commerce . . . of Chicago, 1858* (Chicago, 1859), 22.

One student of the corn-hog cycle concludes that there was a fairly consistent relationship between a rise or fall of the "corn-hog ratio," calculated by dividing the average monthly hog price during the winter by the average monthly corn price in the fall, and an increase or decline in the pack two years later. Hog prices were found to be more important in determining production than corn prices. A rise or fall in the price of whiskey was also a determinant in a farmer's decision to alter his hog production.[39]

---

[37] Cincinnati *Gazette*, 1859, quoted in *De Bow's Review*, XXVIII (January, 1860), 118.

[38] St. Louis *Old School Democrat*, April 19, 1843. The reported hog pack in Ohio declined in 1844-45 by an estimated 110,000 head or 20 per cent. At Cincinnati the pack dropped by 18 per cent. *De Bow's Review*, XII (January, 1852), 67-68.

[39] Thomas S. Berry, *Western Prices Before 1861. A Study of the Cincinnati Market* (Cambridge, Mass., 1943), 244-266, observed that high corn prices caused hog producers to shorten the feeding period and sell earlier than usual. This affected the gross weight of the marketed hogs as well as the quality of the pork. Low pork prices caused a similar reaction. Charles Cist, *The Cincinnati Miscellany, or Antiquities of the West . . .* (2 vols., Cincinnati, 1845-46), II, 331.

The great bulk of pork products that entered into internal commerce took the river route to the South, which was the largest domestic market for the Northwest. The Erie Canal was only of minor value as an outlet for provisions.[40] Cincinnati's barreled pork exports in 1850 alone were four times greater than Buffalo's receipts. Pork destined for the East was generally shipped to New Orleans and then re-exported. Most of the provisions from the Northwest, particularly pork and lard, which were destined for overseas markets traveled the same route. Until the railroads of the northwestern states achieved connections with railroads from the East, Cincinnati and the pork centers in the Ohio valley were dependent upon the river for access to markets. This was the most direct route to the southern market above New Orleans and the cheapest way of reaching the Atlantic coast.

The foreign market for American provisions was not very large until the late 1850's. Even then, the $13 million worth of pork and beef products exported in 1860 was only $3 million more than Cincinnati's exports. In the period 1840-45, as in 1803-05, provisions exports ranged between $2 million and $4 million, with an increase to $9 million occurring in 1846 and slowly rising shipments continuing thereafter.[41] New Orleans was of some importance in the overseas trade in barreled pork, but this was a small factor in the New Orleans provisions trade. In 1846 the United States exported 190,000 barrels of pork and 19,000 tons of lard. New Orleans received 302,000 barrels, 190,000 being shipped by sea to domestic markets and 41,000 exported directly to overseas markets. The domestic market was much the larger. Receipts of lard at New Orleans totaled 150,000 tons, almost eight times greater than total foreign exports of the product.[42]

Cincinnati's pork products found various markets, although it is not possible to determine the proportionate value of each market. The North American coast and the South were dependent upon

---

[40] From 1849 to 1852 Buffalo's receipts of barreled pork averaged under 50,000 barrels annually. The receipts rose from 1853 to 1855, averaging 118,000 barrels, and then dropped to between 60,000 and 70,000 barrels yearly from 1856 to 1860. United States Treasury Department, *Statistics of the Foreign and Domestic Commerce of the United States* (Washington, D.C., 1864), 162.

[41] United States Treasury Department, *Commerce and Navigation. Annual Reports, 1840-60* (Washington, D.C., 1840-60).

[42] Ohio alone exported 330,000 barrels of pork and 15,000 tons of lard in 1846, 50 per cent of it from Cincinnati. *The Ohio Cultivator*, III (April 15, 1847), 58; Treasury Dept., *Commerce and Navigation, AR, 1846*, 10-13; *De Bow's Review*, VI (December, 1848), 437-438.

Northwestern provisions for home consumption. Large orders for lard were received from Mexico. In 1843 the *Niles Weekly Register*, quoting a Cincinnati correspondent, reported that of the 250,000 hogs packed in 1842-43, some 70,000 were used for lard, chiefly for shipment to Marseilles, which received an estimated 3,200 tons. Lard was also packaged for export to the Havana market.[43]

The pork trade at Cincinnati seems to have expanded rapidly in the period 1854-60, after having experienced a rather prolonged downturn in the early 1850's. In 1854 the value of pork exports was recorded at $6.8 million and in both 1857 and 1858 at $9.5 million. In the following two years exports exceeded $10 million.[44]

The industry was also undergoing a major transformation while appearing on the whole to grow. Exports of pork in certain forms, like barreled pork, bulk pork, and barreled lard, declined during the 1850's, while a portion of this drop was compensated for by increasing shipments of pork in other forms. Candles, soaps, and lard oil were shipped in increasing quantities. Pork, bacon, and hams were forwarded in smaller, less bulky packages, and the first live hogs were exported in 1858. It is doubtful if the aggregate increases in these items alone could have resulted in a rising dollar volume of exports, but in conjunction with climbing prices for hogs and pork products an appearance of growth in the packing industry was generated.[45]

However, in the 1850's Cincinnati was in the process of losing its preponderant position in the packing industry. After the mid-1850's there was little real growth in the trade as Cincinnati absorbed a double blow. Her position as a packing center was undercut by the intrusion of east-west railway lines through the center

[43] *NWR*, LXIII (October 1, 1842), 80, LXV (November 25, 1843), 208; *De Bow's Review*, XII (January, 1852), 71.

[44] The hog pack at Cincinnati declined from 498,000 in 1848 to 334,000 in 1851. For the next two years it averaged 343,000. From 1855 to 1859 the average annual pack was 407,000. See sources for Table 12. *Hunt's*, XXXIII (December, 1855), 742, XXXVII (December, 1857), 738-739, XXXIX (November, 1858), 605-608; *De Bow's Review*, XXIX (December, 1860), 782.

[45] *Hunt's*, XXXVIII (January, 1858), 93; Cincinnati Chamber of Commerce, *34 AR, 1882*, 222-224. December prices for hogs rose from $3 to $4 per 100 pounds in 1847-50 to between $5 and $6 in 1858-60. Ohio Commissioner of Statistics, *7 AR, 1863*, 25. Barreled pork was above $16 a barrel from 1856 to 1861. Cincinnati Chamber of Commerce, *34 AR, 1882*, 218. The fall in pork and bacon exports was temporary. After 1868 shipments increased. Boxes of candles and soap rose from 6,400 in 1846 to 85,000 in 1850 and 241,000 in 1860. By that year the soap and candle industry was one of the largest in Cincinnati. *Ibid.*, 128.

of her source of supply. Simultaneously, the production area which served the Queen City felt the competition of areas to the west in the raising of swine. Here too, the role of the railroad was sharply defined.

Cincinnati felt the repercussions of through rail nets more acutely than the state as a whole or even the Miami valley.[46] The railroads made possible the transporting of live hogs and cattle directly to the East.[47] Even in 1854 it was noted that large amounts of hog products were being forwarded directly to Pittsburgh and Wheeling for shipment to the seaboard. It was both cheaper and more convenient for farmers to ship live hogs by rail than to drive them to market or slaughter them at home and then send the dressed hog to a packer. By 1858 railroads had monopolized the transportation of animals and animal products. Ohio's railroads alone carried 1.2 million hogs and 299,000 cattle in that year. The Cleveland, Painesville, and Ashtabula road connecting with lines to New York City carried 403,000 hogs and 116,000 cattle. The Ohio Central carried some 100,000 hogs to Wheeling and a connection with the Baltimore and Ohio Railroad.[48] The livestock and provisions tonnage carried by the B & O from its western terminus rose from 18,000 tons in 1853 to 50,400 in 1854 and 61,500 in 1860.[49]

---

[46] While the hog pack at Cincinnati during the late 1850's was often less than that of the late 1840's, hog production increased in the Miami valley. The 17 major corn counties produced 34 per cent of the state's hog crop in both 1849 and 1859. 7 *Census, 1850,* 863-864; 8 *Census, 1860, Agriculture,* 113-117.

[47] Beef cattle in the Scioto valley, which had formed 16.3 per cent of total beeves in Ohio in 1849, formed 14 per cent in 1859, while the proportion of dairy cows increased. An even more prominent growth in dairying was occurring in the Western Reserve at this time. *Ibid.,* 1850 and 1860; Renick, *Memoirs,* 13-14.

[48] *Cincinnati Price Current,* August, 1854, quoted in *Hunt's,* XXXIII (September, 1855), 212; *ibid.,* XLI (December, 1859), 747-748. The Cleveland, Columbus and Cincinnati Railroad carried 231,000 hogs, the Pittsburgh, Fort Wayne, and Chicago Railroad carried 155,000, and the Little Miami carried 122,000. The total carried does not represent total Ohio exports since hogs from other states are included and some hogs and cattle were probably counted twice if carried over two roads. Columbus, for instance, was intersected by the Cleveland and Cincinnati, the Little Miami, and the Ohio Central, and it is likely that some of the hogs carried on the first two roads were reshipped eastward over the latter.

[49] *Thirty-first Annual Report of the Baltimore & Ohio Railroad Company, 1860* (Baltimore, 1860), 102-105. To the north, the number of swine carried over the Michigan Central increased sharply from 12,000 in 1853 to 37,000 in 1855, 170,000 in 1856, and 243,000 in 1857. Michigan Central Railroad Company, *Fourteenth Annual Report, 1860* (Boston, 1860), 30.

The shift of livestock to rail transportation had a pronounced effect on Cincinnati. By 1856 Cincinnati was receiving a large number of hogs via rail, especially over the Little Miami road. In that year Cincinnati received approximately 90,000 hogs from the Miami line, which was 65 per cent of the total number carried by it. In 1859 Cincinnati received 79 per cent, in 1860 70 per cent, and in 1861 53 per cent of the total live hogs transported by the Little Miami.[50] Prior to the railroad, virtually all of the hogs in the area traversed by the road, above local needs, would have arrived in one form or another at Cincinnati.

Railroads not only opened up a direct connection with the East for the farmers of Ohio, they also gave a competitive advantage to the farmers of Indiana and Illinois over those of Ohio. Farmers in the fertile prairies to the west could raise more corn at less expense than their counterparts in Ohio. Hog production in Indiana and Illinois naturally benefited from this situation. The actual impact came in the decade of the 1860's, when total hog production in Ohio, which had increased from 1.9 million head to 2.2 million from 1849 to 1859, decreased to 1.7 million in 1869.[51] By this time corn and hogs had moved vigorously into the trans-Mississippi West. Cincinnati remained a fairly large center for the pork industry, but its days of preeminence were ended. Another and larger industry had been created at Chicago.

OTHER CENTERS OF THE PORK INDUSTRY

Cincinnati was only one, if the largest, of numerous towns engaged in the slaughtering and packing of hogs. Louisville, at times during the antebellum period, packed as much as 70 per cent of Cincinnati's total cut. The industry grew rapidly after 1840-41, when two packers slaughtered about 32,000 hogs. By 1849-50 the pack had increased to 184,000. Large numbers of hogs were obtained from the river counties of Indiana and those immediately to the north. Marion and Spice Valley townships in Lawrence

---

[50] *First Joint Annual Report of the Directors to the Stockholders of the Little Miami and Columbus and Xenia Railroad Companies, 1856* (Columbus, 1857), 40, *4 AR, 1859,* 36-37, *5 AR, 1860,* 36-37, *6 AR, 1861,* 36-37.

[51] *9 Census, 1870,* VII, 694-708. Indiana's hog production followed the same pattern from 1859 to 1869. But in 1859 both Indiana and Illinois had a larger hog crop than Ohio.

County, Indiana, supplied Louisville with swine. Orange County shipped an estimated 6,000 hogs in 1849, while Crawford and Harrison counties also exported livestock. The pack at Louisville appears to have reached its summit in 1851-52, when 275,000 hogs were slaughtered, and then declined slowly to around 250,000 in 1857-58. Louisville probably obtained fewer hogs from Indiana as the decade progressed and railroads enabled farmers to ship live hogs.[52]

Besides Louisville and Cincinnati, hog packing flourished, though on a smaller scale, at various points in the Ohio valley during the 1840's and the early 1850's. Madison, in Jefferson County, was the porkopolis of Indiana and competed directly with Cincinnati and Louisville for the hogs of southeastern Indiana. The provisions trade at Madison received an important stimulus with the completion of the Madison and Indianapolis Railroad in 1847, which penetrated an area hitherto dependent upon Cincinnati's Whitewater Canal for access to a market. In 1849-50 Madison received via the railroad a total of 146,000 live hogs and 6,500 tons of bulk pork and bacon. Receipts for 1850-51 were estimated at $2.3 million. During the late 1840's and early 1850's, Madison packed between 85,000 and 98,000 hogs annually.[53]

Other centers of the provisions trade in Indiana were located along the Wabash River. The upper Wabash shipped some 70,000 hogs in 1843, most of them reported to originate from Lafayette, Delphi, and Covington. Terre Haute and Lafayette were next to Madison in the size of the annual pack. Lafayette's cut ranged between 35,000 and 45,000 at the turn of the decade while Terre Haute cut from 50,000 to 65,000 annually. In the three years 1849-51, these two Wabash centers and Madison packed between 45 and 55 per cent of Indiana's total cut. Most of the Wabash provisions probably went south, since Toledo shipped less than 40,000

[52] *NWR*, LX (May 8, 1841), 149; Cincinnati *Enquirer*, February 1, 1850; [Chamberlain], *Indiana Gazetteer*, 200, 245, 341; Andrews, "Reports on Trade and Commerce," 725; Gray, *History of Agriculture in the South*, II, 841.

[53] *ARJ*, XXV (February 15, 1851), 102, (September 25, 1852), 613. Packing points developed along the canal, Clinton being one of the largest. In 1849, 62,000 hogs were reported cut at various canal towns. Connersville and Cambridge City packed between 25,000 and 30,000 hogs annually. *Patent Report, 1848*, 639, *1849*, 495, *1851*, 567. Other packing centers along the Ohio existed at Aurora, 26 miles below Cincinnati, and at New Albany and Jeffersonville. The latter two villages were located across the river from Louisville.

barrels of pork in 1851 and the Michigan Southern did not carry significant quantities of provisions until later in the decade.[54]

Meat packing in Illinois was even less concentrated than in Indiana. Until Chicago became the center for Illinois, and eventually for the Northwest, none of Illinois' packing centers were as large as Madison or Terre Haute. The packing was generally performed on either the Mississippi or Illinois rivers, and of the numerous centers, Beardstown on the Illinois and Alton on the Mississippi were the most important.

As in Indiana and Ohio, the bulk of the provisions trade was carried on with the South until railroads began turning a large part of it to Chicago and the East just prior to the Civil War. The value of the pork trade south of Peru on the Illinois River was valued at $1.5 million in 1841. In that year 8,000 tons of pork were received at St. Louis from the Illinois River.[55]

Through the 1840's and early 1850's, Beardstown was the most active packing center in the state, its annual pack averaging 31,000 hogs in the five years 1848-52. Pekin and Peoria, also Illinois River ports, both averaged 22,000 during the same period. On the Mississippi River, Quincy packed approximately as many hogs as Pekin and Peoria, while Alton's cut, only slightly less than Beardstown's, averaged 29,000 annually from 1848 to 1852. Other packing towns included Springfield, Lacon, Canton, Meredosia, and Knoxville. During the four years 1848-51, these Illinois towns were responsible for over 65 per cent of the total pack in the state. But after 1852 or

---

[54] St. Louis *Old School Democrat*, April 22, 1843; Andrews, "Reports on Trade and Commerce," 193. In five months of 1849, 50,700 barrels of pork and 4,300 tons of bacon and lard were reported passing Vincennes on the Wabash and Erie Canal. Considerable quantities passed Vincennes on the river and were not counted. *De Bow's Review*, IX (September, 1850), 337. Toledo's provisions probably came primarily from areas east of Fort Wayne, the upper Miami valley, and the Maumee valley. The nine counties of northwestern Ohio, Lucas, Wood, Hancock, Fulton, Henry, Putnam, Williams, Defiance, and Paulding, raised 158,000 hogs in 1849, which probably was about equal to the provisions demands of Toledo. 8 *Census, 1860, Agriculture*, 113-117.

[55] St. Louis *Old School Democrat*, February 29, 1844; George R. Baldwin, *Report Showing the Cost and Income of a Railroad as Surveyed from Toledo, Ohio, to Chicago, Illinois, Incorporated as the Buffalo and Mississippi Rail-Road* (Toledo, 1847), 49-50. Some of this 8,000 tons probably originated at Mississippi ports such as Quincy, Oquawka, and Keokuk. Quincy packed between 3,500 and 12,000 hogs annually from 1837 to 1841. [Samuel A. Mitchell], *Illinois in 1847; a Sketch Descriptive of the Situation, Boundaries, Face of the Country* . . . (Philadelphia, 1837), 127-128; Carlson, *Illinois Military Tract*, 89.

1853, the proportion dropped steadily as the industry took hold at Chicago. In 1854 Chicago's pack formed 15 per cent of the total slaughtered in the state, and by 1858 Chicago's pack of 100,000 swine amounted to 25 per cent of the total. The following year Chicago packed over 50 per cent, and its monopolization of the industry was virtually complete by the Civil War.[56]

SUMMARY

Through the 1840's and well into the 1850's, the grain trade based on the interior rivers of the Northwest and the great trunk routes of the Ohio and Mississippi continued to perform an essential function in the movement of grain and provisions from producer to consumer. The grain trade down the rivers grew in volume and in value in response to the increasing demands made upon the agricultural wealth of the Ohio valley by southern and eastern consumers. Within the river complex, the state of Ohio was the dominant factor throughout the 1830's and 1840's. As the area in the Northwest which first felt the thrust of settlement and thus emerged from the frontier stage, the upper Ohio valley developed, at an earlier time than regions to the west, a mature and commercially oriented system of agriculture—one equipped to marshal its resources to meet and profit from new demands for foodstuffs.

But as the tide of settlement pushed farther west, while simultaneously ascending the river valleys into central and northern Indiana and Illinois, these areas too entered into the river trade in a vigorous way. The river trade of the lower Ohio valley was decades old by 1850, but it is in the decade of the 1840's that the center of gravity for the river traffic begins to move into the lower Ohio and upper Mississippi valleys. In order to evaluate fully the over-all role of the river system in the continuing growth of the grain trade, it is necessary to pass from Cincinnati to St. Louis, and from the Miami and Ohio rivers to the Wabash, Illinois, and Mississippi.

---

[56] *Patent Report, 1848,* 638, *1849,* 495, *1851,* 568; 7 AR, *Commerce of Chicago, 1858,* 22. The pork trade in Chicago is treated in more detail in Chapter XIII.

The River Complex:
The Foodstuffs Trade of the
Lower Ohio and Upper
Mississippi Valleys, 1840-50

CHAPTER VII

THE PATTERN OF INDIANA'S TRADE

As in previous decades, the grain trade of both Illinois and Indiana during the 1840's was predominantly with the South. After 1842 parts of the upper Wabash valley could reach the lakes over the Wabash and Erie Canal, and after 1848 the Illinois and Michigan Canal opened the lakes to the upper and middle Illinois River valley. But throughout the 1840's, the larger parts of both states continued to ship south over the natural waterways.

The foodstuffs trade of Indiana was less centralized than that of other states. It was conducted independently of any large central market like Cincinnati or St. Louis. Large numbers of smaller towns, located mainly on the Wabash and Ohio rivers, gathered in produce from neighboring areas. Parts of Illinois, particularly those along the Indiana border and the Kaskaskia River, were in a similar situation in regard to marketing. But the major trade activity of Illinois was concentrated between the Illinois and Mississippi rivers. On these rivers commercial towns such as Peoria and Quincy developed. Unlike towns of comparable size in Indiana, these Illinois towns served to collect grain and provisions for shipment to a still larger market—first St. Louis, which then marketed the foodstuffs in the South, or New Orleans. Through most of the 1840's this relationship between the Illinois valley and St. Louis and New Orleans continued undisturbed. But in 1848 completion of the canal from Chicago to the Illinois River disrupted the normal flow of trade.

Thus, by 1848 the southern route was feeling the competition of the lakes throughout the entire breadth of the Old Northwest— from Cleveland and the Ohio Canal in the east, to Toledo and the Wabash and Erie Canal in the middle, to Chicago and its canal in the west. Within the next decade another factor appeared—the railroad, competing with both lake and river, but more effective against the river due to the composition of river traffic.

The corn belt of the East North Central states ran in a westerly direction from the lower and middle Miami valley of Ohio through south central and central Indiana to the middle Wabash valley, where it continued, in a somewhat wider path, to the lower and middle Illinois River counties and eventually the Mississippi. It was largely from this general area, which raised over 50 per cent of the tri-state corn crop in 1859, that the corn and provisions exports of the Northwest originated. It was to this area, at no point more than 125 miles wide, that the South looked for foodstuffs to supplement its own production, and this enormous southern need in turn was partly responsible for the location of the corn belt.[1]

As compared with Ohio and Illinois, Indiana, for the 20 years from 1830 to 1850, devoted least of its land and labor to the cultivation of wheat. But in the decade of the 1850's Indiana's wheat crop grew until it became the second largest in the nation, exceeded only by the crop of Illinois in 1859.[2] During the period 1839-49, the small wheat surplus of Indiana was largely grown in the northern part of the state. The primary stimulus to this was the completion of the Wabash and Erie Canal from Lafayette to

---

[1] *Patent Report, 1850,* 17. In 1859 the three states produced 31 per cent of the corn harvested in the country. 8 *Census, 1860, Agriculture,* 181-185.

[2] *Ibid.*

Toledo. The unusually heavy foreign demand for American food-stuffs between 1846 and 1849 supplied another incentive to wheat producers. But with a total wheat crop in Indiana of 6 million bushels in 1849, the trade could not have been very large.[3]

Corn and wheat production were rather evenly distributed throughout the state. From 1840 to 1860 the northern third of the state produced about 25 per cent of the wheat, the lower and middle Wabash counties about 20 per cent, and the counties in southeastern Indiana's Whitewater River valley about 15 per cent. These proportions were maintained while the state's wheat crop increased from 6 million bushels in 1849 to 16.8 million in 1859. The production of corn displayed a similarly even distribution throughout the state, while the crop rose from 53 million bushels in 1849 to 72 million a decade later. Corn was grown more intensively in the south and wheat received more emphasis in the north.[4]

The surplus of Indiana generally sought the Ohio River until the Wabash and Erie Canal reached Toledo in 1842, although some areas to the northwest utilized the ports of Michigan City and St. Joseph. The two major trade areas facing south were the Wabash valley and the Whitewater valley. The trade of the Wabash River and its tributaries was normally conducted without reliance upon a major port, while in the southeast, Cincinnati furnished a market for such Whitewater counties as Wayne and Franklin. After the opening of the canal, the trade of the Wabash River, especially in wheat, at least to a point around Lafayette, was diverted in part to Toledo. It also made available an alternative route to market for counties like Clinton, Carroll, and Montgomery. Clinton County reported exports of wheat and livestock in excess of $200,000 annually, which were marketed either at Logansport or Lafayette on the canal.[5] If Logansport, the produce went to Toledo; Lafayette shipped in both directions.

In the southeastern part of the state, the Madison and Indianapolis Railroad, completed in 1847, opened a new route to the Ohio River at Madison. Counties such as Clinton, Tipton, Hamilton,

---

[3] Thirty-three counties of Indiana in 1839, and 26 in 1849, produced less than four bushels of wheat per capita. Thus, a large portion of the state was required to import flour.

[4] *6 Census, 1840*, 287-288; *7 Census, 1850*, 755-756, 791-792; *8 Census, 1860*, *Agriculture*, 38-43.

[5] [E. Chamberlain], *The Indiana Gazetteer or Topographical Dictionary of the State of Indiana* (Indianapolis, 1849), 196.

Boone, and Hendricks could utilize this road, which offered strong competition to the Whitewater Canal and Cincinnati. In the late 1840's both Boone and Hamilton counties were reported exporting large numbers of hogs to Madison.[6]

Madison, in Jefferson County, became the largest grain center on the Ohio River between Cincinnati and Louisville as a result of the railroad. It greatly enlarged Madison's sources of supply, as the line traversed several of the more productive counties in the state. Marion, Johnson, and Bartholomew counties were reported shipping produce and provisions valued at $1.1 million in 1849. Bartholomew exported 25,000 hogs, 200,000 bushels of corn, and 10,000 barrels of flour while Johnson shipped 450,000 bushels of grain in 1848-49. In that year the Madison road carried almost $600,000 worth of farm produce to the Ohio River. This figure rose to $1.4 million in 1850 and $2.5 million the next year. At this time Madison was probably receiving more bulk wheat than Cincinnati, and half as much produce.[7]

Although Madison and Cincinnati served as markets for the southeastern corner of Indiana, the Wabash River provided a route to market for the western part of the state, and Toledo tapped the northeastern corner, large areas of Indiana still lacked adequate connections with a market as late as the mid-1850's. Delaware and Jay counties in east central Indiana were both too distant from either Toledo to the northeast or Cincinnati to the southeast to engage in the grain trade extensively. The Indianapolis and Bellefontaine Railroad, a continuation of the Ohio and Pennsylvania road completed in 1853, opened up through connections with Pittsburgh and the East for this area, as other roads radiating from Indianapolis were in the process of doing throughout most of the state.[8]

The trade of Indiana with the South was conducted on a smaller and less organized scale than that of Ohio or Illinois. The absence of a commercial center such as Cincinnati or St. Louis was a disadvantage which hampered the general economic growth of

---

[6] *Ibid.*, 170-171, 242.

[7] *Ibid.*, 160, 276, 305; *ARJ*, XXIV (February 15, 1851), 102, XXV (September 25, 1852), 613. Madison was also reported receiving produce via the Shelbyville and Knightstown Railroad. Cincinnati *Enquirer*, December 4, 1850; Andrews, "Reports on Trade and Commerce," 715.

[8] *Hunt's*, XXX (February, 1854), 257-258. By the early 1850's Indianapolis was the terminus of seven railroads and had direct connections with the major towns along the Wabash and Erie Canal.

the state. Farmers along the Wabash River and its major feeder streams, the East and West forks of the White River, were forced to conduct their grain trade throughout the 1840's without the active financial and marketing facilities available to areas dealing with St. Louis or Cincinnati. Market towns like Lafayette and Terre Haute had neither the financial resources, storage capacity, nor current market information available at larger cities. Indiana farmers were compelled to deal on a direct, individual basis with New Orleans or other southern markets.

Before the railroads channeled large quantities of produce and livestock to the East, the rivers emptying into the Ohio carried virtually all of the surplus that moved south. A large portion of this trade was transported by flatboat. Even in the southeastern section of the state, much produce was shipped directly south instead of being marketed initially at Cincinnati. Counties located along the lower and middle Wabash and its major tributary, the White River, floated considerable quantities of foodstuffs south on flatboats even after steamboats were regularly calling at Terre Haute, Lafayette, and Logansport. Morgan County alone was said to have exported 100,000 bushels of grain and 30,000 hogs on some 30 vessels each freighted with from 50 to 70 tons. Vermillion County, with the Wabash as its eastern boundary, loaded between 200 and 250 flatboats annually through the 1840's. Numerous Ohio River counties, such as Ohio, Jefferson, and Harrison, carried on a remunerative trade with the South and shipped largely by flatboat.[9]

The degree to which Indiana's farmers relied on such transportation is accentuated if the origin of flatboat arrivals at New Orleans is noted. While arrivals at New Orleans declined from 2,792 in 1847 to 547 in 1857, and arrivals from Ohio, Indiana, and Illinois declined in proportion, remaining at 50 per cent of total recorded arrivals during the ten years, flatboats from Indiana formed 46.5 per cent of the northwestern total in 1846-47, 54 per cent during the five years 1848-52, and 65 per cent from 1852 to 1857.[10] At Vincennes in 1849 some 7,300 barrels of flour were counted passing through the dam and lock on flatboats at the falls above the town. But double that quantity was said to have kept to the river, bypassing the lock and thus going uncounted.[11] Un-

[9] [Chamberlain], *Indiana Gazetteer*, 245, 324, 339, 408.
[10] Switzler, "Report on Internal Commerce," 222.
[11] *De Bow's Review*, IX (September, 1850), 337.

known numbers of flatboats from Indiana, and other northwestern states as well, descended interior streams to the Ohio, reached the Mississippi, and sold their goods north of New Orleans. But of all the northwestern states, Indiana probably placed greatest reliance on flatboats, continuing the practice into the 1850's. This condition, in addition to the requirements of the southern market, determined that the produce shipped be limited in quantity and relatively valuable in proportion to weight, thus requiring that corn and wheat be converted into more portable and more profitable forms.

Indiana carried to a maximum the practice, also prevalent in all the northwestern states, of sending its surplus corn to market barreled or on the hoof. Although parts of the upper Wabash had access to Toledo, and the southeastern corner access to Cincinnati, both of which cities used substantial quantities of corn, most of Indiana was unable to reach a market large enough, by virtue of extensive distilling or pork packing, to require a large supply of grain. And freight rates, whether by water or rail, were too high and corn prices too low to allow shipment any great distance. Most of the corn, as in Ohio and Illinois, was fed to livestock, consumed by humans, or manufactured into whiskey at home stills and local distilleries. Dearborn County contained three distilleries which manufactured $200,000 worth of whiskey in 1847-48, some of which probably went to Cincinnati for sale and shipment. The bulk corn that remained to be shipped kept to the waterways and went south. There is no doubt that in many interior points of the Northwest, remote from markets and producing great quantities of corn, the grain was a drug in the market and hardly worth cash at any price. Much of it was probably left to rot in the fields or to furnish fodder for wild animals.[12]

THE PATTERN OF ILLINOIS' TRADE

The problems faced by Indiana's farmers in marketing their crops during the 1840's appeared in many parts of Illinois as well. Most of the corn was consumed on the spot or manufactured into whiskey or meal since it did not pay to ship corn. The bulk of the marketable surplus was consigned to St. Louis or sent directly to the South. Until Chicago's railroads reached the Mississippi, the

[12] Robert Russell, *North America. Its Agriculture and Climate* . . . (Edinburgh, 1857), 123; [Chamberlain], *Indiana Gazetteer*, 245.

counties along that river had no alternative but to ship south, while the counties of the middle and upper Illinois valley could ship north to Chicago over the Illinois and Michigan Canal after 1848. Both St. Louis and Chicago drew their corn supplies from much the same territory during the late 1840's and early 1850's. Yet the traffic was so diffused and the sale of corn in bulk was so limited that even after Chicago became the greatest single corn market in the nation, in the mid-1850's, less than 10 per cent of Illinois' crop was disposed of in bulk at that market, and even less reached St. Louis in its original state. Each year vast quantities of the crop were probably wasted. Most of the corn in Sangamon County was not reaped, but left on the stalk to be consumed by hogs, cattle, birds, and squirrels.[13] The problem here, as elsewhere in the Northwest, was one of transportation costs. Bulk corn could not bear the cost of land freight for much more than 20 or 25 miles, and great numbers of farmers lived beyond this maximum distance from a cash market or a river route to a market. In the interior of the Military Tract, no point was more distant than 45 miles from the Mississippi or Illinois rivers. Yet it was estimated that from 15 to 20 per cent of the value of wheat and corn was absorbed in hauling grain 20 miles to a river town.[14] With the price of corn generally low, the remaining value of the grain was often less than the cost of production.

The decade of the 1840's was not one of uniform prosperity in Illinois. In 1841 poor crops of corn and wheat and a large supply of unmarketable livestock, coupled with low prices, caused some to suggest that farmers turn to the production of hemp, tobacco, or wool.[15] This was at the tail end of a long and harsh depression period. Illinois was still without an outlet to the north. Fairly large crops in 1842-43 served to depress prices further. Supplies in the East from 1841 to 1842 had carried over, and the foreign demand was inactive. Three years later, in 1845, the price of corn was so poor in certain areas of Illinois that farmers found it cheaper to purchase than to raise. There seemed to be no reason for optimism in evaluating the future prospects of agriculture in the state. One source estimated that total production in Illinois in 1841 had de-

---

[13] Russell, *North America*, 117.

[14] Theodore L. Carlson, *The Illinois Military Tract. A Study of Land Occupation, Utilization and Tenure* (Urbana, Ill., 1951), 87.

[15] *Sangamo Journal*, December 24, 1841.

clined since 1839 to a point where the wheat crop was barely large
enough to feed the local population.[16]

At least as early as 1839, the corn acreage of Illinois was twice
that of wheat. Certain areas, though, deviated significantly from
the state norm. The east central and southeastern prairie counties,
encompassing some 40 per cent of the land area of the state, produced 12 times as much corn as wheat. Less than five bushels of
wheat per capita were raised in the entire section, and many counties produced only two or three bushels per capita.[17] The only
outlet for this region was the Wabash River, and this waterway
was too distant from most of the district. There was really no market for corn or wheat. Corn was of greater general utility to a pioneer population and the market that did exist was the southern—
thus the greater emphasis given to that crop. It is probable that a
considerable part of each crop was wasted. Counties to the south,
along the Wabash River, raised the same proportions of corn and
wheat as the prairie counties. Some of the surplus, marketed as
pork and whiskey, was consigned to Shawneetown and Cairo,
where it could be re-exported directly to New Orleans, the lower
Mississippi valley, or St. Louis.[18]

A decade later, in 1849, the east central and Wabash counties
had intensified their specialization in corn. Coles, Edgar, and Vermilion counties produced between 35 and 45 times more corn than
wheat, for which there was still no market in this area. This factor
also resulted in a decline in wheat production in southern Illinois
in general. Whereas in 1839 southern Illinois counties such as Gallatin, Saline, Williamson, Franklin, and Hamilton produced an average of 13 times more corn than wheat, ten years later they pro-

---

[16] J. W. Spencer and J. M. D. Burrows, *The Early Days of Rock Island
and Davenport*, Milo M. Quaife, ed. (Chicago, 1942), 194-195; Cincinnati
Advertiser and Journal, January 13, 1841.

[17] In 1839 the corn-wheat ratio was 6.8, and, as explained in Chapter IV,
15 bushels of wheat per acre and 40 bushels of corn are taken as representative
yields. *6 Census, 1840*, 299-300.

[18] J. M. Peck, *A Gazetteer of Illinois in Three Parts* . . . (Jacksonville, Ill.,
1834), 118, 123, 135. Flatboat arrivals at New Orleans from Illinois were usually less than one-tenth the number of Indiana arrivals. This might be taken to
mean that most of Illinois' produce was disposed of before reaching New
Orleans or that much Illinois produce was carried on Indiana flatboats after
being marketed at a Wabash River town. Other areas of Illinois used steamboats regularly for freighting purposes. The Illinois River valley dealt with
St. Louis rather than New Orleans. St. Louis flatboats were not counted as
originating in the Northwest. Switzler, "Report on Internal Commerce," 222.

duced the startling figure of 130 times more corn.[19] Most areas within these five counties were without access, except by wagon, to the Wabash or Ohio rivers, so that it is extremely unlikely that a grain trade of any proportions developed. Most of the corn which was not consumed locally in one form or another was probably allowed to go to waste.

In the western part of Illinois, between the Illinois River and the Mississippi, a different picture presents itself. In 1839 there had not yet developed any particular concentration in either corn or wheat. This region had superior transportation facilities in its two rivers and the large market of St. Louis to draw off some of its surplus. In the 1840's the upper portions of the Illinois valley began to concentrate more heavily on wheat than corn. This specialization was a response to the developing market at Chicago, and resulted in a similar concentration on wheat in the counties to the west and northwest of Chicago. It was part of a similar pattern occurring in counties all along the more northern stretches of the East North Central states and was called into being by the greater demand in the East for wheat than for corn. The southern demand for corn and provisions goes far toward explaining the relatively greater attention given to corn in lower Illinois valley counties such as Sangamon, Morgan, Cass, and Menard. Certain counties in the middle Illinois valley which could reach either St. Louis or Chicago continued, through the 1850's, to demonstrate no particular concentration on one grain more than the other.[20]

By 1859 the corn-wheat ratio for Illinois was down to just under 5:1, with almost twice as much acreage in corn as in wheat. The counties in east central and southeastern Illinois continued an intensive specialization in corn, while the counties on both sides of the Illinois River planted from three to five times more acreage in corn than in wheat. In these two areas, extending from the Indiana border through central Illinois to the Mississippi River, over 55 per cent of the state's corn crop was produced in 1859. Certain of the western counties in these areas were also engaged in the production of large crops of wheat, although in general the primary wheat area remained in the northern regions of the state, where the largest market was located.[21]

---

[19] *6 Census, 1840,* 299-300.

[20] *Ibid.; 7 Census, 1850,* 730-731; *8 Census, 1860, Agriculture,* 30-35.

[21] *Ibid.; Transactions of the Department of Agriculture of the State of Illinois, 1875,* new series, V (1876), 297.

ST. LOUIS AND THE RIVER TRADE

St. Louis was the great market during the 1840's and into the 1850's for those parts of Illinois within reach of the Mississippi and the Illinois River system. These parts were the most commercially developed regions of Illinois. As early as the 1830's, the trade of St. Louis covered an enormous stretch of territory, including the upper Mississippi and Illinois river valleys. St. Louisians were confident that their central position athwart the major thoroughfare of the old and new West predestined their city to be the paramount commercial metropolis of the West—if not the nation.[22]

The commerce of St. Louis with the upper Mississippi and the Illinois River increased steadily during the 1840's. Total steamboat arrivals at St. Louis rose from 1,476 in 1839 to 2,905 in 1849, while during the same period arrivals from the upper Mississippi jumped from 143 in 1841 to over 600 in 1845-46. During the peak shipping seasons of late fall and spring, from 50 to 100 steamboats called weekly at the port. Smaller packets from the north laden with produce from Wisconsin, Iowa, and Illinois unloaded at St. Louis and took on return cargoes of general merchandise, while the produce was transferred to larger vessels for shipment to the South.[23]

For a good part of the period before the Civil War, St. Louis was the most important market for Illinois in conducting its trade with the South. Moreover, the counties of the Illinois River valley and those bordering the Mississippi were the basic source areas from which St. Louis procured its produce. Of the two areas, the Illinois River valley was more important, since it penetrated to the very heart of Illinois' grain-growing area. St. Louis first established regular communications with Illinois River towns in the late 1820's, when steamboats began making scheduled visits to ports like Naples, Beardstown, Peoria, Pekin, and Peru. These towns devel-

---

[22] *De Bow's Review*, VII (November, 1849), 404, quoting an article in the *Western Journal of Commerce* of St. Louis.

[23] St. Louis *Old School Democrat*, May-June, 1843, February 29, 1844; Mildred L. Hartsough, *From Canoe to Steel Barge on the Upper Mississippi* (Minneapolis, 1934), 57, 69; Frank H. Dixon, *A Traffic History of the Mississippi River System* (Washington, D.C., 1909), 24. In 1846, 881 flatboats and keelboats arrived at St. Louis—600 between August 1 and December 31, and 453 in the last three months of this period. During these fall and early winter months, St. Louis usually received over 50 per cent of her total yearly receipts of grain and flour. Undoubtedly a large number of the flatboats were from the Illinois River and from Illinois ports on the Mississippi. *Hunt's*, XVII (August, 1847), 169, XXIV (March, 1851), 301.

oped a considerable traffic in grain and provisions. Peoria reported 1,286 steamboat arrivals in 1852, while Pekin received grain and provisions valued at $1.5 million. Meredosia and Lacon also assumed active roles in the grain and provisions trade of their hinterlands.

Peoria, the largest of the Illinois River ports, experienced its real growth during the years 1854-58. By 1850 the town was already an important hog-packing center, the cut running at about 27,000 annually. Grain exports were also considerable in that year. Some 628,000 bushels of corn and 265,000 bushels of wheat were exported, while 33,700 barrels of flour were manufactured. By 1856 Peoria's corn receipts reached 3.8 million bushels, of which some 1.3 million bushels were used in the town's eight distilleries. In 1856, 83,000 barrels of whiskey were manufactured. Over 650,000 bushels of wheat and oats were shipped and some 110,000 barrels of flour were ground. Grain and provisions exports, valued at $1.2 million in 1851, had more than tripled by 1857-58.[24]

The growth of Peoria coincides in time quite closely with the rise of Chicago as the primary grain mart of the Northwest. It is likely that substantial quantities of exports from Peoria went north over the Illinois and Michigan Canal. Corn receipts at Chicago rose from 3.3 million bushels in 1851 to 11.6 million in 1858, while those at St. Louis fluctuated between 1 and 2 million bushels during that period. It is probable that the sustained increase in Peoria corn exports was a response to an expanding market at Chicago. Peoria was never of great importance in bulk wheat shipments, but did manufacture and ship a large quantity of flour. Much of this went to Chicago, which was less extensively engaged in milling than St. Louis and therefore more dependent upon outside sources for its flour.[25]

That the Illinois valley was vital to the trade of St. Louis is

---

[24] *Ibid.*, XLI (November, 1859), 647, (December, 1859), 689-694, XXXVII (September, 1857), 306-307; James W. Putnam, *The Illinois and Michigan Canal. A Study in Economic History* (Chicago, 1918), 105.

[25] *Hunt's*, XXVI (April, 1851), 428-430; Chicago Board of Trade, *Nineteenth Annual Report of the Trade and Commerce of Chicago, 1876* (Chicago, 1877), 42-43; St. Louis Merchants' Exchange, *Annual Statement of the Trade and Commerce of St. Louis, 1878* (St. Louis, 1879), 52. St. Louis flour receipts declined after 1858, while Chicago's receipts increased. Peru, Illinois, was reported dealing in over 1 million bushels of grain in 1856. Judson F. Lee, *Transportation as a Factor in the Development of Northern Illinois Previous to 1860* (Chicago, 1917), 51.

substantiated by the valley's contribution to total grain receipts at the Mississippi River port. In 1851 the Illinois River region shipped 964,000 bushels of wheat to the port, or 56 per cent of total receipts.[26] In 1853 Illinois River sources supplied St. Louis with 46 per cent of total wheat receipts, while the upper Mississippi contributed 44 per cent. Forty-one per cent of the corn received at the city originated in the valley, and of 72,000 barrels of pork received in 1853, the Illinois River area sent 36,000. Two years later St. Louis received over 35 per cent of total wheat receipts, over 50 per cent of provisions, and between 75 and 80 per cent of corn from the country along the Illinois River.[27] These figures indicate a declining percentage of wheat receipts from the valley between 1851 and 1855. Sources along the upper Mississippi, primarily Illinois, supplied 52 per cent of wheat receipts in 1853 and 33,000 barrels of pork.[28]

During the 1850's St. Louis suffered a heavy diversion of the grain that she had previously received from parts of the Old Northwest because of lake and railroad competition. The gross impact of this diversion, which was revolutionary, was concealed only by the fact that St. Louis tapped new sources as she was losing her older ones. Thus, her total grain trade continued to grow during the 1850's, as Table 14 should make clear, even while she was becoming of less importance to the Old Northwest. In the early and mid-1850's, some 90 per cent of total wheat and flour receipts arrived via the Mississippi. But in 1856 the river carried only 56 per cent of wheat and flour imports. Railroads from the East touched the Mississippi in the late 1850's. By 1857 Chicago was receiving some 8 million bushels of wheat over the Galena, the Rock Island, the Chicago, Burlington and Quincy, and the Chicago, Alton and St. Louis railroads. Much of this originated in areas which had

---

[26] *Hunt's*, XXVI (April, 1852), 429. As noted earlier, the South experienced a general crop failure in 1851. High prices prevailed at St. Louis which attracted large quantities of grain that ultimately reached the South.

[27] Carlson, *Illinois Military Tract*, 97, fn. 104. Chicago's wheat receipts doubled from 1854 to 1855, while exports tripled. This reflected the great foreign demand generated by the Crimean War. During the same period receipts at St. Louis increased by 50 per cent.

[28] *De Bow's Review*, XVI (April, 1854), 404; *Hunt's*, XXX (April, 1854), 453, 488. Receipts from Alton, Illinois, were probably designated as upper Mississippi River, but much of Alton's shipments consisted of grain and flour received from the Illinois River. In 1853 Alton shipped 27,000 barrels of flour to St. Louis, or 13 per cent of the latter's total receipts, and the same share of corn receipts. Chicago *Daily Tribune*, February 6, 1854.

engaged in a heavy grain trade with St. Louis in previous years. The Rock Island had crossed the Mississippi in 1855, and it reached Grinnell, Iowa, in 1860, while several other roads made trans-Mississippi connections.[29] St. Louis, while engaged in pushing a major railroad in the direction of Kansas City, and other lines to

TABLE 14. AVERAGE ANNUAL RECEIPTS, 1845-49, AND ANNUAL RECEIPTS, 1850-60, AT ST. LOUIS OF WHEAT, FLOUR, CORN, OTHER GRAINS; AND ANNUAL FLOUR MANUFACTURES AT ST. LOUIS (IN THOUSANDS)

Year	Wheat (bu.)	Flour (bbl.)	Flour Mfg. in St. Louis (bbl.)	Corn (bu.)	Other Grains (bu.)
1845–49	1,663	229	224 [a]	733 [b]	–
1850	1,900	293	–	1,665	–
1851	1,713	185	408	2,737	–
1852	1,645	132	383	1,015	–
1853	2,076	201	455	1,147	–
1854	2,126	193	503	–	–
1855	3,313	226	603	–	–
1856	3,747	323	678	939	1,030
1857	3,281	574	663	2,486	1,831
1858	3,836	687	826	892	2,028
1859	3,569	485	873	1,640	1,633
1860	3,556	443	839	4,250	2,333

[a] The figure is for 1846 only.
[b] All grain, excluding wheat, 1845/49-53.
Sources: Hall, *The West*, 252-253; Andrews, "Reports on Trade and Commerce," 729; *Lippincott's Gazetteer*, 1028; St. Louis Merchants' Exchange, *Trade and Commerce, 1878*, 50-52.

the north and southwest, secured her first connection with a road leading toward the East Coast with the completion of the Ohio and Mississippi to Vincennes in 1855.[30]

The extension of railroads to the Mississippi and trans-Mississippi country also curtailed shipments reaching St. Louis from

[29] In 1857 the C. B. & Q., the Galena, and the Rock Island transported 2.6 million bushels of corn to Chicago. *Seventh Annual Review of the Trade and Commerce . . . of Chicago, 1858* (Chicago, 1859), 11-14; B. Henry Meyer *et al.*, *History of Transportation in the United States Before 1860* (Washington, D.C., 1948), 549; "Report of the Bureau of Topographical Engineers, 1856," *House Executive Documents*, 35 Cong., 1 Sess., No. 2 (1856), Serial 943, 340.

[30] *De Bow's Review*, XXI (July, 1856), 87. Railroad communications had an immediate effect on flour receipts at St. Louis. In 1857, 15 per cent came by rail; in 1859, 33 per cent. Dixon, *Traffic History of the Mississippi River System*, 34.

sources in Wisconsin and Minnesota.[31] The quantities received were probably not very significant, since the latter did not produce a surplus until the mid-1850's. By that time railroads from Chicago, Milwaukee, and Racine were approaching the Mississippi to intercept a large part of the supplies sent down the river. By the late 1860's Minneapolis–St. Paul was a flour market in its own right, competing with the cities to the southeast for the grain of the intervening territory west into Iowa. The completion of railroads from Lake Michigan ports to the Twin Cities made it unnecessary to export grain via the Mississippi.

The time-span during which St. Louis was able to tap Wisconsin for grain supplies was also quite limited. Although the *Niles' Weekly Register* quoted a notice from a St. Louis paper in 1818 advertising for sale 300 barrels of fine, bolted flour manufactured at Prairie du Chien, Wisconsin's southwestern regions were almost uninhabited prior to the 1840's.[32] During the next decade settlement converged largely on the southeastern lands of Wisconsin, which did not produce a large surplus until the mid-1850's. Shortly thereafter railroads gave Wisconsin's Mississippi River ports access to markets on Lake Michigan. Crawford County, Wisconsin, reported in 1851 that for several seasons its wheat crop had exceeded the internal demand and dealers were sacking wheat for the St. Louis market.[33] Within six years the Milwaukee and Mississippi Railroad reached Crawford County and an outlet east was provided. Before the Civil War intervened, the upper Mississippi had been connected with railroads to the East at a number of points and considerable traffic was diverted from St. Louis.

Throughout this development, while the volume of traffic in foodstuffs at St. Louis rose, the actual patterns of traffic were revolutionized. Sources east of the Mississippi, along the river bank itself and into the Illinois valley country, shifted their trade from St. Louis to Chicago, while the railroads made serious inroads into produce originating along the upper Mississippi. The quantities

---

[31] St. Louis opened up communications with the Minnesota territory in 1820 when steamboats reached the Falls of St. Anthony. But it was not until the late 1830's that population in that district warranted a regular commercial exchange between St. Louis and St. Paul. In the early 1840's some 40 to 45 steamboats arrived at St. Paul each season. In 1858 the number of arrivals totaled 1,068. *NWR*, XVIII (July 15, 1820), 360; Hartsough, *Canoe to Steel Barge*, 54-55; Louis C. Hunter, *Steamboats on the Western Rivers. An Economic and Technological History* (Cambridge, Mass., 1949), 45.

[32] *NWR*, XVI (May 29, 1819), 240.

[33] *Transactions of the Wisconsin State Agricultural Society*, I (1851), 145.

carried by river diminished steadily in the immediate pre-war years. The war itself provided the coup de grace to the river trade by cutting off the lower Mississippi valley from the Union. By 1878 all river traffic to St. Louis was supplying the town with only 7 to 10 per cent of its total grain receipts. The Illinois River contributed less than one-half of the river total. St. Louis continued to receive a large portion of its grain from southern Illinois, but it was carried to the city by rail, while increasing quantities were obtained from the West. Thus, sources for grain west of the river were tapped to compensate for the loss of sources to the east. Moreover, whereas in the early and mid-1850's virtually all of the grain exports from St. Louis had traveled down the Mississippi to the South, by 1878 56 per cent went east via railroad.[34]

St. Louis supplied an enormous area with grain and merchandise. The introduction of the steamboat had greatly extended the area with which St. Louis could have direct commercial dealings. By the 1840's this region included both the upper and lower Mississippi valley, the Ohio valley, and the country through which the Cumberland and Tennessee rivers flowed, as well as regions to the west and southwest. In the grain trade the excellent business and financial connections developed by St. Louis with New Orleans and the general southern market allowed St. Louis to assume the role of middleman between northern producers and southern consumers. The farmers and grain dealers of the upper Mississippi valley, the Illinois River valley, and southern Illinois had few business connections with the South, and had not the ability to concentrate or package produce or provisions in the form and quantities necessary to supply the southern demand. St. Louis provided these services.[35]

St. Louis and New Orleans engaged in a large trade, and one of the major items in the traffic was foodstuffs sent from the Mis-

[34] St. Louis Merchants' Exchange, *Trade and Commerce, 1878*, 51. Henry C. Hubbart, *The Older Middle West. 1840-1880* . . . (New York, 1936), 80-81, maintains that one-third of the surplus of the upper Mississippi was still going to St. Louis in 1860. This is unlikely in view of the great quantities of grain received at Milwaukee and Chicago by rail and canal during the late 1850's and the substantial increase in receipts experienced by those two ports.

[35] Switzler, "Report on Internal Commerce," 53. St. Louis' flour was preferred in the South and graded especially for consumption in the area bordering on the Cumberland, Tennessee, White, Red, and lower Mississippi rivers. During the last half of the 1850's, St. Louis was the largest milling center in the nation and her flour was regarded as the best produced in the country. James Hall, *The West: Its Commerce and Navigation* (Cincinnati, 1848), 103;

souri city to New Orleans. This commerce had been carried on for decades, but it grew rapidly in importance during the 1840's and reached its highest significance during the 1850's.

It would be difficult, if not impossible, to determine with precision what part of the wheat, flour, and corn which was delivered at New Orleans was shipped from St. Louis, and it would be even more difficult to discover the ultimate destination of that part of St. Louis' shipments which was not sent to New Orleans. During the five years 1841-45, St. Louis flour exports averaged 160,000 barrels annually, while New Orleans received an annual average of 498,000 barrels. For the four years 1846-49, St. Louis shipped an average of 400,000 barrels yearly, while New Orleans received an average of 1,044,000 barrels. For the entire nine years shipments from St. Louis were between 32 and 38 per cent of total New Orleans flour receipts, and in 1851 shipments were 69 per cent of receipts.[36] During the two-week period October 31–November 13, 1848, steamboats from St. Louis carried to New Orleans 21,000 barrels of flour, or 5 per cent of total annual shipments and 3 per cent of total annual receipts. In the same two-week period in 1851, New Orleans received 15,000 barrels of flour from St. Louis via steamboat, or 1.5 per cent of the total yearly receipts and 3 per cent of the yearly shipments.[37] It is probably safe to assume that at least one-half of the grain exports from St. Louis in the 1840's were received at New Orleans, forming there between 25 and 30 per cent

Isaac Lippincott, *A History of Manufactures in the Ohio Valley to the Year 1860* (Chicago, 1914), 163; Charles B. Kuhlman, *The Development of the Flour-Milling Industry in the United States with Special Reference to the Industry in Minneapolis* (Boston and New York, 1929), 83-84. By the 1850's St. Louis milled about twice as much flour as was received from outside sources.

[36] *Hunt's,* IX (August, 1843), 159; *De Bow's Review,* V (April, 1848), 371; Andrews, "Reports on Trade and Commerce," 729; [John Hogan], *Thoughts About the City of St. Louis, Her Commerce and Manufactures, Railroads, &c.* (St. Louis, 1854), 14; *8 Census, 1860, Agriculture,* clvi.

[37] *The Daily Picayune* (New Orleans), October 31–November 14, 1848, October 31–November 14, 1851. About the same ratio applies to corn. Most of the bulk wheat received at New Orleans came from St. Louis. In 1851 barreled pork exports from St. Louis were one-third, and lard one-quarter, of New Orleans' receipts. The remainder of St. Louis' shipments went to towns such as Memphis, Vicksburg, and Natchez on the lower Mississippi, and Nashville on the Cumberland. *Patent Report, 1852,* 427. At Vicksburg, grain and provisions were reshipped to the interior via the Vicksburg and Jackson Railroad. In 1849-51 that road carried an aggregate of 42,000 barrels of flour and 3,500 tons of meat, some 50 per cent going to Jackson. *De Bow's Review,* IX (October, 1850), 455-456, XI (December, 1851), 595. After 1853 flour from St. Louis could reach Nashville by the Louisville and Nashville Railroad.

of the total receipts. During the mid and late 1850's, the importance of the cities to one another as market and source probably intensified as Cincinnati, which had been New Orleans' other major source, directed progressively larger quantities of grain and provisions to the East.

The Nature of the Trade at New Orleans

In 1850 the total commerce of the Mississippi River system was approaching a value estimated at $400 million, or 175 per cent more than the value of the total exports of the United States. Of this Mississippi commerce, the share of New Orleans was $97 million, while her exports of $37.6 million were equal to 28 per cent of total American domestic shipments overseas.[38] In 1840 exports of wheat and flour from New Orleans consigned to foreign destinations were the equivalent of about 15 per cent of total United States exports in those items. In 1849, although both receipts and

Table 15. Annual Up-River Receipts at and Exports from New Orleans of Flour, Corn, and Pork, 1840-49 (in thousands)

	Receipts			Exports		
Year	Flour (bbl.)	Corn (bu.)	Pork (bbl.)	Flour (bbl.)	Corn (bu.)	Pork (bbl.)
1840 [a]	486	1,332	121	–	–	47 [c]
1841	496	1,377	217	311	–	80
1842	440	1,881	244	272	878	187
1843	521	2,130	205	339	1,681	160
1844	503	1,587	413	300	511	393
1845	533	1,481	217	279	550	181
1846	838	4,125	369	573	2,354	273
1847	1,618	7,871	302	1,320	6,301	231
1848	707	4,718	256 [b]	473	3,061	318
1849	1,013	4,889	551	778	3,667	466

[a] Bulk wheat receipts were under 400,000 bushels except in 1845-46 and 1848.
[b] 14,000 hogsheads of pork were received in 1848 and 18,000 in 1849.
[c] This figure includes only those to New York, Boston, Philadelphia, and Baltimore.
Sources: Receipts—Switzler, "Report on Internal Commerce," 195-202; *8 Census, 1860, Agriculture*, clvi. Exports—*The Ohio Cultivator*, I (January 15, 1845), 12; *NWR*, LXV (October 7, 1843), 88; *De Bow's Review*, I (June, 1846), 493, VI (December, 1848), 437-438, VII (November, 1849), 421; *Hunt's*, VII (October, 1842), 391, IX (December, 1843), 570, XI (November, 1844), 419, XIII (October, 1845), 370.

[38] Switzler, "Report on Internal Commerce," 204, 377; Evans, "Exports, Domestic and Foreign," Table 4, 75-76.

exports had increased, as Table 15 points out, the share of the foreign trade at New Orleans was under 10 per cent.[39] However, in absolute terms, New Orleans did register an increase in the quantity of flour exported to foreign markets after 1846. But the domestic trade with the cities along the middle and north Atlantic coast remained the major destination for New Orleans' shipments.

As has already been shown, the activity experienced after 1845 in the grain and provisions trade was a direct result of an expanded foreign demand. In the four years 1842-1845, before this demand developed, 60 per cent of the flour, 75 per cent of the corn, and over 90 per cent of the pork exported from New Orleans was sent to domestic markets, mostly on the Atlantic coast. During the subsequent four years, 1846-49, at the height of the foreign demand, only 5 per cent less flour and 5 per cent less pork went to domestic markets, while 34 per cent less corn went to home ports. Part of this was re-exported. This is purely a decline in relative terms, for the export trade increased in volume. It illustrates the continuing centrality of the home market for New Orleans.[40]

The trade in grain and provisions at New Orleans developed at different rates during the decade. In general, the provisions trade was almost wholly attuned to the domestic market, and, as such, was less susceptible than the grain trade to the constantly shifting foreign demand for American foodstuffs. Thus, its course during the decade was less erratic than that of the grain trade.[41] The advances made in the provisions trade were much weightier in terms

---

[39] *De Bow's Review*, VII (November, 1849), 421; Evans, "Exports, Domestic and Foreign," Table 2, 23.

[40] See sources for Table 15. In 1847 only 17 per cent of the flour and 13 per cent of the corn exported from New Orleans was destined for domestic markets. Boston's receipts of flour from New Orleans rose from 75,000 in 1845 to 122,000 in 1846, and from 210,000 in 1848 to 303,000 in 1849. During the five years 1845-49, New Orleans supplied approximately 20 per cent of Boston's total flour receipts. Boston generally re-exported 10 to 15 per cent of total receipts. *Hunt's*, XXI (November, 1849), 539; *Patent Report, 1851*, 535.

[41] During the peak export year, 1847, 82 per cent of New Orleans' provisions exports were consigned to domestic markets. A small portion of this probably was re-exported. The following notes New Orleans' receipts of bulk pork and lard for selected years.

Year	Bulk pork (in thousands of lbs.)	Lard (in thousands of kegs and bbls.)
1832	4,114	153
1835	7,161	259
1841	9,744	321
1849	10,274	489

Switzler, "Report on Internal Commerce," 195-202, 216-217.

of dollar volume. In 1842 flour and grain receipts were valued at $2.5 million while provisions were estimated at $3.2 million, the former making up 7 per cent and the latter 9 per cent of the value of all receipts. In 1845 the dollar value of the grain trade had increased to $2.6 million, but its proportionate value had declined to 4.5 per cent. In the following year provisions receipts had risen to $8 million and grain to $7 million. But by 1852 flour and grain were worth only 6 per cent of total receipts, while provisions receipts at $15.5 million composed 15.8 per cent of the total, and had formed at least 14 per cent since 1848.[42]

New Orleans does not seem to have suffered perceptibly, as of 1850, from the dynamic growth of the Great Lakes grain trade, accomplished primarily through the agency of such port cities as Cleveland, Sandusky, Toledo, Detroit, and, to a lesser degree, Milwaukee and Chicago. The latter two ports were in the early stages of their career, while the Lake Erie ports had, through their canals and railways, tapped regions which previously were relatively unproductive. The radical increase in the demand for American foodstuffs in the latter part of the 1840's stimulated production in many areas of the Northwest. The lake trade received most of its additional grain from Ohio and Michigan, for northern Illinois, northern Indiana, and Wisconsin were less settled and less agriculturally advanced than Ohio and Michigan, and thus less capable of expanding production to meet a given market demand. The more densely settled, commercially and agriculturally developed regions in the southern sections of Ohio, Indiana, and Illinois, which habitually shipped south and produced the commodities demanded by the South, were capable of concentrating and specializing their agricultural efforts to produce an enlarged grain crop. The activity of the trade to New Orleans is the palpable product of this effort.

Nevertheless, there were developments, visible and already operational in the Northwest, which were to effect a profound change in the grain trade of New Orleans in the following decade. The initial consequences were encountered by New Orleans in the late 1840's. At this time the most prominent threat to New Orleans'

---

[42] Andrews, "Reports on Trade and Commerce," 756-757; *Hunt's*, XXIII (December, 1850), 659, XXXIII (November, 1855), 602; Hall, *The West*, 190, 216. The pronounced decline in pork receipts from 1846 to 1848 does not seem to reflect the situation for all provisions. Lard, barreled pork, and ham and bacon receipts all increased during these years. Neither did the abnormally high quantities of corn received in 1846-47 result in a decline in the over-all western hog pack, which rose from 875,000 in 1846 to 1.4 million in 1850.

grain trade was the Illinois and Michigan Canal, for any factors that worked to divert grain from St. Louis would have their ultimate impact at New Orleans.[43] The canal did have adverse effects at specific times on receipts at St. Louis. The decline in wheat and flour receipts at St. Louis from 1848 to 1852 was attributed, in part, to the operation of this canal. The marked decline in corn receipts in 1852 was blamed on the extraordinary low stage of water in the upper rivers in the summer and fall of 1852, causing much grain in the north to take the railroad route to Lake Michigan markets.[44] But it was also noted that in the spring of 1852 much of the corn in store along the river north of Beardstown was committed to Chicago. Grain dealers of the lake port had advanced as much as 20 cents a bushel to merchants and producers at Pekin and Peoria, and reportedly they held warehouse receipts for at least half the grain at the latter market.[45]

The implications of the growing strength of northern financial resources in the competition for the grain trade were not lost on those who were concerned over New Orleans' future. It was observed in 1851 that New York commission houses and grain dealers were flooding the rich regions of Ohio, Indiana, and Illinois with eastern bank notes advanced to packers, millers, and western grain merchants, on produce to be shipped east.[46] Together with improved transportation facilities, the system of cash advances enabled farmers to market their crops soon after harvest. Prior to the railroad, farmers who were unable to dispose of their crops before the freeze were compelled to hold the produce through the winter. This put a great strain on the limited financial resources of most producers, who needed an immediate return on their productive

---

[43] The most substantial threats, of course, were the railroads, already approaching the Ohio River and Lake Erie from the Atlantic coast, and their connection with east-west lines which were being constructed, and with north-south lines far advanced in construction or already completed.

[44] Flour receipts declined at St. Louis from 387,000 barrels in 1847 to 132,000 in 1852, while corn dropped from 2.7 million bushels in 1851 to 1 million the following year. *ARJ*, XXXI (July 3, 1858), 427.

[45] *Ibid.*, XXV (April 17, 1852), 245. During these years New Orleans receipts, except in 1850, were substantially higher than in the period 1840-45, but not quite as high as in the four years 1846-49. Supplies from sources other than St. Louis compensated for any decline that may have occurred in receipts from the latter city. Flour exports at Cincinnati rose between 1850 and 1852. *Thirty-fourth Annual Report of the Cincinnati Chamber of Commerce and Merchant's Exchange . . . 1882* (Cincinnati, 1882), 155.

[46] *De Bow's Review*, XI (November, 1851), 521.

efforts to carry them through the winter. These factors also enabled grain dealers to accumulate produce through the winter, and store it until lake transportation opened up in the spring. In the days before large sums of eastern money became available to help finance the movement of grain, many dealers were forced to hurry off their shipments to New Orleans during the late fall and early winter. *De Bow's Review* thought that the banking facilities of the East were at least as instrumental in diverting trade from New Orleans as were the new routes opening up between the interior and the Atlantic seaboard.[47] To be sure, financial strength was of critical importance in the growth of a port such as Chicago, but it would seem that the extension of transportation facilities into the interior, and the consequent enlarging of the area from which supplies were obtained, was the more basic prerequisite. An expanding trade area attracted capital which led to further expansion, but the growth came initially through the agency of transportation improvements.

Despite the fact that New Orleans had great financial resources and was the center of an immense exchange operation, a dispro portionate share of her active capital was committed to the trade in cotton and, to a lesser degree, sugar, molasses, and tobacco. Moreover, New Orleans functioned, in part, as a staging center for grain that was destined for northern cities, and in a sense performed a role similar to that of Buffalo and Oswego.

For much of the traffic New Orleans was not a market. A substantial part of the produce entering New Orleans was never offered for sale there. New Orleans was a place of transhipment for grain purchased in the more southerly regions of the Northwest by eastern dealers. Even some of the grain destined for overseas was purchased directly in the interior rather than at the New Orleans market. In such instances the only profits accruing to New Orleans were derived through transferring the produce from river to ocean-going vessels.[48]

Much of the produce actually sold at New Orleans did not

---

[47] *Ibid.*; Thomas S. Berry, *Western Prices Before 1861. A Study of the Cincinnati Market* (Cambridge, Mass., 1943), 495, fn. 56, states that the "American Express Company alone imported $975,000 in currency and $1,200,-000 in coin to be paid out [in the West] for hogs."
[48] New York *Tribune*, January 14, 1842; St. Louis *Old School Democrat*, March 15, 1843. Much the larger part of produce, southern staples, and foreign or domestic imports arriving at or departing from the port of New Orleans was

redound to the direct benefit of New Orleans either. The purchasing power gained through a sale at New Orleans, and the South as well, was normally used to pay for or purchase goods of non-southern origin, largely eastern manufactures. New Orleans before the 1850's carried on a profitable business as a distributor of eastern merchandise to the Northwest. During this period the purchasing power from a sale of foodstuffs was often returned to New Orleans. But in the middle 1850's eastern merchandise began to move directly by rail to western distributors, thus bypassing New Orleans.

In terms of services and facilities offered to shippers, New Orleans' grain market was far inferior to the northern grain centers. Freight rates from the Northwest to New Orleans evidenced a significant decrease from 1815 to 1840, as greater numbers of larger steamboats plied the western waters. The over-all costs of shipping foodstuffs from Cincinnati to New York City via the Ohio and Erie Canal, Lake Erie, and the Erie Canal, or via Pittsburgh to Philadelphia, were not substantially less than by way of New Orleans. By the northern route, the freight per barrel of flour in the late 1840's averaged about $1.35, while the rate via New Orleans averaged $1.47, half of which was charged from New Orleans to New York. In the early 1840's rates via New Orleans had been some 20 cents less per barrel.[49] But even though freight rates over the rivers remained competitive with the lake route, New Orleans did not get the benefit. For, in addition to freight charges, shippers using the southern route were compelled to pay higher premium rates for insurance than prevailed on the lakes. One source estimated that this added another 12 to 20 cents per barrel to the cost of freighting flour to New York via New Orleans.[50]

Another serious disadvantage to the grain trade at New Or-

carried in shipping registered at other ports than New Orleans. That port, as the South in general, was dependent upon other places for shipping, and had been since Colonial days. The ocean-going vessels calling at New Orleans were largely owned either on the north Atlantic coast or in Great Britain. One-half of the tonnage owned by New Orleans consisted of steamboats employed mostly in the cotton trade. *Lippincott's New and Complete Gazetteer of the United States* (Philadelphia, 1854), 795.

[49] *De Bow's Review*, III (February, 1847), 101; Berry, *Western Prices*, 88, Appendix B, Tables 9 and 10, 561.

[50] Between Chicago and Buffalo, from spring to September, the premium was 1½ per cent; from September to October 1, 1¾ per cent. From Buffalo to New York the premium was generally about ¼ per cent. Premiums often increased another ¼ to ½ per cent after October, when rough weather on the

leans was the acute lack of storage facilities. As at St. Louis, the warehouses were a considerable distance from the wharves, and not nearly commodious enough to handle the vast quantities of northern and southern commodities passing through the port. Many shippers were reluctant to pay the drayage and storage costs for grain or flour destined for foreign or coastwise export, in which case the commodities were exposed to the damp climate or searing heat at New Orleans and to sudden changes in the weather. At best, the produce was covered by tarpaulins in the event of rain. A considerable quantity of flour was soured or otherwise injured by such exposure. Produce and provisions taken to the warehouses experienced rough handling. In 1847, for instance, it was reported that some 200,000 sacks of shelled corn were damaged between wharf and warehouse. As a result of deterioration, New Orleans flour often brought from 25 to 50 cents per barrel less at New York than similarly graded flour from the lakes.[51] The profits derived from the sale of flour were reduced by just the amount that anticipated risk, as reflected in insurance costs, or actual damage lowered the price of the product.

Conditions were aggravated if the market was slow, or if sufficient shipping was lacking. Great piles of merchandise and produce covered the wharves, and that part of the produce which had not been sold or consigned in advance had to be disposed of by individual bargaining, since there were no public warehouses or auction rooms,[52] and since the grain trade itself was of secondary importance compared with the commerce in the great southern staples. Flatboats caught in a sated market were often forced to lay over for considerable periods of time, and pay additional levee fees.[53]

---

lakes could be anticipated. At the most, then, the premium would reach 2½ per cent from Chicago to New York City. From Galena to New York via the Mississippi the premium was 6½ per cent, 4 per cent of which was charged against the voyage to New Orleans. Produce from Alton and Quincy was charged between 3 and 3¼ per cent to New Orleans. *Hunt's*, II (January, 1840), 78-80. Often insurance was not available, or only at prohibitively high rates, for flatboat shipments to New Orleans from the upper waters. *De Bow's Review*, III (February, 1847), 101.

[51] *Ibid.*, 103-104; Harold Sinclair, *The Port of New Orleans* (New York, 1942), 168-169.

[52] *Ibid.*

[53] *Hunt's*, II (May, 1840), 425-426. Flatboats, fully or partly laden, paid an initial fee of $10. Those with commodities for the local market were exempt from the levee dues, but after a stay of 12 days, fees were charged for any

New Orleans, as early as 1840, was losing part of the market in Illinois, Indiana, and Ohio, but this loss was concealed in the statistics of volume, because new markets replaced the old ones. Part of the loss resulted from the reluctance of shippers to face the obstacles and shortcomings inherent in the traffic with New Orleans. The new markets were oriented to New Orleans only so long as there existed no alternatives to the use of the river system for their transport. When alternatives became available, they soon began to swing away from New Orleans also. The commerce of New Orleans rested on tradition and on the city's strategic geographic location. As the 1850's were to show, these factors proved an inadequate defense against the encroachment of competing routes. Even though the grain and provisions trade reached new peaks both of volume and of dollar value from 1855 to 1861, the days of New Orleans as a great grain entrepot were numbered by 1860.

SUMMARY

The grain economy of the East North Central states began to experience, during the 1840's, the initial stages of what was in the subsequent decade to alter sharply the pattern of its trade. Even as early as 1840 and 1841, the first signs of an impending revolution were noticeable as Cleveland, through the agency of the Ohio Canal, dipped into the Ohio valley and diverted foodstuffs from the river to the lake route. Some three years later, a similar diversion occurred in the area of the upper Wabash, and, as the decade ended, Chicago and St. Louis were rivals for the grain trade of the Illinois valley. From the eastern border of Ohio to the Mississippi River, the lake and river routes were engaged in a strenuous competition for the grain trade of the Old Northwest.

The foodstuffs trade of the river experienced a steady growth during the 1840's, even though the customary areas of supply for the river trade were suffering from increasing encroachment by the lake ports. The river traffic was steadily losing out relative to lake traffic, but growth was possible, and the impact of this loss was

---

additional time spent at their assigned berth. Many flatboats tied up outside of the corporate limits of New Orleans to avoid paying these fees, and an additional one levied against those vessels broken up and sold within the incorporated limits of the port, but this more or less isolated them from the market and made it more difficult to dispose of their wares.

much reduced by the importance of the local market in the South. Corn was the staple crop of large areas in the more southern regions of the Northwest, and this crop, in its concentrated forms, was shipped in great quantities to the South for local consumption. The growth of this southern trade, and that of New Orleans, is a measure of the importance of this regional market.

Between the time when the rivers served to give the East North Central states an avenue to the outside world and the time when they lost out to the canals and railroads, there was an intermediate stage during which they continued to have importance in connecting parts of the Northwest with a vast regional market. This was at a time when domestic commerce was far more important than foreign trade anyway. And home demand was the real key to the river traffic of the last antebellum decade.

Aspects of the Foreign Trade in Grain

CHAPTER VIII

In the antebellum years, the foreign trade of the United States reflected in its composition the dominance which agriculture and industries dependent upon agriculture exercised upon the American economy. In only one year, 1855, did agricultural exports form less than 80 per cent of the total value of domestic exports. Although products of the farm and plantation were predominant in the foreign trade, this is not to say that foreign trade as a whole assumed a central position in the economic growth of the nation. Nor is it true that the foreign trade in grain and grain products, including provisions, formed a major part of total exports. At a later stage of our history, the export trade in foodstuffs became an important part of American exports and a major factor in the grain economy. In the 1890's exports of wheat and flour alone formed around 15 per cent of the total value of exports, compared to 5 per cent in both 1859 and 1860. Exports of wheat and flour averaged 1 bushel for every 2.75 produced in 1890-99, which offers dramatic contrast to exports of 1 bushel for every 10 produced in 1860.[1] Before the Civil War, the foreign grain trade was not a dominant element in either the American economy or in the economy of the East North Central states.

Between 1815 and 1860 the overseas trade did not grow at a steady rate. In the three years prior to 1818, the foreign trade displayed an activity not again matched until the 1830's. Domestic exports rose from $45.9 million in 1815 to $73.8 million three years later. Exports then dropped to $43.6 million in 1821 and dull times in foreign commerce continued for the next decade. Recovery came haltingly. The average annual value of exports in the five years 1826-30 was $54.7 million, 8 per cent less than the average from 1815 to 1820. Moderate but steady progress followed between 1831 and 1845. Exports exceeded $100 million in 1835 and then fluctuated between $90 and $100 million until 1847. In the latter year $150 million worth of goods went to foreign markets. Substantial progress followed between 1847 and 1860. Exports moved sharply upward to $213 million in 1854 and $316 million in 1860.[2]

Although one student of the foreign grain trade maintained that between 1835 and 1860 the activity of the trade was of considerable importance in colonizing the interior lowlands of the Great Lakes, this is assigning a significance to the trade which it did not merit.[3] For most of the antebellum period, grain formed but a small part of a small foreign trade. At no time after 1821 did the grain trade compose as much as 20 per cent of the total value of exports. Cotton and tobacco at no time made up less than 50 per cent of the trade. During the five-year period 1856-60, the total value of grain exports reached an annual average of $37 million, over three and a half times greater than the annual average from 1803 to 1807. Yet in the earlier period, exports of grain products

---

[1] Evans, "Exports, Domestic and Foreign," Table 5, 78-87, Table 7, 116; Isaac M. Rubinow, *Russian Wheat and Wheat Flour in European Markets* (Washington, D.C., 1908), 15.

[2] Evans, "Exports, Domestic and Foreign," Table 4, 75-76, Table 5, 78-87, Table 9, 207. During the 1820's the general foreign trade and the grain trade were substantially smaller than in the period 1795-1802.

[3] Herbert J. Wunderlich, "Foreign Grain Trade of the United States, 1835-1860," *The Iowa Journal of History and Politics*, XXXIII (January, 1935), 29.

equaled 23 per cent of total exports, compared to 13 per cent in
the later period.[4]

As to the components of the grain trade, wheat flour for the
entire period formed over 50 per cent of the value of shipments,
and in the years prior to 1850 flour made up well over 65 per cent
and bulk wheat contributed less than 10 per cent. After 1847 the
proportion of bulk wheat in the total value began to rise. By 1854
bulk wheat exports were equal to 31 per cent of the total value and
in 1861 the export value of bulk wheat exceeded that of flour. The
proportion of corn and corn meal to the total value of the overseas
grain trade fluctuated between 10 and 15 per cent from 1815 to
1860, except during the years of great foreign demand between
1845 and 1849, when the annual average value of corn exports
formed 29 per cent of total exports of breadstuffs.[5]

The foreign grain trade was unable to absorb more than a
small fraction of the grain which American farmers produced.
Throughout the entire period after 1820, the domestic market expanded at a more rapid and constant pace than the foreign.[6] A
rough measurement of the relative importance of the foreign and
domestic grain trade is possible if the ratio between total receipts

---

[4] Between 1856 and 1860 provisions exports added some $13 million
yearly to the foodstuffs trade. This was a marked increase from the period between 1820 and 1840, when exports were well under $5 million annually. Dur-
ing the five years before the war, when the value of provisions formed 5 per
cent of total exports, Cincinnati alone exported $10 million worth of meat prod-
ucts, and Chicago, in 1858, exported close to $7 million worth. United States
Treasury Department, *Commerce and Navigation. Annual Report. 1848* (Washington, D.C., 1848), 10-13, *AR, 1849,* 10-13, *AR, 1856-60; Seventh Annual
Review of the Trade and Commerce . . . of Chicago, 1858* (Chicago, 1859), 36.

[5] Evans, "Exports, Domestic and Foreign," Table 2, 20-23, Table 7, 113-
116. This was caused by two years in which corn exports were enormous: 16
million bushels of corn, plus corn meal, valued at $18.6 million in 1847, and
$9 million worth in 1849. Most of this went to England, and especially Ireland
during the famine years of 1847-48.

[6] The data available for measuring the foreign grain trade is considerably
more comprehensive concerning value, composition, volume, and destination,
than the data available concerning the domestic trade. It is known that large
quantities of breadstuffs were imported into New England, the South, and parts
of New York and Pennsylvania, but none of the shares can be precisely meas-
ured. In neither the foreign trade nor the domestic is it possible to tell how
much of the grain originated in the East North Central states. But one can say
with some certainty that the domestic trade in foodstuffs was much more important to the economy of the country and to the Northwest than was the foreign trade.

of wheat and flour at a specific number of markets and total wheat and flour exports is computed.[7] This is done in Table 16.

The relative stability evidenced during the years 1815-24 and the rather accentuated movement during the subsequent ten years

TABLE 16. BIENNIAL RATIO OF WHEAT AND FLOUR RECEIPTS AT VARIOUS MARKETS TO TOTAL WHEAT AND FLOUR EXPORTS, 1815-50

Years	Ratio	Years	Ratio
1815–16	1.5	1833–34	3.1
1817–18	1.0	1835–36	4.2
1819–20	1.7	1837–38	6.2
1821–22	1.8	1839–40	2.4
1823–24	1.8	1841–42	2.5
1825–26	2.4	1843–44	3.8
1827–28	2.6	1845–46	3.1
1829–30	2.5	1847–48	2.4
1831–32	2.3	1849–50	4.0

Sources: Evans, "Exports, Domestic and Foreign," Table 2, 23-32, Table 7, 115-116; M'Culloch, *Dictionary*, I, 686; Treasury Dept., *Statistics of Foreign and Domestic Commerce*, 179-180; 8 *Census, 1860, Agriculture*, clvi, cxlvi; *Hunt's*, VI (February, 1842), 183, XX (February, 1849), 215, XXI (November, 1849), 539, XXV (December, 1851), 732, XXXVIII (March, 1858), 340.

represents a contrast between a period with production areas remote from markets and the fairly sudden emergence of a new market in the South and the appearance of means of reaching markets in the Northeast. The initial growth in the domestic market, from 1824 to 1827, came as a result of increased receipts at New York City. Thereafter, general stability prevailed until New York receipts again rose steeply in 1833-34. The first increase represented the productive gains in western New York, and the latter represented the productive gains in Ohio, the fruits of which were reaching the Erie Canal in rising volume during the early 1830's.[8]

---

[7] The receipts-export ratio would be most meaningful if it could be derived from a series representing receipts with constant components between 1815 and 1860. But this was not possible. The ratio in Table 16 includes inspections at Philadelphia, New York, Baltimore, New Orleans, and the Richmond area from 1815 to 1838. From 1839 to 1850 the receipts used in deriving the ratio include those at Boston, Philadelphia, New Orleans, Baltimore, and, instead of inspections at New York, wheat and flour arriving at tidewater via the Erie Canal.

[8] Flour inspections at New York increased from 250,000 barrels in both 1820 and 1821 to over 500,000 in 1826, and over 640,000 in each of the three years 1827-29. Inspections surpassed 1 million barrels in 1833. In that year

The relative importance of the foreign grain trade was at its lowest ebb at the end of the 1830's.[9] Thereafter, foreign grain exports rose slowly during the early 1840's and rapidly during the peak years of foreign demand in the late 1840's. In the decade of the 1850's exports fluctuated radically, but the low points in the cycle were generally higher than certain peak years in preceding periods. But even with the obvious rise in the quantities of wheat and flour shipped overseas, the foreign grain trade did not progress as rapidly as the domestic.[10]

In expressing their concern over the obvious lack of overseas markets for American cereals, contemporaries noted that New England alone consumed about as much flour as was destined for overseas.[11] The problem of foreign markets did not cease to be less acute even after 1846 and the opening of the English market to the free movement of foreign grain, for then American grain was forced to compete with European and Middle Eastern cereals for the English trade. The foreign grain trade of the United States did not achieve a preferred position in the world market until many years after the Civil War. At best, America served as an auxiliary source

---

Buffalo received just over 500,000 bushels of wheat and flour from the Northwest, or about 10 per cent of New York's inspections. J. R. M'Culloch, *A Dictionary, Practical, Theoretical, and Historical, of Commerce and Commercial Navigation*, Henry Vethake, ed. (2 vols., Philadelphia, 1852), I, 686; *Hunt's*, XXIV (April, 1851), 451.

[9] The ratio, 6.2:1, for 1837-38 distorts the picture considerably since it represents a period in which universal crop failures in the United States compelled many seaboard ports to import foreign breadstuffs.

[10] The ratio of receipts to exports from 1856 to 1860 at New Orleans, Philadelphia, Richmond, Baltimore via the Baltimore and Ohio Railroad, and at various lake receiving centers was as follows:

Year	Ratio	Year	Ratio
1856	2.4	1859	3.7
1857	1.7	1860	4.2
1858	2.6		

[8] *Census, 1860, Agriculture*, clvi; *Hunt's*, XXXVIII (March, 1858), 349; United States Treasury Department, *Statistics of the Foreign and Domestic Commerce of the United States* (Washington, D.C., 1864), 177-178; *De Bow's Review*, XXV (October, 1858), 468; *Thirty-fourth Annual Report of the Baltimore & Ohio Railroad Company, 1860* (Baltimore, 1860), 102-105.

[11] If this assessment is correct, and there is no evidence to dispute it, the ratios given in Table 16 could have a factor of one added for each two-year period until 1839-40. For in those years the component markets are lacking a New England representative. *NWR*, XXXIII (November 3, 1827), 149; *Hunt's*, VI (February, 1842), 183.

of supply for the English, and it did not penetrate the European continent in strength until the late 1880's.[12]

A century before the economic triumph of the United States as a dominant force in the grain markets of the world, Tenche Coxe, writing in 1794, maintained that Great Britain and Europe would soon be dependent upon grain supplies from the American republic.[13] Although it was quite obvious throughout the antebellum period that Coxe's optimism was unfounded, contemporaries did not agree as to the reasons. Many observers blamed the slow growth of the trade on discriminatory tariffs levied against American produce by European nations. Before 1846 the English Corn Laws were singled out as a basic deterrent to the expansion of the foreign grain trade.[14] Others argued that the fundamental obstacle to growth lay not in tariff walls but in the nature of the markets, actual or potential, available to the United States.[15] The merits of this latter argument require further scrutiny.

The overseas area experiencing the most rapid growth in population and wealth was Western Europe. But this region had no need for American grain supplies. France and the Germanics were quite self-sufficient throughout the antebellum years. France was forced by reason of crop failures and the Crimean War to import large supplies of grain from 1853 to 1857. In the last two years of that period the United States exported a total of 8.9 million bushels of wheat and flour, valued at over $13 million, to France. This was considerably greater than the total volume or value exported to France in the entire period since 1800. Another part of the Euro-

---

[12] Wunderlich, "Foreign Grain Trade of the U.S.," 73-74, asserts that one significance of the grain trade "was the gradual recognition of our foreign grain trade, by Spain, France, and England as necessary to their food supply. This recognition had been established by 1865." But this is not so. Before the Civil War the United States, although important, was but a secondary source of supply for England, of but negligible importance to France, and of no consequence to Spain. Even in the 1890's American foodstuffs penetrated the French and Spanish markets but occasionally. By this time, however, the United States was the primary source of English cereal imports.

[13] Tenche Coxe, *A View of the United States of America, in a Series of Papers, Written at Various Times Between the Years 1787 and 1794* (Philadelphia, 1794), 146-147, 234-235.

[14] *NWR*, XXXV (November 22, 1828), 401; *Hunt's*, XII (May, 1845), 427; *The Ohio Cultivator*, I (September 15, 1846), 143.

[15] *Fisher's National Magazine and Industrial Record*, II (April, 1846), 1046; Ezra C. Seaman, *Essays on the Progress of Nations, in Civilization, Productive Industry, Wealth and Population* (New York, 1852).

pean market where American grain fared poorly was in Spain and Portugal. This market had been primary in Colonial days, but was lost when America left the British Empire. It suddenly reappeared in phenomenal size in 1812-13, and then as quickly evaporated.[16] Still another potentiality, it might be supposed, was Belgium and Holland, but any demand existing there did the United States little good, since the Baltic regions and Russia were capable of supplying the needs of these countries. Continental Europe was no market for American grain until well after the Civil War.[17]

England, however, did import an appreciable amount of American grain. It occupied this exceptional position because, of all the European nations, it alone was fairly consistently dependent upon outside sources for its food supply, and because, of all the markets with great potential, it was the only one to which the United States gained occasional entrance.[18] Consequently, the tariff policies of Great Britain took on a more intrinsic significance, from the viewpoint of the United States, than those of the European nations which could feed themselves.

The Corn Laws, which were of seventeenth-century origin, were devised to protect British producers against the competition of foreign cereals. As amended from 1822 until their repeal in 1846, they imposed upon foreign grain a sliding scale of duties which decreased as the price per quarter of grain in the English market rose.[19] Until 1846 this system was subjected to constant criticism

---

[16] *De Bow's Review*, XXI (October, 1856), 430-431; *Hunt's*, XLII (October, 1860), 404-405; Treasury Dept., *Commerce and Navigation, AR, 1856, 1857*, 20-23.

[17] During the late 1850's the United States found, for the first time, a limited and temporary market in these places. Belgium received $1.3 million in American breadstuffs in 1854, and in 1856 Belgium, Holland, and the Hanse Towns received cereals worth $2.6 million. In 1898-99 the United States shipped 17.9 and 18.3 million bushels of wheat to Belgium, just under 10 per cent of total exports, and about 40 per cent of Belgium's total imports. Treasury Dept., *Commerce and Navigation, AR, 1854, 1856*, 14-23; Rubinow, *Russian Wheat*, Table 27, 47.

[18] England became a rather consistent grain-importing country during the early 1760's.

[19] In the revision of 1822, foreign wheat was entirely excluded until the price reached 70 shillings. In 1828 a new act repealed those preceding and fixed a sliding scale of duties starting at 34s. when wheat was at 52s. and decreasing to 1s. when wheat reached 73s. a quarter. Subsequent amendments liberalized the duties, and in 1842 a maximum duty of 20s. was exacted when wheat dropped as low as 50s. per quarter. David G. Barnes, *A History of the English Corn Laws from 1660 to 1846* (New York, 1930), 139, 174, 200-201, 250-252.

in the United States. Many contemporaries, as well as modern students of the Anglo-American trade in grain, agreed with a correspondent writing to *The Ohio Cultivator* in 1846, upon the repeal of these laws, that "with the ports of Great Britain . . . now nominally free, we shall easily get rid of our surplus produce. . . ."[20] This viewpoint seems to be borne out if the extent of the British market for American foodstuffs in 1841-45 is compared with that between 1846 and 1850.

In the earlier period, exports of breadstuffs to England averaged $738,000 annually, and had not surpassed $1.2 million since 1820. Between 1846 and 1850 the figure rose phenomenally to $13.9 million. Grain exports to England composed more than 10 per cent of America's total domestic exports. American flour shipments to England skyrocketed from 35,000 barrels in 1845 to 969,000 in 1846, and 2.4 million the following year. Corn exports experienced an astounding growth, reaching 15.5 million bushels in 1847, while wheat exports to England rose from 2,000 bushels in 1845 to 2.5 million in 1847. During the single year 1847, fully 40 per cent of England's imports of wheat and flour originated in the United States.[21]

But although these changes coincided with the repeal of the Corn Laws, it does not follow that repeal was the causative factor in this sudden upsurge in American exports to England. The operative factors were the disastrous failure of the Irish potato crop, the short crop in England which raised the price of wheat to 105 shillings at one point, and the simultaneous failure of grain crops in Europe, particularly in France.[22] The stimulus to the trade was English extremity, not the repeal of the tariffs.

Moreover, the position of preponderance achieved by the

---

[20] *The Ohio Cultivator*, I (September 15, 1846), 143. Emory R. Johnson et al., *History of Domestic and Foreign Commerce of the United States* (2 vols., Washington, D.C., 1915), I, 231, stated that "the repeal of the English Corn Laws . . . gave a great stimulus to the cereal production and trade of the United States by opening a larger market for American grain." Wunderlich, "Foreign Grain Trade of the U.S.," 73-74, and Thomas P. Martin, "The Staff of Life in Diplomacy and Politics During the Early Eighteen Fifties," *Agricultural History*, XVIII (January, 1944), both agree. The latter argues that repeal enabled the United States to assume a position of equality with European producers.

[21] Evans, "Exports, Domestic and Foreign," Table 4, 75-76, Table 5, 78-80, Table 9, 207, Table 10, 215-218; Treasury Dept., *Commerce and Navigation, AR, 1821-60.*

[22] *Hunt's*, XXX (March, 1854), 363, XLIII (October, 1860), 404-405.

United States in the English market in 1847 was not maintained thereafter. While British imports from 1849 to 1852 surpassed the quantities purchased in 1847, the share devolving upon the United States dropped from 40 per cent in 1847 to 9 per cent in 1848, and remained between 11 and 17 per cent during the three years 1849-51.[23] England, after 1847, turned to her customary sources of food-stuffs in Europe—France, the Germanies, and Russia—and to a fairly new one developing in the Middle East, while America's share of this lucrative trade returned to its pre-famine position.

Now it is quite true that although the United States had failed to improve her status in the English corn trade relative to other grain-producing countries, the quantities shipped from America never returned to the lower levels of 1841-45, except in 1850 and 1855. It is also true that the total value of American exports of breadstuffs to England rose after 1846, increasing from an annual average for the five years 1846-50 of $13.9 million to $14.5 million for the five years 1856-60.[24] But simply because this progress occurred after the Corn Laws were repealed is no historical sanction for attributing to the latter event, as some tend to, an overwhelming causative role.

Rather, the higher levels were maintained, just as the initial peak in 1847 was reached, due to a succession of crises, man-made and natural, affecting England's sources of supply. War and crop failures resulted in a volume of wheat and flour exports from the United States in 1853 and 1854 forming 26 per cent of England's total imports. In 1856 American wheat and flour exports rose to the highest point attained before the Civil War. But by 1859 the American portion had declined to 20 per cent, just about where it had been a decade earlier.[25] With an increased English demand at a time when Britain's customary sources of supply had failed, or, because of war, were inaccessible, it would have been strange indeed if the Anglo-American trade in grain had not risen precipi-

---

[23] Total English imports of wheat and flour reached 35.7 million bushels in 1847. The United States supplied 14.6 million of this. In the three years 1849-51 England imported a total of 119.6 million bushels, of which only 16.3 million originated in the United States. *Ibid.*, XXXI (July, 1854), 106, XL (June, 1859), 728, XLI (December, 1859), 739; Seaman, *Essays on the Progress of Nations*, 222.

[24] Treasury Dept., *Commerce and Navigation, AR, 1846-60.* Between 1846 and 1860 the total value of breadstuffs exports to the United Kingdom remained fairly stationary.

[25] *Ibid., 1850-60; Hunt's*, XXXIII (October, 1855), 460-461, XXXV (December, 1856), 742, XLI (December, 1859), 739.

tately. In this light, the repeal of the Corn Laws becomes one of a series of interrelated events which combined to raise American exports to England in the 1850's to higher levels than in previous years. Of all the European markets, then, it was only in the English that the position of the United States improved appreciably. And even there it was by no means a strong position that had been attained, for America had not advanced relative to other competitors for the English trade.

There were a few markets where the United States was dominant and had been for some time. However, these markets—in the West Indian islands and South America—were not dynamic. They had either a static demand, such as the West Indies, or were soon, as in certain areas of South America, to be self-sufficient and often to become the active competitors of the United States in the world grain market. Furthermore, in most of these relatively nearby markets, the interest of the East North Central states was negligible, not only because the trade was small in absolute terms, but because it was handled by ports which received little or no western produce.

Between 1842 and 1858, Baltimore, Richmond, and Alexandria supplied some 70 per cent of the foodstuffs received by the West Indies from the United States.[26] New Orleans' exports were largely confined to Cuba, which received from 15 to 25 per cent of its foreign flour from the Mississippi River port before 1840, and often as great a proportion as 70 to 90 per cent between 1840 and 1850. But it was in the provisions trade with the West Indies, and particularly with Cuba, that New Orleans, and therefore the Old Northwest, had the greatest interest. Lard exports to Cuba increased from between $700,000 and $800,000 in the 1840's to as high as $2 million in 1858.[27] New Orleans was able to dominate

---

[26] *Ibid.*, VIII (April, 1843), 383, XIX (August, 1848), 196-199, XXXVIII (April, 1858), 423; *De Bow's Review*, XIV (May, 1853), 474; *Patent Report, 1848*, 777-780, *1850*, 541. It is possible that a portion of Baltimore's exports was of western origin after the Baltimore and Ohio Railroad touched the Ohio River in 1853. But by this time the West Indies were taking only about 10 per cent of the total export value of breadstuffs.

[27] Cuba was of greatest importance as a market for breadstuffs from 1821 to 1825, when some $700,000 worth arrived annually from the United States. Normally, Cuba received the great bulk of its flour and meal from Spain. In 1838-42 Cuba imported flour valued from $2.4 to $2.8 million annually, of which about 18 per cent originated in America. In this market, high tariffs discriminated against non-Spanish breadstuffs. *Hunt's*, XIII (October, 1845), 332; *De Bow's Review*, V (May, 1848), 460; Treasury Dept., *Commerce and Navigation, AR, 1821-60; The Daily Picayune* (New Orleans), November 5, 1850.

this trade by virtue of her large provisions traffic with centers of the pork industry in the Old Northwest.

The produce market in South America was of little value to the Northwest. During the 1840's and 1850's Richmond and Petersburg mills generally accounted for between 25 and 30 per cent of total Brazilian imports and above 40 per cent of total South American flour imports. The greatest part of the remainder was shipped by Baltimore. From 1845 to 1852 South America received between 35 and 45 per cent of its flour from Baltimore. The Richmond-Baltimore area, then, supplied over 80 per cent of South America's flour requirements and about 75 per cent of total Brazilian imports. Brazil was the largest market for American foodstuffs in the Western Hemisphere excepting the British North American colonies. In 1858 New Orleans was reported to have shipped some 70,000 barrels of flour to South American countries, which imported a total of 590,000 barrels from other American ports. This was of minimal importance not only to South America but also to New Orleans, the latter's exports exceeding 1 million barrels in 1858. During the period 1853-60, New Orleans exported more than 25 per cent of her total flour shipments to markets other than domestic, England, or Cuba only in 1854 and 1857. Thus, the quantities consigned to South America and the West Indies could not have been very substantial.[28]

The United States, then, was in an advantageous position only in those markets which experienced the least internal growth. In England, the largest importing nation in the world, the United States was an auxiliary source of supply. In 1847, when England's primary sources for foodstuffs had failed, the United States was still capable of supplying only some 40 per cent of the English requirement. This suggests that America's productive capacity fell far short of being able to supply the total English need. The foreign grain trade of the United States was of minor importance primarily because large and consistent markets were lacking. The foreign demand was so irregular, and the trade so precarious, that it was virtually impossible for producers to make a real adaptation to meet it.

[28] *Hunt's*, VIII (April, 1843), 383, XIX (August, 1848), 196-199, XX (January, 1849), 53, XXXI (November, 1854), 600, XXXVIII (April, 1858), 423, XLII (August, 1860), 231; *De Bow's Review*, XIV (May, 1853), 474, XIX (December, 1855), 702, XXV (November, 1858), 423, XXVIII (June, 1860), 720; *Patent Report, 1848*, 777-780, *1850*, 441; Treasury Dept., *Commerce and Navigation, AR, 1858*, 8-49, *1859*, 24-41, *1860*, 24-41.

Throughout the entire first quarter-century of the Federal Union's existence, the foreign grain trade fluctuated violently in response to the vicissitudes of the French revolutionary and Napoleonic wars. It was the policy of the belligerent powers to prohibit supplies of food from flowing to the colonial outposts of their opponents—located primarily in the West Indies. Markets appeared and disappeared according to the shifting fortunes of war, making the trade hazardous at all times. The over-all consequences of the war were probably deleterious to the grain trade, despite the transient gains made in supplying France and the French and Spanish West Indies during the 1790's, or the Iberian Peninsula from 1811 to 1813.[29] The trade with the Peninsula was a most striking illustration of the sudden emergence and sudden disappearance of a market.

In Colonial days the grain trade with Spain and Portugal had been quite large, although after independence it was only of irregular importance.[30] But during the period of the Peninsular Wars, 1811-13, with French and Allied armies contesting for the supremacy of the region, exports of American grain products rose at an astounding rate. Abnormally high prices and the complete dependence of both the British armies and the Peninsular population upon American grain supplies combined to raise the exports of flour to that area from some 80,000 barrels in 1808 to 192,000 in 1809, mostly to Portugal. The figure jumped to 835,000 in 1811, or

---

[29] From 1793 to 1796 France received a total of 2.2 million bushels of wheat and flour from the United States. This was some 300,000 bushels more than the total shipped to France for the subsequent 50 years. The wars forced both France and Spain to open their Caribbean ports to the produce of America. The French islands received as much as 320,000 barrels of flour in 1793 but this fell off to 39,000 in 1799. The Spanish islands took as much as 21 per cent of America's flour exports in 1799, but only about 10 per cent during the next 15 years. Evans, "Exports, Domestic and Foreign," Table 2, 22-23, Table 5, 78-80; *American State Papers: Documents, Legislative and Executive* (38 vols., Washington, D.C., 1832-61), *Commerce and Navigation*, I, 26-31, 113-123, 226-235, 304-308, 424-430; David Macpherson, *Annals of Commerce, Manufactures, Fisheries, and Navigation with Brief Notices of the Arts and Sciences Connected with Them* . . . (4 vols., London, 1805), IV, 216-217, 532-533; Timothy Pitkin, *A Statistical View of the Commerce of the United States of America* . . . (2nd ed., New York, 1817), Table 2, 149-150; Henri Sée, "Commerce Between France and the United States, 1783-1784," *American Historical Review*, XXXI (July, 1926), 735-736.

[30] The United States exported some 125,000 barrels of flour annually to Spain between 1790 and 1795, and in 1803-05. Only in 1802-03 did American flour reach Portugal in comparable volume—114,000 barrels and 148,000 barrels. *American State Papers. Commerce and Navigation*, I, 26-31; Pitkin, *A Statistical View*, Tables 1 and 2, 147-150.

57 per cent of America's flour exports, and 987,000 in 1813, or 78 per cent of flour shipments. During the next three years, trade with the Peninsula diminished rapidly—only a total of 320,000 barrels of flour were shipped to that destination—and then the trade vanished. The interest of the Northwest in this trade was minute. New Orleans, between 1811 and 1813, shipped only 66,000 barrels of flour to the Peninsula, out of a total American export of 2.7 million barrels.[31]

As noted previously, England made only intermittent use of America as a source of foodstuffs, but was of great significance in the total foreign trade of the United States.[32] But in years such as 1831 and again in 1840, a sizable market did open up in England for American grain. The earlier year fell about midway in a four-year cycle of poor English crops. From 1829 to 1832 Great Britain imported some 40 million bushels of wheat and flour. Of this total, the United States supplied 8 million bushels, or 20 per cent. In 1838-41 another period of deficient crops forced imports up from less than a million bushels annually between 1833 and 1836 to 14.7 million bushels of wheat and flour in 1838 and between 19 and 23 million bushels in each of the next three years. Of a total import during the five years 1838-42 of 100 million bushels of wheat and flour, only 6.7 million originated in the United States. Over 50 per cent of the American exports arrived in 1840, a year in which continental sources of supply experienced short crops.[33] But such market demand as this, and the even greater one caused by the Irish famine, could not be counted on by American producers. Before America could expect to supply great quantities of grain to Eng-

---

[31] *Ibid.; American State Papers. Commerce and Navigation*, I, 995. See W. Freeman Galpin, "The American Grain Trade to the Spanish Peninsula, 1810-1814," *American Historical Review*, XXVIII (October, 1922), 24-44, and "The Grain Trade of New Orleans, 1804-1814," *Mississippi Valley Historical Review*, XIV (March, 1928), 496-507.

[32] By the 1850's England was receiving between 60 and 65 per cent of total American exports. Total exports from the United States increased from a five-year annual average of $5.5 million in 1821-25 to an average of $278.2 million in 1856-60. During those five years England received an average of $173.5 million each year, compared to about $24 million yearly during the 1820's. Cotton was the number one item in this expanding trade. Evans, "Exports, Domestic and Foreign," Table 5, 78-80, Table 10, 215-218.

[33] *Hunt's*, XII (May, 1845), 427; M'Culloch, *Dictionary*, I, 477; Thomas Tooke, *A History of Prices and of the State of the Circulation, from 1793 to 1837* . . . (2 vols., London, 1838), II, 196-205; Seaman, *Essays on the Progress of Nations*, 290; Barnes, *English Corn Laws*, 219-220, 243; Treasury Dept., *Commerce and Navigation, AR, 1843-45*, 14-21.

land, not only had English crops to be poor, but European supplies had to be deficient as well. When American farmers prepared for these conditions and they did not eventuate, or increased production on the basis of temporary English demand, they often suffered losses and were thereafter reluctant to try to anticipate this market. Rumors of an English shortage in 1828 stimulated great activity in American ports, but the shortage did not develop as predicted. Numerous grain dealers took losses on shipments to England. "And so, we fear," one onlooker commented ruefully, "endeth this nine hundred and ninety-ninth British bubble, extending itself into the very interior of our country and injuring many innocent persons." [34]

Most of these shortages, prior to the Irish famine, did not have a strong impact on the East North Central states. But it appears that the English demand of 1840 did stimulate an augmented movement of grain from the Northwest along the lake route. Total receipts of wheat and flour at Buffalo and Oswego increased from 2.5 million bushels in 1839 to 5 million in 1840. Receipts of wheat and flour at Cleveland rose from 2.8 million bushels to 4.7 million during the same period.[35] And the great foreign demand of 1846-47 stimulated such productive increases in the Northwest that, as estimated previously, it was enabled to supply a minimum of 46 per cent of total American exports. Since the Northwest was the granary of the nation, there is reason to maintain that from 1847 to 1860 at least one-half of total foreign wheat and flour exports originated in the East North Central states.

Another crisis in England's grain supply occurred in 1854 and 1855, during the Crimean War, when England found itself fighting against one of its major grain suppliers. At the very beginning of this conflict in 1853, an American editor, in noting the connection between poor crops in England and France and the Russo-Turkish controversy, wrote: "Brighter prospects were never before held out to the agricultural world of America than at present. All the wheat and corn that the present crop can produce, is certain to find a ready market at greatly advanced prices." [36] These expectations were realized in 1853 and 1854 as total American exports of wheat and flour reached 18.4 million and 28 million bushels, over 50 per

---

[34] *NWR*, XXXV (November 22, 1828), 401.

[35] Treasury Dept., *Statistics of Foreign and Domestic Commerce*, 161, 179-180; *Hunt's*, V (September, 1841), 287, VIII (March, 1843), 276.

[36] *De Bow's Review*, XV (September, 1853), 309.

cent of which were consigned to England.[37] At the same time, while exports from Chicago more than doubled, increasing from 1 million bushels in 1852 to 2.8 million in 1854, and exports at Milwaukee increased by over 150 per cent, lake exports from the Northwest surged from some 16 million bushels in 1848-50 to between 20 and 22 million bushels of wheat and flour in 1852-53 and 24 and 25 million in 1855 and 1856. Exports from New York advanced from 3.8 million bushels of wheat and flour in 1850 to 10.8 million in 1854.[38] Considering the volume of northwestern wheat and flour moving over the lake, it is likely that much the larger part of New York's exports were of northwestern origin. And considering the fact that New York and New Orleans were dependent upon the Northwest for the bulk of their grain supplies, and that these ports, from 1852 to 1856, were responsible for 55 per cent of total American exports of wheat and flour, it is reasonable to assume that the Northwest, at a minimum, contributed 50 per cent of the total.[39]

In 1856 blight and rain cut the English crop short again at the very time when France, normally a supplier for Britain, was herself importing foodstuffs, and when less than good crops were being harvested in the Germanies for the second consecutive year. In that year a total of 16.8 million bushels of American wheat and flour were consigned to England. In 1857 and 1858, while English imports remained at high levels, exports from America were cut in half and halved again by 1860, when only 4 million bushels were directed to England.[40] The English market was not to be relied upon by American producers.

---

[37] Evans, "Exports, Domestic and Foreign," Table 7, 115-116; Treasury Dept., *Commerce and Navigation, AR, 1853-54*, 14-17.

[38] Chicago Board of Trade, *Nineteenth Annual Report of the Trade and Commerce of Chicago, 1876* (Chicago, 1877), 43; Milwaukee Chamber of Commerce, *Fifth Annual Report for the Year 1862* (Milwaukee, 1863), 20; Table 4 above; *Fourth Annual Report of the Chamber of Commerce of the State of New York for the Year 1861-1862* (New York, 1862), 326-328.

[39] Northwestern wheat and flour was also exported from Baltimore, Philadelphia, and Boston. The first two cities received from 2 to 3 million bushels of wheat and flour annually from Ohio River sources between 1853 and 1856. Boston received northwestern grain from both New Orleans and her railroad connection with the Erie Canal. Moreover, some quantities of American cereals were shipped via Canada.

[40] *Hunt's*, XL (June, 1859), 728, XLI (December, 1859), 739, LXIII (October, 1860), 404-405; Treasury Dept., *Commerce and Navigation, AR, 1856-60*.

The very irregularity of the market was sufficient to throw a port into a state of feverish and often impetuous activity whenever any chance bit of information was received hinting at English shortages. Although one contemporary argued that the foreign market had but little effect on wheat and flour prices,[41] most contemporary and modern students disagree.[42] At New Orleans, in 1840, flatboat owners were forced, according to reports, to reduce their prices due to the absence of a foreign demand.[43] News at Cincinnati of the great English scarcity in 1846-47 pushed flour prices up from $3.00 to over $5.00, while flour at New Orleans rose from about $5.00 in 1847 to a monthly average of $6.80 in the next year. At the time of the Crimean War, wheat could not be purchased at Chicago for less than $1.40 per bushel. Flour quotations at New York advanced from around $4.50 in 1852 and the first half of 1853 to $7.75 in January, 1854, and $9.87 in the following September. Flour prices at Baltimore and New Orleans also reacted sharply. Flour at Baltimore reached $8.75 in September, 1854, and the average monthly price at New Orleans in 1854 was $7.60. By 1858, with a diminished foreign demand, prices had declined at Baltimore and New York to less than $5.00 a barrel.[44]

It would appear, then, that a definite correlation existed between an increased foreign demand for American grain for any given year or years and the movement of cereals over the routes leading from the Northwest, and prices at grain entrepots both in the interior and on the seaboard. Prices rose swiftly with an active and expanding foreign market, and declined when a contraction came. A large foreign demand was also reflected in a greatly accelerated grain traffic over the lakes. During the Crimean War, ports from the western end of the lakes through Buffalo to tidewater reacted swiftly to the opportunities opening up in Europe. For the ports to respond with such large increases of grain exports

[41] Seaman, *Essays on the Progress of Nations*, 358.

[42] Wunderlich, "Foreign Grain Trade of the U.S.," 75, held that the foreign demand, fluctuating as it did from 1835 to 1860, raised the prices of American grain. Peter T. Dondlinger, *The Book of Wheat. An Economic History and Practical Manual of the Wheat Industry* (New York, 1908), and Ernest L. Bogart, *Economic History of American Agriculture* (New York, 1923), both see the world market as exerting a dominant influence on American prices.

[43] *The Daily Picayune*, January 12, 1840.

[44] "Report of the Secretary of Treasury, 1855," *House Executive Documents*, 34 Cong., 1 Sess., No. 10 (1856), Serial 846; *Hunt's*, XXVIII (February, 1854), 236, XXXVIII (January, 1858), 92, (February, 1858), 206, (April, 1858), 422, (June, 1858), 737-738.

depended ultimately upon an expanded production in the areas from which they obtained supplies.

Grain from the Northwest, destined for overseas shipment, generally traveled over the customary routes—by the lakes to Buffalo or Oswego and then to New York, or by river to New Orleans. But throughout most of the period after 1815, there was available to Americans along the Great Lakes an alternate and indirect route through Canada to the British Isles. At the same time, a foodstuffs market of growing importance developed in the Maritime Provinces. During the years after 1825, British North America was of consistently greater importance to the foreign grain trade of both the United States and the Northwest than the British West Indies or Brazil.[45]

Between 1815 and 1830, and to a lesser degree from 1831 to 1845, Canada was assigned a crucial role as England attempted to cause the transfer of the greater share of the carrying trade of American goods to English and colonial ports. As part of this attempt, an effort was made to establish, at various ports along the St. Lawrence River and in the Maritime Provinces, great entrepots receiving British manufactured goods for distribution to the United States and American produce for shipment to England and the West Indies.

Regulation of this trade was handled in two ways. By 1815 the inland, domestic trade was under the regulatory control of the provincial governments, while trade between American and Canadian seaports was within the cognizance of the government in London. The provincial governments actively sought American foodstuffs and other raw materials by allowing the importation of these goods duty free. As a result, American exports to British North America reached over $3.2 million in 1816, three times that of any prior year, and included 133,000 barrels of flour. In 1820 almost 200,000 barrels of American flour entered Canada and the Maritime Provinces.[46]

---

[45] In 1821-25 the annual average value of exports to the north was $405,-000, or 6.6 per cent of total grain exports, while in 1856-60 the average equaled 19 per cent of the total, and was valued at $7.1 annually. Provisions exports to the colonies reached $2 million in 1860. Treasury Dept., *Commerce and Navigation, AR, 1821-60.*

[46] Pitkin, *A Statistical View*, 297; Secretary of the Treasury, "The Amount and Description of Merchandise Exported to, and Imported from the British American Colonies," *House State Papers*, 19 Cong., 2 Sess., Document 144 (1826-27), Serial 155, 36-44.

Then British policy changed. The Canadian Trade Act of 1822 imposed duties upon American produce entering Canada which were stiffened in 1825. As a result, trade between Canada and the United States languished during most of the 1820's. The trade improved from 1826 to 1829 as foreign flour warehoused at Quebec was granted an imperial preference if shipped directly to the British West Indies. But the levels reached were still far below those of 1816-20.[47]

In 1831 there was a liberalization of the regulations governing the Canadian grain trade with the United States. American grain could again enter Canada duty free. Flour, as a manufactured product, was subject to a duty. If the grain was manufactured into flour in Canada, it would be transhipped to a British market, where it was treated as colonial flour and therefore was subjected to a much lower rate of duty than that imposed upon foreign produce. This act continued until 1842. In this way certain quantities of grain produced in the Northwest reached England during the 1830's. But as the Northwest was not engaged in a grain trade of very large dimensions over the lakes at this time, it is likely that the volume was quite small. Ohio reaped most of the benefit from the situation.

In the same year that the new regulations went into effect, the Welland Canal opened, but the trade displayed little improvement from 1830 to 1839. At no time during those years did it reach 200,-000 barrels of flour, and it surpassed 150,000 barrels only in 1830 and 1833, while plunging to as low as 23,000 and 29,000 barrels during the disastrous American crop years of 1837-38. At the same time, Canadian exports declined to under 250,000 bushels of wheat and flour.[48] This, for the most part, was a reflection of the meager market existing in England during those years.

---

[47] D. G. Creighton, *The Commercial Empire of the St. Lawrence, 1760-1850* (Toronto, 1937), 235-239. A. L. Kohlmeier, *The Old Northwest as the Keystone of the Arch of the American Federal Union. A Study in Commerce and Politics* (Bloomington, Ind., 1938), 8-9, maintains that this preference, plus an act which created some free ports in the British West Indies and Canada, stimulated the grain trade between the United States and Canada to the north and New Orleans and the British islands to the south. The trade to the north was of small dimensions and it is difficult to see any substantial progress before 1840. To the south, the grain trade at New Orleans was dormant from 1820 to 1827, and, although flour exports to the British West Indies increased from 37,000 barrels in 1822 to between 110,000 and 133,000 barrels from 1824 to 1826, it is likely that the Chesapeake Bay region furnished most of the supplies.

[48] "Papers Relating to Trade with the British Colonies," *Senate Docu-*

In 1841 it was reported that receipts at New York from the interior were lighter than in past seasons due to large quantities of western grain being diverted to Canada for shipment to England. Exports to Canada reached some 3.2 million bushels of wheat and flour in 1840, the first year in which bulk wheat shipments were of any significance.[49] Cleveland shipped an estimated 400,000 bushels of grain to Canada, and Rochester shipped 200,000. Grain traffic through the Welland Canal rose to 3.0 million and 2.6 million bushels of wheat and flour in 1840 and 1841, while Canadian exports climbed to above 2.3 million during the latter year.[50] This activity was largely a response to a greatly amplified English demand, which, though tapering off from 1843 to 1846, rose thereafter to still higher levels.

New tariff regulations in 1842 and 1843, which placed duties on American produce exported to Canada, abruptly curtailed this promising trade. Then, in 1846, the Corn Laws were repealed and colonial preferences abandoned. These acts prevented an increase in trade to Canada even when the British market was growing. Exports of flour to British North America fluctuated between 275,000 and 375,000 barrels from 1841 to 1849 while wheat never exceeded 1 million bushels and was normally below 600,000.[51] The advantages of shipping through Canada disappeared with the repeal of the Corn Laws.

The British North American market was most important to the United States when the foreign grain trade, in particular with England, was least important to the American economy. The cereal trade with British North America suffered further diminution from 1850 to 1853. In fact, between 1850 and 1853, greater quantities of wheat and flour were imported by the United States from Canada, in bond and for re-export to other markets, than vice versa.[52]

---

ments, 21 Cong., 2 Sess., Document 20 (1831), Serial 203, 28-32; H. A. Innis and A. R. M. Lower, eds., *Select Documents in Canadian Economic History, 1783-1885* (Toronto, 1933), 265-266; Treasury Dept., *Commerce and Navigation, AR, 1827-38.*

[49] *The Cultivator*, VIII (September, 1841), 152. Receipts arriving at tidewater via the Erie Canal declined from 12 million bushels of wheat and flour in 1840 to 10 million in 1841 and 9.8 million the next year. Treasury Dept., *Statistics of Foreign and Domestic Commerce*, 179-180; Treasury Dept., *Commerce and Navigation, AR, 1840*, 220-225.

[50] *NWR*, XL (May 8, 1841), 147; Hugh G. J. Aitken, *The Welland Canal Company. A Study in Canadian Enterprise* (Cambridge, Mass., 1954), 142; *Hunt's*, XIX (October, 1848), 422.

[51] Treasury Dept., *Commerce and Navigation, AR, 1841-49.*

[52] *Ibid., 1850-53.*

Before 1830 British North America produced barely enough foodstuffs for home needs. The Maritime Provinces never attained agricultural self-sufficiency and received most of their supplies from the United States even after Canada was producing a surplus for export. A good portion of the little that Canada did export originated in the United States, or was at least released for overseas shipment by importing American cereals for home consumption. Canada exported an aggregate of 9.9 million bushels of wheat and flour from 1841 to 1845, while the United States was exporting 10.2 million bushels to British North America, of which Canada received 6.3 million. Thus, fully two-thirds of Canadian exports were composed of or released by American grain. These shipments to Canada were equal to only 8.5 per cent of the total shipped over the Great Lakes by the Northwest. Although the volume of trade with Canada increased between 1855 and 1860, averaging 2.4 million bushels of wheat and flour annually, the movement of American exports down the St. Lawrence amounted to only about 10 per cent of that reaching tidewater over the Erie Canal.[53] The latter was less than the full amount reaching the eastern seaboard of the United States, for considerable quantities of flour were using rail rather than canal transportation.

There were several reasons why Canada failed to divert a large portion of the lake grain trade from American grain centers, despite some apparent advantages enjoyed by Canadian markets. Of the advantages, the most important was the generally favorable freight differential offered by the Welland Canal route, enabling western produce to be carried to tidewater via the St. Lawrence more cheaply than by any competing route. However, this advantage was negated by many other considerations. For one, freight from New York to Liverpool was cheaper than from Quebec because New York, due to its large imports, had considerably more shipping at its disposal than Quebec. Moreover, lake vessels preferred the New York route because return freights were more certain at Buffalo or Oswego than at Montreal or Quebec.[54] Nor could the Canadian

---

[53] Innis and Lower, *Documents in Canadian History*, 266; *Fisher's National Magazine*, II (April, 1846), 1046; Table 4 above; Treasury Dept., *Statistics of Foreign and Domestic Commerce*, 101; Treasury Dept., *Commerce and Navigation, AR, 1841-60*.

[54] In 1856 it was estimated that freight per barrel from Chicago to Quebec was some 20 to 40 cents cheaper than from Chicago to New York via Oswego. From Chicago to Liverpool via New York flour cost an estimated $1.05 per barrel and 30 cents more via Quebec. *Hunt's*, XXXV (August, 1856), 158-159.

cities match the financial facilities available at Buffalo or Oswego, backed as they were by New York's financial resources and often by English houses as well.[55] Harmful as these factors were to the Canadian grain trade, Canada would have labored under a tremendous disadvantage even had they been equalized, for they were really not the operative causes of her inferiority. The real difference lay in the fact that the great foodstuffs market was located in the northeastern part of the United States, where substantially more was consumed than exported. Compared to that market, the supplies required by the Maritime Provinces were paltry indeed.

For the regions of the East North Central states using the lakes, the route through Canada was only of minor importance compared with the Erie Canal or the railroads paralleling the canal. And for large areas of the Northwest, Canada was of no importance at all. For the most part, the cereal surplus of these states entering the foreign trade was shipped from New York or New Orleans. In the year ending September, 1861, the United States exported 2.5 million barrels of flour and 25.5 million bushels of wheat to Great Britain. Of this enormous export, New York shipped 68 per cent of the flour and 80 per cent of the wheat. Out of 11.7 million bushels of corn consigned to England, New York supplied 8.6 million. The bulk of this originated in the Northwest. New Orleans exported 1.4 million bushels of corn but only insignificant quantities of wheat and flour.[56] For New Orleans this represented a sharp decline.

As Table 17 points out, the foreign grain trade of New Orleans was generally much less important than the grain trade with domestic markets along the Atlantic and Gulf coasts. Only in the years which brought a greatly enhanced English demand did the foreign trade at New Orleans assume great significance relative to the domestic trade. In 1841, 1846, and 1847, the English demand was reflected there by increased shipments to foreign ports.[57]

---

[55] Treasury Dept., *Statistics of Foreign and Domestic Commerce*, 102, quoting from the Canadian Ministry of Finance, *Trade and Navigation Report, 1862*. This report argued that the chief cause of Canada's failure to divert more American grain from the East was the absence of sufficient competition among forwarders engaged in the St. Lawrence trade and in the financial and shipping strength of New York.

[56] New York Chamber of Commerce, *4 AR, 1861-62*, 326; Switzler, "Report on Internal Commerce," 382. Chicago, Milwaukee, and Detroit were also engaged in the direct shipment of wheat and flour overseas, but the quantities, though growing, were still relatively small.

[57] In 1841, out of a total export of 311,000 barrels of flour, 184,200 went

During the 1850's, and most noticeably after 1853, the British market became of less importance to New Orleans than the flour market at other foreign ports. Exports of flour rose from 1851 to 1858. That portion destined for non-British foreign ports rose at

TABLE 17. NEW ORLEANS TOTAL ANNUAL FLOUR EXPORTS, TOTAL FLOUR EXPORTS TO FOREIGN PORTS (NOT INCLUDING GREAT BRITAIN), AND TOTAL FLOUR EXPORTS TO GREAT BRITAIN, 1851-60 (IN THOUSANDS OF BARRELS)

Year	Total Flour Exports	Total Flour Exports to Foreign Ports	Total Flour Exports to Great Britain
1851	583	59	206
1852	545	70	139
1853	520	71	180
1854	586	237	190
1855	346	60	27
1856	729	189	100
1857	905	308	73
1858	1,053	222	268
1859	606	112	0
1860	387	80	6

Sources: *De Bow's Review*, XI (December, 1851), 643-644, XIII (November, 1852), 511, XV (November, 1853), 527, XVII (December, 1854), 623, XXI (November, 1856), 513, XXIII (October, 1857), 374, XXV (November, 1858), 566, XXVII (October, 1859), 479, XXIX (December, 1860), 663; *Hunt's*, XXXIII (November, 1855), 604.

the same rate, while exports to British ports, except in 1858, actually declined.[58] By 1860 total exports at New Orleans going to non-British ports had dropped rapidly, while exports to England were insignificant. The decline is all the more striking if it is noted that receipts of flour at New Orleans were around 1 million barrels in 1859 and 1860.

The sudden reversal in the upward trend of total grain exports can be explained in part by the decline in shipments to New York, Boston, and Philadelphia from New Orleans. All three of these cities

to foreign ports, primarily England. The following year New Orleans exported close to 300,000 barrels, while the quantity consigned to foreign ports stood below 100,000. This proportion held true until 1846 and 1847, when another great English need raised foreign shipments to 49 per cent and 80 per cent of total flour exports. *NWR*, LXV (October 7, 1843), 88; *De Bow's Review*, VI (December, 1848), 437-438.

[58] Britain continued to be the major market for exports of corn from New Orleans until 1857 and 1858, when shipments fell off considerably. Pork exports also diminished.

were receiving increasing quantities of grain supplies directly from
production centers in the West, while those supplies reaching New
Orleans seem to have been destined largely for the southern market. But there seems to be no satisfactory explanation for the sudden disappearance of the trade in grain with Great Britain, particularly at a time when shipments of cotton from New Orleans were
flourishing and a relatively active grain trade with England existed.
In 1860, while New Orleans shipped 86,000 barrels of flour overseas, New York exported 1.1 million barrels and 1.8 million bushels
of wheat, and this was a comparatively lean year in New York's
grain trade.[59]

New York, after the late 1820's, was the largest grain-exporting
center in the United States. During the 1830's and early 1840's, the
overseas grain trade at New York, like that of the nation as a whole,
experienced little if any growth. In 1830 and 1831 New York exported less than 400,000 barrels of flour. In 1845 exports of 469,000
barrels of flour and 305,000 bushels of wheat represented 40 per
cent of total American wheat and flour exports. That the domestic
market was growing much more rapidly is indicated by the fact
that flour inspections rose from 650,000 barrels in 1827 to more than
1 million in 1838. Then, in 1846, flour exports shot up to 1.1 million
barrels, and to twice that amount in the following year, while wheat
shipments in 1847 were ten times those of 1845, and corn exports
reached 6.9 million bushels.[60]

Most of this grain, as well as that leaving New Orleans, was
of northwestern production. For the two years 1846-47 New York's
wheat and flour exports were equal to 52 per cent of total American
exports, while New Orleans furnished 24 per cent of the wheat and
flour and 48 per cent of the corn exports, which had attained 18
million bushels. For all grains, New York and New Orleans supplied 68 per cent of total exports.[61] Table 18 records the percentage
share of the grain trade held by New York and New Orleans and
other ports during the 1850's.[62]

---

[59] Treasury Dept., *Commerce and Navigation, AR, 1860,* 348-349.

[60] M'Culloch, *Dictionary,* I, 686; *Hunt's,* XII (February, 1845), 186-187,
XV (July, 1846), 89, XLIII (November, 1860), 613; *Patent Report, 1845,* 371-
373.

[61] *Hunt's,* XLIII (November, 1860), 613; *De Bow's Review,* VI (December, 1848), 437-438; Evans, "Exports, Domestic and Foreign," Table 2, 20-23.
Most of New York's corn came from New Jersey and New York, although some
came from New Orleans.

[62] In certain years, 1852, 1853, 1856, and 1860, the percentage totals in

Table 18 shows the degree to which New York dominated the grain trade during the 1850's. The table also attests to the slow but steady diminution of the foreign trade at New Orleans. Also it points to the growing importance of direct overseas shipments of

TABLE 18. ANNUAL PERCENTAGE OF TOTAL U.S. EXPORTS OF WHEAT AND FLOUR SHIPPED FROM SELECTED CITIES, 1851-60

Year	New York	New Orleans	Balti-more	Rich-mond	Phila-delphia	Boston	Chicago Detroit Milwaukee
1851	27	11	17	–	14	6	–
1852	51	6	18	12	10	8	–
1853	49	7	16	13	12	10	–
1854	40	8	10	8	12	3	–
1855	37	6	–	–	–	–	–
1856	70	5	12	9	5	3	2
1857	45	6	7	7	7	2	5
1858	50	12	9	6	5	4	9
1859	41	4	12	8	7	6	13
1860	70	3	11	7	5	7	10

Sources: Table 17 above; New York Chamber of Commerce, *4 AR, 1861-62,* 326-328; Evans, "Exports, Domestic and Foreign," Table 2, 20-23; *De Bow's Review,* XIV (May, 1853), 474, XXV (October, 1858), 468, XXVIII (May, 1860), 332; *Hunt's,* XXV (December, 1851), 732, XXVIII (March, 1858), 349, (April, 1858), 423; Treasury Dept., *Commerce and Navigation, AR, 1854-60*; Charles B. Kuhlman, *The Development of the Flour-Milling Industry in the United States with Special Reference to the Industry in Minneapolis* (Boston and New York, 1929), 66.

wheat and flour from the center of production itself, the Old Northwest, which can be considered as a rough index of the expansion of trade, commerce, and agricultural production occurring in the East North Central states during the 1850's.

In 1860 total exports of wheat and flour were above 17 million bushels, while the crop in the Northwest in 1859 was just short of 80 million bushels of wheat. Of this total production, some 40 million bushels passed over the Erie Canal to tidewater; another 14 million arrived at eastern receiving centers other than Buffalo or Oswego; and almost 4 million bushels reached Baltimore and Philadelphia via rail. In addition to this, some 5 million bushels passed down the Mississippi to New Orleans, although very little of this reached foreign markets and a part of the receipts were from areas

Table 18 are in excess of 100 per cent. This is because some of New York's and Boston's flour originated at New Orleans, while New York shipped flour to Boston and received some from Richmond, as did Philadelphia.

other than the Northwest.[63] Thus, approximately 60 million bushels of northwestern wheat, or over three times more than total exports, found their way to various parts of the East and South. New York, New Orleans, Chicago, Detroit, and Milwaukee shipped 83 per cent of total exports in 1860. On the basis of this and the enormous volume of northwestern grain moved in 1860, it would seem reasonable to assert that the East North Central states, in 1860, supplied 80 per cent of the total foreign exports of wheat and flour. This would be the equivalent of about 15 per cent of the total crop produced in 1859. Thus, by 1860, while the stake of the Northwest in the domestic market was paramount, the interest in the foreign market was not inconsiderable.

In absolute terms the advance of the overseas grain trade was obvious. Exports of wheat and flour, estimated at 3 million bushels in 1770, reached 17 million in 1860, and had been as high as 33 million in 1857. But considering that 90 years had elapsed, this advance does not appear particularly noteworthy. In 1770 grain exports composed 20 per cent of total American exports, while between 1820 and 1860 the proportion was as high as 19 per cent only between 1846 and 1850, and was only 13 per cent during the 1850's.

The market situation for the United States had not undergone a marked improvement since 1790. America was at best an auxiliary source of supply for the markets with the greatest growth potential. In terms of volume, the United States was able to sell larger quantities of grain in England after 1846 than it had previously. But the United States supplied about the same proportion of Britain's grain imports in the 1850's that it had in the 1790's. And the English market was extremely precarious and subject to dangerous fluctuations.

To the East North Central states, the foreign market was of slight value until the late 1840's. Even after 1846 this market did not grow as rapidly as the domestic, compared to which it was of secondary importance, although greater quantities of grain were reaching foreign consumers, and even though the Northwest was supplying considerably more than one-half of total American exports of cereals. The foreign trade in grain was not a major factor, during the antebellum years, in the economies of either the United States or the East North Central states.

---

[63] Evans, "Exports, Domestic and Foreign," Table 7, 116; *8 Census, 1860, Agriculture,* clvi, 184-185; Treasury Dept., *Statistics of Foreign and Domestic Commerce,* 177-178; Baltimore & Ohio Railroad, *34 AR, 1860,* 102-105.

The Distribution of the
Grain Culture in the Northwest
During the Fifties

CHAPTER IX

Before proceeding with a discussion of the grain trade during the last antebellum decade and to place in perspective the general development of the grain culture in the Old Northwest, it seems advisable to examine the volume and the distribution of wheat and corn at the beginning of the decade of the 1850's and again at the end, both for the region as a whole and for the states as separate units.

Wheat production had made notable strides in the East North Central states by 1859, in which year a crop of 173 million bushels was equal to 46 per cent of total production in the United States. This compared with a contribution of 37 per cent in 1849 and 31 per cent in 1839. During each of the census periods, the Northwest produced significantly more wheat per capita than any other section, the figure reaching 11.5 in 1860, while for the United States as a whole it was 5.5.[1] This fact prompted the *Cincinnati Railroad Record* to note that, without the Northwest, the United States would have no surplus of grain, and to conclude that "the feeding power, therefore, is in the Northwest."[2]

While the Northwest, as a section, expanded its production of wheat more rapidly than the remainder of the United States, and more rapidly than population increased within the five-state area, the relative contribution from each state to total sectional production underwent a significant change during the antebellum years.

The most conspicuous trend outlined in Table 19 is the con-

TABLE 19. PERCENTAGE OF WHEAT PRODUCTION, BY STATE, TO TOTAL PRODUCTION OF WHEAT IN THE EAST NORTH CENTRAL STATES, 1820-59

State	1820	1830	1839	1849	1859
Ohio	78	70	63	36	19
Indiana	13	20	15	16	21
Illinois	8	9	13	24	30
Michigan	–	1	8	12	10
Wisconsin	–	–	–	10	20

Sources: See Table 2.

sistent and rapid decline in the relative importance of Ohio's wheat production to total regional production after 1839. The decennial figures, in fact, may exaggerate the full extent of the decline in Ohio, for production in the initial year of this comparison, 1849, was less than in 1847 or 1851, as shown by exports, which exceeded production in 1849. The fluctuations throughout the decade of the 1850's carried production from as high as 25 million bushels in 1851 and 1857 to as low as 12 million in 1854 and 15 million in 1859.[3] In spite of the large differences in individual yearly wheat crops,

---

[1] Individually, the five East North Central states did not, in any of the census periods from 1839 to 1859, rank one through five in wheat per capita. In 1839 Virginia, Pennsylvania, and Maryland followed Ohio and Michigan and preceded Illinois and Wisconsin Territory. In 1849 Iowa, Virginia, and Maryland produced more wheat per capita than Ohio or Indiana. Ten years later Oregon and California produced more wheat per capita than all the northwestern states save Wisconsin. Minnesota and Iowa had a greater ratio than Indiana, Michigan, or Ohio; and Maryland, Virginia, and Delaware were ranked before Ohio, the latter in twelfth position in the wheat per capita ranking.

[2] *Cincinnati Railroad Record* (n.d.) quoted in *Hunt's*, XXIX (December, 1853), 770.

[3] The acreage planted in wheat was estimated at 1.7 million acres in 1851 and 1.8 million in 1859, and had dropped as low as 1.4 million in 1854. Corn production oscillated quite violently too. In 1849 some 60 million bushels were produced, and in 1860 91.5 million. But production declined to as low as 50

the fact that wheat acreage remained between 1.6 and 1.8 million acres during the decade indicates a certain degree of stability, or at least a cessation of rapid growth in wheat production.

Contemporaries blamed the generally poor wheat crops in Ohio on various factors, some working together against the farmer in certain years, and cumulatively causing a harmful decline in the yield of wheat per acre during the decade.[4] One authority asserted that the principal reason for declining yields was the existence of farms too large for the amount of labor available and therefore worked improperly and haphazardly. This source considered a farm excessive in size if over 320 acres.[5] For the most part, poor crops seem to have been due to several harsh winters causing considerable winter kill, to the destructive activities of insects which ruined entire crops in some areas, and to drought. In 1859 wheat crops were severely damaged by June frosts in many areas of central and southern Ohio. The corn crop also suffered from frost in 1859, and, despite the fact that much new land had been sown with corn, the yield in that year was only 28 bushels of corn per acre, while in a good year like 1853 the yield per acre reached 40.[6]

While wheat did poorly and corn did but moderately well dur-

---

million bushels in 1858. During the entire decade, 1848-59, the acreage given over to corn, in contrast to wheat, rose steadily from 1.5 million acres in 1850 to 2.4 million in 1859. Poor corn crops during the decade were the result of poor yields to a greater extent than was the case for wheat, although poor wheat yields were quite evident in 1854 and 1859. Ohio Commissioner of Statistics, *Third Annual Report to the Governor, 1859* (Columbus, 1860), 17; Ohio Secretary of State, *Annual Report to the Governor for the Year, 1871* (Columbus, 1872), 131.

[4] The yield per acre for wheat was:

Year	Yield	Year	Yield
1850	17.3	1858	10.3
1851	15.2	1859	7.5
1854	8.0	1860	12.7
1856	10.0	1861	10.3
1857	14.0		

Ibid.; Ohio Commissioner of Statistics, *3 AR, 1859*, 17.

[5] Ohio State Board of Agriculture, *Fourteenth Annual Report, 1859* (Columbus, 1859), 563. This is a rather dubious explanation if unqualified. In 1860, of 179,889 farms in Ohio, 29 per cent were from 20 to 49 acres, and 36 per cent from 50 to 99 acres, or 65 per cent between 20 and 99 acres. Another 23 per cent fell into the 100- to 499-acre category, most of these being under 400 acres. Ohio Secretary of State, *AR, 1871*, 328-329. The assertion that many farms were worked in a slovenly manner had a good empirical basis, but a farm of 50 acres was as susceptible to mismanagement as one of 320 acres.

[6] *Patent Report, 1855,* 195, *1861,* 265-266; Ohio Commissioner of Statistics, *3 AR, 1859,* 97-99; Ohio Secretary of State, *AR, 1871,* 135; W. A. Lloyd,

ing the decade, the production of other grains, particularly oats, increased; the number of hogs and cattle increased; and dairying became more important, especially in the Western Reserve and Scioto valley.[7] Farming made progress during the decade even though wheat raising appears to have advanced but slightly, if at all. But the rate of advance had slowed down. Between 1840 and 1850 an estimated 7 million acres were added to the amount of land in farms; during the following decade the amount of new land added was under 3 million. By 1849 the proportion of land in farms to the total land surface of Ohio was 69 per cent; a decade later, 81 per cent; and in 1880, 94 per cent.[8] The striking gains in productivity were being made in states to the west of Ohio.

In 1849 the wheat belt of Ohio lay generally in the north central part of the state, particularly in the middle and upper Muskingum valley, but by 1858-59 the distribution of wheat culture was spread more evenly throughout the state, except in the Western Reserve district of Ohio, which produced only 7.4 per cent of the crop in 1858, with 15 per cent of the population. The rather even spread of wheat production in 1858 is noted below in terms of the percentage of the population and the percentage of the state crop produced in a defined geographical area.[9]

	Per cent wheat	Per cent corn	Per cent population
Muskingum valley	24.1	21.4	19.4
Scioto valley	15.0	24.7	13.2
Miami valley	26.0	23.9	24.6
Maumee valley	14.8	8.8	12.6

J. I. Falconer, and C. E. Thorne, *The Agriculture of Ohio* (Wooster, Ohio, 1918), 131-132. Of the 2.7 million acres of new land brought into cultivation between 1849 and 1850, about 900,000 acres were devoted to corn, and about 100,000 occasionally devoted to wheat. Much of the older wheatland was converted into meadow and pasture rather than cornfields and some of the newer lands went for grazing also. The number of livestock in Ohio advanced from 3.3 million head in both 1839 and 1849 to 3.8 million in 1859. The gain was evenly divided between hogs and cattle. Ohio State Board of Agriculture, *12 AR, 1857*, 61.

[7] *Ibid.*; *14 AR, 1859*, 221-222. Lloyd, Falconer, and Thorne, *Agriculture of Ohio*, 140-143, note that the average value of land in farms for all Ohio rose from $19.23 per acre in 1850 to $33.12 in 1860.

[8] *NWR*, LX (May 15, 1841), 172; Ohio Secretary of State, *AR, 1871*, 330-331; *10 Census, 1880, Agriculture*, III, xi. There was proportionately less land improved in Ohio during the 1850's than in the other East North Central states.

[9] The Western Reserve was reported importing wheat in 1858. Ohio State

The Miami valley counties produced 350,000 more bushels than the Muskingum valley on less acreage. Most of the increase in the Miami valley resulted from the growth of wheat production in the northern counties, continuing a trend which had its beginnings during the 1840's. Production in the Muskingum valley declined from 33 and 31 per cent of the state's wheat in 1839 and 1849 to 24 per cent in 1859. The contribution of the Miami valley continued to rise—from 17.9 per cent in 1839 to 19.8 per cent in 1849 and 26 per cent in 1858.[10]

At the same time the Miami valley's share of the corn crop decreased, between 1849 and 1858, although total production in the valley increased. Meanwhile the proportion of corn raised in the Muskingum valley rose, thus distributing corn production throughout the state, since the percentage grown in the other sections remained quite stable over the nine years.[11]

In Indiana there was no question as to the growth in both wheat and corn production between 1849 and 1859. In spite of alternating years of drought beginning in 1854, wheat and corn crops reached 16.8 and 71.5 million bushels respectively in 1859. This was an increase of 171 per cent over the wheat crop of 1849 and of 54 per cent for corn. Considerable quantities of Indiana's wheat were reported moving over the Pittsburgh, Fort Wayne, and Chicago Railroad in 1859-60, to supply deficiencies in Ohio.[12]

As noted in a previous chapter, the wheat and corn crops of Indiana were not specialized along very sharply delineated geographical lines. There was no overriding commitment by an area within the state to a single crop as was developing in parts of Illinois, or as had been the case in Ohio during the 1830's and 1840's. Both corn and wheat were more or less evenly distributed throughout the state in 1849, with the north producing slightly more wheat and the south more corn. By 1859 corn had moved into some of the

Board of Agriculture, *14 AR, 1859*, 557; Ohio Commissioner of Statistics, *3 AR, 1859*, 111-113. The Muskingum valley produced 35 per cent of the rye, oats, and barley grown in Ohio in 1858.

[10] The Scioto valley increased its share of the crop from 6.7 per cent in 1849 to 15 per cent in 1858, while the Maumee's share rose slightly from 12 to 14.8 per cent, and that of the Western Reserve declined from 11 per cent to 7.4 in 1858. *Ibid.*

[11] Ohio Commissioner of Statistics, *3 AR, 1859*, 111-113.

[12] *7 Census, 1850*, 755-756; *8 Census, 1860, Agriculture*, 38-43; *Patent Report, 1861*, 269; *Hunt's*, XLII (June, 1860), 700.

northern counties while wheat moved south, so that the spread of both crops became even more uniform.[13]

Of all the East North Central states, none displayed more substantial development during the 1850's than Illinois. The wheat crop grew by 147 per cent between 1849, with the crop at 9 million bushels, and 1859, when the crop was reported at 23.8 million. Illinois was the leading wheat state in the nation, and, with the corn crop estimated at 115 million bushels in 1859, the foremost corn state as well.[14]

The amount of land in farms increased from 12 million acres in 1848, or 35 per cent of the total land surface in Illinois, to 20.9 million acres in 1860, or 59 per cent of the land surface. An even greater gain was made in improved acreage, which increased from 5 million acres in 1850 to 13 million acres ten years later, while 67,-000 new farms were opened up during the period.[15] The total farm acreage of each county was consistently much larger, frequently as much as three to five times, at the end of the 1850's. Much of this growth was directly attributable to the impact of the Illinois Central Railroad. Along the whole extent of country crossed by the road, numerous towns came into existence. One contemporary compiled a list of 57 towns lying along the route of the Illinois Central, of which 35 were not in existence in 1850 and the population of which increased from 8,000 in 1850 to 40,600 in 1856.[16]

At the beginning of the decade, some thought was given to

---

[13] The breakdown by size of Indiana's farms was quite similar to that in Ohio. In the former, 37 per cent were from 20 to 49 acres, compared to 29 per cent in Ohio, and 30 per cent were between 50 and 99 acres, compared to 36 per cent in Ohio. Ohio Secretary of State, *AR, 1871,* 328-329.

[14] 7 *Census, 1850,* 730-731; 8 *Census, 1860, Agriculture,* xxix. An even larger corn crop, approaching 139 million bushels, was reported in 1855. Frederick Gerhard, *Illinois as It Is; Its History, Geography, Statistics, Agriculture* (Chicago, 1857), 390. Illinois produced 13.8 bushels of wheat per capita in 1859 and was surpassed only by Wisconsin's 20 bushels per capita. For Illinois the 1859 figure represented an advance from 11 bushels per capita in 1849.

[15] Ohio Secretary of State, *AR, 1871,* 328-331.

[16] Gerhard, *Illinois as It Is,* 417. For a detailed account of the impact of the Illinois Central, see Paul W. Gates, *The Illinois Central Railroad and Its Colonization Work* (Cambridge, Mass., 1934). In spite of the great improvement the new railroad effected in east central Illinois, the area developed slowly during the 1850's. Much of the land remained too distant from the Illinois Central or the east-west lines which intersected it. The drainage problem proved especially serious. In some counties as much as 80 per cent of the land required tiling and ditching before it could be farmed intensively. *Ibid.,* 239; Margaret B. Bogue, *Patterns From the Sod. Land Use and Tenure in the Grand Prairie, 1850-1900* (Springfield, Ill., 1959), 13-17.

the disadvantages of extensive wheat cultivation in Illinois. In the southern areas of the state, especially along the eastern border, the corn crop expanded at a much faster pace than wheat. Even in the northern wheat belt second thoughts about the heavy commitment to wheat were not lacking. One writer asserted that "husbandry, in northern Illinois, is now in a state of active transition, from the Old hundred-acre wheat fields, to moderate stock and dairy farms, and a variety of products for market instead of the *one,* which seventeen years experience has shown to be the most uncertain, and—except occasionally (and then from accidental causes)—the least profitable of all standard crops in northern Illinois." [17] But in the early 1850's the position of wheat suddenly improved. There was a series of good wheat crops, coupled with the rapid extension of railroad facilities throughout the state, and then, in 1853-55, the heavy foreign demand caused by the Crimean War sent wheat prices to unprecedented heights.[18] There followed a period of partial or total crop failures in both wheat and corn caused by heavy spring rains and June frosts aggravated by insect ravages. Even in 1859, with the wheat crop at 23 million bushels, barely 10 bushels per acre were produced, and in the following year the land devoted to wheat declined by 300,000 acres. A reassessment of the crop situation was again in order, and this time a reduction of wheat production in northern Illinois did follow, lasting through the 1860's and into the 1870's.[19]

In other sections of the state, however, wheat production increased after 1850, most strikingly in the south, which until then had often produced as much as 70 to 80 times more corn than wheat. Between 1850 and 1860 a notable transition occurred, as southern Illinois expanded the acreage devoted to winter wheat. A group of 17 Illinois counties, including Bond, Fayette, Effingham, and Jasper, and all counties to the south of these except those bor-

---

[17] *Transactions of the Wisconsin State Agricultural Society,* I (1851), 300.

[18] Illinois correspondents reported wheat prices ranging from 75 cents to $1.40 per bushel in 1855. *Patent Report, 1855,* 192-193. Flour prices at St. Louis averaged $7.50 per barrel during 1855, at New York $9.00, and at New Orleans $9.30. *Hunt's,* XXXVIII (January, 1858), 92, (February, 1858), 206, (June, 1858), 737-738; "Report of the Secretary of Treasury, 1855," *House Executive Documents,* 34 Cong., 1 Sess., No. 10 (1856), Serial 840.

[19] *Hunt's,* XLII (May, 1860), 643; Gates, *The Illinois Central Railroad,* 256-257; Chicago Board of Trade, *Fourteenth Annual Report of the Trade and Commerce of Chicago, 1871* (Chicago, 1872), 28; W. C. Flagg, "The Agriculture of Illinois, 1683-1876," *Transactions of the Department of Agriculture of the State of Illinois, 1875,* new series, V (1876), 308-310.

dering on the Mississippi, Ohio, and Wabash rivers—in other words, 17 interior counties—produced 1.26 bushels of wheat per capita with a corn-wheat ratio of 55:1 in 1849. A decade later the corn-wheat ratio had narrowed to 10:1, and seven bushels of wheat per capita were produced.[20]

A number of factors probably worked together to stimulate wheat production in this area. The use of winter wheat itself, with a yield generally more fruitful than the spring variety and with its earlier harvest period, was of some advantage. In southern Illinois most of the harvesting was still done by hand, although to the north the new Manny and McCormick reapers were cutting a considerable portion of the grain by the late 1850's. In McHenry County it was reported that nearly all the harvesting was done by machinery as early as 1854. Northern Illinois was alleged to have purchased approximately one-fourth of the total number of McCormick reapers sold between 1849 and 1857.[21] In southern Illinois, however, many farms were not of sufficient size to warrant the purchase of a reaper, and even the hire of one during harvest cost an estimated 75 cents an acre. At 15 bushels of wheat per acre this would amount to a charge of 5 cents per bushel—a steep price to pay with wheat normally under $1.[22] The threshing was done mostly by horses, and often in the field. The sowing of winter wheat at least allowed the farmer to handle this crop before spring crops were ready for harvest. Manual labor predominated in the south during the threshing season, even though threshing machines of various types were available. For one, threshing machines were expensive and often did not perform the separating and winnowing processes satisfactorily, if at all. Then, too, at least one agricultural authority maintained that threshing by machine often cost as much as 10 cents per bushel, and that barley and oats could be threshed more cheaply by flail than machine.[23] In any event, very

---

[20] 7 *Census, 1850,* 730-731; 8 *Census, 1860, Agriculture,* 30-35.

[21] *Patent Report, 1854,* 139; Robert Russell, *North America. Its Agriculture and Climate* . . . (Edinburgh, 1857), 115; Paul W. Gates, *The Farmer's Age: Agriculture 1815-1860* (New York, 1960), 287-288. Leo Rogin, *The Introduction of Farm Machinery in Its Relation to the Productivity of Labor in the Agriculture of the United States During the Nineteenth Century* (Berkeley, Calif., 1931), 78-79, estimates that west of the Alleghenies more than 70,000 reapers were in operation by 1858 and that by 1860 about 70 per cent of the wheat harvested in that area was cut by machine.

[22] *The Prairie Farmer,* XX (September 8, 1859), 148.

[23] *Sangamo Journal,* January 5, 1841; Solon Robinson, ed., *Facts for Farmers; also for the Family Circle* . . . (2 vols., New York, 1865), II, 682-683.

few farmers in southern Illinois, or for that matter anywhere in Illinois, could afford to pay 15 cents per bushel of wheat for reaping and harvesting. Since the unit cost rose steadily higher in proportion as the crop was less (or as the fixed cost was spread over a small number of bushels), the use of expensive machinery was even less economically justifiable for the small farmer than for the large.

More significantly, however, the rapid growth of wheat production was a response to improved market conditions and advances in transportation, the latter giving to the interior farmers of Illinois access to markets in three different directions. Farmers along the line of the Illinois Central could ship either to Chicago or Cairo, on the Ohio River, with the former the preferred route. Intersecting the Illinois Central, as well as the Chicago, Alton and St. Louis Railroad, the two being the north-south lines, were a number of east-west roads including the Ohio and Mississippi, completed from St. Louis to Vincennes by 1856, and soon after to Cincinnati. The other east-west roads were the Peoria and Oquawka, the Terre Haute and Alton, and the Great Western. The cross-state railroads were primarily feeders for the north-south routes and thus, in effect, feeders for Chicago's growing trade.[24] St. Louis continued to derive some advantage from the Ohio and Mississippi rivers, and southern Illinois still supplied the Missouri city with considerable quantities of grain even after the Civil War. It was also possible for producers or dealers along the east-west lines which had Indiana connections to ship directly east through Pittsburgh or Wheeling, but it is unlikely that much grain was so routed since it was still considerably less expensive to ship north to the lakes and via water to New York City or south to New Orleans and other southern markets.

Progress in the raising of wheat in southern Illinois did little to change the relative position of the north as the center of wheat production in the state. Ten of the leading 11 wheat counties in 1859 were situated to the north of Stark and Putnam counties. The ten produced 34 per cent of the crop of 1859 with 14 per cent of the population, utilizing only 12 per cent of the total land surface of Illinois. While counties such as Lake, Du Page, and La Salle were among the first 10 in wheat production in 1849, they were not among the leading 25 in 1859, all of which produced at least 300,-

---

[24] *De Bow's Review,* XXI (July, 1856), 87; Gates, *The Illinois Central Railroad,* 87.

000 bushels of wheat. The dominant wheat area, while remaining in the north, had moved west into the Rock River valley, partly as a result of the construction of the Rock Island Railroad from Chicago. Some counties in the lower Illinois River valley, such as Knox, Pike, and Tazewell, outproduced northern counties that were among the leaders in 1849.[25]

To the north of Illinois lay Wisconsin, of all the East North Central states the most deeply committed prior to the Civil War to a wheat economy. In 1859 the wheat crop was estimated at 15.8 million bushels, three times that of 1849, and in the following year the crop was reported at 27 million bushels. The average yield per acre reached above 20 in that year, and 35 bushels of wheat per capita were produced. This represented an enormous productive effort, and a tremendous gain over the previous decade.[26]

During the 1850's the immense land surface of Wisconsin remained largely virgin territory. In 1850 only 8 per cent of the total land surface of Wisconsin was in farms, and ten years later the figure had just surpassed 20 per cent, doubling again by 1880.[27] During the decade of the 1850's, land in farms increased by almost 5 million acres, while the number of improved acres rose by 2.7 million. This tendency to take up more land than could be efficiently cultivated was singled out as a major source of evil in the wheat economy. Too frequently, one observer remarked, "immigrants . . . tempted by the low price of land . . . purchased a larger quantity of land than they are able to pay for. . . . When pay day comes around . . . they are obliged to raise money at such an enormous rate of interest as must prove ruinous in the end." [28] Under such circumstances, farmers required a speedy return for their labor, which the cultivation of wheat afforded since the crop usually commanded cash at some price, or at least its equivalent value in credit. As an inhabitant of Columbia County described the process:

---

[25] The other county was St. Clair, one of the major source areas of St. Louis. The ten leading counties included McHenry, Winnebago, Stephenson, Carroll, Ogle, De Kalb, Whiteside, Lee, Henry, and Bureau. *8 Census, 1860, Agriculture,* 30-35.

[26] *Ibid.,* 166-167; *Transactions Wisconsin Agricultural Society,* VI (1860), 52-55.

[27] Ohio Secretary of State, *AR, 1871,* 328-331; *10 Census, 1880, Agriculture,* III, xi.

[28] John Gregory, *Industrial Resources of Wisconsin* (Milwaukee, 1855), 61.

"The greater part of our citizens came here poor, consequently could raise wheat easier than anything else, that staple requiring a less outlay in cash than stock of any kind. . . . A great many have anticipated good crops and have purchased teams, tools, and made improvements on time, expecting to meet their engagements with their crops: but instead . . . have been obliged to loan money at a high rate of interest and now [are] in straightened circumstances." [29] The cry went up to diversify, particularly during the poor crop seasons of the early 1850's. The chancellor of the University of Wisconsin, the president of the Kenosha County Agricultural Society, and many others called on Wisconsin's farmers to extend the cultivation of corn, oats, barley, and flax and introduce stock raising, dairy cattle, and sheep.[30]

In the mid-1850's an improved crop picture, the extension of railroads into the interior of Wisconsin, high prices at lake ports, and a great influx of immigrants took the edge off the urgency behind the plea for diversification. It was estimated that the amount of land in cultivation in 1857 was double that of 1850. The average cash valuation per acre of farmland in Wisconsin increased from $9.50 in 1850 to $16.59, mostly as a result of advances made after 1854.[31] Between 1858 and 1860 the acreage sown with wheat increased from 600,000 to 1.1 million while wheat production more than tripled. If anything had occurred during the decade to modify the condition of farming in Wisconsin, it was an even more intensive specialization in wheat rather than the reverse.[32]

Between 1849 and 1859 the geographical distribution of wheat did not alter significantly in Wisconsin. In the earlier year, the southeastern counties of the state were the most productive. In the years prior to 1849, wheat moved into the third and fourth tiers of counties, as far north as Fond du Lac and Green Lake. In 1859 the ten leading wheat counties included Racine, Walworth, and Rock in the first tier, Waukesha, Jefferson, and Dane in the sec-

---

[29] *Transactions Wisconsin Agricultural Society*, I (1851), 133.

[30] *Ibid.*, 36-37, 112-113; Gregory, *Industrial Resources of Wisconsin*, 61.

[31] John G. Thompson, *The Rise and Decline of the Wheat Growing Industry in Wisconsin* (Madison, 1908), 338-339; *Transactions Wisconsin Agricultural Society*, VI (1860), 51.

[32] The corn crop also made notable gains during the decade, increasing from 2 million bushels in 1849 to 7.5 million in 1859 and 12 million the next year. Wheat acreage was almost four times that of corn and two and a half that given to other grains in 1860. *Ibid.*, 52-55.

ond, Dodge and Columbia in the third, and Fond du Lac and
Green Lake in the fourth. Within this area 60 per cent of the crop
was raised, but a shift in intensity of production occurred between
1849 and 1859. In 1849 Rock and Walworth counties produced 33
per cent of the state crop, while in 1859 and 1860 the share was
14 per cent. The four northernmost counties of the above ten, located in the third and fourth tiers, produced 15.3 per cent in 1849
and 27.5 per cent a decade later. Each of the leading ten counties
raised over 500,000 bushels in 1859, and five of them over 1 million.[33] The culture of wheat within the ten-county area was more
evenly proportioned than in prior years.

The ten leading wheat counties of Illinois, in the north, and
the first ten wheat counties of Wisconsin formed a contiguous area
encompasing some 14,000 square miles, or about 14 per cent of the
total area of both states. The commitment to and concentration
upon wheat cultivation made this the area of greatest density of
wheat production in the United States. In 1859 the total crop of
this region represented 45 per cent of the total produced in Illinois-
Wisconsin, 22 per cent of East North Central production, and over
10 per cent of the wheat grown in the United States. The 17.8 million bushels raised in the 20 counties were equal to 34.2 bushels
per capita, double that of Illinois-Wisconsin, triple that of the East
North Central states, and almost seven times greater than that in
the United States. Production in these 20 counties exceeded the
total wheat and flour exports of the United States in both 1858 and
1860, and the surplus available from the 20 counties, probably in
excess of 14 million bushels, was the equivalent of 80 per cent of
wheat and flour exports in 1860.[34] It was from this area that Chicago and Milwaukee obtained their grain supplies.

The above 20 counties alone produced twice as much wheat
in 1859 as Michigan, the least important of the East North Central
states in terms of the grain trade. Michigan's wheat crop of 1859
was surpassed by each of the northwestern states and was less than
that of Virginia, Pennsylvania, and New York. Although Michigan
added some 1.5 million improved acres between 1850 and 1860,
over 80 per cent of the increase came after 1854, and available crop
figures indicate that only a fraction of this was converted to wheatlands, while somewhat more was probably employed in the raising

---

[33] 8 *Census, 1860, Agriculture*, 30-35, 165-167, 184-185.
[34] *Ibid.*; Evans, "Exports, Domestic and Foreign," Table 7, 116.

of corn.[35] Compared with Wisconsin or Illinois, this represented a retreat in the wheat economy.

Michigan farmers in the 1850's, according to a Lenawee County inhabitant, discovered wheat culture to be the least remunerative of agricultural pursuits. The cost of raising wheat, excluding the expense of harvesting, was estimated at between 40 and 55 cents a bushel, while harvesting frequently cost from 5 to 10 cents. With wheat normally under 80 cents per bushel and frequently as low as 65 to 70 cents, this left little after the cost of transportation was deducted. As the decade of the 1850's advanced, reports from Michigan describing the depredations of insect pests appeared frequently. Some Michigan farmers undoubtedly discovered that over twice as much corn could be raised as wheat with no more labor and expense, while the price of corn was generally more than 50 per cent that of wheat.[36]

In both 1849 and 1859 relatively more wheat was grown in southeastern Michigan than in other sections, but distribution was not as uneven in the latter year. Wheat was grown in fairly uniform amounts along the entire southern tier of counties, from Lake Erie to Lake Michigan, and the counties in the four southernmost tiers produced more than 13 bushels of wheat per capita. Above the fourth tier and in the Upper Peninsula, insufficient wheat was raised to supply even two bushels per capita, so this area probably imported wheat from elsewhere to make up the deficiency. It is known that the counties above the fourth tier raised but 580,000 bushels of wheat, while using some 3.3 million in the manufacture of approximately 660,000 barrels of flour. Most of the wheat for

---

[35] In both 1848 and 1853 wheat acreage was assessed at about 470,000 acres. In the latter year a crop of 7 million bushels was reported, while in 1859 and 1860 state and federal census enumerators recorded 8.3 and 8.1 million bushels and the crops were considered as normal, as was the crop of 1853, which yielded 15 bushels per acre. Using this yield as representing a good crop, the acreage in both 1859 and 1860 was probably about 550,000 acres. The corn crop in 1853 was estimated at 7.6 million bushels and raised on 327,000 acres, and was considered good, as was the crop of 1859, which reached 12.3 million bushels. At 25 bushels of corn per acre, the 1860 crop probably required some 494,000 acres. *Patent Report, 1849*, 553; Michigan Department of State, *Census and Statistics of the State of Michigan, May, 1854* (Lansing, 1854), 393; Ohio Secretary of State, *AR, 1871*, 330; 8 *Census, 1860, Agriculture*, 76-77.

[36] On new lands, the initial cost per bushel would be somewhat higher, even though the yield might be greater than from older lands. Breaking up new land cost from $4 to $5 per acre. *Patent Report, 1851*, 411-413, *1853*, 133, *1854*, 128, 143-144; Russell, *North America*, 100-101.

this flour had to be supplied from other areas, probably southern Michigan.[37]

Viewed as a section, the East North Central states experienced a rapid growth of grain production, and agriculture in general, during the ten years preceding the Civil War, as they had also, for that matter, in the decade of the 1840's. By 1860 the region did, in fact, deserve to be referred to as the "feeding power" of the nation. The growth over 25 years had been fairly steady, as was to be expected when large numbers of settlers, aided by striking technological advances, moved into an area of unsurpassed fertility and productive potential. But the obvious progress of the section should not obscure the distinctive rates of growth experienced by the states constituting the section, or by areas within the states. Prior to the early 1850's most of the agricultural advance was attributable to the development of grain production, transportation, and marketing improvements, and regional crop specialization in Ohio and, to a lesser extent, Indiana and Michigan. In the 1850's, however, both Ohio and Michigan reached a relatively stable plateau of grain production, while simultaneously in Ohio the production of wheat and corn was dispersed more evenly throughout the state, and the raising of livestock, including sheep, took an added importance in such districts as the Western Reserve and Scioto valley. In Ohio by the 1850's, with most parts fairly well settled and economically mature, the railroads had less effect on production than in less settled and more youthful areas in states to the west, although the railroads did exert a sharp influence on the direction the trade in grain followed at certain points in Ohio.

In Illinois and Wisconsin, particularly the former, the great function of the railroad as an agent of settlement and as a cause of expanded production was attested to by the growth of wheat production in southern Illinois, the intensification of the wheat economy in areas of the northern wheat belt penetrated by railroads such as the Rock Island or Galena road, the phenomenal activity exhibited along the line of the Illinois Central, and most strikingly by the explosive growth experienced in the grain trade at Chicago.

In a sense, the decade of the 1850's defines the period in which the East North Central states achieved real primacy in the production and shipment of grain in the United States. At no time after the Civil War was the grain trade of the Old Northwest as impor-

[37] 8 *Census, 1860, Agriculture,* 76-77; *Michigan Census, 1860,* 307-314.

tant, relative to other sections, as during the late 1850's and early 1860's. By 1870 other sections to the west of the Mississippi were emerging as the major grain regions in the nation. The Northwest produced 46 per cent of the nation's wheat in 1859. Ten years later, production in Ohio, Indiana, and Wisconsin was larger by 10 million bushels, while Michigan's wheat crop doubled and Illinois' increased by 7 million bushels, amounting to an increase of 49 million bushels for the section. In spite of these increases, the share of these five states in the national production had fallen to 44 per cent. During the same period, the proportion of the national corn crop produced in the Old Northwest remained stationary. The center of the production of grain, particularly of wheat, was again shifting to the West.

The Diversion of the
River Trade of the Northwest
During the Fifties

CHAPTER X

The 1850's witnessed what many writers are wont to call a diversion of the grain trade from the South to the East. It is important, when speaking of diversion, to arrive at some acceptable definition of the term. Insofar as it is applied to the trade in grain with the South, it can mean either that the southern route via the Mississippi to New Orleans and an ultimate destination elsewhere was becoming of less relative or absolute importance to the Northwest, or that the southern consuming market for northwestern grain contracted during the 1850's, or some combination of the two.

Because of this potential ambiguity, care must be taken in any analysis of the relation between the East North Central states and the South to distinguish between the trade with the South and the use of southern river routes as a means of reaching other markets, overseas and domestic—the latter including both northern and southern grain-importing centers. One authority on the commercial history of the United States, in an all-encompassing statement, wrote: "A History of the trade between the North and the South from 1830 to 1860 is . . . little more than an account of the commerce on the Mississippi." [1] This, of course, is so greatly oversimplified that it loses its value as a description of a trade which followed numerous paths, among which the Mississippi was paramount for certain phases of the trade and of little or no significance for others, and of generally less importance as an avenue to market in the 1850's than during previous periods.

Of these two aspects of the southern trade, that relating to the southern market, including the demand at New Orleans, is initially a problem of measurement. Between 1849 and 1859, did the southern market actually contract or was it perhaps expanding at one point while diminishing at another? This, in short, demands that the sticky problem of southern agricultural self-sufficiency be faced.

A determination of the relative importance of the Mississippi route to market can also be accomplished by means of measuring certain components of the trade, most obviously at New Orleans, the grain trade of which can be compared with that of northern grain centers; or at a center such as Cincinnati, which furnished a large proportion of the produce and provisions floated on the Mississippi during the decades preceding 1850. It should also be possible to analyze the grain production trends in the more southerly parts of the East North Central states to see whether the exportable surplus increased or declined during the years between 1849 and 1859. If the surplus increased while the volume of goods utilizing the Mississippi decreased, either absolutely or relatively, even if the absolute increase of surplus was slight, the question of alternate methods of reaching ultimate markets must be considered, and would revolve primarily around the development of rail transportation and its role as both a local and intersectional carrier of grain.

Reference has been made in Chapter VI to the state of grain production in the South and an effort was made to demonstrate that there was an actual deficiency of corn existing in the South. There also existed a large deficiency in wheat, although it is inaccurate to assume, as some writers do, that all of the South was de-

---

[1] Emory R. Johnson *et al.*, *History of Domestic and Foreign Commerce of the United States* (2 vols., Washington, D.C., 1915), I, 241.

pendent upon other sources for its foodstuffs, or that the dependent areas remained constant throughout the antebellum years.[2]

The per capita production of wheat in the South increased from 3.06 bushels in 1849 to 3.68 in 1859. This was partly a result of gains in wheat production experienced in Virginia and Maryland, total production for both states increasing from 15.6 million bushels in 1849 to 19.2 million in 1859, and wheat per capita rising from 7.77 bushels in 1849 to 8.62 a decade later. In the remaining southern states, including North and South Carolina, Georgia, Alabama, Mississippi, Louisiana, Florida, and Texas, wheat production rose from 4.9 million to 11.8 million in the ten years while wheat per capita increased from 1.09 in 1849 to 1.99 in 1859.[3] What did this mean in terms of a deficiency in wheat?

For the eight states, as a group, there was a marked decline in the number of bushels required to fulfill home consumption needs between 1849, when some 6.9 million bushels were required, and 1859, when a deficiency of 4.9 million bushels is estimated.[4] The decline is largely accounted for by the attainment of self-sufficiency in North Carolina, and the approach to this condition in Georgia. The latter increased its wheat production from 1 million bushels in 1849 to 2.5 million in 1859, which was only some 250,000 short of actual needs, compared with a shortage of 1.2 million ten years earlier. South Carolina also seems to have taken a long stride toward self-sufficiency in grain. Charleston, for instance, through its railroad connections with the interior, became independent of northern breadstuffs, and exported almost 100,000 barrels of flour

---

[2] Herbert J. Wunderlich, "Foreign Grain Trade of the United States, 1835-1860," *The Iowa Journal of History and Politics*, XXXIII (January, 1935), 33, assumes an even distribution of wheat consumption throughout the country and the over-all dependence of the South on other localities for its wheat. Contemporaries credited the South with consuming much less wheat per capita than the North. Consumption estimates ranged from four to seven bushels per capita for the North and in the following discussion 3.5 bushels per capita is assumed to represent southern consumption.

[3] *7 Census, 1850*, lxxxii-lxxxvii; *8 Census, 1860, Agriculture*, 184-185.

[4] This rough estimate has been arrived at for each state by taking the total production minus 10 per cent for seed and feed, the results of which should approximate that available for home consumption, and then comparing it to a figure representing consumption requirements. This was arrived at by taking a 3.5-bushel requirement for each white and one bushel for each slave. As far as the white requirements are concerned, 3.5 may be too high for some areas in the interior fairly isolated from markets, while it may be too low for tidewater regions or southern cities. Neither does it make an adjustment for a rising per capita consumption over the ten-year period.

and 424,000 bushels of wheat in 1858. This market had previously been supplied from New Orleans and Baltimore.[5]

The areas of the South which continued as markets for grain from the Northwest included Texas, Louisiana, Florida, Alabama, and Mississippi. In these states the demands remained fairly level between 1849 and 1859. The deficiency in Florida and Louisiana increased from some 1.5 million bushels in 1849 to 2 million in 1859, while the deficiency in Alabama and Mississippi declined from 2.7 to 2.3 million bushels and in Texas from 560,000 to 330,000 in the ten years. Even within this southwestern and Gulf Coast area the actual needs varied considerably from place to place and time to time. Mississippi required large amounts of corn and wheat due to protracted drought in the summer of 1850, but just a year earlier, Vicksburg was reported exporting close to 100,000 bushels of corn downstream.[6]

Although immense strides were made in the cultivation of grain in certain areas of the South, resulting in an increasing self-sufficiency for those areas, other regions continued to require grain supplies from outside sources to supplement their own production. In those areas which improved their degree of self-sufficiency, railroads stretching from seaboard cities into the interior probably were the major stimulus. As in the Northwest in earlier decades, areas remote from transportation facilities felt little inducement to produce a surplus of wheat. But with railroads knitting together the back-country farmer and seaboard city, as at Charleston, a market was furnished to the producer and a new form of commerce to the port.

Taking all these trends into account, it is clear that a fairly large southern market for northwestern breadstuffs continued to exist up to the Civil War, along with an even larger southern need for provisions and corn. Since the over-all southern importation of grain did not really diminish during the decade there is every reason to speak with precision regarding the diversion of grain from

---

[5] Savannah, Georgia, became a grain-exporting port in the 1850's. In 1855-56 some 800,000 bushels of wheat were shipped, principally coastwise. Charleston's efforts to tap western trade were first centered on the Blue Ridge Railroad from Charleston to Knoxville, Tennessee, where it united with roads running to Lexington and Cincinnati. Connections were also made with Chattanooga, Memphis, Nashville, and Louisville. Most of Charleston's provisions still came from New Orleans or Baltimore. *De Bow's Review*, XVII (November, 1854), 541, XXII (April, 1857), 443, XXV (October, 1858), 471.

[6] *Patent Report, 1850*, 17; *De Bow's Review*, XI (December, 1851), 599.

the South during the 1850's. Whatever the extent of the diversion, it was not from the South as a market for northwestern agricultural goods, but a diversion of grain from the southern route down the Mississippi and through New Orleans to alternate avenues of commerce. This traffic went largely to the railroads leading either to the Great Lakes or to such western terminals of eastern railroads as Wheeling and Pittsburgh, or especially into the interior of the South. A recent student of the Old Northwest, in pointing out the continued importance of the South to Illinois farmers, also raised the question of the degree to which other modes of transportation replaced the Mississippi River system as an avenue to market by stating that in the latter part of the 1850's the Illinois Central Railroad, with shipping connections at Cairo, Illinois, had to a very considerable extent surpassed the upper Mississippi River system in carrying agricultural goods to the South.[7]

This conclusion exaggerates the immediate impact of railroads in the upper Mississippi valley. In 1859 the Illinois Central carried 350,000 bushels of grain and 27,000 barrels of flour to Cairo while St. Louis received 67 per cent of its flour via river, or 324,000 barrels, as well as upwards of 4 million bushels of grain. Compared to this, or to the 1.2 million bushels of wheat and flour and 794,000 bushels of corn which the Illinois Central moved to Chicago, the amount moving south via rail seems small indeed, and hardly justifies the contention that the Central had replaced the Mississippi in transporting grain to the South.[8] But it does focus attention on the increasing use of railroads in the 1850's, at the expense of movement along both rivers and canals. Not only did the grain traffic on the Ohio and Mississippi feel the effects of railroad competition, but the role of interior rivers and canals changed from that of feeding the larger rivers to that of feeding railroads intersecting the streams. Regarding the canals, this is less applicable for the canals

---

[7] Paul W. Gates, *The Illinois Central Railroad and Its Colonization Work* (Cambridge, Mass., 1934), 274-275. It is assumed that this does not mean through shipments directly to southern markets by means of the railroad connection with the Mobile and Ohio Railroad, which was completed to Baton Rouge in 1857. Statistics regarding the volume of grain carried by this line, if they are available, have not been consulted.

[8] *Ibid.*, 275; Frank H. Dixon, *A Traffic History of the Mississippi River System* (Washington, D.C., 1909), 34; St. Louis Merchants' Exchange, *Annual Statement of the Trade and Commerce of St. Louis, 1878* (St. Louis, 1879), 50-52; *Seventh Annual Review of the Trade and Commerce . . . of Chicago, 1858* (Chicago, 1859), 7-14.

feeding lake ports than for those terminating at the Ohio River, but in both cases there was a noticeable diminution of traffic during the 1850's and especially along the southern sections. As to railroads, those in the South in the 1850's were active competitors of the rivers, and to the extent that they succeeded in this rivalry, the grain traffic to the South over the rivers experienced a diversion. In the North, however, railroads served to swell the volume of grain traveling over the lakes, and were not serious competitors for the through grain traffic until after the Civil War. But at two points in the progress of grain from producer to consumer, the railroads did impinge upon the traffic of traditional carriers. In the West the railroads competed with such canals as the Ohio, Wabash and Erie, and Illinois and Michigan for the grain traffic moving toward lake ports such as Cleveland, Toledo, and Chicago, and at the eastern end of the lakes railroads competed effectively with the Erie Canal in the carriage of certain commodities to seaboard cities.

Railroads had begun to offer some competition to river routes in the transportation of grain in the 1830's, and the rivalry had continued during the succeeding decade.[9] However, it did not really become a major factor in the grain trade until the 1850's, when the large eastern roads such as the Pennsylvania, Baltimore and Ohio, New York and Erie, and the consolidated lines forming the New York Central reached the lakes or the Ohio River, where they connected with the grain ships or where they made connections with western railroads. At this time, diversion of grain traffic from customary routes became a possibility and the railroad took on a more than local significance in the grain trade of the Northwest.[10]

Before proceeding directly to the problem of measuring the diversion of grain from the southern to northern routes, or from

[9] The Baltimore and Ohio Railroad carried between 150,000 and 260,000 barrels of flour annually from 1832 to 1839 and competed with both the Potomac River and the Chesapeake and Ohio Canal. *Thirty-fourth Annual Report of the Baltimore & Ohio Railroad Company, 1860* (Baltimore, 1860), 102-105. In the late 1830's, traffic on the B & O was increased by feeder lines from the interior of Virginia, such as the Winchester and Potomac Railroad, which reached the B & O at Harper's Ferry in 1836 and was soon connected with Richmond, thus affording farmers along its lines market opportunities either at Baltimore or Richmond. *The American Farmer*, August 21, 1839; *NWR*, XL (July 16, 1831), 340, LXII (July 30, 1842), 344.

[10] Wunderlich, "Foreign Grain Trade of the U.S.," 49, maintains that railroads before the Civil War were of little practical use in the grain trade. It seems, however, that railroads were of considerable value in the conduct of the trade, at first on local levels, but increasingly on intersectional levels.

river to rail or lake, it may be helpful to make certain general observations which can serve as guideposts in this and subsequent
discussions. Between 1853 and 1860 the total railroad mileage of
the United States increased immensely, growing from 15,500 to
about 30,000, while that in the Northwest rose from 25 per cent of
the total mileage to about 35 per cent. In Illinois the progress was
most striking as the mileage jumped between 1852 and 1858 from
95 to 2,700, or 30 per cent of the track in the East North Central
states. At the same time there were numerous points at which the
railroad and the rivers or canals were engaged in vigorous economic competition for the carrying trade in general, and for grain
in particular. At the eastern end of the Great Lakes, the New York
and Erie and New York Central were making harmful inroads upon
the flour traffic of the Erie Canal. In 1853 these two roads carried
1.2 million tons of freight compared to 4.2 million shipped over the
canal. In 1865 the two roads together were carrying a larger tonnage than the canal, and by 1880 three times more tonnage moved
over the railroads than over the canal.[11]

To the south, a decline in the importance of steamboats and a
general falling off in river traffic was discernible at least as early as
the middle 1850's. The historian of the steamboat on western rivers
states that the 1850's were marked by depression and misfortune
for the steamboat interests, which soon relegated them to a minor
economic role. Whatever the steamboats lost meant not only a loss
of river traffic to rail traffic but also a change in the direction of
traffic, since most of the railroads ran north to the lakes or east-
west. An important advantage of the railroad was its ability to
move goods during all seasons, while steamboat traffic was subject
to interruption by freezing rivers or low water, the latter occurring
quite frequently during the 1850's.[12] It would seem that steamboats
suffered the greatest loss sometime after 1855, since before that
period there is no evidence of a diminishing traffic. In 1855 the

---

[11] *ARJ*, XXVII (November 4, 1854), 697, XXXII (January 1, 1859), 2;
Frederick Gerhard, *Illinois as It Is; Its History, Geography, Statistics, Agriculture* (Chicago, 1857), 132-133; Henry V. Poor, *Sketch of the Rise and Progress
of the Internal Improvements and of the Internal Commerce of the United
States . . .* (New York, 1881), xlii-xlvi.

[12] Louis C. Hunter, *Steamboats on the Western Rivers. An Economic and
Technological History* (Cambridge, Mass., 1949), 481-482, places great weight
on the causative role of a series of "low-water depressions" in the 1850's in dis-
crediting river transportation and diverting traffic to the railroads.

steamboat tonnage passing the Louisville Canal was the highest in its history, and arrivals and departures at major river towns, such as St. Louis, Louisville, and Cincinnati, had yet to fall off significantly, while the tonnage of steamboats constructed on western waters reached a peak of 37,000 tons in 1857 compared to 28,000 in 1849. Moreover, the setback experienced by steamboats probably related more to the Ohio and upper Mississippi rivers than to the lower Mississippi, since the main commodity handled there was cotton, and the lone railroad paralleling the river did not offer dangerous competition. But along the upper rivers the railroads were making severe encroachments upon the trade of traditional routes. It was noted that the eastern seaboard was not so dependent on summer and fall navigation for its foodstuffs as formerly, since northern railroads were transporting large winter supplies.[13]

One of the reasons sometimes advanced in accounting for the relative decline in importance of the Mississippi River route was that the surplus from the part of the Old Northwest which generally shipped via the river had not increased between 1849 and 1859.[14] If this were true, it alone would account for the relative decline in grain traffic by way of the Mississippi as compared with traffic over routes whose supply area was continuing to increase production—as the more northern regions did increase, except in Ohio, from 1849 to 1859. If the production in the normal supply areas of the river routes were still increasing, then the explanation for the static condition of the river trade must lie entirely in the success of competing modes of transportation.

In general, production in the southern regions of Ohio, Indiana, and Illinois did increase. For Ohio it is necessary to qualify this statement by noting that the state as a whole, as mentioned in the previous chapter, maintained fairly stable wheat production levels. In fact the older wheat belt in the upper and middle Muskingum River valley lost some of its predominance, while wheat

---

[13] *10 Census, 1880,* IV, 671-672; Dixon, *Traffic History of the Mississippi River System,* 19; *Hunt's,* XXXVII (December, 1857), 720. Rudolph A. Clemen, "Waterways in Livestock and Meat Trade," *American Economic Review,* XVI (December, 1926), 650-652, maintains that meat traffic over water declined during the 1850's as railroads reached points normally shipping provisions via the rivers.

[14] A. L. Kohlmeier, *The Old Northwest as the Keystone of the Arch of the American Federal Union. A Study in Commerce and Politics* (Bloomington, Ind., 1938).

became a more important crop in the southeast, which customarily shipped via the river. For the state as a whole, the production of wheat per capita declined from over seven bushels in 1849 to six and a half in 1859. The corn crop increased by 12 million bushels, over 80 per cent produced south of the Maumee valley and Western Reserve districts of Ohio.[15]

In Indiana, that portion of the state south of a line running from Richmond in the east through Indianapolis to the Illinois boundary made much more substantial gains in wheat production than northern Indiana. As Table 7 indicates, the northern 40 per cent of Indiana produced 42 per cent of the total crop in 1849. In the next decade the wheat crop expanded from 6.2 million to 16.8 million bushels in 1859. The 30 northern counties produced 5 million bushels, or 30 per cent; thus, production in the south demonstrated greater growth during the decade than in the north. The production of wheat per capita, at 6.3 bushels in 1849, doubled by 1859. The exportable surplus actually increased more rapidly in the southern half of the state than in the northern.

How Indiana's surplus left the state is difficult to ascertain. By the late 1850's it had the alternatives of following older routes via the Wabash and Erie Canal to either Toledo or Evansville, or the Whitewater Canal to Cincinnati, or traversing any of several railroads running both north and south and east and west. It is likely that the Ohio River counties of Indiana and the next tier or two to their north continued to ship south by water, especially those counties along the lower Wabash River. But even here alternate routes directly to the East or the lakes were available. At Evansville, the southern terminus of the Wabash and Erie Canal, railroad connections existed with Vincennes and Crawfordsville, and through them to the lakes. In 1858 Evansville's exports via railroad and river included 360,000 bushels of grain, 62,000 barrels of flour, and 50,000 barrels of pork.[16] The proportion going in any given direction is not clear, but that some was shipped over the railroads to the north and east is certain. Before the railroads, all of the surplus went by water. Probably grain shipments over such Indiana railroads as the Madison and Indianapolis or New Albany and Salem, both terminating at the Ohio River, went largely to

---

[15] *7 Census, 1850,* lxxxii-lxxxvii; *8 Census, 1860, Agriculture,* 184-185.
[16] *Hunt's,* XXXIX (December, 1858), 688.

swell the river trade until connections with east-west lines were made. The same would be true of interior grain markets such as Vincennes.[17] Irrespective of the direction by which the surplus of southern Indiana traveled to market, however, the crucial fact remains that this surplus did grow between 1849 and 1859.

The same was true for southern Illinois. Here a remarkable expansion of the wheat crop was achieved during the 1850's. Southern Illinois changed its position from an area often dependent upon outside sources for its wheat and flour to an area producing a considerable surplus for export, and one from which St. Louis drew a good portion of its grain supplies once the Ohio and Mississippi Railroad was completed from Vincennes to the Mississippi. Southern Illinois started to furnish St. Louis with an increasing volume of grain just at the time when grain from the Illinois River valley and upper Mississippi began to move eastward via railroad instead of proceeding to St. Louis. The railroad was probably instrumental in the development of the grain trade in those parts of southern Illinois which were some distance from any navigable streams.[18]

It is possible to conclude, then, with some certainty, that grain traffic over the Mississippi route did not fail to keep pace with that of the eastern or northern routes because of a slackening in production in its supply areas. In fact, the southern regions of Indiana and Illinois made their most notable gains in production during the 1850's, and far from experiencing a lag in the production of an exportable surplus, raised the per capita production of wheat to a point where, for the first time, a significant quantity of wheat was available for shipment. If the Mississippi River system suffered a setback in its position as a major route to market, it was not because the area which fed it did not progress but because new, efficient, and economical avenues to markets were available. Nowhere was the alteration in traditional patterns of trade more apparent than at Cincinnati.

In 1851 the *Cincinnati Price Current*, comparing the commerce of Cincinnati with that of Great Lakes ports for 1848 and 1850,

[17] *ARJ*, XXV (September 25, 1852), 613. Vincennes was reported shipping a total of 50,000 barrels of flour, 62,000 barrels of pork, 300,000 bushels of wheat, and over 1 million bushels of corn and oats via the Wabash and Erie Canal in 1851 and 1852. The direction is not indicated, but most of it probably went south, as exports had in the past. *Ibid.* (September 4, 1852), 566.

[18] *Hunt's*, XXX (April, 1854), 443.

concluded that "not only is the commerce of Cincinnati rapidly increasing, but . . . the time is near at hand when it must *command the entire trade* of Ohio and Indiana, notwithstanding the great efforts to maintain the ascendancy of the Atlantic ports." [19] Commerce and industry had indeed advanced rapidly at Cincinnati throughout the 1830's and 1840's. The value of products manufactured at Cincinnati increased from $16 million in 1840 to $46 million in 1850, while the aggregate value of all imports and exports rose from some $15 million in 1839 to over $100 million in 1847, and $180 million in 1860.[20] Much of this trade was due to Cincinnati's strategic function as a distributing center for eastern manufactured goods, such southern staples as cotton and sugar, and foreign articles such as coffee. But among the articles of purely domestic production and manufacture, pork, whiskey, and flour were dominant in the trade of Ohio's Queen City.

Much has been written concerning the revolutionary change in the direction which Cincinnati's trade took in the middle 1850's, and the impression often received is that Cincinnati's dependence upon the river as an avenue of commerce ceased, suddenly and completely, having been replaced by a dependence upon railroads.[21] This was not the case, however. In 1855 over 80 per cent of the total value of both imports and exports and 92 per cent of the total tonnage utilized the river. During the remainder of the decade, this overwhelming dependence upon the river did lessen, but the river retained its importance to the commerce of Cincinnati. The total number of arrivals and departures of steamboats increased from around 5,000 in 1850 to 5,400 in 1856 and 5,900 in 1859, while the whole tonnage of steamers and barges running between Cincinnati and other ports rose from 49,000 in 1850 to 82,500 in 1856, before declining to between 60,000 and 66,000 tons from 1858 to 1861. Most of this tonnage was employed in trade with the

---

[19] Quoted in *De Bow's Review*, X (May, 1851), 555.

[20] Charles Cist, *Cincinnati in 1841: Its Early Annals and Future Prospects* (Cincinnati, 1841), 84; *Thirty-fourth Annual Report of the Cincinnati Chamber of Commerce and Merchants' Exchange . . . 1882* (Cincinnati, 1882), 75. Between 1847, when exports and imports surpassed $100 million, and 1855, there was little change in the value of Cincinnati's commerce. The aggregate value dropped to $90 million in both 1852 and 1853 and hovered around $100 million in both 1854 and 1855. In 1856 the total value reached $126 million, and thereafter the gain was progressive.

[21] Dixon, *Traffic History of the Mississippi River System*, 34; R. B. Way, "The Commerce of the Lower Mississippi in the Period 1830-1860," MHVA *Proceedings* (1918-19), 65.

lower Mississippi.[22] There was a decline in the use of the river after the mid-1850's which affected certain commodities to a greater degree than others. Among those most heavily influenced by the coming of the railroad were grain and flour, and in these commodities the diversion from river to rail was virtually complete.

As Table 12 indicates, the grain and flour trade of Cincinnati demonstrated no striking gains during the 1850's. After reaching a peak in 1847, when grain and flour valued at $3.2 million were exported, a decline followed, and the total value of grain exports did not match the 1847 figure until 1854, when $3.8 million worth was shipped from Cincinnati.[23] Thereafter there was a general increase of value in the grain trade, reaching over $6 million in 1856. Quantitatively the peak came in 1858, when over 600,000 barrels of flour were shipped.[24]

In the early days of railroad development at Cincinnati, and other commercial centers as well, railroads served primarily in two capacities: first, as feeders of raw materials to Cincinnati for local use or re-export, either in their original state or, as with corn and wheat, in processed forms; and second, as routes over which Cincinnati distributed manufactured or imported products to the interior. In its first capacity, then, the railroad was an adjunct of the river, in the same commercial sense that the interior rivers and canals were, and it was as a rival of these other tributary transportation networks that the railroad first engaged in competition for the carrying trade. The early railroads were functionally limited because they were for the most part north-south lines, projected to connect the Ohio River with the Great Lakes. The major eastern

[22] "Report of the Bureau of Topographical Engineers, 1856," *House Executive Documents*, 35 Cong., 1 Sess., No. 2 (1856), Serial 943, 339; Cincinnati Chamber of Commerce, *34 AR, 1882*, 104-106.

[23] The total value of grain exports in 1854 exceeded that of 1847 not because of a quantitative increase in shipments, but because of a price increase caused mostly by the Crimean War. Wheat, worth about $1.00 per bushel in 1847, was approaching $1.50 in 1854; corn rose from about 33 cents to 40 cents; and flour climbed from around $5.00 to $5.50. *Hunt's*, XXIII (October, 1850), 343, XXXI (November, 1854), 601-603; Ohio Commissioner of Statistics, *Seventh Annual Report to the Governor, 1863* (Columbus, 1864), 25.

[24] Cincinnati Chamber of Commerce, *34 AR, 1882*, 155, 162-169, 171; *Hunt's*, XXXVI (October, 1856), 477-478, XXXIX (November, 1858), 605-606. Corn receipts displayed the largest increase over the decade. Almost all of the receipts were transformed in Cincinnati, either to pork or whiskey, so very little bulk corn was exported. Wheat receipts, too, rose during the decade from some 300,000 to 400,000 bushels in 1850-55 to over 1 million bushels in each year thereafter to 1860, except 1857.

lines had not yet made connections with trans-Appalachian terminals or with the east-west lines which were being constructed to
meet them. But when this extension of eastern roads to the Ohio
River or Great Lakes was completed, and when a junction with
western roads was realized, then the economic functions of the
railroads were enlarged and transformed, since they now existed as
parallel and competing routes, bidding to replace the traditional
paths to market—the lakes, the Erie Canal, and the Ohio River.

The railroads, terminating at Cincinnati from the middle 1840's
through the early 1850's, operated to expand the interior area from
which agricultural products were received and to which manufactured articles were sold. As previously observed, the railroads competed so effectively with the Miami Canal and the Whitewater
Canal that the latter was eventually abandoned, while the amount
of flour received at Cincinnati over the former declined from as
much as 40 to 60 per cent of total receipts in 1845-51 to less than
15 per cent in 1857-60. Between 1847 and 1850 the Little Miami
Railroad supplied Cincinnati with some 23 per cent of its flour and
15 per cent of its grain receipts. In 1845 and 1846 the road carried
almost 60,000 barrels of whiskey to Cincinnati, or 17 per cent of
total receipts.[25]

The grain traffic at this time was almost entirely toward Cincinnati, and it remained so until 1854-55. The trade south via the
river appeared impregnable in the late 1840's and early 1850's.
Even though the completion of through routes from Atlantic coast

---

[25] *ARJ*, XX (January 9, 1847), 28; Cincinnati Chamber of Commerce, *34
AR, 1882*, 256. Whiskey was an important part of Cincinnati's commerce. The
trade was based on receipts from interior rectifying points rather than production at Cincinnati. This was especially true from the 1840's through the mid-
1850's, for bulk corn cost more proportionately to ship to Cincinnati than it did
in the form of spirits or pork. In the late 1850's the distilling industry did expand at Cincinnati and receipts and exports of whiskey rose steadily. Receipts
increased from 187,000 barrels in 1850 to a decade peak of 582,000 barrels in
1857, and, although a downswing followed, annual average whiskey receipts
for 1856-60 equaled 419,000 barrels. Annual average exports amounted to 164,-
000 barrels for the five years 1846-50 and 335,000 for 1856-60. Much of this
was marketed in Arkansas, Mississippi, and Louisiana. The value of whiskey
exports increased from $1.5 million in 1850 to $4 million in 1857 and $5.3 mil-
lion in 1859. At this date it was a more valuable article of export than flour and
grain, and worth about one-half the value of Cincinnati's pork and provisions
industry. *The Ohio Cultivator*, III (April 15, 1847), 59; *Hunt's*, XXVII (November, 1852), 568, XXXVII (December, 1857), 738-741, XLI (October,
1859), 495-498; Thomas S. Berry, *Western Prices Before 1861. A Study of the
Cincinnati Market* (Cambridge, Mass., 1943), 205.

cities was just a matter of time, and even though rail connections with the main lines were in the process of construction, or at least on the drawing board, many observers did not anticipate the impact which completion of this process would have on western trade. A Cincinnati correspondent of *Hunt's Merchants' Magazine* wrote that in a comparison between routes to New Orleans or to New York from Cincinnati, "although there is a difference of 500 miles in favor of New York, yet on the untaxed waters of the Ohio and Mississippi, a barrel of flour is carried 1,500 miles in a flat-boat for fifty cents, being less than the toll charged by the States of Ohio and New York on 613 miles of canals, besides the sum required to remunerate . . . transporting the barrel 1,010 miles, and the inconvenience and delay occasioned by 1,239 feet of lockage." [26] The striking point here is that railroads were not even considered as a factor in the competition between New York and New Orleans for the produce of the West. Within a few years such an omission would have been inconceivable.

In 1845, 45 miles of railroad were operating in Ohio. Three years later six times this mileage existed, and in 1852 over 1,400 miles crisscrossed the state. By 1856 some 2,500 miles of road were completed and 2,000 miles were in progress.[27] Ohio had rail connections with every section of the nation, and virtually every county in the state was served by at least one road. The consequences of this development upon Cincinnati's trade with the South were unavoidable in the sense that railroads offered shippers advantages in speed, convenience, safety, uninterrupted seasonal traffic, and eventually rates—advantages which river transportation could not hope to equal. Nor could river facilities offer compensatory gains in other aspects of the trade. Railroads afforded shippers quick and sure carriage directly to the major points of consumption on the Atlantic coast.[28]

Between 1845 and 1853 a minimum of 65 per cent of the flour exported from Cincinnati went south, and probably a good deal

---

[26] *Hunt's*, XXIII (November, 1850), 505.

[27] *ARJ*, XIX (January 3, 1846), 8, XXVI (January 1, 1853), 1; *Hunt's*, XXXV (December, 1856), 766.

[28] Berry, *Western Prices*, 93, summarizes it succinctly: ". . . successive reductions in rail time were diminishing the risk of loss and reducing insurance rates, and commissions and storage expenses at New Orleans were saved by shipping directly [East]. The time of arrival could better be predicted, and both the railway and telegraph made possible a narrower and safer margin of profit."

more, either to New Orleans or other down-river ports. In 1851 and 1852, 97 per cent of the flour moved south from Cincinnati, along with 80 per cent of bulk meat, 97 per cent of beef, 96 per cent of corn, and 83 per cent of lard exports. In 1853 about 80 per cent of the flour and grain went south, but a new factor intruded in significant proportions for the first time—over 19 per cent of the flour moved north and east either by canal and railroad or by the Ohio River. In the next year the movement in this new direction increased, at the expense of the southern route. In 1854 only 47 per cent of the flour went downstream while 25 per cent was shipped up-river and 27 per cent was carried by either rail or canal, with the latter a minor factor. In the following year the revolution in commercial connections involving the grain trade was complete: only 5 per cent of the flour was shipped south while 33 per cent went up-river and 62 per cent moved over railroads or the Miami Canal. During the period 1856-60, the South received as much as 25 per cent of Cincinnati's flour exports only in 1858.[29] In 1856, 1859, and 1860 the South received only from 3 to 8 per cent of Cincinnati's flour exports. In less than three years the importance of New Orleans and the South to Cincinnati's grain trade, insofar as they were reached via river, was eliminated, and Cincinnati faced squarely to the East. The pork and provisions trade experienced a slightly less thorough rerouting. In 1857 some 55 to 65 per cent of pork and lard exports were shipped over railroads from Cincinnati, while the share reaching New Orleans was under 20 per cent. Most of the remainder probably went up-river.[30]

After 1853, then, the bulk of Cincinnati's grain and provisions shipments traveled over the Miami Canal, by railroads, or to up-river ports where through connections were available to Philadelphia or Baltimore. Of these routes, rail soon was dominant. It was possible, once the Cincinnati and Marietta Railroad was completed in 1856, to reach the Baltimore and Ohio Railroad directly from Cincinnati without using the Ohio River. Even before 1856, grain using the canal or the railroads probably was routed to Pittsburgh

---

[29] In 1861, during the Sumter crisis, exports to the South reached 37 per cent as dealers shipped as much and as rapidly as possible to avoid being caught with a large inventory if the crisis worsened.

[30] *De Bow's Review*, IX (December, 1850), 653, XII (January, 1852), 90, XIV (February, 1853), 183, XXI (November, 1856), 516, XXIV (January, 1858), 66; *Hunt's*, XXIX (December, 1853), 743, XXXVII (December, 1857), 743; Cincinnati Chamber of Commerce, *34 AR, 1882*, 162-169.

or Wheeling rather than to the Great Lakes. A substantial quantity of grain and flour utilized the Little Miami Railroad and its connection with the Ohio Central, which moved west from Wheeling. Connections were also possible at Mansfield with the Pennsylvania and Ohio Railroad from Pittsburgh.[31]

The role of the Little Miami, initially one of transporting agricultural produce to Cincinnati, had reversed itself in regard to many farm products. Whereas in the late 1840's and early 1850's most of the flour traveling over the line moved to Cincinnati, by 1859 and 1860, out of a total of 411,000 barrels of flour carried, 357,000 were eastbound. A similar diversion applied to wheat, whiskey, and provisions. Only in live-hog traffic did westbound traffic, to Cincinnati, surpass eastbound. From 1857 to 1859 the Indianapolis and Cincinnati Railroad supplied Cincinnati with greater quantities of flour than the Little Miami, and equal quantities of corn and hogs. Other lines, such as the Cincinnati and Dayton and Marietta and Cincinnati railroads, also carried produce and provisions in both directions.[32]

The extent to which through railway connections with the East diverted grain traffic from Cincinnati altogether, instead of merely rerouting this traffic, is problematical. Annual receipts and exports seem to indicate that no such diversion occurred. After 1855, flour, wheat, and corn receipts displayed some growth, at the very time when the pre-war impact of railroads should have been most apparent. If the export and import statistics are interpreted in terms of the absence of marked growth, instead of evidence of slight and unsteady growth—and the figures are susceptible to both approaches—the explanation of the lack of growth for Cincinnati would appear to lie in the oscillation in production in southeastern Ohio and the relatively stable amount of land sown with wheat

---

[31] The Little Miami and Columbus and Xenia Railroad was a major carrier for Cincinnati. In 1853, the first year in which exports via rail and canal were of any significance, the road transported 60 per cent of the flour. By 1859, 25 per cent of total flour exports from Cincinnati traveled over the Little Miami, and 20 per cent in both 1860 and 1861. Between 1856 and 1861 the Little Miami normally transported about 50,000 barrels of whiskey and 35,000 barrels of pork and beef eastward from Cincinnati. *First Joint Annual Report of the Directors to the Stockholders of the Little Miami and Columbus and Xenia Railroad Companies, 1856* (Columbus, 1857), 40, *4 AR, 1859,* 36-37, *5 AR, 1860,* 44-45, *6 AR, 1861,* 36-37.

[32] *Ibid.* (for each year); *Report of the Indianapolis & Cincinnati Railroad Company, 1859* (Cincinnati, 1860).

rather than in the possibility that grain which had generally gone to Cincinnati had begun to utilize the existing rail connections with the East or Lake Erie, thus bypassing the river city.

Still, there were some indications that the flow of grain from areas previously supplying Cincinnati did alter its direction. Columbus, Ohio, for example, received more flour from way stations on the Little Miami than was shipped through Columbus from Cincinnati in 1859 and 1860. For both years, 108,000 barrels of flour were carried from Cincinnati to Columbus and points east of Columbus, while the latter town received 351,000 barrels from points along the Little Miami between Cincinnati and Columbus. In the early 1850's this traffic was normally directed toward Cincinnati. Points in Highland County, east and slightly north of Cincinnati, which had previously shipped produce to Cincinnati, were reported exporting to Chillicothe in 1859, a route made practical by the construction of the Marietta and Cincinnati Railroad. At Marietta connections could be made with the Parkersburg, Virginia, branch of the Baltimore and Ohio Railroad, or at Chillicothe the Ohio Canal could be taken to Cleveland, or the produce could be freighted north to Lake Erie over the Sandusky, Mansfield and Newark Railroad.[33]

Thus, in the mid-1850's, a radical alteration occurred in the direction in which the grain trade at Cincinnati moved. Although rail connections with the East existed before 1853, it was only in the latter year that substantial quantities of Cincinnati's produce deserted the route to the South in favor of those leading directly to the East Coast. It was precisely in 1853 that the Baltimore and Ohio Railroad achieved its connection with the Ohio River, a year after the Pennsylvania line reached Pittsburgh.

Between 1852 and 1856 grain traffic over the Baltimore and Ohio grew steadily, rising from 600,000 barrels of flour and 21,000 tons of grain, livestock, and provisions in 1852 to 911,000 barrels of flour and 89,000 tons of grain, livestock, and provisions in 1856. After 1855 at least 50 per cent of the total tonnage of agricultural products carried over the road originated from the western terminals, and often as high as 65 per cent in a year such as 1858, when the road carried 986,000 barrels of flour, of which 682,000 were of

---

[33] Little Miami Railroad, *4 AR, 1859*, 36, *5 AR, 1860*, 44, *6 AR, 1861*, 36; *Hunt's*, XXIX (December, 1853), 759-760, XXXV (December, 1856), 766; Ohio State Board of Agriculture, *Fourteenth Annual Report, 1859* (Columbus, 1860), 178-179.

western origin. In addition to the Baltimore road, the Pennsylvania Railroad transported 150,000 barrels of flour east from Pittsburgh in 1853, 200,000 in 1854, and between 340,000 and 350,000 barrels in both 1859 and 1860. The Baltimore and Ohio and the Pennsylvania together carried a total of 806,000 barrels of western flour in 1859 and 702,000 in 1860.[34]

It is not possible to relate this traffic with any precision to that moving east from Cincinnati. As pointed out above, in the first years that through connections to Baltimore were available, the proportion of Cincinnati flour shipped east rose from some 3 per cent in 1852 to 20 per cent in 1853 and 42 per cent in 1854. Thereafter, the proportion was at least 65 per cent. It is likely that the Baltimore and Ohio received a part of the flour moving out of Cincinnati via railroad, and most of the flour shipped to up-river ports. The latter approach accounted for between 22 and 35 per cent of Cincinnati's exports in 1854-61, and an annual average for the eight years of 28 per cent. If all of the flour carried up-river from Cincinnati was eventually freighted east over the Baltimore and Ohio Railroad, in the five years 1856-60 it would amount to about 30 per cent of the total quantity of western flour moved by that carrier during those years.[35]

The redirection of Cincinnati's grain and provisions exports at the expense of the southern route had a considerable effect on the commercial relationship maintained with New Orleans. As early as 1850, when receipts of flour at the latter city were only one-half those of 1849, *De Bow's Review* discovered the cause in the "increased facilities for reaching the Atlantic markets through the Canals and railroads which Northern enterprise is constantly . . . extending." [36] Until 1855, however, considerable quantities of

---

[34] Baltimore & Ohio Railroad, *34 AR, 1860*, 102-105; *ARJ*, XXVII (May 6, 1854), 278; *Hunt's*, XXXII (February, 1855), 243; United States Treasury Department, *Statistics of the Foreign and Domestic Commerce of the United States* (Washington, D.C., 1864), 138-139.

[35] B & O Railroad, *34 AR, 1860*, 102-105. There is no evidence that grain or provisions from Cincinnati found their way to Pittsburgh and the Pennsylvania Railroad, but in view of the fact that the westward extension of the Pennsylvania Railroad intersected roads coming from Cincinnati at Mansfield and Bellefontaine, it seems likely that some traffic flowed in that direction, and it is likely that some of the farm produce moving up-river passed Parkersburg or Wheeling for the Pittsburgh market.

[36] *De Bow's Review*, IX (December, 1850), 660. In this particular year lower receipts resulted largely from deficient crops in many areas of southern Illinois, Indiana, and Ohio, as well as short southern crops, which probably diverted some supplies from New Orleans to other southern markets.

farm produce from Cincinnati continued to seek New Orleans. In 1855 this traffic almost vanished. In the early 1850's Cincinnati furnished New Orleans with some 30 to 35 per cent of her flour and between 40 and 50 per cent of her provisions. From 1849 to 1853 an annual average of 25 per cent of New Orleans' flour receipts originated at Cincinnati. In 1854 this had dropped to 17 per cent, and the annual average for 1855-61 was 4 per cent, while in 1857 less than 20 per cent of pork and lard receipts came from the Ohio River market. As far as the grain trade was concerned, Cincinnati and New Orleans had ceased to be significant to one another. Whereas in one week in January, 1850, Cincinnati forwarded 1,600 barrels of flour to New Orleans, in 1855 only 10,000 were shipped during the entire year.[37]

During the initial stages of this realignment there was some correspondence between falling Cincinnati shipments to New Orleans and declining receipts at New Orleans, as indicated below.[38] It will be noticed that Cincinnati's total flour exports declined also.

Year	Cincinnati's flour exports to New Orleans	Total Cincinnati flour exports	Total flour receipts at New Orleans
	(in thousands of barrels)		
1852	310	408	927
1853	203	313	807
1854	149	333	874
1855	10	199	673
1856	33	509	1,121

Also, receipts of pork, lard, and bulk pork, bacon, and hams declined at New Orleans from 1853 through 1857.[39] During roughly these same years, the hog pack in the West increased from between 1.1 and 1.5 million hogs in 1850-52 to between 2.1 and 2.4 million from 1853 to 1856, while the pack at Cincinnati rose from 324,000 hogs in 1851 to 421,000 in 1854, and fluctuated from 350,000 to

---

[37] *ARJ*, XVIII (January, 1845), 77; *Hunt's*, XXXVII (December, 1857), 743; Cincinnati *Enquirer*, January 5, 1850.

[38] See sources cited in fn. 30 above; *8 Census, 1860, Agriculture*, clvi. Corn receipts at New Orleans were steady.

[39] Barreled pork declined from 316,000 barrels in 1853 to 243,000 in 1857; lard from 268,000 barrels, tierces, and hogsheads to 196,000 in 1857; bulk meats from 281,000 pounds and 97,000 hogsheads, boxes, and casks in 1853 to 7,760 pounds and 81,000 packages in 1857. Switzler, "Report on Internal Commerce," 195-202, 216-218.

450,000 during the remainder of the decade.[40] On the basis of these generally corresponding trends, it might be inferred that the incipient effects of the sudden new course upon which Cincinnati's grain trade embarked were entirely detrimental to the grain trade at New Orleans. This conclusion seems reinforced if it is recalled that from 1852 to 1855 the amount of flour received at or manufactured in St. Louis increased steadily from 515,000 barrels to 830,000 barrels. The grain trade at New Orleans more than recovered in 1856, partly as a result of heavy receipts from St. Louis, where over 1 million barrels of flour were received or manufactured.[41] But New Orleans never recovered the grain trade from Cincinnati.

After 1855 the grain trade at New Orleans achieved previously unexcelled levels, both in the volume and the value of the traffic. The decade of the 1850's was extraordinarily profitable for all phases of commerce at New Orleans. The value of total receipts, at $96 million in 1850, passed $100 million the following year, and for the next ten years expanded at a rate averaging 7.8 per cent annually, until it reached $185 million in 1860. Exports during the same period advanced from $37 million in 1850 to $107 million in 1860.[42] However, this commercial prosperity was, to an even greater degree than in the past, based on an astounding growth in receipts and exports of bulk cotton, and to a lesser degree sugar, molasses, and tobacco—all staple products of the South.

Between 1846 and 1850 the total value of cotton, sugar, molasses, and tobacco receipts formed some 60 to 65 per cent of total receipts at New Orleans. This proportion increased to 71 and 72 per cent in 1852 and 1853, and rose still further, reaching 77 per cent in both 1859 and 1860. In 1860 cotton worth $109 million, sugar worth $18 million, and molasses and tobacco valued at $14.6 million passed down-river to New Orleans, which was rapidly becoming a purely southern commercial center, with its economic affluence ever less dependent upon trade with the Old Northwest.[43]

---

[40] See Table 13.

[41] St. Louis Merchants' Exchange, *Trade and Commerce, 1878*, 50.

[42] Switzler, "Report on Internal Commerce," 209-210, 377.

[43] Andrews, "Reports on Trade and Commerce," 750-757; Switzler, "Report on Internal Commerce," 209-210. As the 1850's progressed, *De Bow's Review* devoted less and less space to statistical studies of the upper Mississippi valley. Fewer abstracts of reports dealing with the trade and manufacturing of northwestern communities appeared, as each issue was focused more intensively on the state of the South in general, and New Orleans in particular.

What this meant in terms of the grain and provisions trade of the Old Northwest with the Crescent City was not, as one student has asserted, the continuation of a trade remaining stable in value.[44] Nor was it the case, as another student has maintained, that "the receipts of flour and other important staples at New Orleans failed to increase during the decade [1850's]." [45] Receipts of flour reached 1.5 million barrels in 1858, a quantity exceeded only in 1847, and were in excess of 1 million barrels in 1856-57, 1859, and 1861. Corn receipts rose too, reaching 3.8 million bushels in 1861. The total value of grain and flour reaching the town rose from $5 million in 1850 to $15 million in 1856, a sum equaled in 1857 and 1860. Still, grain and flour forming 6 per cent of the total value of receipts in 1850 retained the same share in 1860. Only in a relative sense did the grain trade remain stable; in an absolute sense it grew. The provisions trade, on the other hand, lost ground, both relatively and absolutely. Provisions contributed $15.5 million, or 15.8 per cent of the total value of receipts in 1852. Thereafter a steady reduction ensued—to $10.3 million or 6.1 per cent in 1858, and $6.5 million or 3.5 per cent in 1860.[46] Whereas in the late 1840's the provisions trade at New Orleans had been of greater value both totally and relatively than the grain trade, the situation was reversed by 1860.

The provisions trade apparently never recovered from the initial setback experienced when Cincinnati began to ship east rather than south. No other sources of supply arose to compensate for the loss of a major part of Cincinnati's provisions exports. Other packing centers in the Northwest which might have filled the gap were enabled, as railroads penetrated their vicinity, to ship directly east, or to lake ports, or, as seemed to be the case for a number of smaller slaughtering centers, to foresake packing entirely and ship live hogs to larger centers either in the West or on the Atlantic coast. For grain, after a temporary decline, St. Louis seems to have made up in quantity about the amount lost from Cincinnati. St. Louis was able to supply increasing quantities of grain and flour

[44] Edward C. Kirkland, *A History of American Economic Life* (3rd ed., New York, 1951), 227-228.

[45] Berry, *Western Prices*, 49.

[46] *Hunt's*, XXIII (December, 1850), 659, XXXIII (November, 1855), 602; *8 Census, 1860, Agriculture*, clvi; Switzler, "Report on Internal Commerce," 209-210; *Lippincott's New and Complete Gazetteer of the United States* (Philadelphia, 1854), 796; Isaac Lippincott, *A History of Manufactures in the Ohio Valley to the Year 1860* (Chicago, 1914), 180.

to New Orleans in spite of diminishing receipts from the Illinois River valley and the upper Mississippi, partly because of the expansion of wheat production in southern Illinois, but largely due to enlarged grain crops west of the Mississippi. It is also probable that part of the increasing crops of wheat and corn in Indiana, particularly in the southern regions and along the lower Wabash, found their way over the traditional route to New Orleans and the South. But it does appear not only that the grain trade of New Orleans declined in its relative importance to the Northwest, but also that the area supplying New Orleans contracted east of the Mississippi, while it expanded west of that river until secession destroyed the trade entirely.

Some writers maintain that throughout the 1850's New Orleans' interest in the coastwise trade in grain and provisions declined, largely as a result of the diversion of the grain trade from the Mississippi River, and that after the mid-1850's western produce moving south was wholly for local consumption and not for export.[47] But this distorts the true picture, for except in years of heavy foreign demand for American foodstuffs, such as 1841, 1847, and 1853-54, over 60 per cent of the flour exported from New Orleans was consigned to domestic ports, as noted below.[48]

Year	Per cent	Year	Per cent
1841	41	1853	20
1842–46 ave.	61	1854	26
1847	17	1855–61 ave.	67
1848–52 ave.	71		

The domestic market was even more important for the pork trade. From 1840 to 1844, an annual average of 64 per cent of New Orleans' pork exports were consigned to New York, Boston, Philadelphia, and Baltimore. During the subsequent five years, 1845-49, of an annual average export of 257,000 barrels of pork, 87 per cent went to domestic markets, with similar proportions applicable in 1850, 1851, and 1853. Exports of pork from New Orleans declined after 1853, dropping to 178,000 barrels in 1856, 132,000 in 1858, and 53,000 in 1860. But domestic markets retained their primacy, and

---

[47] Dixon, *Traffic History of the Mississippi River System*, 34; Thomas D. Odle, "The American Grain Trade of the Great Lakes, 1825-1873," *Inland Seas*, VII (Winter, 1951), 244-245.

[48] *Hunt's*, IX (December, 1843), 570, XIII (October, 1845), 370; *De Bow's Review*, VI (December, 1848), 437-438, VII (November, 1849), 421, XI (December, 1851), 643-644. See Table 17 for 1851-60.

from 1856 to 1860 an annual average of 97 per cent of New Orleans'
pork exports went to home ports. The proportion received by New
York and Boston declined from 65 per cent in 1854 and 75 per cent
in 1855 to 5.5 and 6 per cent in 1859 and 1860. A similar decline in
the proportion of flour shipped to New York and Boston occurred,
but, as with pork, only in the last year before secession.[49]

Throughout the decade of the 1850's, there was a marked increase in the proportion of total flour receipts ultimately utilized
to fill domestic requirements, either local, southern, or northern.
In 1851, 72 per cent of the flour received at New Orleans remained
in the United States. In 1856, 75 per cent did so, and in 1859-60,
90 per cent was used domestically.[50] The markets at New York and
Boston, in spite of improved connections with production centers
in the Northwest, continued to be primary to New Orleans until
1860, although New Orleans was relatively of less importance to
those cities as a source of flour. In fact, exports of flour to those
two cities actually increased during the 1850's, both relative to
total exports and in quantity. In the five years 1848-52, an annual
average of 43 per cent of New Orleans' flour exports were consigned to New York and Boston. This plunged to 16 and 7 per cent
in 1853 and 1854, due to heavy foreign demands occasioned by the
Crimean War. But from 1855 to 1859 the annual average was 47
per cent, which indicated that Boston and New York more than
recovered their previous degree of importance to New Orleans.
Only in 1860 occurred the change which some writers maintain
had been taking place throughout the 1850's—the market on the
north Atlantic coast virtually disappeared. But until that year, this
was hardly the case.[51]

---

[49] See sources cited for fn. 48 above.

[50] The difference between receipts of flour and exports of flour was consumed at New Orleans or reshipped to up-river markets; this quantity plus exports to New York, Boston, Baltimore, Philadelphia, and other American cities
is taken to represent flour consumed domestically, although a part of it was
probably re-exported from the Atlantic coast ports named above.

[51] Boston received some 14 per cent of total flour receipts from New
Orleans in 1859. This compares favorably, in terms of the mutual importance
of the two cities to each other's grain trade, with the percentage received at
Boston in earlier years, as noted below.

Year	Per cent	Year	Per cent
1839	11	1849	31
1841	10	1851	11
1845	9	1852	8
1848	20		

The condition of the grain trade at New Orleans with refer-ence to the over-all commercial development of the city is less difficult to summarize than that of the relative position of New Orleans in the grain trade of the United States. In the first place, receipts of the great southern staples grew much more rapidly than the trade in grain and provisions, the latter failing to keep pace even with grain and declining both relatively and totally, until it was a negligible factor in 1860. The traffic in both grain and provi-sions at New Orleans suffered severely from the initial shock of Cincinnati's redirected agricultural trade. Grain traffic recovered as new sources of supply appeared to fill the vacuum created by the departure of Cincinnati from the scene. The provisions trade failed to recuperate. This specific instance of a diversion of grain traffic from the route leading to New Orleans resulted in an actual loss in provisions and in a much slower and less substantial rate of growth in the grain trade at New Orleans, which nevertheless achieved fairly high levels of volume and value during the late 1850's. Here it is a matter of what would have developed had it not been for the constantly augmented quantities of grain moving eastward over rail or lake from areas which had normally shipped through New Orleans. As the mileage of railroads increased in the Northwestern states, and as the possibilities of shipping to the East entirely by rail or using railroads to reach the Great Lakes spread to more and more interior areas, the incentive to ship by the Mis-sissippi River diminished. While receipts of wheat and flour at Buffalo increased from 9.1 million bushels in 1850 to 16.3 million in 1859, and exports from Chicago rose from 1.3 million to 10.5 million bushels, receipts at New Orleans experienced an increment of less than 2 million bushels within the same period. Even though the export of grain from New Orleans to East Coast cities retained its importance relative to receipts and total exports at New Orleans until 1860, the latter was rapidly becoming of minor importance to northeastern cities as a source of produce.

It is entirely likely that, had not the Civil War intervened, the

New Orleans also supplied some 10 per cent of the corn received at Boston. The remainder generally originated in Virginia and Maryland, in addition to some received from New York and Pennsylvania. *Hunt's*, VI (February, 1842), 183, XX (February, 1849), 215, XXI (November, 1849), 539, XXV (Decem-ber, 1851), 732; *De Bow's Review*, XIV (March, 1853), 254-256; Charles B. Kuhlman, *The Development of the Flour-Milling Industry in the United States with Special Reference to the Industry in Minneapolis* (Boston and New York, 1929), 65.

New Orleans grain trade would have vanished except insofar as foodstuffs were required to fill local consumption requirements, and these might very well have been supplied by way of the Atlantic coast or from areas in the South producing a surplus, such as the vicinity of Savannah, which could reach New Orleans by a coasting trade. In the year 1860 the domestic market along the north Atlantic coast was of no significance and the foreign trade of minimal importance. Thus, at this time New Orleans had become, economically as well as otherwise, a southern city.

Railroads and the Grain Trade of the Lake Erie Ports from 1850 to 1860

CHAPTER XI

Between 1850 and 1860 the focal point of the grain trade on the Great Lakes shifted from Lake Erie to Lake Michigan. Viewed in terms of the decade, this shift in centrality occurred gradually, but from the perspective of the several decades in which Lake Erie's trade was dominant the transition was rather abrupt. It was the natural consequence of the swift settlement and development of Wisconsin and the northern and north central regions of Illinois.

The population in both Wisconsin and Illinois more than doubled from 1850 to 1860, while that of the remaining northwestern states rose by 30 per cent. Along with rapid settlement went rising levels of grain production, until by 1860 the greatest wheat-growing region in the United States straddled the Wisconsin-Illinois border. Expanding population and production were inextricably bound up with the construction of thousands of miles of railroads, reaching out from ambitious Lake Michigan ports into their immediate hinterlands, beyond to the Mississippi River, and eventually to the trans-Mississippi West.

While Milwaukee and Chicago engaged in strenuous economic competition in their efforts to engross the lion's share of the grain trade, and while these markets progressed rapidly in their relative importance and total contribution to the grain trade of the Great Lakes, older grain entrepots like Cleveland, Sandusky, and Detroit became increasingly sensitive to the westward movement of the grain trade. Not only was the center of grain production shifting ever westward, but the new lands being put into production yielded greater quantities of grain at less cost than the heavily worked lands in parts of Ohio and Michigan, and the railroads afforded the new farmers access to the Great Lakes, thus placing their grain in competition with that of the regions inland from Lake Erie. The grain trade of Lake Erie ports was also damaged by the extension of through routes from the East which cut in behind them, giving to farmers in areas penetrated by those lines the alternative of shipping directly east by rail instead of to Lake Erie and thence to a grain depot at the eastern end of the lakes. To a certain extent the forces which, in an earlier period, enabled ports like Cleveland, Detroit, or Sandusky to eliminate the effective competition of Ashtabula, Monroe, and Milan-Huron now acted in favor of grain centers farther west and at the expense of those located on Lake Erie.[1] In 1842 Ohio supplied 48 per cent of the total wheat and flour receipts at Buffalo, and Michigan contributed another 20 per cent. The next year Ohio and Michigan supplied fully 80 per cent of Buffalo's receipts. By 1857 the proportion had fallen to 22 per cent, representing a considerable quantitative decline as well.[2]

The degree to which preponderance in the grain trade shifted from Lake Erie to Lake Michigan is expressed in Table 20, used in conjunction with Tables 4 and 10.

The new dominance of Lake Michigan was by no means of overwhelming proportions, and was achieved only in the middle of the 1850's. Until 1854 Ohio and Michigan still contributed over

---

[1] Toledo was an exception, primarily because of her connection with rich areas of north and north central Indiana, the latter only coming into its own in wheat production during the 1850's.

[2] *Hunt's*, VIII (May, 1843), 529, XI (August, 1844), 133, XL (May, 1859), 600.

60 per cent of total lake exports, and, as noted earlier, it was an augmented production in Ohio and Michigan between 1850 and 1853 that accounted for the pronounced rise in the lake grain trade during that period. But in 1855 the proportion supplied by Lake Erie fell below 50 per cent, and from 1856 to 1860 remained be-

TABLE 20. TOTAL ANNUAL EXPORTS OF WHEAT AND WHEAT FLOUR FROM ALL LAKE ERIE AND LAKE MICHIGAN PORTS, BY STATE, 1853-60 [3] (IN THOUSANDS OF BUSHELS)

Year	Ohio	Indiana	Illinois	Michigan	Wisconsin	Total
1853	10,998	1,029	1,560	4,482	2,561	20,630
1854	6,404	720	2,865	2,604	1,892	14,385
1855	8,053	1,270	7,115	3,957	4,436	24,831
1856	7,330	1,409	9,445	3,017	4,626	25,927
1857	8,305	1,251	10,144	3,387	4,653	27,640
1858	10,899	1,875	11,202	3,628	6,861	34,465
1859	10,753	1,633	10,597	3,529	7,560	34,072
1860	13,383	2,411	15,892	6,452	11,288	49,426

Sources: C. P. McClelland and C. C. Huntington, *History of the Ohio Canals. Their Construction, Cost, Use and Partial Abandonment* (Columbus, Ohio, 1905), Appendix J, 175-176; 8 *Census, 1860, Agriculture*, cxlix; Chicago *Daily Tribune*, March 27, 1854; *De Bow's Review*, XXVI (April, 1859), 453; United States Treasury Department, *Statistics of the Foreign and Domestic Commerce of the United States* (Washington, D.C., 1864), 150; *Hunt's*, XXVIII (March, 1853), 363, XXIX (October, 1853), 512, XXXVI (November, 1850), 556-559, XI, (March, 1859), 300, (May, 1859), 701, XLII (April, 1860), 428-429; Chicago Board of Trade, *Nineteenth Annual Report of the Trade and Commerce of Chicago, 1876* (Chicago, 1877), 43; Milwaukee Chamber of Commerce, *Fifth Annual Report for the Year 1862* (Milwaukee, 1863), 20.

[3] In arriving at Toledo's contribution for 1854 and 1856, exports were estimated on the basis of known receipts over the Miami and Erie and the Wabash canals, which normally brought about 25 per cent of Toledo's total flour receipts and 50 per cent of the wheat. These receipts, minus a small portion retained for domestic use, were exported. In 1855-57 exports from ports such as Sandusky, Milan-Huron, Venice, etc., are estimated at 2 million bushels on the basis of a known decline from previous levels. In 1858-60 the figure is assumed to be 1.5 million on the basis of reports that, excepting Cleveland, all other ports on Ohio's lake shore exported an amount equal to 20 per cent of the wheat and flour shipped from Toledo. Cleveland's contribution in 1859-60 was calculated on the basis of receipts in which railroads carried two times as much wheat and flour to Cleveland as the Ohio Canal, the latter figure alone being known for 1859-60. In 1854 and 1858 the estimated exports are out of line with production figures reported by state enumerators. In both cases the suggested figure for exports would leave too little for home consumption if the state figures are accurate. Most probably, the exports are a little high and total production low.

Most of the wheat and flour originating in Indiana utilized either Toledo or Chicago if destined for the lakes. But it was reported in 1857 that Buffalo received 10 per cent of her flour and wheat from Indiana, so this proportion

tween 40 and 43 per cent of the total. This was by no means a negligible share of the trade, however, and in terms of the total value of all categories of lake trade, the commerce of Lake Erie, while no longer furnishing two-thirds as in 1851-52, contributed at least 50 per cent in 1860.[4]

For the most part, the loss of ascendancy by Lake Erie was the result of a stabilization of wheat acreage in Ohio and Michigan after 1853 or 1854. The noticeable fluctuations in both production and exports reflected not only market conditions but the relative success or failure of crops grown on a constant acreage. In Wisconsin and Illinois, on the other hand, poor crop yields in any given year were often compensated for by an increased acreage sown with wheat, enabling total production to rise fairly steadily in spite of none too bountiful yields per acre. Numerous were the complaints of Ohio producers to the effect that the cost of producing a bushel of wheat was twice that of farmers in Illinois and Wisconsin. But in years when wheat rose above $1.50 a bushel and then hit $2.00, and a barrel of flour reached $8.00 or $9.00, even farmers who estimated the cost of raising a bushel of wheat at 90 to 93 cents could expect a profit from their crop. Unfortunately, wheat rarely remained at a dollar for very long.[5]

The stable wheat acreage in the interior areas, from which ports like Cleveland, Sandusky, and Detroit drew their grain supplies, prevented those ports from expanding their grain trade to any great extent, and, indeed, made the trade more precarious than at earlier periods, when the effects of a poor crop were ameliorated by yearly additions to the previous wheat acreage. An obstacle to growth in the grain trade also existed, as has been suggested pre-

---

was used to calculate the quantities representing Indiana's lake trade, the remainder being an unknown portion of Ohio and Illinois exports. Illinois exports are based entirely on those from Chicago. Michigan's are based on exports from Detroit plus known receipts at Chicago of wheat and flour via the Michigan Southern and Michigan Central railroads, some of which were from Indiana.

Wisconsin's exports were reached by assuming that exports from Milwaukee represented, as they did in 1852 and 1858, about 70 per cent of the state total. A certain portion of Wisconsin grain is represented in the Illinois column, as part of the 500,000 bushels of wheat and flour received at Chicago via the Chicago, St. Paul and Fond du Lac Railroad in 1857 was undoubtedly of Wisconsin origin, and the Chicago and Milwaukee road also carried some of Wisconsin's grain to Chicago.

[4] Andrews, "Reports on Trade and Commerce," 222, 227, 245.

[5] *Patent Report, 1854*, 146; Ohio Commissioner of Statistics, *Seventh Annual Report to the Governor, 1863* (Columbus, 1864), 25; *Hunt's*, XXXV (December, 1856), 748.

viously, in the completion of through rail routes from the East Coast to Chicago. These roads, the Pittsburgh, Fort Wayne, and Chicago, the Lake Shore–Michigan Southern lines, the Michigan Central–Great Western complex, and the Ohio and Pennsylvania Railroad enabled producers along their routes to ship directly to the East and avoid the grain centers in the Northwest. Before 1860 the effect of these roads was more or less limited, in regard to through grain traffic, to those portions of the lines passing in the rear of Cleveland and Sandusky, and even at these places, before the Civil War, the role of the railroad in supplying grain more than balanced the diversion of grain from such ports by other railroads.

The period of greatest growth in the grain trade at Cleveland had occurred in the 1830's. Receipts of wheat and flour increased from 340,000 bushels in 1830 to 2.8 million in 1839, and 4.6 million the following year. Thereafter, down to the Civil War, as Tables 6 and 21 indicate, receipts and exports followed an uncertain path, fluctuating radically at times, and over the course of 20 years demonstrating no perceptible progress. The initial growth at Cleveland followed closely upon the completion of the Ohio Canal and its numerous feeder canals, which allowed Cleveland to draw its grain supplies from the prolific lands of the upper and middle Muskingum valley. Even though Cleveland was the major grain-forwarding center on the Great Lakes as late as 1854, and in the years 1851-52 shipped 7.3 and 6.6 million bushels of wheat and flour, her days of ascendancy were strictly numbered, for her receipts were dependent upon a wheat acreage that was not increasing during the 1850's. Moreover, the relative importance of the grain trade lost ground rapidly during the 1850's. In the 1840's grain exports were normally worth about 50 per cent of total exports. This proportion had declined to some 25 per cent by 1851, and dropped still lower as the grain trade failed to demonstrate lasting growth. Other commodities assumed an increasing importance and caused total exports to advance from $12 million in 1851 to $76 million in 1855.[6]

Throughout most of the antebellum years, Cleveland received by far the greatest portion of her grain from the Ohio Canal, while a small part reached Cleveland by wagon or in coasting vessels

---

[6] "Improvement of the Navigation of the Northern and Northwestern Lakes, etc.," *House Reports,* 34 Cong., 1 Sess., No. 316 (1856), Serial 870, 6-7; Andrews, "Reports on Trade and Commerce," 168-169; *Hunt's,* X (March, 1844), 293.

from other lake ports. But in the early 1850's a rising quantity of grain began to reach Cleveland by railroad. This was accompanied by a decline in receipts via canal. At the same time, total dollar receipts on the Ohio Canal, after reaching a peak of some $700,000 in 1851, entered upon a steady and rapid decline to less than $100,-000 in 1861. The railroads were rapidly making the Ohio Canal obsolete.[7]

At Cleveland a number of lines converged: two—the Cleveland and Toledo Railroad and the Cleveland, Painesville, and Ashtabula Railroad—paralleled the lake shore.[8] Another, the Cleveland and Mahoning road, was designed to penetrate the Mahoning River valley, and passed through Warren, Niles, Girard and Youngstown, to the southeast of Cleveland, while the Cleveland and Pittsburgh also ran through southeastern Ohio. The Cleveland, Medina and Tuscarawas road ran almost straight south. Cleveland was connected with Cincinnati by two lines; one, the Cleveland, Columbus and Cincinnati, was completed in 1851; the second, through Zanesville, had advanced 65 miles by 1856.[9] All of the north-south roads were intersected at some point by the major east-west lines coming from Wheeling or Pittsburgh.

From the mid-1850's, Cleveland received a growing proportion of her grain by rail. In 1854 the Cleveland and Pittsburgh line carried 27,000 barrels of flour, 177,000 bushels of wheat, and 110,-000 bushels of other grain to Cleveland. In the same year, the Cleveland, Columbus and Cincinnati road deposited 1.6 million bushels of grain at Cleveland, along with 303,000 live animals and

---

[7] Statistics representing receipts at Cleveland generally include only those from the Ohio Canal. Before 1852 receipts showed an excess over exports, which was natural since some had to be retained for local use. But in 1852 there is an export excess of some 600,000 bushels of wheat and flour. This suggests that grain was reaching Cleveland by railroad. In 1853 the excess of exports over imports reached 1.8 million bushels. C. P. McClelland and C. C. Huntington, *History of the Ohio Canals. Their Construction, Cost, Use and Partial Abandonment* (Columbus, Ohio, 1905), Appendix F, 170.

[8] *Report of the Directors of the Cleveland and Toledo Railroad Company, 1854* (New York, 1854), 3. This road was formed by the union of the Junction Railroad and the Toledo, Norwalk and Cleveland Railroad in September, 1853. *Hunt's,* XXXV (December, 1856), 766.

[9] *ARJ,* XXVI (October 29, 1853), 693; *Hunt's,* XXXV (December, 1856), 766. The Cleveland and Pittsburgh road erected a 250,000-bushel grain warehouse at Cleveland in 1853 and added a line of propeller steamers in 1856 between Cleveland and Detroit. Cleveland and Pittsburgh Railroad Company, *Sixth Annual Report, 1854* (Cleveland, 1854), 27; *9 AR, 1857,* 11.

15,000 tons of meat products.[10] It was also reported that dressed hogs in large quantities were reaching Cleveland from as far as Lafayette and Terre Haute, Indiana. In 1856 some 70,000 barrels of flour and large quantities of grain arrived via the Cleveland and Pittsburgh road, while some 17,000 tons of freight came over the lines of the Cleveland and Toledo road. By 1857 about one-half of Cleveland's flour receipts and two-thirds of the wheat arrived by rail. At the same time unknown quantities were leaving Cleveland via rail.[11]

In 1858 Toledo was the largest grain center on Lake Erie and by 1860 the second most important in the East North Central states, surpassed only by Chicago in the total quantity of grain shipped. In that last year of peace, Toledo shipped 8.8 million bushels of wheat and flour, a million bushels less than Milwaukee's exports, but the latter exported only 140,000 bushels of corn, oats, and rye, while Toledo forwarded some 5.3 million bushels of corn. The steady growth of the grain trade centered at Toledo and the large traffic attained by 1860 were largely the result of the striking advance in wheat cultivation in Indiana during the 1850's and the ability of Indiana's farmers to reach the Toledo market via rail and canal. Toledo also received corn from as far west as Vermilion County, Illinois.[12]

Railroads carried a swelling volume of grain and provisions to Toledo during the 1850's, while the proportion coming over the Wabash and Erie and Miami and Erie canals declined in consequence of the expanding rail facilities. Still, in 1862, the canals were by no means obsolete and they delivered between 20 and 25 per cent of the wheat and flour reaching Toledo. This was about the same proportion carried in 1860, when the canals carried 1.9 million of the 8.8 million bushels of wheat and flour received at Toledo, but a considerable decline from 1852, when 3.2 million of 4.3 million bushels arrived via canal.[13]

[10] Cleveland and Pittsburgh Railroad, *7 AR, 1855; ARJ*, XXVIII (March 24, 1855), 183.

[11] Cleveland and Pittsburgh Railroad, *9 AR, 1857*, 11; *Report of the Directors of the Cleveland and Toledo Railroad Company, 1863*, 29; *Hunt's*, XL (March, 1859), 300.

[12] *Patent Report, 1854*, 123. Here it was observed that the prairie farmers of this region usually sold their corn in the shock to cattle feeders since the price at the Wabash and Erie Canal was normally less than the feeders paid.

[13] United States Treasury Department, *Statistics of the Foreign and Domestic Commerce of the United States* (Washington, D.C., 1864), 155.

Among the major lines serving Toledo were the Cleveland and Toledo and the Dayton and Michigan railroads. The latter, almost complete in 1858, ran directly south from Toledo and tapped the same region previously penetrated by the Miami and Erie Canal.

TABLE 21. ANNUAL SHIPMENTS OF WHEAT, FLOUR, AND CORN AT CLEVELAND AND TOLEDO, 1851-60 (IN THOUSANDS)

Year	Cleveland			Toledo[a]		
	Wheat (bu.)	Flour (bbl.)	Other (bu.)	Wheat (bu.)	Flour (bbl.)	Corn (bu.)
1851	2,141	656	907	1,640	243	2,775
1852	3,500	760	967	2,813	416	4,107
1853	2,624	796	471	2,100	327	–
1854	–	377	1,061	–	–	–
1855	537	408	440	1,701	273	4,267
1856	438	587	626	1,976	464	–
1857	490	334	272	1,446	336	–
1858	681	519	370	2,343	466	1,993
1859	–	–	–	2,313	688	714
1860	–	–	–	5,272	720	5,334

[a] 1853 is based on canal receipts which in prior years contributed 65 per cent of the flour and 80 per cent of the wheat received at Toledo. Both 1856 and 1857 are based on canal receipts, which in 1858 and 1859 furnished 25 per cent of flour and 50 per cent of wheat receipts. In 1859-60 receipts are used.

Sources: Andrews, "Reports on Trade and Commerce," 168-169, 189-190; Chicago *Daily Tribune*, March 27, 1854; *Patent Report, 1855*, 410; *De Bow's Review*, XXVI (April, 1859), 453; *8 Census, 1860, Agriculture*, cxlix; *Hunt's*, XXVIII (March, 1853), 363, 477, XXIX (October, 1853), 512, XL (March, 1859), 300, (May, 1859), 701.

This road appears to have been a relatively unimportant factor in Toledo's grain trade prior to 1861. Much more important was the Toledo and Wabash road running parallel to the Wabash and Erie Canal, and in operation by 1857 along the entire route from Toledo to a point on the Illinois border east of Williamsport, Indiana. It is entirely likely that some of the produce from the area around Danville, Illinois, and Williamsport, Indiana, which normally traveled south via the Wabash and Erie Canal to Evansville and a southern market, was diverted northeast to Toledo with the coming of this road. The canal had already served to divert grain from the southern route to Toledo from as far west as Lafayette, and the railroad served to extend this distance farther west. While it is known that the 500,000 bushels of wheat and flour that left Logansport in 1852 went north over the Wabash and Erie Canal, and in later years over the Toledo and Wabash line, the direction which shipments from Terre Haute took is not clear. By the mid-1850's Terre Haute was on the line of the Terre Haute and Indianapolis, the Alton and Terre Haute, the Evansville and Illinois, and the Terre Haute and Richmond, so that possibilities existed for shipping either to Toledo, Chicago, or Cincinnati.[14]

The major rail route from which Toledo derived its mounting grain receipts was the Michigan Southern and Northern Indiana Railroad, running from Chicago through South Bend, Indiana, and southern Michigan to Toledo, and which established through connections to Chicago in 1852. Along the line of this road, Toledo and Chicago competed for the agricultural produce of the intervening territory. It seems that Toledo was more successful in capturing the traffic of this route. The total tonnage carried by the line increased from 232,000 in 1856 to 399,000 in 1860. Of this, 38 per cent was consigned to Toledo in 1856, 43 per cent in 1857, and 73 per cent in 1860. In 1858 and 1859, 90 per cent and 77 per cent of the freight moving east was composed of goods classified as vegetable or animal.[15] During the latter years of the 1850's, the Michigan Southern transported to Toledo over 50 per cent of total flour receipts and between 36 and 44 per cent of wheat receipts, while the Toledo and Wabash system brought between 40 and 50 per cent of total corn receipts compared with 12 per cent carried

	Michigan Southern RR.			Toledo and Wabash RR.		
Year	Flour (bbl.)	Wheat (bu.)	Corn (bu.)	Flour (bbl.)	Wheat (bu.)	Corn (bu.)
	(in thousands)			*(in thousands)*		
1858	253	940	266	73	343	875
1859	380	1,024	–	98	336	352
1860	395	1,950	–	–	–	–
1862	883	2,851	–	–	–	–

[14] The Toledo and Wabash was formed in 1858 by the consolidation of the Toledo and Wabash Railroad of Ohio and the Wabash and Western Company of Indiana. *First Annual Report of the Toledo and Wabash Railway Company to the Stockholders, 1859* (Toledo, 1860), 7; *ARJ*, XXVI (June 11, 1853), 378.

[15] *Report of the Board of Directors of the Michigan Southern and Northern Indiana Rail-Road Companies, 1853* (New York, 1853), 6-7, *1859*, 17, *1863*, 37.

by the Michigan Southern in 1858. The quantities carried by both roads to Toledo for several years are noted below: [16]

Most of Toledo's exports were shipped via Lake Erie during the 1850's. The town was connected with both the New York Central and New York and Erie railroads by steam propeller lines of some six to ten vessels each. Connections were also available with Oswego and other Lake Ontario markets, as well as Ogdensburg. The larger part of exports went, as formerly, to Buffalo. In 1851 some 90 per cent of the flour, 50 per cent of the wheat, and 60 per cent of the corn exported from Toledo was consigned to Buffalo. Similar proportions still held in 1857.[17] Certain amounts of grain were also reported moving east via the Cleveland and Toledo road, but for the most part shipments east over railroads were composed of provisions and livestock. Some 165,000 live hogs were shipped east by rail in 1859, a considerable increase over the 23,000 live hogs shipped in 1851. At least part of the 100,000 barrels of pork received at Toledo in 1859 also went east via rail.[18]

By 1860, then, both Cleveland and Toledo were heavily dependent upon railroads for their grain receipts, and, correspondingly, less dependent upon the existing canal networks. Diversion of traffic from the canals seems to have been a more rapid process at Cleveland than Toledo, for as late as 1862 the Wabash and Erie Canal carried 217,000 barrels of flour, 3 million bushels of wheat, and 738,000 bushels of corn to Toledo.[19] Normally, considerably more corn than wheat took the water route, since it was of much less value than wheat but cost about the same to ship.[20] Since Toledo was a far greater depot for corn than Cleveland, it was

---

[16] Toledo and Wabash Railway, *1 AR, 1859,* 7, 20; *Hunt's,* XL (May, 1859), 699-700; Treasury Dept., *Statistics of Foreign and Domestic Commerce,* 155. Over 90 per cent of the flour arriving via the Toledo and Wabash originated at Logansport, Lafayette, Peoria, and Fort Wayne.

[17] Andrews, "Reports on Trade and Commerce," 108, 111, 133; *Hunt's,* XL (May, 1859), 601.

[18] *ARJ,* XXVIII (October 27, 1855), 674-675; *Hunt's,* XLII (May, 1860), 609; Andrews, "Reports on Trade and Commerce," 193; Treasury Dept., *Statistics of Foreign and Domestic Commerce,* 155.

[19] *Ibid.*

[20] For this reason, as well as because of the generally low price of bulk corn, as much of the grain as possible was turned into pork or whiskey. It was estimated that in Ohio some 66 per cent of a corn crop was used for stock feeding, and another 20 per cent was utilized in distilleries. Ohio Commissioner of Statistics, *2 AR, 1858,* reported that Ohio distilleries consumed 11.7 million bushels of corn in 1858, or 23 per cent of the crop; *Hunt's,* XXIV (May, 1851), 618. Charles T. Leavitt, "Transportation and the Livestock Industry of the Middle West to 1860," *Agricultural History,* VIII (January, 1934), 20-23, as-

natural that the canal should continue to serve Toledo, after the Ohio Canal became a rather minor factor in the trade of Cleveland. Both communities constructed railroads directly into the country from which the canals obtained their freight and at the same time initiated the practice of shipping a part, albeit a small one, of their grain via rail to the East. The major difference between the towns was that Toledo drew its supplies from a region which greatly expanded its production of grain during the 1850's, while the area which contributed to Cleveland's grain exports maintained a relatively uniform level of production. Cleveland also had more to fear from railroads passing immediately to her rear through the upper and middle Muskingum valley. These lines probably diverted some grain to Wheeling and Pittsburgh from regions equidistant between Cleveland and those Ohio River cities.

The Michigan Southern's great rival to the north, the Michigan Central road, served Detroit, and since both carriers depended to a certain extent upon the agricultural produce of the same area, Toledo and Detroit were to that degree competitors in the grain trade. Detroit and Chicago, too, were served by the Central, which passed from Chicago through Calumet City, Illinois, Michigan City, Indiana, New Buffalo, Michigan, Kalamazoo, Battle Creek, and Ann Arbor to Detroit. In 1853 the Great Western Railroad of Canada was opened, giving the Central a through route to both the New York Central and New York and Erie at Niagara Falls. At Hamilton, Ontario, the Great Western connected with the Canadian Trunk Railroad, thus making Toronto, Montreal, Quebec, and Portland, Maine, accessible by rail to shippers in the Northwest.[21]

The grain trade at Detroit, in the 1850's, corresponded in its

---

serted that due to the rising price of corn in Ohio in the 1850's, farmers could not afford to feed it to hogs, so that much more corn during the 1850's was sold as a cash crop. Moreover, railroads had so increased land values as to make it unprofitable to raise swine. Yet the *Cincinnati Price Current*, August, 1852, quoted in *Hunt's*, XXVIII (November, 1852), 558, reported that corn was high due to the high price of hogs, which served as an inducement to increase the supply of the latter. During the 1850's the price of corn at Cincinnati did rise from some 33 to 35 cents in 1850-51 to around 43 cents in 1855 and 45 cents in 1860. Hogs per 100 pounds also rose from under $4.00 in the late 1840's to as high as $6.85 in 1858 and $5.25 in 1860. Ohio Commissioner of Statistics, 7 *AR, 1863*, 25. Since both corn and hogs were rising in value, and whiskey as well, it would seem that the earlier reasons for concentrating the corn in other forms would retain their validity, especially since railroads now made it possible to ship livestock directly to the East.

[21] Michigan Central Railroad Company, *Eighth Annual Report, 1854* (Boston, 1854), 20; *Fifth Annual Review of the Trade and Commerce . . . of Chicago, 1856* (Chicago, 1857), 60-61.

frequently oscillating movement with that of Cleveland, and reflected, as did the Cleveland trade, a generally stable level of production in the areas from which grain supplies were derived. Exports of wheat and flour, which reached 3.4 million bushels in 1847, exceeded that figure only once during the 1850's, when close to 4 million bushels were shipped in 1855. In other years, exports fluctuated between 3.1 and 3.3 million bushels, and dropped as low as 2.5 million in 1854. In 1860 and 1861, however, in response to another enormous English demand, exports rose to 5.6 million and 8.1 million bushels.[22]

At Detroit, railroads assumed an earlier and greater importance in supplying grain than at either Cleveland or Toledo, since a major canal did not terminate at Detroit as was the case with the Ohio ports. In shipments also, railroads seem to have served even more prominently if compared to Toledo or Cleveland, both of which continued to send the bulk of their produce to the East via Lake Erie.

The Michigan Central was the major carrier to Detroit, and, as observed in a previous section, supplied some 55 to 65 per cent of Detroit's flour receipts during the 1840's. During the 1850's the proportion received at Detroit via the Central increased to around 70 per cent in 1856 and over 75 per cent in the years 1857-59. Virtually all of the incoming wheat at Detroit arrived over the railroad, as did the major part of the relatively small corn receipts. The wheat and flour that did not travel the Central line arrived for the most part via the Detroit and Milwaukee route, which transported 17 per cent and 14 per cent of Detroit's flour receipts in 1857 and 1859. The little remaining came via wagon and coasting vessels, with small quantities also carried by the Erie and Kalamazoo Railroad from Toledo. At Chicago the Central delivered between 20,000 and 50,000 bushels of wheat and flour from 1853 to 1857, and 122,000 bushels in 1858, the latter representing about 5 per cent of the total wheat and flour transported by the road.[23]

---

[22] *Hunt's*, XVI (February, 1847), 191, XXXVI (November, 1856), 556-559; Andrews, "Reports on Trade and Commerce," 198-199; Treasury Dept., *Statistics of Foreign and Domestic Commerce*, 158.

[23] In 1857 the Detroit and Milwaukee carried 83,000 barrels of flour to Detroit, while the Central transported 375,000 out of the 483,000 barrels received at Detroit. In 1859 the former road carried 85,000 barrels and the Michigan Central 458,000 out of total receipts of 605,000 barrels. *Hunt's*, XXXV (November, 1856), 557-559, XXXVIII (May, 1858), 581, XLII (April, 1860), 421. The figures representing receipts via the Michigan Central do not correspond

Some of the grain received at Detroit was used to supply the lumber regions to the north in Michigan's Upper Peninsula. By 1855 the Sault Ste. Marie Canal was open and grain and provisions could reach Lake Superior. In 1859 Detroit was reported shipping 12,000 barrels of flour and some 3,000 barrels of pork and beef through that waterway. For the most part, grain seems to have moved north into Lake Superior until 1860, rather than south from that lake.[24] A considerable quantity of Detroit's flour found its way into Canada, along with some corn for purposes of whiskey manufacture. In this trade, the Michigan Central's connection with the Great Western Railroad was of considerable significance. In 1854 and 1855 approximately 35 per cent of the flour shipped from Detroit traveled on the Great Western road, and in 1857 the same proportion still held. Over one-half of corn exports were carried by that line in 1857, but only 9 per cent of the wheat shipped from Detroit utilized rail services while the bulk of the wheat went via Lake Erie, 80 per cent being consigned to Buffalo in 1857.[25]

In the grain trade of the large markets treated in this section, railroad facilities played an important part in carrying the grain to Lake Erie, and, as in the case of Detroit, served as a major alternative route for moving flour to ultimate points of consumption, although Lake Erie retained its position as the primary route even at Detroit. This function, as a carrier from the centers of production to final consuming centers, was not to become a common role of the railroads until after the Civil War, but the initial stages of

with those furnished in Michigan Central Railroad, *14 AR, 1860*, 30, as the latter accumulated its figures by the calendar year while the Detroit newspapers from which *Hunt's* obtained its information were referring to figures between July and June of a given crop year. Some of Detroit's corn came from Illinois. It is not clear why the Detroit market attracted corn from such a distance. Michigan Central Railroad, *14 AR, 1860*, 30; *5 AR, Commerce of Chicago, 1856*, 20, *7 AR, 1858*, 7, 11-12.

[24] Most of the south-flowing commerce consisted of iron and copper ore. Archer B. Hulbert, *The Paths of Inland Commerce. A Chronicle of Trail, Road, and Waterway* (New Haven, Conn., 1920), 166, wrote that in the decade preceding the Civil War, exports of wheat from Lake Superior rose from 1,400 bushels to 3.2 million bushels, while in 1859 nearly 7 million bushels of corn and oats were shipped from the lake. These estimates seem quite excessive. Minnesota produced only 2.1 million bushels of wheat and 2.9 million bushels of corn in 1859, and a good portion of the surplus went south along the Mississippi to points where eastern railroads touched the river. Furthermore, of the 16 million bushels of corn received at Buffalo-Oswego, Chicago supplied at least 75 per cent.

[25] *Hunt's*, XXXV (November, 1856), 566, XXXVIII (May, 1858), 577, XL (May, 1859), 601, XLII (April, 1860), 428-429.

its development are apparent at points like Detroit and areas to the east of Cincinnati during the 1850's. The western railroads, both in the eastern and western regions of the Old Northwest, served primarily to transport grain from interior centers, near points of production, to central depots on the Great Lakes. There the grain was transferred to lake vessels and shipped to various receiving centers at the eastern end of the lakes, where railroads entered into competition with the canals and with each other for the grain traffic to the East Coast. Prior to the Civil War, then, the impact of railroads was felt in two of the three stages of transportation through which agricultural produce passed in its journey from producer to American consumer.

In their capacity as carriers of grain in the initial stage of the trade—from farm to northwestern grain market—the impact of each road upon the regions which it traversed varied according to the time and place that service was inaugurated. As subsequent pages will attempt to point out, there seems to have been a certain distinction between the consequences of the coming of railroads to Ohio and parts of Indiana and their development in Illinois and Wisconsin. The railroads had a considerably more impulsive, dynamic, and developmental effect upon the grain trade at Chicago and Milwaukee than at Cincinnati, Cleveland, and Toledo.

The Advent of Railroads
in Illinois and Wisconsin

CHAPTER XII

The rapid growth of population in Wisconsin and Illinois in the 1850's led inevitably to an increase in the production of grain, since farming and activities dependent upon agriculture were the paramount economic activities of the region. But population increase in itself is not enough to explain the remarkable levels of grain production achieved in either state during the decade. Some other factor had to be present—a factor offering farmers of both states a concrete inducement to expand grain cultivation to a point in 1859 where Illinois produced 13.8 bushels of wheat per capita and Wisconsin 20, thus stimulating a remarkable advance of the grain trade centered at both Milwaukee and Chicago.

In 1848 such a factor appeared in Illinois and Chicago in the form of the Illinois and Michigan Canal, which enabled Chicago to draw a large part of its grain supplies from the country between

Chicago and the upper Illinois River valley. This transportation improvement, of particular importance to the corn trade of Chicago, did little to advance the wheat and flour trade, which was based to a large degree on counties not served by the canal and dependent upon wagons or such streams as were available to carry their produce to Chicago. Milwaukee's dependence upon the wagon trade was similar, and though both towns entered actively into the construction of plank roads into the interior, this did little to expand the area from which grain supplies were procured. A new development was necessary, not only to enlarge the area maintaining commercial relations with the Lake Michigan ports, but to accelerate the production of grain by offering economic incentives to farmers far removed from the lake shore. Such an incentive appeared in the form of the Galena and Chicago Union Railroad, which began to deliver grain at Chicago's wharves in 1848. In 1849 there were 53 miles of railroad in Illinois, and in 1852 56 miles in Wisconsin. In 1852 Illinois boasted 296 miles, and one year later 777 miles. By 1858 this latter figure had reached 2,682 miles, while Wisconsin's track increased to 130 in 1853 and 775 in 1858.[1]

The growth of the rail net radiating from Chicago to the West and converging upon Chicago from eastern approaches was particularly impressive after 1852, when, in six years, some 2,700 miles were added to the rail system of Illinois. As of 1854, it was estimated that 1,626 miles of railroad led into Chicago.[2] By the end of the decade as least 3,000 miles of railroad terminated there. In 1852 the Michigan Central reached Chicago, providing through rail service to New York. In the same year the Michigan Southern obtained entrance to Chicago, and five years later the Pittsburgh, Fort Wayne, and Chicago route was completed.[3]

Construction of the Galena and Chicago Union Railroad, Chicago's pioneer road, and long the most important grain carrier, was begun in 1848 but had advanced only 42 miles to Elgin by 1850. Three years later it was completed to Freeport, where it used the tracks of the Illinois Central to reach Galena. Connections were also secured with Dunleith, opposite Dubuque, Iowa, on the Mississippi River, in 1855. A second line of the Galena left the Free-

---

[1] *ARJ*, XXVI (January 1, 1853), 1, XXVII (January 7, 1854), 12.

[2] William Brass, *The Railroads, History, and Commerce of Chicago* (Chicago, 1854), 15.

[3] *Hunt's*, XLII (June, 1860), 698-699.

port branch at St. Charles, cut laterally across Kane and De Kalb counties, passed along the northern edge of Lee County, and crossed Whiteside County to the town of Fulton on the Misissippi River. This branch was completed in December, 1855, and later became the main line of the Chicago and Northwestern Railroad. A junction was also obtained between the Galena road and the Wisconsin Central by means of the Fox River Valley Railroad extending north from Elgin, which permitted the Galena road and Chicago to tap the southern tier of Wisconsin counties. Beloit, Wisconsin, was also reached by a branch which was later extended to Madison.

In 1854 the Chicago, Burlington and Quincy Railroad was opened. This road was formed by a consolidation of three shorter lines, and ran west from Chicago to Batavia, turned south to Aurora and southwest through Mendota to Galesburg, and ultimately to Burlington, Iowa. At Galesburg, the Quincy and Chicago Railroad, formerly the Northern Cross, connected Galesburg with Quincy on the Mississippi River. By 1856 the C. B. & Q. had penetrated some 200 miles into Iowa by means of the Burlington and Missouri Rail road.

The Chicago and Rock Island Railroad, an extension of the Michigan Southern, was operating along its entire 181 miles by 1854. This road ran from Chicago through Joliet, Ottawa, La Salle, Peru, and Bureau, along the line of the Illinois and Michigan Canal, and from Bureau to Moline and Rock Island. The Peoria and Bureau Valley road connected with the Rock Island at Bureau and paralleled the Illinois River to Peoria. At that town, connections were made over the Peoria and Oquawka to a third point on the Mississippi River. From Rock Island, the main line also had connections with the interior of Iowa via the Mississippi and Missouri road. Another line running southwesterly was the Chicago, Alton and St. Louis route, through Joliet, Bloomington, Lincoln, Springfield, and Alton.

The last great road serving Chicago was the Illinois Central, the first land grant railroad, constructed between 1851 and 1857. This road ran north from Cairo through Carbondale to Centralia, where it branched off in two directions—the western branch continuing to Decatur, Bloomington, and a junction with the Alton road, La Salle, Dixon, where it crossed the Galena, Freeport, and Galena; the eastern branch running from Centralia through Mattoon, Urbana, and Kankakee to Chicago. The eastern line traversed some of the most fertile, most isolated, and least developed lands in Illinois.[4]

Chicago was also active in pushing her rail connections into Wisconsin. By 1857 the Chicago and Milwaukee road, through Waukegan, Kenosha, and Racine, was completed. A second road to the northwest, part of which was later incorporated into the Chicago and Northwestern Railroad, was the Chicago, St. Paul and Fond du Lac line. The southern division was completed to Janesville, Wisconsin, where connections were available with the Milwaukee and Prairie du Chien line (formerly the Milwaukee and Mississippi), and the Racine and Mississippi road. South of Fond du Lac junction with the southern branch was made, by 1860, through Watertown, and the road had been pushed north of Fond du Lac around the western shore of Lake Winnebago to the head of the Fox River. From there connections were available via steamer with Green Bay.[5]

While Chicago was thrusting its rail connections in the direction of the Mississippi and through the very hinterland of Milwaukee and Racine, the Wisconsin communities were not inactive in promoting the construction of rail networks to the Mississippi at points within Illinois as well as Wisconsin. Racine was the first to achieve a direct rail connection with the Mississippi by extending the Racine and Beloit road to Freeport and Savanna, Illinois.[6] Milwaukee inaugurated a major cross-state road in 1850 in the Milwaukee and Mississippi. Seventy miles of the road were in operation in 1852, and it was completed through Madison to Prairie du Chien in 1857. There arrangements were made for two lines of steamers to run daily between Prairie du Chien and St. Paul, Minnesota.[7]

Milwaukee sought to develop a commerce with the third and

---

[4] *Fifth Annual Review of the Trade and Commerce . . . of Chicago, 1856* (Chicago, 1857), 52-60.

[5] 6 AR, Commerce of Chicago, 1857, 34-35; *Transactions of the Wisconsin State Agricultural Society,* VI (1860), 68-70. Navigation was opened along the Fox River Improvement from Lake Winnebago to Green Bay in 1856. This outlet to Lake Michigan served farmers in central Wisconsin until railroads from the south penetrated the area. The Chicago and Milwaukee road planned an extension along the western shore of Lake Michigan into the Green Bay country.

[6] *Hunt's,* XXXVI (May, 1857), 554.

[7] Andrews, "Reports on Trade and Commerce," 375; Daniel S. Curtiss, *Western Portraiture, and Emigrants Guide: A Description of Wisconsin, Illinois, and Iowa; with Remarks on Minnesota and Other Territories* (New York, 1852), 40; John Gregory, *Industrial Resources of Wisconsin* (Milwaukee,

fourth tier of counties through the agency of the La Crosse and Milwaukee Railroad, which ran to the southern tip of Lake Horicon, then west through Portage, where the Wisconsin River was bridged, and on to La Crosse. As at Prairie du Chien, steamboat service with the upper Mississippi was initiated. La Crosse suffered, however, from the lack of elevators and less efficient facilities for handling grain than were available at Prairie du Chien or Dunleith. Another important line serving Milwaukee was the Milwaukee, Watertown and Baraboo Valley Railroad, which was approaching Sauk County in 1860.[8]

A striking feature of the railroad development outlined above was the degree to which roads centering at Milwaukee, Chicago, and Racine connected, thus allowing farmers and dealers a choice of markets. Chicago was not only competing for Wisconsin's grain in the immediate rear of markets like Milwaukee and Racine, but was actively engaged in an effort to tap central Wisconsin, while both Milwaukee and Chicago cast covetous eyes on the expanding crops and lucrative trade in metal ore and lumber of upper Wisconsin and Minnesota. Simultaneously, Wisconsin's main cities sought and secured outlets through Illinois to the Mississippi River. Officials of the Chicago and Northwestern line complained in 1862 that higher prices at Milwaukee were diverting much grain from Chicago to the former market. A year earlier the Chicago, St. Paul and Fond du Lac road diverted to Chicago over 40 per cent of the flour and approximately 70 per cent of the provisions originally shipped over the Racine and Mississippi Railroad.[9]

The coming of railroads did far more than merely establish new routes to the markets at Chicago or other railroads. The railroads, to a certain extent, revolutionized the established pattern of the grain trade. Prior to the advent of such quick transportation, most interior producers or local dealers were forced to haul the crops to market by wagon, or, if fortunate enough to reside in the vicinity of the canal or a navigable river, to deposit the crop at some staging point along the waterway, where it was either re-

---

1855), 277; *Eighth Annual Report of the Directors of the Milwaukee and Mississippi Rail Road Company, 1856* [in 1860 renamed the Milwaukee and Prairie du Chien Railroad] (Milwaukee, 1857), 12.

[8] *Report of the Receiver of the La Crosse and Milwaukee Railroad . . . 1860* (Milwaukee, 1861), 5, 20; Milwaukee Chamber of Commerce, *Second Annual Report for the Year 1859* (Milwaukee, 1860), 11.

[9] Chicago and North Western Railway Company, *Third Annual Report, 1862* (Chicago, 1862), 6-7; *Third Annual Report to the Trustees in Possession of the Racine and Mississippi Railroad, May, 1862* (Racine, Wis., 1862).

shipped to a larger market—Chicago or St. Louis—or sent directly
south via flatboat or steamboat, bypassing the larger markets entirely. Storage and transfer facilities at such depots were usually
of a primitive kind. Rough sheds or bins usually housed the grain
and then only in small lots, for grading techniques were not sophis-
ticated enough to allow the storage of similar grades together.
Transportation along the waterways was slow and uncertain, market information often unreliable, and cash payments at these centers infrequent. Shipments were possible only in small quantities
also, as much as a steamboat or canal barge could haul, and poor
storage arrangements necessitated the added expense of sacking
bulk grain or corn in order to prevent spoilage—which occurred
nonetheless.

A prominent feature of the pre-railroad era was a fairly pronounced concentration or centralization of the grain trade in the
interior regions of the Northwest. Massillon, Terre Haute, and Peoria developed first as canal towns and as original receiving centers
for grain to be shipped elsewhere. Considering the huge expanse
of territory designated as the Old Northwest, such original receiving centers were relatively scarce. Although there were innumerable flatboat landings along the navigable streams, it is doubtful
if much commerce or commercial exchange was accomplished at
those obscure landings. With the avenues of trade limited to rivers
and canals, only towns lying directly along such routes could gen-
erate much commerce, and in Illinois the most important commercial centers, Alton, Quincy, Peoria, or Beardstown, developed rapidly along the Mississippi and Illinois rivers, while Chicago's
growth in the early and mid-1840's was less than remarkable. The
completion of the Illinois and Michigan Canal did little to alter
the composition of the established centers of commerce. It did
serve to stimulate trade at Peru, Pekin, and Peoria, for instance,
but these towns had a prior trade based on the Illinois River. The
Illinois and Mississippi river ports were dominant and a few dealers
at these few markets handled much of the grain trade in its first
stages.[10]

---

[10] Much of the grain trade was unreported. Millers were widespread
throughout the state, generally following population movement, as did country
stores. Both millers and storekeepers, as noted previously, performed an important function in the initial stages of the trade. Probably much of the 3 million
bushels of grain received at Peoria, for instance, in 1856 was brought in by
millers or storeowners and represented the productive efforts of innumerable
farmers.

Such conditions—a scarcity of markets, difficulty in reaching them, inadequate facilities to handle grain, limited financial resources—could not but affect the farmer in deciding how much land to devote to each crop and how to dispose of the crops when harvested. At Naperville, 35 miles west of Chicago, corn could be hauled by team to the lake port for about 12 cents a bushel if the roads were serviceable.[11] But even when corn was as high as 50 cents—and in 1857 and 1858 wheat was at that price—the 38 cents remaining had to pay for the farmer's time in getting the crop to market, and the initial cost of producing the corn. This left the farmer with but a meager profit. A farmer living farther west than Naperville would not even make the attempt to haul bulk corn to market, but would feed it all to his livestock, which could stand the cost of freight better than corn. Wheat was preferred as the cash crop since, although corn cost no more to freight than wheat, the latter grain was normally two or three times more valuable per unit of volume than corn. The arrival of the Galena road in the vicinity of Naperville increased the margin of profit per bushel of corn and extended the distance over which corn, other cereals, provisions, and livestock could be transported economically.

The advent of rail transportation effected a significant dispersal of the grain trade in the interior, while it fostered an even greater concentration at secondary receiving centers like Chicago, Milwaukee, and Toledo. In the interior, at towns in the areas where production centered, the railroad contributed to a proliferation of individuals dealing in grain. Before the railroad, a few men at major points had done the bulk of the produce business. Such individuals normally purchased grain from producers or from smaller dealers such as country storeowners during the fall and were then compelled to store the produce from November, or the close of water navigation, to April and the spring thaw. At that time, additional supplies could be procured from farmers who had held their crops over the winter in order to obtain better prices or because of an inability to market it following the harvest. Holding grain over the winter demanded adequate financial resources or substantial credit, and probably a combination of both. With the railroad, produce men became as "thick as potato bugs." Anyone with $250 could purchase a carload of wheat and ship it to Chicago or

---

[11] The maximum load for a two-horse team was about 50 bushels. At 50 cents per bushel, this would bring $25, minus $6 for freight. It would probably have involved a journey of three days.

Milwaukee. The same possibilities were present in the provisions trade.[12]

Farmers could now haul their wheat to the nearest railroad depot for sale to a local dealer, who was often an agent for a produce merchant at the secondary market. Grain dealers traveled around the countryside buying up the crop prior to harvest.[13] One such produce merchant set up business along the Illinois Central tracks in Williamson County. Wheat originating in both Jackson and Franklin counties was hauled by wagon to this point. This dealer shipped by the carload to Chicago and also sold carloads to other dealers, who then were responsible for getting the wheat up north. By 1857 business was so profitable that permission was solicited and received from railroad officials to erect a grain shed equipped with scales. In that area the harvest was good in 1857 and the dealer bought largely, paying cash and distributing, as the merchant maintained, "amongst the farmers more money than had ever before been seen or heard tell of in the same length of time in this county. They brought their wheat in by the wagon load, and took home for it a dollar a bushel in gold." [14]

To a certain extent, such activity was unprecedented in many areas of the state, particularly in the south, which until the 1850's had been noted for concentration on corn, so heavy that many parts of southern Illinois were actually compelled to import wheat and flour. This condition prevailed to an even greater extent in the east central prairie counties. In the vicinity of Urbana, Champaign County, it was estimated that within a circuit of 15 miles, more than 20,000 acres were sown with wheat, double the amount of all the land previously cultivated. A French Canadian colony developed the town of Assumption, 25 miles south of Decatur, with such rapid growth resulting between 1858 and 1861 that by the latter year an estimated 500,000 bushels of corn were shipped over the Illinois Central line. This was a trade that had not existed at all

---

[12] J. W. Spencer and J. M. D. Burrows, *The Early Days of Rock Island and Davenport*, Milo M. Quaife, ed. (Chicago, 1942), 271; Robert Russell, *North America. Its Agriculture and Climate* . . . (Edinburgh, 1857), 115-116.

[13] Paul W. Gates, *The Farmer's Age: Agriculture 1815-1860* (New York, 1960), 414, wrote that "Farmers were no match for the wily buyers. . . . Rarely were farmers offered a competitive price . . . and too often were they reminded that the only alternative to the price offered was a long trip to market with its time-consuming delays, expenses, and uncertainties."

[14] Milo M. Quaife, ed., *Growing Up with Southern Illinois, 1820 to 1861, from the Memoirs of Daniel Harmon Brush* (Chicago, 1944), 213-214, 229.

previously. Along the line of the Illinois Central, including both the main line and the Chicago branch, the acreage in wheat increased from 549,000 acres in 1855 to 1.3 million in 1859, while that in corn rose from 1.1 million to 2.1 million acres.[15]

The railroad had its effect on all aspects of the grain trade. Grain could be shipped more quickly and safely to Chicago. Instead of arriving in small wagon loads or canal boat lots, it arrived in large quantities, and since the carrier could not afford idle cars, it required speedy handling, which in turn necessitated the building of large grain elevators with automatic loading and unloading equipment. It further required that grain be carried by grade from the original point of departure and stored by grade at the secondary market, rather than being handled, as it was in the 1840's, in separate units as numerous as there were owners of grain. Officials of the Chicago and Northwestern Railroad in 1860 estimated a company loss of some $10,000 to $20,000 a month because of inadequate grain storage facilities at Chicago which prevented the road from holding grain in store until lake navigation commenced in the spring.[16]

It is possible, of course, to overstate the consequences resulting from the widespread introduction of rail transportation. Certain markets in Illinois, such as Peoria, based the foundations of their commerce upon river communications with St. Louis. Then came the canal and an enlargement of commercial opportunities, followed by railroads which wisely sought to run their lines through established centers of population and trade or through areas which, though lacking establishment, awaited only the railroad to create a commerce. It cannot be said with assurance that in an established area, such as Peoria, the increase of grain imports and exports from 1 million bushels in 1850 to 3.3 million in 1858 resulted from rail connections.[17] Undoubtedly the Illinois and Michigan Canal supplied the initial developmental impetus. The railroads sustained and contributed to further growth. But in places like Morrison in

---

[15] Gerhard, *Illinois as It Is; Its History, Geography, Statistics, Agriculture* (Chicago, 1857), 237; Paul W. Gates, *The Illinois Central Railroad and Its Colonization Work* (Cambridge, Mass., 1934), 237, 301. According to these figures over one-half of the total wheat acreage harvested in 1860 was along the Central lines. This seems unlikely and it is probable that the wheatlands along the railroad are exaggerated.

[16] *Circular to the Bond and Stockholders of the Chicago and North Western Railway Company* (New York, 1861), 6.

[17] *Hunt's*, XLI (December, 1859), 693-694.

Whiteside County, on the Fulton branch of the Chicago and Galena, where grain exports of some 200,000 bushels were recorded in 1859, or at Urbana, where some 300,000 to 400,000 bushels of wheat were shipped in 1856, or Assumption, the railroads created a trade.[18] In this sense, roads which created such a commerce had an impact both more elemental and developmental than roads constructed in Ohio, which, for the most part, followed established lines of commerce, passed through settled and fairly mature areas, and afforded the farmers the opportunity to ship in one dierction rather than another. Ohio had passed through a stage of canals with one function and of railroads with a somewhat different one. The canals of Ohio generally performed the pioneering function of opening up new lands for settlement and providing these areas with a route to markets. The railroads of Ohio greatly improved the transportation facilities of established areas and commercial centers. In Illinois the railroads performed both functions.

Not all of Illinois' railroads had such a developmental impact. The Chicago, Burlington and Quincy and the Chicago, Alton and St. Louis passed through much of the Illinois River valley, previously settled, with established commerce, and able even before the railroads either to ship south to St. Louis or, after 1848, north over the canal to Chicago. The rail connections with Chicago provided alternate routes to market. It is true, however, that the coming of railroads, even through older areas of the state, thrust into the commercial life of the state some hamlets, like Galesburg on the C. B. & Q. Railroad, which had previously been of no significance whatsoever. But there still seems to be a difference between the over-all effects of such roads and of those like the Illinois Central, which actively colonized a previously unsettled region. The Central was constructed on the theory that the establishment of a connection with large markets would make the land lying along its route so desirable as to attract settlers, and that the cost of construction would be paid by selling to such settlers part of the 2.5 million acres granted to the road.[19]

The 12 counties through which the two main sections of the Galena and Chicago Union Railroad passed experienced rapid

---

[18] Gerhard, *Illinois as It Is*, 416; Judson F. Lee, *Transportation as a Factor in the Development of Northern Illinois Previous to 1860* (Chicago, 1917), 40.

[19] In 1855-56 the road sold over 800,000 acres of land. Gerhard, *Illinois as It Is*, 401-408.

growth between 1850 and 1860, yet in certain phases the advance was less rapid than for the state as a whole. While it is not possible to say with exactness that the railroad caused this progress, it is most probable that the role of the railroad was preponderant.[20] Seven of these counties were among the 15 leading wheat producers in the state by 1859.[21]

Most striking was the increase in improved acreage over the decade. In 1849, 43.5 per cent of all the land in farms in the 12 counties was improved. In 1859 the total quantity of improved acreage, rising from 1 million acres in 1849 to 2.4 million, formed 74.3 per cent of the total land in farms. This latter category rose from 2.3 million to 3.3 million acres. The remainder of the state also demonstrated a notable increase along these lines, the total land in farms increasing from 11 million acres in 1849 to 20.9 million ten years later, while improved acreage stood at 13 million acres in 1859, 8 million more than in 1849. The proportion of improved acreage to total land in farms for the state was at 60 per cent in 1859. The Galena counties, while putting new land into farms at a less rapid pace than the rest of the state, transformed it into improved acreage more quickly, so that the area of the 12 Galena counties was more intensively cultivated than the remainder of Illinois.

The rise in land values along the Galena road was impressive. For the 12 counties, the cash value of land in farms rose from $20.7 million in 1849 to $77.5 million in 1859. But for the state as a whole the rise was even more marked: the cash value estimated at $408.9 million in 1859 represented an increase of 325 per cent since 1849. In the Galena counties most of the increase in value occurred after 1853, which lends support to the suggestion that the role of the Galena road was primary in the economic development of the area. For nine of the counties, the assessed value was $14.1 million in

---

[20] The Galena counties include Boone, Carroll, Cook, De Kalb, Jo Davies, Kane, Kendall, McHenry, Ogle, Stephenson, and Winnebago. Of these, the two main sections of the Galena did not touch Ogle or Carroll. Ogle was intersected by the Galena branch of the Illinois Central, which met the southern line of the Galena road at Dixon, Lee County. A branch line from Savanna, on the Mississippi River, to Freeport gave Carroll County a connection with the Galena road.

[21] They were, in order, Ogle (1), De Kalb (4), Stephenson (5), Winnebago (6), McHenry (10), Carroll (11), and Kane (15). The 12 counties produced 27 per cent of the state's wheat in 1859 compared to 37.7 per cent in 1849. Some of the remaining counties which were among the top 15 in 1849 were replaced by counties in the Rock River valley. Except where noted, this discussion is based on the Federal Census, 1850 and 1860.

1850. In 1853 it amounted to $20 million, an annual advance of
11.8 per cent.[22] The assessed value reached $52 million in 1860, a
yearly increment of 18.4 per cent. It was after 1853 that the Galena
road was pushed through most energetically to the Mississippi
River.

The Rock River valley counties also experienced a great advance in the production of wheat between 1849 and 1859.[23] By
1859 five of the counties were among the leading 15 wheat-producing counties in the state.[24] Whereas in 1849 this group produced
911,000 bushels of wheat or 9.3 per cent of the state crop, in 1859
4.1 million bushels or 17.1 per cent of the state crop originated in
the Rock River country, which, if added to the Galena counties,
accounted for 44 per cent of the state crop in 1859. Wheat raising,
remaining concentrated in the north, moved into the western counties largely as a result of the Rock Island Railroad, while the Galena
road was also of service to such counties as Lee and Whiteside.

In such areas the impact of railroads was of the most basic
kind. Without railroads, even though the land were peopled and
a strong demand for grain at attractive prices might exist at distant
points, no significant trade could grow up. If the farmer lacked
quick and cheap access to market places—if a six-day trip with 40
bushels of wheat from Ogle County, Illinois, brought $20—he
would produce at less than full capacity, at levels but little higher
than would be required to fulfill the limited needs of the local
market. Land would lie idle, which meant that valuable capital
resources were idle. Land would remain ill-cared for, a waste of
capital resources. The local economy would fail to expand, which
normally results in an eventual contraction. In these circumstances,
the railroad provided the essential catalytic action for growth. Railroads induced growth by bridging the existing market gaps within
sections and between sections. Marengo, on the northern branch
of the Galena road, constructed four warehouses with a total capacity of 240,000 bushels. Further, a railroad meant more than a
route to market. It meant jobs to construct, maintain, and operate
the road and the warehouses. It stimulated a more intensive and

---

[22] These counties included Boone, Du Page, Jo Davies, Kane, Kendall,
Lake, Ogle, and Winnebago. *De Bow's Review,* XXII (December, 1854), 603.

[23] These counties included Rock Island, Mercer, Knox, Stark, Henry,
Whiteside, Lee, and Bureau.

[24] They were, in order, Bureau (2), Lee (7), Whiteside (8), Henry (9),
and Knox (14).

efficient utilization of land, capital, and labor. It permitted farmers along the line of the Milwaukee and Prairie du Chien to import some of the newfangled contrivances which enabled a farmer to harvest ten acres a day instead of two or three.

To the degree that railroads accomplished the above and in addition allowed farmers to ship their produce 500 miles, at less expense than a team could haul it 100 miles, to a port on the lake shore providing a convenient and cheap route to the East—to that degree the railroad created a commerce which previously had but a tenuous existence.

The Impact of Railroads
on the Grain Trade of the
Lake System from 1850 to 1860

CHAPTER XIII

In 1860 it is possible to speak of the grain trade of Lake Michigan solely in terms of the produce pouring out from the harbors of Chicago and Milwaukee. These bustling cities experienced a truly meteoric rise during the 1850's, both in the grain trade and in general commerce. The period of most notable growth occurred after 1853 or 1854. Milwaukee, for instance, had a total export trade of only $5.3 million in 1854. This more than doubled, reaching $12.5 million in the following year, and in 1860 grain exports alone were valued at about $12 million. At Chicago the advance was even more remarkable. In 1851 the value of total exports stood at $5.3 million; two years later it was at $21 million; by 1860, it had reached $72.7 million. In 1847 Cincinnati's exports and imports totaled $100 million, or 25 times those of Chicago. In 1860 the total value of exports and imports at Cincinnati reached $180 million, only $10 million more than at Chicago. The value of grain exports from Chicago rose from between $2 million and $3 million during the late 1840's and early 1850's to $12 million in 1858 and $21.7 million in 1860, not including another $6 million in provisions exports.[1]

Reference has been made to the doubling of population in Illinois and Wisconsin between 1850 and 1860, and to the enormous increase in the production of grain. Wheat production in Illinois rose from 9.4 million bushels in 1849 to 23.8 million in 1859, and corn from 57.6 million bushels to 115 million. In Wisconsin the wheat crop grew from 4.2 million to 15.6 million bushels and, while corn increased too, it was of little importance to the grain trade of Wisconsin or the receiving markets serving its farmers. It will be recalled that the greatest wheat region in the country lay in a group of some 20 Wisconsin and Illinois counties bisected by the Illinois-Wisconsin border.[2]

It is certain that the railroads had a sharp and invigorating effect on the economic development of Wisconsin, both in the interior and in the lake ports. As Table 22 indicates, the grain trade at Milwaukee rose sharply during the 1850's, especially after 1852. Milwaukee's mills manufactured some 65,000 barrels of flour in 1852 and above 150,000 in 1858. An important brewing industry took hold in the 1850's and some 75,000 barrels of ale and beer were manufactured in 1856, twice the quantity turned out in 1852. A fairly large milling industry developed at Madison. Sauk County contained several sizable milling towns. Baraboo, Wisconsin, was reported turning out some 600 to 800 barrels of flour weekly, much of which was consigned to Boston. In Lafayette County, on the Illinois border, while the assessed valuation of improved lands actually declined from 1849 to 1853 and remained steady from 1854 to 1856, the valuation increased by 74 per cent between 1857 and 1858. During the latter two years, a railroad was constructed running from Mineral Point, Iowa County, the immediate northern neighbor of Lafayette County, through Lafayette into northern Illinois and

---

[1] *Patent Report, 1854,* 476, *1855,* 407; Milwaukee Chamber of Commerce, *Fifth Annual Report for the Year 1862* (Milwaukee, 1863), 20; *Seventh Annual Review of the Trade and Commerce . . . of Chicago, 1858* (Chicago, 1859), 36; Andrews, "Reports on Trade and Commerce," 218; John S. Wright, *Chicago: Past, Present, Future. Relations to the Great Interior, and to the Continent* (2nd ed., Chicago, 1870), 152.

[2] *7 Census, 1850,* 701-702, 730-731, 917, 931; *8 Census, 1860, Agriculture,* 30-35, 102-103, 166-167.

a connection with the Galena and the Racine and Mississippi roads.[3] A tremendous expansion of wheat cultivation occurred in the four east central counties of Fond du Lac, Winnebago, Marquette, and Green Lake. While production in Wisconsin rose 265 per cent from 1849 to 1859, it multiplied by six and a half times in those four counties, increasing from 309,354 bushels to 2.3 million. In 1859 this represented 15.1 per cent of the state crop compared with 7 per cent in 1859. Bushels of wheat produced per capita had been about 14 for the state and only 9 in the four counties in 1849. A decade later, although the per capita figure for the state reached 20, it attained 28 in the four counties, with Fond du Lac producing 36 and Green Lake 47 bushels of wheat per capita.[4] There seems little reason to doubt that this rate of growth, eclipsing even the striking advance made by the state as a whole, was basically the result of railroad penetration into this region. It was this region which the Chicago and Northwestern sought to tap in constructing its lines to Oshkosh, in Winnebago County. And by 1860 a line from Sheboygan, on Lake Michigan directly east of Fond du Lac, was pushing into this territory as well.

Milwaukee, by the middle or late 1850's, was completely dependent upon the railroads for its grain supply. In 1858 total receipts of wheat reached 4.8 million bushels, 4.1 million being delivered by rail along with 186,000 of the 206,000 barrels of flour received at Milwaukee. In 1859 railroads carried 90 per cent of the wheat and flour entering the port.[5]

The Milwaukee and Prairie du Chien Railroad was the leading carrier of Milwaukee's grain. In 1858 and 1859 the road reported wheat traffic amounting to 2.3 and 2.2 million bushels. All but about 100,000 bushels in each year ultimately reached Milwaukee. The completion of the road to Prairie du Chien in late 1857 proved an immediate boon to the traffic on the road. Whereas in 1856 and 1857 the line hauled between 30,000 and 40,000 barrels of flour and 1.5 to 1.6 million bushels of wheat, the quantity of flour carried more than doubled by 1859 and wheat traffic rose by 55 per cent.

---

[3] *De Bow's Review*, XVII (November, 1854), 533-534; *Hunt's*, XLI (September, 1859), 316-318; Daniel S. Curtiss, *Western Portraiture, and Emigrants Guide: A Description of Wisconsin, Illinois, and Iowa; with Remarks on Minnesota and Other Territories* (New York, 1852), 161; *Transactions of the Wisconsin State Agricultural Society*, VI (1860), 304, 330-331.

[4] *7 Census, 1850*, 931; *8 Census, 1860, Agriculture*, 166, 167.

[5] Milwaukee Chamber of Commerce, *2 AR, 1859*, 11, 16.

That the connection with Prairie du Chien was instrumental can be seen more clearly in 1860. In that year the road shipped eastward 177,000 barrels of flour and 6.4 million bushels of wheat, along with 3,900 tons of provisions. Of this, 25 per cent of the flour, 50 per cent of the wheat, and over 50 per cent of the provisions originated at Prairie du Chien. On the basis of the performance in 1858 and 1859, it is assumed that all of the wheat and 90 per cent of the flour were consigned through to Milwaukee. For the years 1858-60 Milwaukee received 47, 41, and 70 per cent of total wheat receipts, and 32, 31, and 50 per cent of flour receipts via this road. An unknown quantity went to Chicago.[6]

Most of the wheat shipped eastward from Prairie du Chien probably originated either in Iowa or in Minnesota. In 1860 all of the Wisconsin counties bordering on the Mississippi River, which would have furnished Prairie du Chien with the bulk of Wisconsin wheat, produced 1.1 million bushels. Some 50,000 people inhabited those counties. At a minimum consumption of four bushels per capita, more than 200,000 of this production would have been consumed locally, leaving only 900,000 bushels as surplus available for export. But Prairie du Chien shipped 3.1 million bushels, and 800,000 bushels originated at La Crosse, the western terminus of the La Crosse and Milwaukee Railroad. It would appear, therefore, that some 3 million bushels of the 4 million shipped from Prairie du Chien and La Crosse must have been of non-Wisconsin origin. Moreover, it is known that both towns shipped some grain downriver to towns in Illinois where connections were made with Chicago's roads.[7]

The La Crosse and Milwaukee line was the second largest grain carrier for Milwaukee. Most of the grain and flour carried by the road was consigned through to Milwaukee. In 1858, of 1.1 million bushels of wheat transported, 782,000 arrived at Milwaukee, along with 70 per cent of the flour. Some of the wheat was probably diverted at the junction with the Chicago and Northwest-

---

[6] *Ibid.*, 16; *Tenth Annual Report of the Directors of the Milwaukee and Mississippi Rail Road Company, 1858* (Milwaukee, 1859), 28, *11 AR, 1859*, 26-28. Of a total of 159,000 barrels of flour shipped over the road, 89 per cent reached Milwaukee. This road was renamed the Milwaukee and Prairie du Chien Railroad in 1861. *First Annual Report of the Milwaukee & Prairie du Chien Railway Company for 1861* (Milwaukee, 1862).

[7] *Ibid.*; *Report of the Receiver of the La Crosse and Milwaukee Railroad . . . 1860* (Milwaukee, 1861), 5, 20; *Hunt's*, XLIII (October, 1860), 476.

ern Railroad. In 1858 and 1859 Milwaukee received 16 and 24 per cent of its total wheat receipts and 36 per cent of the flour via the La Crosse route.[8] In 1858, then, 63 per cent of Milwaukee's wheat receipts were supplied by the Prairie du Chien and the La Crosse routes, and in 1859, 64 per cent. In 1860 the La Crosse road carried 2.8 million bushels of wheat and 161,700 barrels of flour, and in 1862 6 million bushels of wheat and 330,000 barrels of flour.[9] The proportion received by Milwaukee is unknown, but on the basis of previous experience it is likely that the bulk of it was consigned to Milwaukee.

The Milwaukee, Watertown and Baraboo Valley road was of some importance also; it carried 11 per cent of Milwaukee's wheat in 1858 and 13 per cent the following year. In 1859 the Milwaukee Chamber of Commerce made particular note of the fact that receipts via the Chicago and Milwaukee Railroad had increased over 1858, although the quantities received via this road were negligible compared to those already noted.[10]

In addition to the roads crossing the state from Milwaukee, the Racine and Mississippi Railroad passed from Racine through Darien and Beloit and then turned southwest to Freeport, Illinois. A certain portion of the grain carried over this line was diverted to Chicago and Milwaukee. Most of Racine's receipts over the road probably originated between the home station and Beloit. Racine received some 1.5 million bushels of wheat over the road in 1861.[11]

The great bulk of Milwaukee's grain exports went via Lake Michigan until well after 1860. In the years immediately following the war, about one-half of the flour exported traveled via rail, but

---

[8] *ARJ*, XXXII (April 23, 1859), 257; Milwaukee Chamber of Commerce, *2 AR, 1859*, 16.

[9] *Report of the Receiver of the La Crosse and Milwaukee Railroad, 1860*, 20-23, *Report, 1862*. Among the items moving west in 1860 were 498 tons of agricultural implements. While not a large quantity, it represents an important service supplied by railroads. Before railroads, interior farmers were generally dependent for their implements upon local manufacturers. With railroads appearing in Illinois and Wisconsin coincidentally with the beginning of large-scale manufacture of mechanized equipment, such as Manny's and McCormick's reapers, interior farmers were able to purchase these machines some distance from the point of manufacture.

[10] Milwaukee Chamber of Commerce, *2 AR, 1859*, 5. The Milwaukee and Chicago carried 149,137 bushels of wheat and 6,600 barrels of flour to Milwaukee in 1859 compared with 83,680 bushels and 520 barrels in 1858.

[11] Freeport, Illinois, was reported shipping 380,000 bushels of wheat via the Racine road in 1861. *Third Annual Report to the Trustees in Possession of the Racine and Mississippi Railroad, May, 1862* (Racine, Wis., 1862).

in 1858-59, out of 481,000 barrels of flour shipped, only 40,000 traveled by railroad. As in the past, Buffalo received the greater part of Milwaukee's grain exports. In 1858 and 1859 Buffalo received 57 and 55 per cent of Milwaukee's wheat receipts and Oswego 23 and 28 per cent. About 60 per cent of the flour shipped from Milwaukee went to Buffalo.[12]

Between 1849, when Milwaukee exported 1.8 million bushels of wheat and flour valued at almost $2 million, and 1860, when wheat and flour worth some $12 million left the port, the quantitative increase was 8 million bushels, or 380 per cent. Among the

TABLE 22. ANNUAL SHIPMENTS OF WHEAT, FLOUR, AND CORN AT CHICAGO AND MILWAUKEE, 1850-60 (IN THOUSANDS)

	Chicago			Milwaukee		
Year	Wheat (bu.)	Flour (bbl.)	Corn (bu.)	Wheat (bu.)	Flour (bbl.)	Corn (bu.)
1850	834	101	469	298	100	22
1851	438	72	3,847	317	52	126
1852	636	61	5,032ᵃ	575	93	743
1853	1,206	71	4,831	957	104	504
1854	2,307	117	6,626	1,809	145	1,015
1855	6,298	163	7,518	2,642	182	209
1856	8,364	216	11,130	2,762	188	10
1857	9,846	260	6,815	2,581	228	4
1858	8,850	470	7,726	3,994	299	675
1859	7,167	686	4,349	4,634	283	405
1860	12,402	698	13,700	7,569	457	140

ᵃ 1852-53 include rye, oats, and barley.
Sources: Chicago Board of Trade, *Nineteenth Annual Report of the Trade and Commerce of Chicago, 1876* (Chicago, 1877), 43; Milwaukee Chamber of Commerce, *5 AR, 1862*, 20; United States Treasury Department, *Statistics of the Foreign and Domestic Commerce of the United States* (Washington, D.C., 1864), 150.

many factors which stimulated this advance—population growth, a rising demand for grain along the East Coast, a fairly active foreign trade, and generally high prices for grain products—none would seem more basic than the construction of a comprehensive railroad network throughout the state. This was true, to an even more decided degree, of Chicago and Illinois.

The growth of the grain trade centered at Chicago between

[12] Canada received 12 per cent of flour shipments in both 1858 and 1859, while Oswego and Ogdensburg each received some 6 per cent. Milwaukee Chamber of Commerce, *2 AR, 1859*, 12, 16.

the years 1850-52 and 1860 was phenomenal. In 1850, 1.8 million bushels of wheat, flour and other grains left Chicago. In 1860, 30.8 million bushels of grain and flour and in the next year 50.3 million bushels were exported. This was almost 10 million bushels more than the total foreign exports of the United States in 1857, the peak year of the pre-war period, and 80 per cent of the 68 million bushels exported in 1861.

This spectacular growth at Chicago should not obscure—although it tends to by its sheer size—the fact that the 1850's were not unattended by economic crises, recurrent crop failures, and plunging prices. Nor, on the other hand, should it be assumed that such progress was inevitable or that it represented the effects of a natural growth process. Chicago, unlike New Orleans, did not serve passively as a reception center for grain. Nature created the main channel for the commerce of New Orleans and little was done to improve or promote its augmented use. Man, in large measure, constructed the arteries of trade upon which the prosperity of Chicago was based, by digging up the earth to make canals and spiking iron rails into the ground; and having created them, man energetically improved and expanded the initial works to make even more efficient tools by which to ply his trade.

The decade did not open auspiciously for the grain trade at Chicago. A series of winter wheat failures in the northern counties of Illinois and Wisconsin and a static foreign demand depressed the grain trade and caused receipts at Chicago to fall off sharply from the levels reached in 1847-49. Relief came in 1854. A new foreign demand, occasioned by the Crimean War, was accompanied by good crops, while the rapid extension of railroads into the interior continued apace. By 1855 the Chicago, Burlington and Quincy was penetrating the upper portion of the Illinois Military Tract; the Galena road was at Freeport; the Rock Island was completed; and construction of the Illinois Central was progressing through the prairie counties of central Illinois. The expanding market brought enormous prices and profits and filled Chicago's harbor with ships. Between August 1 and December 1, 1854, one speculator made over $200,000. Wheat could not be purchased for less than $1.40 per bushel.[13]

---

[13] Chicago *Daily Tribune*, February 23, 1854, reported 56 vessels in the harbor with a capacity for 650,000 bushels of grain. J. W. Spencer and J. M. D. Burrows, *The Early Days of Rock Island and Davenport*, Milo M. Quaife, ed. (Chicago, 1942), 268.

Then came the end of the war and a marked decline in the foreign market. Prices of produce fell sharply, a drop which was disastrous to many grain dealers. The speculator who had reaped a profit of $200,000 lost an equivalent amount in the fall of 1855.[14] Shortly thereafter, the Panic of 1857 ensued and low prices prevailed in a stagnant market burdened by good crops. A reduction of supply, caused by poor crops in 1858, did not relieve the situation, as low prices continued. Receipts at Chicago fell off sharply.[15] The Chicago, Burlington and Quincy reported that traffic in wheat and flour fell off 45 per cent and corn 28 per cent from 1857-58 to 1858-59. Wheat and flour was exported from Chicago to areas normally furnishing Chicago with produce.[16] By 1859 supplies were quite depleted at Chicago, the previous crop being so scanty that little was carried over. The crop of 1859 was good and a considerable quantity of it was reported marketed before April, 1860. By that month some 5 million bushels of corn had already been sold. The stickiness of wheat prices hindered the movement of that grain somewhat. It was noted that farmers throughout the fall of 1859 were storing their grain, waiting for a better price. Grain already at Chicago showed little movement, since the price margin between Chicago and the East was reported to be insufficient to warrant shipment. Vessels were observed in the harbor that had been seeking freight unsuccessfully for some period of time.[17] By the end of the year 1860, activity at the market had improved, and grain worth $21.7 million moved out of Chicago to eastern destinations. Most of this grain, as in preceding years, arrived at Chicago over some segment of its vast railroad network.

---

[14] *Ibid.*, 269-270.

[15] This is not apparent in Table 22, which is based on figures gathered from January 1 to December 31. On an August-to-August basis, the crop failure and decline in receipts is obvious, and is noted below:

Grain	1857–58	1858–59
Flour (bbl.)	534,730	502,230
Wheat (bu.)	13,873,053	5,118,668
Corn (bu.)	7,005,745	5,891,800
Oats (bu.)	2,340,181	723,149

Hunt's, XLI (October, 1859), 509.

[16] Chicago, Burlington and Quincy Railroad Company, *Fifth Annual Report, 1859* (Chicago, 1860), 13; *Hunt's*, XLI (October, 1859), 509-510. It was reported that from 50 to 65 per cent of the winter wheat crop was killed in La Salle County, leaving insufficient grain on hand for local consumption. *The Prairie Farmer*, XIX (June 30, 1859), 406.

[17] *Ibid.* (May 19, 1859), 313, XX (September 1, 1859), 137; *Hunt's*, XLII (May, 1860), 643.

In one phase of Chicago's growing industry, meat packing and livestock, there is a remarkable correlation between expansion within the industry and expansion of the railroad net. In 1851-52 the hog pack at Chicago was slightly over 22,000, less than the pack at Peoria, Beardstown, or Alton. In the following season the pack at Chicago more than doubled, surpassing that of any other packing center in the state. By this time the Galena and Chicago Union Railroad had extended to the upper reaches of the Rock River. Of total receipts amounting to 79,000 hogs, some 53,000 were packed in Chicago and 11,000 sent East via rail. The Galena road carried 58 per cent of total receipts and the Rock Island 18 per cent, while small numbers of hogs arrived via the Michigan Central and Illinois Central railroads. The progress of the trade after 1853-54 is indicated in Table 23. In the season of 1860-61, the

TABLE 23. ANNUAL RECEIPTS OF LIVE AND DRESSED HOGS AT, HOGS PACKED AT, AND LIVE HOGS SHIPPED FROM CHICAGO, 1854-55 to 1860-61, 1866-67

Year	Total Receipts Live and Dressed	Total Hogs Packed	Total Live Hogs Shipped
1854–55	138,565	73,694	52,881
1855–56	308,539	80,380	187,763
1856–57	220,702	74,000	103,074
1857–58	214,223	99,662	88,546
1858–59	530,000	280,500	192,913
1859–60	271,000	–	110,246
1860–61	392,864	505,000[a]	227,164
1866–67	1,341,656	–	672,769

[a] 1861-62 pack.

Sources: 7 *AR, Commerce of Chicago*, 22, 24-27; *The Prairie Farmer*, XIX (January 6, 1859), 16; Wright, *Chicago*, 164-165; Chauncey M. Depew, ed., *One Hundred Years of American Commerce, 1795-1895* (2 vols., New York, 1895), II, 385.

pack at Chicago exceeded Cincinnati's and formed about 23 per cent of the total western cut. In 1848 Chicago packed 10 per cent of the state total, in 1853 15.4 per cent, and in 1857 19.5 per cent. One year later Chicago's portion stood at 22 per cent, and in 1859 47 per cent.[18]

_____

[18] *Ibid.*, XXVIII (May, 1853), 564, XXXII (June, 1855), 690; *Chicago Daily Tribune*, March 27, 1854. See sources cited for Tables 13 and 23. Until 1856, receipts of dressed hogs exceeded those of live hogs. Thereafter the latter surpassed dressed receipts by some two or four times. As Chicago's packing facilities expanded, and as packing became more and more centered at Chicago, all processes were accomplished in the city and proportionately less slaughtering and packing was done at other points.

During the first half of the 1850's, the Galena road was the major carrier of Chicago's pork supplies, and it was upon this traffic that the industry based itself. Until 1855-56 the Galena road transported about 65 per cent of Chicago's total receipts of live and dressed hogs.[19] Thereafter the Chicago, Burlington and Quincy and the Chicago, Alton and St. Louis roads were the dominant livestock and provisions carriers. This was a logical succession in that the Galena road penetrated an area heavily committed to wheat while the C. B. & Q. and the Alton roads passed through predominantly corn-growing areas. In 1858 the C. B. & Q. supplied 70 per cent of the dressed hogs and 39 per cent of the live hogs, while the Alton road carried 29 per cent of the live hogs, and the Illinois Central 18 per cent of the live hogs received at Chicago.[20] During the years 1858-59 and 1860-61, the proportion of Chicago's hog receipts arriving over the C. B. & Q. remained about the same as in 1857-58.[21]

Before the railroad became a factor in the grain and provisions trade of Chicago, approaches to the town from the interior consisted of roads and, after 1848, the Illinois and Michigan Canal. The latter avenue provided a real stimulus to the trade at Chicago since it allowed Chicago to tap other than contiguous counties and so expand the volume of grain handled in its market. For the most part, the canal's greatest importance lay in giving a predominantly corn-raising region access to market. The wheat-raising counties to the west of Chicago, along the Wisconsin border, were mainly dependent upon wagon transportation until the Galena and Chicago Union Railroad pentrated the region. In 1850 the Galena road and the canal supplied Chicago with more than one-half of the 1.1 mil-

---

[19] 7 *AR, Commerce of Chicago,* 24-27.

[20] *Ibid.,* 27. Theodore L. Carlson, *The Illinois Military Tract. A Study of Land Occupation, Utilization and Tenure* (Urbana, Ill., 1951), 131-132, wrote that the completion of the C. B. & Q. in the state through the tract greatly stimulated beef and hog raising. As to hogs, the number in the state increased from 1.9 million in 1849 to 2.5 million in 1859. This latter figure had been reached previously in 1854 and 1856, while the number of head declined from 1849 to 1.1 million in 1852. So the increase was not steady, but fluctuated considerably during the decade. By 1859 the counties through which the Burlington route passed raised 7.8 per cent of the state total, compared with 7.1 per cent in 1849. The counties which the Alton road served raised 10.5 per cent in 1849 and 11.3 per cent in 1859. Hog production in the Burlington and Alton counties grew but slightly faster than for the state as a whole. 7 *Census, 1850,* 730-731; 8 *Census, 1860, Agriculture,* 30-35; Wright, *Chicago,* 164-165.

[21] Chicago, Burlington and Quincy Railroad, *5 AR, 1859, 6 AR, 1860, 7 AR, 1861.*

lion bushels of wheat received. The remainder came in via wagon. Just two years later, however, 55 per cent of total wheat receipts arrived via rail. Thereafter, the railroads completely engrossed the traffic in wheat and flour.[22]

In the corn trade, however, the canal continued to have an economic significance in the grain trade of Chicago throughout the 1850's. As observed previously, the canal enabled Chicago to draw supplies of corn from an area which had in the past utilized the market at St. Louis. The rivalry between Chicago and St. Louis for the agricultural surplus of the Illinois valley was one of the first instances of a diversion of grain from the southern route to the northern. The increasing penetration of railroads based at Chicago into this area resulted in a pronounced decline of receipts at St. Louis from the Illinois valley, and completed a process which the canal inaugurated and continued to foster during the decade.

One student of Chicago's commerce has asserted that the Rock Island road, which paralleled the canal up to the point where the Illinois River turned south at Bureau, absorbed a major share of the canal's traffic and contributed to its declining economic importance during the late 1850's.[23] In terms of the grain trade, this statement requires some qualification. In the first place, the canal continued to be the most important single carrier of corn in the state, and in the second place, it does not appear that the Rock Island road diverted a significant quantity of grain from the canal.

From 1851 to 1854, that is, before the Rock Island became operational, the canal carried an average of 2.9 million bushels of corn each year, while Chicago's receipts averaged 5 million. During this period, the other major carrier was the Galena road, over which Chicago received an average of 820,000 bushels annually. The rest came in via teams.[24] Thus, the canal supplied some 55 per cent of total corn receipts. As indicated in Table 24, the Galena road was a larger carrier of corn than the Rock Island for most of the period. In 1847 the Chicago, Burlington and Quincy road sup-

---

[22] The canal furnished 308,000 and the railroad 262,000 bushels of wheat. Chicago *Daily Tribune*, December 28, 1850; 5 AR, *Commerce of Chicago, 1856*, 31.

[23] Wyatt W. Belcher, *The Economic Rivalry Between St. Louis and Chicago, 1850-1880* (New York, 1947), 35. A canal was eventually cut through from Bureau to the Mississippi at Rock Island, so the Rock Island Railroad paralleled it along its entire route.

[24] 5 AR, *Commerce of Chicago, 1856*, 31, 7 AR, *1858*, 14; *Hunt's*, XXVI (April, 1852), 429-430.

plied Chicago with a larger quantity of corn than either the Galena or Rock Island roads. Receipts via the C. B. & Q. increased from 1.9 million bushels in 1860 to 3.5 million in 1861.[25] Corn was also arriving in larger quantities via the Illinois Central and the Chicago, Alton and St. Louis roads. But as late as 1861 the canal still

TABLE 24. TOTAL RECEIPTS OF CORN AT CHICAGO AND RECEIPTS OF CORN VIA THE ILLINOIS AND MICHIGAN CANAL AND THE ROCK ISLAND AND GALENA RAILROADS, 1854-61 (IN THOUSANDS OF BUSHELS)

Year	Total Corn	Receipts via Canal	Receipts via Rock Island	Receipts via Galena
1854	7,491	4,501	565	2,084
1855	8,532	3,566	350	3,762
1856	11,888	5,407	1,114	3,587
1857	7,409	4,123	407	354
1858	8,260	4,735	372	742
1859	5,401	–	431	1,003
1860	15,212	4,336	–	–
1861	29,385	11,735	–	–

Sources: *5 AR, Commerce of Chicago, 1856,* 31, *7 AR, 1858,* 14; Chicago Board of Trade, *19 AR, 1876,* 43.

carried 40 per cent of the enormous quantity of corn received at Chicago.[26]

The canal also carried about 50 per cent of Chicago's receipts of oats, barley, and rye, which were between 2 million and 4 million bushels annually from 1854 to 1861. But in the transport of wheat and flour the canal's utility to Chicago did suffer relatively, for the railroads secured the great bulk of this traffic. Between 1855 and 1859 the canal carried between 800,000 and 1 million bushels of wheat and less than 50,000 barrels of flour. This was about twice the quantity carried between 1848 and 1854, but Chicago's receipts had increased by almost five times during the same interval.[27] The

[25] In 1857 the C. B. & Q. was second only to the canal as a carrier of corn to Chicago. Chicago, Burlington and Quincy Railroad, *5 AR, 1859, 6 AR, 1860, 7 AR, 1861.*

[26] Belcher, *Economic Rivalry Between St. Louis and Chicago,* 69, in estimating the quantity of grain received at Chicago via railroad in 1852, 1854, and 1856, uses total receipts and neglects to point out that of the 22.2 million bushels of corn received at Chicago during those three years, all of which are treated as railroad contributions, 11.7 million arrived via canal. The same error exists in Belcher's estimates of wheat and flour receipts at Chicago via rail; total receipts are taken to equal railroad receipts.

[27] *5 AR, Commerce of Chicago, 1856,* 31, *7 AR, 1858,* 14-15; Chicago Board of Trade, *Nineteenth Annual Report of the Trade and Commerce of Chicago, 1876* (Chicago, 1877), 43.

relative uniformity of volume of wheat and flour carried over the canal in the later 1850's is also partly attributable to the less intensive cultivation of wheat in the counties through which the canal passed as compared to other areas. Nevertheless, the canal was of great value to the grain trade of Chicago during the entire decade. While Chicago received 23.8 million bushels of all grains and flour in 1858, the canal transported 5.9 million, or about 25 per cent of total receipts, and at least the same proportion in 1861.[28] But while this shows that the canal was still important, it also illuminates the dominant position that the railroads had attained by the Civil War.

In 1849 Chicago received 262,000 bushels of wheat and flour via rail. From December 1, 1860, to January 12, 1861, the Chicago and Northwestern road alone carried 352,000 bushels of wheat and flour, and the Galena line transported 407,000 bushels to Chicago.[29]

The Galena road was the largest carrier of wheat and flour serving Chicago, since the main line and its branches penetrated the most important wheat-raising country in the state. Traffic in wheat and flour on this road increased rapidly, and during the four years 1856-59, 35 per cent of the total wheat and flour received at Chicago arrived over this line.[30] The second largest carrier prior to the war was the C. B. & Q. Some 20 per cent of the wheat received at Chicago, between 1857 and 1861, arrived over this system. As with the Galena road, the quantity of wheat carried as flour was much less than that carried in bulk. Railroads made it more efficient to transport bulk grain, which freight cars handled more effectively than barrels in terms of space utilization. Moreover, with steam-powered, automatic unloading and loading facilities available at Chicago, it was an easier and cheaper process to unload and reload bulk grain than flour. Between 1856 and 1859, 95 per cent of the wheat and flour traffic over all the railroads represented bulk wheat. For the C. B. & Q., between 1857 and 1861, the proportion was 90 per cent.

The grain traffic was of paramount importance to the railroads

---

[28] Chicago received 54.1 million bushels of grain in 1861. The canal carried 11.7 million bushels of corn, or 23 per cent, plus an unknown quantity of wheat, flour, and other grains.

[29] Chicago *Daily Tribune*, December 28, 1850; *Circular to the Bond and Stockholders of the Chicago and North Western Railway Company* (New York, 1861), 8.

[30] *Hunt's*, XXVI (April, 1852), 428; *5 AR, Commerce of Chicago, 1856*, 20, 7 AR, 1859, 7-12; Chicago Board of Trade, *19 AR, 1876*, 42.

of this period. Manufactured goods composed most of the west-bound freight of the Illinois roads, while farm produce formed the greater part of the eastbound traffic. For the C. B. & Q., grain, provisions, and livestock in 1859, 1860, and 1861 represented 73, 70, and 75 per cent of eastbound tonnage, which rose from 183,000 tons in 1859 to 339,000 in 1861. On the Milwaukee and Mississippi Railroad wheat and flour alone represented between 66 and 78 per cent of total tonnage moved east from 1853 to 1860.[31] It is probable that for most roads agricultural produce accounted for some 75 per cent of the tonnage carried and of the revenue received, although lines such as the Galena derived a considerable tonnage from other raw materials, in its case lead; and lumber and metal ores attained increasing importance as railroads penetrated northern Wisconsin and Minnesota.

Among the other railroads leading to Chicago, the Rock Island, the Chicago, Alton and St. Louis, and the Illinois Central carried large quantities of wheat to Chicago during the late 1850's. In 1855-57 the Rock Island moved about 1 million bushels annually from an area previously isolated from the main channels of commerce. Receipts via the Illinois Central amounted to some 800,000 bushels of wheat during the same three years, and surpassed 1 million in 1858. Receipts of wheat from the Alton road approached 1 million bushels in 1858. Much smaller quantities came by way of the Chicago and Milwaukee and the two Michigan railroads, but the Chicago, St. Paul and Fond du Lac line transported to Chicago 815,000 bushels of all grains, 50 per cent in wheat, in 1857, and about 350,000 bushels of wheat in 1858. Most of this originated between Chicago and Janesville, Wisconsin, and some of it consisted of grain first shipped from the West via the Racine and Mississippi road.[32] By 1860 fully 75 per cent of the wheat and flour received at Chicago came via rail. But in the next stage of movement in the grain trade—that of shipping the goods to the East—the railroad's role was not of critical importance. Only a small fraction of exports left by rail.

Shipments of wheat and flour from Chicago in 1860 represented about 70 per cent of the Illinois wheat crop of 1859. Exports

---

[31] Chicago, Burlington and Quincy Railroad, *5 AR, 1859, 6 AR, 1860, 7 AR, 1861*; Milwaukee & Prairie du Chien Railroad, *1 AR, 1861*.

[32] *5 AR, Commerce of Chicago, 1856,* 20, *6 AR, 1857,* 34-35, *7 AR, 1858,* 11-12; Wright, *Chicago,* 52-53.

via rail accounted for but a minute part of the total and included mostly small lots of flour consigned to various way stations.[33] In 1858 only 721,000 bushels of wheat and flour, 65 per cent representing flour, were exported via rail out of total exports of 11.3 million bushels. The remainder left Chicago by Lake Michigan. Between 1853 and 1858, of the 42 million bushels of corn shipped from the city, more than 90 per cent went via the lake. An even larger proportion of shipments of oats utilized the lake route.[34]

The economics of transportation determined that, through railroads notwithstanding, the lake route to the East retain its overwhelming predominance as the major avenue to market for grain. It was too expensive to ship bulk wheat to the East Coast via rail. Lake freight rates per bushel of wheat experienced a definite reduction from Chicago to Buffalo and Oswego between 1854 and 1858. In 1854 the rates on wheat to Buffalo ranged from 11 to 15 cents per bushel and to Oswego from 16 to 20 cents. By 1858 the rate to the former market was generally between 4 and 6 cents, while to the latter the prevailing rate was from 6 to 7 cents. Rates remained in this range through 1860.[35] From Buffalo to New York, the toll on a bushel of wheat declined from 6.4 cents in 1857 to 4.1 cents in 1848, while freight charges remained at 4 cents during the latter half of the decade.[36] From Chicago to New York, then, the tariff on a bushel of wheat routed over the lakes and through the Erie Canal was between 8 and 10 cents compared with 17 to 24 cents in 1854. From Chicago to New York via rail the shipper paid between 34 and 38 cents per bushel during the late 1850's.[37]

By the end of the decade the difference in freight rates on grain from Chicago to Buffalo, and from ports on Lake Erie to

[33] William Brass, *The Railroads, History, and Commerce of Chicago* (Chicago, 1854), 58.

[34] The Michigan Central carried 36 per cent of the exports, all flour, and the Michigan Southern carried 20 per cent. 3 *AR, Commerce of Chicago, 1855,* 9, 7 *AR, 1858,* 11-14.

[35] *Ibid.,* 37; George G. Tunnell, "Report to the Bureau of Statistics on Lake Commerce," *House Documents,* 55 Cong., 2 Sess., No. 277 (1898), Serial 3679, 28.

[36] In an unsuccessful effort to meet railroad competition, canal tolls on flour were reduced from 22.9 cents to 14.9 cents. Freight charges also declined from between 25 and 30 cents per barrel in 1850-54 to about 23 cents in 1857 and 19 to 20 cents in 1858. *Hunt's,* XXXIX (July, 1858), 123.

[37] Tunnell, "Report on Lake Commerce," 28. Since wheat was the most valuable grain in proportion to its bulk, the rail-lake differential completely precluded significant rail shipments of corn and, more particularly, of oats.

Buffalo, seems to have been negligible, even though the water distance was at least three times as great from Chicago. The traveler Hugh S. Tremenheere noted that the cost of transporting a barrel of flour from Chicago or Milwaukee to Buffalo was only a few cents more per barrel than from Cleveland. In 1851 freight from Detroit to New York via the Erie Canal cost 80 cents per barrel, while in 1855 it was 86 cents from Chicago over the same route. From Detroit to New York, freight rates per bushel of wheat were reported between 8 and 10 cents in 1857, the same as from Chicago.[38] This rate equality, in addition to the lower cost of production in Illinois and Wisconsin, gave farmers in those states a competitive advantage over farmers in Ohio and Michigan in supplying the eastern market, which was soon to work in a similar way to the advantage of farmers in the trans-Mississippi West.

The enormous stores of grain accumulated in Chicago during the winter months kept a large fleet active when navigation opened up in the spring. Before the Civil War, most of the grain was moved in sailing vessels, even though there was a rapid growth in the numbers and tonnage of lake steamers. Vessels of all types—barks, brigs, schooners, and steamers of both paddle and propeller variety—carried the grain down the lakes. During the 1850's three-masted schooners capable of carrying some 16,000 bushels of grain, assisted by smaller schooners with a capacity of 11,000 to 15,000 bushels, moved most of the grain to the East. The tonnage of lake shipping increased from 212,000 in 1851 to 400,000 tons in 1860.[39] The increased efficiency in handling grain at both ends of the lakes made each ton of shipping more valuable in 1860 than 1850, since the saving of time in loading and unloading grain had made it possible for a single vessel to make a larger number of trips. In the early 1840's it required some six to nine days to unload a vessel carrying 15,000 bushels, while in 1860 this task was accomplished in two or three hours.

---

[38] Hugh S. Tremenheere, *Notes on Public Subjects, Made During a Tour in the United States and in Canada* (London, 1852), 77; *ARJ*, XXIV (January 4, 1851), 16; *Hunt's*, XXXV (August, 1856), 155-156; Robert Russell, *North America. Its Agriculture and Climate* (Edinburgh, 1857), 130.

[39] Tremenheere, *Notes Made During a Tour*, 77; Chicago *Daily Tribune*, February 23, 1854; Ralph G. Plumb, "Lake Michigan Navigation in the 1850's," *Inland Seas*, VII (Winter, 1951), 231; Andrews, "Reports on Trade and Commerce," 49; United States Treasury Department, *Statistics of the Foreign and Domestic Commerce of the United States* (Washington, D.C., 1864), 144.

In the late 1850's, as in previous years, the great bulk of Chicago's grain and flour exports was consigned to either Buffalo or
Oswego. Of total wheat exports equaling 18.7 million bushels in
1857-58, 9.5 million bushels went to Buffalo, while 5.3 million bushels were directed to Oswego. Another 1.8 million bushels were consigned to Montreal and Kingston, the latter port, at the head of
the St. Lawrence, receiving 67 per cent of this quantity. At Kingston the grain could be directed on down the St. Lawrence, or, if
manufactured into flour, shipped to Cape Vincent and its rail connections with New England. In 1858 some 1.7 million bushels of
wheat were consigned directly to European markets. Direct shipments of this type occurred with increasing regularity after 1855.[40]

The mode of shipment and the points of destination for flour
were quite unlike those for bulk wheat. Some 20 per cent of total
exports of flour went east over the Michigan Central and Michigan
Southern railroads. Virtually none of Chicago's flour was consigned
to Oswego, since it was primarily a terminus for bulk wheat and
a flour-manufacturing center. Some 256,000 barrels of flour of the
730,000 exported from Chicago in 1857 and 1858 were forwarded
to Buffalo. The remainder of the flour was sent to Ogdensburg,
Montreal, and Collingswood, Canada; the latter market was the
eastern port of call for a line of propellers established at Chicago
in 1858.[41]

The method of conveyance and the destination of corn exports
from Chicago was similar to that of wheat, since the conditions of
shipment for bulk grain controlled them both. Of the 46.4 million
bushels of corn shipped during the six years 1853-58, over 90 per
cent went out on lake vessels. In 1850 and 1851 a total of 5.3 million bushels of corn were consigned to Buffalo, and in 1857-58, out
of exports totaling 14.1 million bushels, 8.1 million went to Buffalo,
while 3.6 million were forwarded to Oswego. The remainder went
to Ogdensburg and various Canadian ports. More than 80 per cent
of the oats shipped were consigned to the Erie Canal port.[42]

Chicago and Buffalo, during the 1850's, were the dominant

---

40 *6 AR, Commerce of Chicago, 1857,* 8; *7 AR, 1858,* 9; United States
Treasury Department, *Commerce and Navigation. Annual Report. 1858* (Washington, D.C., 1858), 349-351; Russell, *North America,* 108.

41 *6 AR, Commerce of Chicago, 1857,* 12, *7 AR, 1858,* 7, 9, 36.

42 Elbert J. Benton, *The Wabash Trade Route in the Development of the
Old Northwest* (Baltimore, 1903), 103, fn. 52; *6 AR, Commerce of Chicago,
1857,* 9, *7 AR, 1858,* 14-15.

factors in their respective grain trades. More than half of Chicago's exports of wheat and corn went to Buffalo, while more than 50 per cent of the wheat and 65 per cent of the corn entering Buffalo's harbor came from Chicago. At Oswego a similar dependence upon Chicago prevailed. Chicago shipped about 30 per cent of its wheat to the Lake Ontario port and some 45 per cent of Oswego's wheat imports originated at Chicago. Twenty-five per cent of Chicago's corn was consigned to Oswego. This was equivalent to 75 per cent of total receipts at that terminus.

The trade in grain at Buffalo and Oswego followed a pattern dictated by the generally rising volume of shipments from ports on Lake Erie and Lake Michigan. Static or declining shipment of cereals from Cleveland, Sandusky, and Detroit were more than compensated for by the swelling grain exports of Chicago, Toledo, and Milwaukee. As Table 25 indicates, Buffalo's preeminence in

TABLE 25. TOTAL ANNUAL RECEIPTS OF WHEAT, FLOUR, AND CORN AT BUFFALO AND OSWEGO, 1853-60 (IN THOUSANDS)

	Buffalo			Oswego		
Year	Wheat (bu.)	Flour (bbl.)	Corn (bu.)	Wheat (bu.)	Flour (bbl.)	Corn (bu.)
1853	5,420	976	8,066	4,354	391	–
1854	3,511	740	10,109	2,492	167	2,632
1855	8,022	937	9,711	5,366	225	2,861
1856	8,466	1,126	9,633	8,382	203	3,589
1857	8,334	846	5,714	5,383	101	2,004
1858	10,672	1,536	6,622	6,595	97	2,914
1859	9,235	1,420	3,114	4,875	65	807
1860	18,502	1,122	11,386	9,652	121	5,019

Sources: Treasury Dept., *Statistics of Foreign and Domestic Commerce*, 161, 177-178; ARJ, XXVII (January 21, 1854), 43; *Hunt's*, XXXVIII (April, 1858), 475, XL (May, 1859), 547-549.

terms of Oswego, its major competitor, was more solidly based in 1860 than in 1853.

Oswego's relative position as a receiving center for northwestern grain declined over the decade while Buffalo's position remained the same. In both 1853 and 1860 Buffalo received 50 per cent of total lake exports. Oswego's share, 30 per cent in 1853, had declined to 20.6 per cent by 1860. A partial explanation is found in the superior facilities, financial and otherwise, available at Buffalo. A rising proportion of the flour received at Buffalo and Oswego traveled to tidewater by rail instead of by canal in the 1850's. Buffalo was the western terminus of both the New York Central and the Western railroads. More handling was required to ship flour to Oswego and then by rail to the East than was required to ship to Buffalo, or to Dunkirk, the western terminus of the New York and Erie road. The consequence was a decline in flour receipts at Oswego, from 1853 to 1860, equivalent to a loss of 1.3 million bushels of wheat. The rise of receiving centers like Dunkirk operated to prevent Oswego's grain trade from keeping pace with the growth of the total grain trade of the Great Lakes, as well as to keep Buffalo's trade from doing more than advance at a similar rate. While receipts at Oswego advanced but slightly after 1856, from 9.3 million bushels of wheat and flour to 10.2 million in 1860, receipts at other receiving centers, not including Buffalo, rose from 11.5 million bushels to 14.7 million.[43]

By 1852 the beginning of what was to become a significant diversion of traffic from the Erie Canal was having its first repercussions. In that year a decrease in shipments of flour from Buffalo via the Erie Canal was attributed to the competition of the Buffalo and Rochester Railroad, later a part of the Central system. The following year, although the newly formed New York Central and the New York and Erie lines carried less than 10 per cent of the eastbound tonnage carried by the canal, the Central transported almost 200,000 barrels of flour from Buffalo. More was offered to the road but a lack of cars prevented its acceptance. Other roads carried some 100,000 barrels. This accounts for the decline in Buffalo's flour shipments via canal from 959,000 in 1852 to 658,000 in 1853.[44]

The total tonnage carried by the New York Central and the Erie roads increased steadily after 1853. In 1854 the two railroads carried 31 per cent as much tonnage as that moved by the Erie Canal. In 1865 it was over 70 per cent, and by 1870 railroad tonnage surpassed that of the canal. The canal, however, remained a significant factor in the trade with the West.

---

[43] These centers included Rochester, Dunkirk, Suspension Bridge, Ogdensburg, Cape Vincent, and Montreal. Treasury Dept., *Statistics of Foreign and Domestic Commerce*, 177-178.

[44] *Hunt's*, XXVIII (March, 1853), 311, XXX (March, 1854), 311-314, XLII (January, 1860), 118; Henry V. Poor, *Sketch of the Rise and Progress of the Internal Improvements and of the Internal Commerce of the United States* . . . (New York, 1881), xxii.

Over the seven-year span, each route increased the tonnage carried, but the course of the Erie Canal traffic was generally downward for four of the seven years. Each route also added to the volume of vegetable foods transported, but only with the canal was there a rise in the proportion of vegetable foods carried relative to total tonnage. This reflected the differing components, within the general classification of vegetable food, which each carrier moved. The canal lost most of the flour traffic to the railroads while it retained bulk grain. In the year ending September 30, 1856, the New York Central road carried 1.9 million barrels of flour, all but 482,000 being carried during the season of canal navigation. During the same year, the canal transported only 76,476 barrels of flour. But of 8.3 million bushels of wheat received at Buffalo in 1857, 6.6 million were shipped over the canal while only 727,000 traveled over the Central and the Erie rail lines.[45] This type of freight was a new feature in the rail traffic up to that time, and it prompted the construction at Buffalo by the New York Central of a large grain elevator, equipped with automatic machinery capable of unloading a lake vessel and loading a train of grain cars in less time than one car could be loaded manually.[46] By 1861 the Erie Canal was carrying only about 10 per cent of the flour shipped east from Buffalo, but it completely dominated the traffic in bulk grain, shipments of wheat rising from 13.9 million bushels in 1860 to 23.7 million in 1861, and to 27.7 million in the next year. Corn traffic rose from 10.3 million in 1860 to 22.4 million in 1862. The railroads made scarcely a dent in this traffic.

The Central dominated the flour traffic from Buffalo, and as Table 26 indicates had surpassed the New York and Erie Railroad in total tonnage by 1857. A good part of the flour carried by the Central was consigned to it directly from the West, and some of this arrived over the Michigan Central–Canada Western route. The larger portion of western flour consigned to the Central arrived via lake vessels, some of which the railroad employed to maintain connections with up-lake ports.

Freight classified as animal products was an essential part of the traffic of both the Central and the Erie lines. From 1854 to 1861

[45] *Hunt's*, XXXVII (September, 1857), 375, XXXVIII (June, 1858), 704; *ARJ*, XXXI (May 1, 1858), 283.

[46] Solon Robinson, ed., *Facts for Farmers; also for the Family Circle* . . . (2 vols., New York, 1865), II, 696.

this category composed between 19 and 24 per cent of the total tonnage carried by the Central, and about the same for the Erie railroad. Vegetable and animal products composed almost one-half of total tonnage, the bulk of which was carried eastward. Before 1853 most of the provisions were shipped via canal while the live-

TABLE 26. TOTAL TONNAGE AND TOTAL VEGETABLE TONNAGE CARRIED BY THE ERIE CANAL AND THE NEW YORK CENTRAL AND NEW YORK AND ERIE RAILROADS, 1854-60 (IN THOUSANDS OF TONS)

Year	Erie Canal		New York Central		New York and Erie	
	Total	Vegetable[a]	Total	Vegetable	Total	Vegetable
1854	4,166	997	550	156	743	136
1855	4,023	993	670	245	842	156
1856	4,116	1,154	933	283	983	170
1857	3,344	551	1,076	276	978	146
1858	3,665	898	926	302	817	178
1859	3,782	1,781	1,088	250	869	170
1860	4,650	1,659	1,366	343	1,140	202

[a] This category includes all grains, meal, flour, and vegetables.
Sources: Poore, *Internal Improvements and Internal Commerce of the United States*, xlii-xlvi; *Reports of the President and Superintendent of the New York and Erie Railroad, 1855* (New York, 1855), 91, 100; New York Central Railroad Company, *Annual Reports, 1854-61* (Albany, 1854-61).

stock went via railroad throughout the 1850's. In 1853 Buffalo received some 172,000 barrels of pork and beef and shipped 135,000 over the Erie Canal. The remainder was probably shipped by rail. Thereafter, to 1860, while receipts at Buffalo failed to increase, the tonnage of animal products carried by the Central almost doubled. In 1856, of over 60,000 barrels of pork received at Buffalo, 28,000 cleared on the canal, and in the next year, with receipts unchanged, canal shipments dropped to 9,000 barrels.[47]

Both the Erie Canal and the eastern railroads, then, performed in quite separate and distinctive ways essential functions in the grain and provisions traffic of the East North Central states. At Buffalo the trade was shared by the two transportation systems. The canal retained the bulk grain which the railroads could not carry as cheaply. The railroads monopolized the freight provided by flour, provisions, and livestock, where higher rates were eco-

[47] New York Central Railroad Company, *Annual Reports, 1854-61* (Albany, 1854-61); Poore, *Internal Improvements and Internal Commerce of the United States*, xlii; Treasury Dept., *Statistics of Foreign and Domestic Commerce*, 162; *Hunt's*, XXX (March, 1854), 321, XXXVIII (June, 1858), 704.

nomically justified either by the higher value of the commodity in proportion to its bulk or by the perishability of the product, which could be minimized by rail shipment. The railroads actively sought the flour trade and were successful in taking the larger part of it from the canal, just as in the early and mid-1840's the Western Railroad from Boston to Albany diverted a portion of the flour previously passing down the Hudson River. In 1851 the various railroads between Buffalo and Albany reduced the freight on flour from $1 to 60 cents per barrel, just 7 cents more than tolls and freight together on the canal. Thereafter, the railroads cut their rates to levels comparable to the tolls alone on the water route. This narrowed the freight differential sufficiently to loosen the canal's prior hold on flour. Consequently, flour was carried by rail in both summer and winter months. More than 70 per cent of the Central's flour and 50 per cent of the New York and Erie's flour was transported during the season of canal operation.[48]

Railroad connections between Oswego and the main rail lines to the East effected a diversion of flour from the canal, but to a lesser degree than at Buffalo. During the late 1850's about one-half of the flour leaving Oswego took the canal route, as did all the wheat and corn. It is entirely likely that some of the flour was transferred from canal to railroad at Syracuse. At Dunkirk, the grain trade from the beginning was dependent upon its position as the lake terminal of the Erie Railroad. By 1857, of the 354,000 barrels shipped east from Dunkirk, 30 per cent had arrived via rail, and of the 145,000 hogs received, 134,000 came by rail.[49] At Ogdensburg, Cape Vincent, and Suspension Bridge, the trade was based on railroad connections with Canada, New England, and the New York railroads. At Suspension Bridge, located a few miles below Niagara Falls, the International Railroad Suspension Bridge connected the Great Western Railroad of Canada with both the New York Central and a branch of the New York and Erie diverging from the main line at Elmira. A line also connected with Buffalo. At this point, flour receipts, at 304,000 barrels in 1856, reached 650,000 in 1860, and 875,000 barrels two years later. This impor-

---

[48] *Ibid.*, XXV (December, 1851), 762, XXXVII (September, 1857), 375, XXXIX (July, 1858), 123; *ARJ*, XXVI (April 16, 1853), 242; *Reports of the President and Superintendent of the New York and Erie Railroad, 1855* (New York, 1855), 91, 100.

[49] *Hunt's*, XXXVII (July, 1857), 39, XXXVIII (March, 1858), 356, XL (May, 1859), 547.

tant railhead also received more than 1.5 million bushels of oats, rye, and barley in each year from 1856 to 1862. Some of the flour probably originated on the Michigan Central Railroad, connecting with the Great Western at Detroit, since it is known that 35 per cent of the flour shipped from Detroit went via the Great Western.[50] This was an important instance of the use of through railroad connections in conducting the grain trade.

SUMMARY

In the 1850's the impact of railroads, both on the grain trade and on the general development of the East North Central states, particularly Illinois and Wisconsin, was unmistakable. No factor stands out more prominently in explaining the growth of large sections of these two states and the rapid advance in grain receipts and exports at Milwaukee and Chicago. Areas hitherto isolated were brought into contact with large markets. The Rock River counties of Illinois and the counties in the Lake Winnebago region of Wisconsin were of little consequence in the commerce of their states until the railroads provided them with access to markets on Lake Michigan. There was a close correlation between the time of greatest activity in the foodstuffs trade at Milwaukee and Chicago and the years of most energetic railroad construction in the period prior to the Civil War.

By 1860 Milwaukee was completely dependent upon the railroads for her grain supply, as was Racine. Chicago was slightly less so, as the Illinois and Michigan Canal continued to furnish greater quantities of corn than any of the railroads. But in the wheat, flour, and provisions traffic the canal was only a minor factor. Railroads not only permitted Chicago and Milwaukee to exploit the natural and agricultural resources of their states, but promoted a vigorous economic competition between the two grain centers. Railroads based at Milwaukee and Racine crossed into Illinois, while Chicago pushed her roads into the very rear of those Wisconsin towns. Both Milwaukee and Chicago displayed a keen interest in securing rail connections with the trans-Mississippi region. Both cities derived substantial quantities of grain from rail-

---

[50] Treasury Dept., *Statistics of Foreign and Domestic Commerce*, 177-178; *Hunt's*, XXXV (November, 1856), 566, XXXVIII (May, 1858), XL (May, 1859), 601, XLII (April, 1860), 428-429.

heads on the Mississippi River, where grain produced in Iowa and Minnesota, some of which had flowed to St. Louis in the past, was intercepted and carried to Lake Michigan ports.

During the decade, then, railroads came to dominate the first stage of the domestic grain trade of the East North Central states. This involved carrying farm commodities from the centers of production to secondary markets like Milwaukee and Chicago, where the goods were forwarded to the East. Exceptions would include the share of the corn traffic retained by the Illinois and Michigan Canal and the Wabash and Erie Canal at Toledo. At the same time, the railroads were dependent upon agricultural goods for the bulk of their east-bound freight. In this first stage, the railroads were instrumental in subverting the position of the river complex as a prominent factor in the grain trade of the Northwest.

In the second stage of the movement of foodstuffs from producer to consumer, the lake route continued to dominate. Hardly any grain utilized through rail routes to the East, as rail transportation could not compete with the low freight rates prevailing on the lakes in the 1850's. Most of the flour was shipped over the lakes also. At Detroit, however, the first substantial indications of a through flour trade were perceptible. And some of the flour which arrived at Dunkirk came via rail from the Lake Erie shore of Ohio. Throughout the Northwest an increasing volume of livestock and provisions sought all-rail connections with the East Coast.

In the third stage of the traffic, the arrival of foodstuffs at the various receiving centers at the eastern end of the lakes again brought the railroads into active operation. At certain receiving ports such as Dunkirk, Ogdensburg, and Suspension Bridge, rail connections were the only routes available to the East, and for this reason increasing quantities of flour sought those ports. The traffic in bulk grain was slight at these railheads. Virtually all of the wheat and corn was carried to tidewater, as in the past, on the Erie Canal. In spite of the competition of other receiving ports, Buffalo retained its preeminence in the lake grain trade, while Oswego lost ground. At both ports the railroads were active and successful competitors for the flour and provisions trade. The canal retained its significance due to its ability to carry bulk grain more economically than railroads and due to its greater capacity for handling the increasing shipments of bulk grain pouring from the East North Central states.

Railroads in the short space of six or seven years became essential factors in the first and last stages of the grain trade, while signs of their potential usefulness in the intermediate stage were apparent at Detroit, and perhaps even more obviously along the rail lines connecting Cincinnati with the Baltimore and Ohio Railroad.

Dominant in most aspects of the first stage, expanding their role in the second, and crucial in certain phases of the third stage, the railroads, during the 1850's, became of controlling importance, on local, sectional, and intersectional levels, in the development of the grain trade throughout the entire area of the East North Central states.

BIBLIOGRAPHY

Primary Sources

FEDERAL, STATE, AND LOCAL PUBLICATIONS AND DOCUMENTS

FEDERAL

Albert Gallatin. "Report on Roads and Canals, Communicated to the Senate, April 6, 1808." *American State Papers*, vol. 37, *Miscellaneous*, I, 724-921.

Secretary of the Treasury. "The Amount and Description of Merchandise Exported to, and Imported from the British American Colonies." *House State Papers.* 19 Congress. 2 Session. Document 144 (1826-27). Serial 155.

"Papers Relating to Trade with the British Colonies." *Senate Documents.* 21 Congress. 2 Session. Document 20 (1831). Serial 203.

"The Annual Amount of Trade and Commerce on the Upper Mississippi River, 1844." *Senate Executive Documents.* 28 Congress. 1 Session. No. 242 (1844). Serial 434.

"Statistics of the Agriculture and Manufactures, Domestic Trade, Currency, and Banks of the United States." *Senate Documents.* 28 Congress. 2 Session. Document 21 (1844). Serial 450.

Israel D. Andrews. "Reports on the Trade and Commerce of the British North American Colonies and upon the Trade of the Great Lakes and Rivers." *House Executive Documents.* 32 Congress. 2 Session. Document 136 (1853). Serial 622.

"Report of the Secretary of Treasury, 1855." *House Executive Documents.* 34 Congress. 1 Session. No. 10 (1856). Serial 846.

"Improvement of the Navigation of the Northern and Northwestern Lakes, etc." *House Reports.* 34 Congress. 1 Session. No. 316 (1856). Serial 870.

House Executive Documents. 35 Congress. 1 Session. No. 2 (1856). Serial 943.

United States Treasury Department. *Statistics of the Foreign and Domestic Commerce of the United States.* Washington, D.C. Government Printing Office. 1864.

Charles H. Evans. "Exports, Domestic and Foreign, from the American Colonies to Great Britain, from 1697 to 1789, Inclusive. Exports, Domestic and Foreign, from the United States to All Countries, from 1789 to 1883, Inclusive." *House Miscellaneous Documents.* 48 Congress. 1 Session. No. 49. Part 2 (1884). Serial 2236.

W. F. Switzler. "Report on the Internal Commerce of the United States." *House Executive Documents.* 50 Congress. 1 Session. No. 6. Part 2 (1888). Serial 2552.

George G. Tunell. "Report to the Bureau of Statistics on Lake Commerce." *House Documents.* 55 Congress. 2 Session. No. 277 (1898). Serial 3679.

Isaac M. Rubinow. *Russian Wheat and Wheat Flour in European Markets* (U.S. Department of Agriculture, *Bulletin 66*). Washington, D.C. United States Department of Agriculture, Bureau of Statistics. 1908.

American State Papers: Documents, Legislative and Executive. 38 vols. Washington, D.C. 1832-61.

Annals of Congress. 11 Congress. 2 Session. 1809-10.

Bureau of the Census. *Historical Statistics of the United States. Colonial Times to 1957.* Washington, D.C. Government Printing Office, 1960.

Federal Census. 1840-1900.

United States Commissioner of Patents. *Annual Reports on Agriculture.* Washington, D.C. 1840-60.

Reports of the Topographical Bureau. 1840-60.

United States Treasury Department. *Commerce and Navigation. Annual Reports.* Washington, D.C. 1821-60.

STATE

Transactions of the Department of Agriculture of the State of Illinois with

Reports from County Agricultural Societies. 1853-1918 (vols. I-VIII entitled *Transactions of the Illinois State Agricultural Society*).

Indiana State Board of Agriculture. *Third-Fifth Annual Report, 1853-56.* Indianapolis. 1853-56.

Michigan Department of State. *Census and Statistics of the State of Michigan, May, 1854.* Lansing. 1854.

Ohio Commissioner of Statistics. *Third-Seventh Annual Report to the Governor of Ohio, 1859-63.* Columbus. 1860-64.

Ohio Secretary of State. *Annual Report to the Governor for the Year, 1871.* Columbus. 1872.

Ohio State Board of Agriculture. *Twelfth, Fourteenth Annual Report, 1857, 1859.* Columbus. 1858, 1860.

Transactions of the Wisconsin State Agricultural Society. 1851-60.

LOCAL

Third (1854)–Seventh (1858) Annual Review of the Trade and Commerce and of the Public and Private Improvements of the City of Chicago. Chicago. 1855-59.

Chicago Board of Trade. *Fourteenth (1871), Nineteenth (1876) Annual Report of the Trade and Commerce of Chicago.* Chicago. 1872, 1877.

Thirty-fourth Annual Report of the Cincinnati Chamber of Commerce and Merchants' Exchange for the Commercial Year Ending August 31, 1882. Cincinnati. 1882.

Milwaukee Chamber of Commerce. *Second, Fifth Annual Report for the Year 1859, 1862.* Milwaukee. 1860, 1863.

Fourth Annual Report of the Chamber of Commerce of the State of New York for the Year 1861-1862. New York. 1862.

St. Louis Merchants' Exchange. *Annual Statement of the Trade and Commerce of St. Louis, 1878.* St. Louis. 1879.

NEWSPAPERS AND PERIODICALS

NEWSPAPERS

Albany, N.Y. *The Cultivator.* 1834-44, 1853-60.

Baltimore, Maryland. *The American Farmer.* 1839.

Chicago *Daily Tribune.* 1849-54.

Chicago. *The Prairie Farmer.* 1859-60.

Cincinnati *Advertiser and Journal* (Cincinnati *Enquirer*, April, 1841). 1840-50.

Cleveland *Plain Dealer.* 1844-45.

Columbus, Ohio. *The Ohio Cultivator.* 1845-48.

Maumee City, Ohio. *Maumee River Times.* 1843-47.

New Orleans. *The Daily Picayune.* 1838-40, 1846, 1848, 1851.

New York *Tribune.* 1841-42.

Springfield, Illinois. *Sangamo Journal.* 1840-42.

St. Louis *Old School Democrat.* 1843-44.

PERIODICALS

Baltimore. *Niles Weekly Register.* 1811-49.

New Orleans. *De Bow's, the Commercial Review of the South and West.* 1846-60.

New York. *The American Annual Register.* 1825-33.

New York. *American Railroad Journal. Steam Navigation, Commerce, Mining, Manufactures.* 1831-59.

New York. *Fisher's National Magazine and Industrial Record.* 1845-46.

New York. *Hunt's Merchants' Magazine.* 1839-60.

RAILROAD REPORTS AND LITERATURE

George R. Baldwin. *Report Showing the Cost and Income of a Railroad as Surveyed from Toledo, Ohio, to Chicago, Illinois, Incorporated as the Buffalo and Mississippi Rail-Road.* Toledo. 1847.

Thirty-first (1857), Thirty-fourth (1860) Annual Report of the Baltimore & Ohio Railroad Company. Baltimore. 1857, 1860.

Chicago, Burlington and Quincy Railroad Company. *Annual Reports, 1855-61.* Chicago. 1855-61.

Report of the Directors of the Chicago, Burlington and Quincy Railroad Company, 1859-61. Chicago. 1859-61.

Chicago and North Western Railway Company. *Annual Reports, 1859-62.* Chicago. 1859-62.

Circular to the Bond and Stockholders of the Chicago and North Western Railway Company. New York. 1861.

Cleveland and Pittsburgh Railroad Company. *Annual Reports, 1853-57.* Cleveland. 1853-57.

Exhibit of the Condition and Prospects of the Cleveland and Pittsburgh Rail Road. Cleveland. 1850.

Report of the Directors of the Cleveland and Toledo Railroad Company, 1854, 1857, 1863. New York and Cleveland. 1854, 1857, 1863.

Documents Relating to the Organization of the Illinois Central Rail-Road Company. 2nd ed. New York. 1852.

The Illinois Central Railway: A Historical Sketch of the Undertaking. . . . London. 1855.

Illinois Central Railway. *Report to the Shareholders, June, 1858.* London. 1858.

Report of the Indianapolis & Cincinnati Railroad Company, 1859. Cincinnati. 1860.

First Annual Report of the Marietta & Cincinnati Railroad Company, 1850. Chillicothe. 1851.

Report of the Receiver of the La Crosse and Milwaukee Railroad to the Bondholders and Other Creditors . . . 1860, 1862. Milwaukee. 1861, 1863.

Fourth Annual Report of the Directors to the Stockholders of the Columbus and Xenia R.R. Company, 1853. Columbus, Ohio. 1854.

First (1856)–Sixth (1861) Joint Annual Report of the Directors to the Stockholders of the Little Miami and Columbus and Xenia Railroad Companies. Columbus and Cincinnati. 1857-62.

Michigan Central Railroad Company. *Fourth (1850)–Fourteenth (1860) Annual Report.* Boston. 1850-60.

Report of the Board of Directors of the Michigan Southern and Northern Indiana Rail-Road Companies, 1853, 1859, 1863. New York. 1853, 1859, 1863.

Eighth (1856)–Eleventh (1860) Annual Report of the Directors of the Milwaukee and Mississippi Rail Road Company. Milwaukee. 1857-60.

First Annual Report of the Milwaukee & Prairie du Chien Railway Company for 1861 [the old Milwaukee and Mississippi]. Milwaukee. 1862.

The New York Central Railroad Company. *Annual Reports, 1854-61.* Albany. 1854-61.

Report of the Directors of the New York and Erie Railroad Company, 1853. New York. 1853.

Reports of the President and Superintendent of the New York and Erie Railroad, 1855. New York. 1855.

The Ohio and Mississippi R.R. Its Vital Importance to the Prosperity of Cincinnati. Cincinnati. 1855.

Report to the President and Directors of the Ohio and Pennsylvania Rail-Road Company, 1848. Philadelphia. 1849.

Ohio and Pennsylvania Railroad. *Annual Report, 1850.* Pittsburgh. 1850.

Fourth (1860)–Fifth (1861) Annual Report of the Board of Directors of the Pittsburgh, Fort Wayne and Chicago Rail Road Company. Pittsburgh. 1861-62.

Statistics and Estimates Relative to the Pittsburgh and Steubenville Railroad. . . . New York. 1857.

Third Annual Report to the Trustees in Possession of the Racine and Mississippi Railroad, May, 1862. Racine, Wis. 1862.

Report to the Stock and Bond Holders of the Sandusky, Dayton and Cincinnati (Late Mad River and Lake Erie) Rail Road Company, 1860. Sandusky, Ohio. 1860.

First Annual Report of the Toledo and Wabash Railway Company to the Stockholders, 1859. Toledo. 1860.

CONTEMPORARY LITERATURE
REMINISCENCES AND MEMOIRS

Milo M. Quaife, ed. *An English Settler in Pioneer Wisconsin. The Letters of Edwin Bottomley, 1842-1850* (Wisconsin Historical Publications. Collections, XXV). Madison. Wisconsin State Historical Society. 1918.

Milo M. Quaife, ed. *Growing Up with Southern Illinois, 1820 to 1861, from the Memoirs of Daniel Harmon Brush.* Chicago. The Lakeside Press. 1944.

W. P. and Julia P. Cutler, eds. *Life, Journals and Correspondence of Reverend Manasseh Cutler.* 2 vols. Cincinnati. R. Clarke and Co., 1888.

Timothy Flint. *Recollections of the Last Ten Years.* Boston. Cummings, Hilliard, and Company. 1826.

Governor Thomas Ford. *A History of Illinois from Its Commencement as a State in 1818 to 1847.* Milo M. Quaife, ed. 2 vols. Chicago. The Lakeside Press. 1943.

H. S. Fulkerson. *Random Collections of Early Days in Mississippi.* Baton Rouge, La. Oldo Claitor. 1885.

William Cooper Howells. *Recollections of Life in Ohio from 1813 to 1840.* Cincinnati. The Robert Clarke Company. 1895.

Letters of William Pelham Written in 1825 and 1826. Reprinted in Harlow Lindley, ed. *Indiana as Seen by Early Travelers. A Collection of Reprints from Books of Travel, Letters and Diaries Prior to 1830* (Indiana Historical Collections, III). Indianapolis. Indiana Historical Commission. 1916.

William Renick. *Memoirs, Correspondence and Reminiscences.* Circleville, Ohio. Union-Herald Book and Job Printing House. 1880.

J. W. Spencer and J. M. D. Burrows. *The Early Days of Rock Island and Davenport.* Milo M. Quaife, ed. Chicago. The Lakeside Press. 1942.

TRAVEL LITERATURE

John M. Baker. *A View of the Commerce Between the United States and Rio De Janeiro, Brazil.* Washington, D.C. Office of the *Democratic Review.* 1838.

Duke Karl-Bernhard, Duke of Saxe-Weimar Eisenach. *Travels Through North America, During the Years 1825 and 1826.* 2 vols. in 1. Philadelphia. 1828.

Morris Birkbeck. *Letters from Illinois.* Philadelphia. M. Carey & Son. 1818.

Morris Birkbeck. *Notes on a Journey in America from the Coast of Virginia to the Territory of Illinois: With Proposals for the Establishment of a Colony of English, Accompanied by a Map Illustrating the Route.* Dublin. J. Ridgway. 1818.

William Cobbett. *A Year's Residence in America.* Boston. Small, Maynard & Co. 1824.

George Coggeshall. *Voyages to Various Parts of the World Made Between the Years 1799 and 1844.* New York. D. Appleton & Co. 1851.

Henry Bradshaw Fearon. *Sketches of America. A Narrative of a Journey of Five Thousand Miles Through the Eastern and Western States of America; with Remarks on Mr. Birkbeck's 'Notes' and 'Letters.'* 2nd ed. London. Longman, Hurst, Rees, Orme, and Brown. 1818.

Elias Pym Fordham. *Personal Narrative of Travels in Virginia, Maryland, Pennsylvania, Ohio, Indiana, Kentucky; and of a Residence in the Illinois Territory: 1817-1818.* Frederic Ogg, ed. Cleveland. The Arthur H. Clark Company. 1906.

[Charles Fenno Hoffman]. *A Winter in the West.* 2 vols. New York. Harper & Brothers. 1835.

James F. W. Johnston. *Notes on North America, Agricultural, Economical, and Social.* 2 vols. Boston. Charles C. Little and James Brown. 1851.

John Melish. *Travels in the United States of America, in the Years 1806 & 1807, and 1809, 1810, & 1811; Including an Account of Passages Betwixt America and Britain, and Travels Through Various Parts of Great Britain, Ireland, and Upper Canada.* 2 vols. Philadelphia. T. & G. Palmer. 1812.

William Oliver. *Eight Months in Illinois, with Information to Immigrants.* Newcastle-upon-Tyne. 1843. Chicago. Walter M. Hill. 1924.

Robert Russell. *North America. Its Agriculture and Climate, Containing Observations on the Agriculture and Climate of Canada, the United States, and the Island of Cuba.* Edinburgh. Adam and Charles Black. 1857.

Patrick Shirreff. *A Tour Through North America Together with a Comprehensive View of the Canadas and the United States as Adapted for Agricultural Emigration.* Edinburgh. Oliver and Boyd. 1835.

James Stuart. *Three Years in America.* 2 vols. 3rd ed. Edinburgh. Robert Cadell. 1833.

David Thomas. *Travels Through the Western Country in the Summer of 1816.* Auburn, N.Y. David Rumsey. 1819.

Reuben Gold Thwaites, ed. *Early Western Travels, 1748-1846.* 32 vols. Cleveland. The Arthur H. Clark Co. 1904-07.

Hugh Seymour Tremenheere. *Notes on Public Subjects, Made During a Tour in the United States and in Canada.* London. John Murray. 1852.

C. F. Volney. *View of the Climate and Soil of the United States of America to Which Are Annexed Some Accounts of Florida, the French Colony on the Scioto, Certain Canadian Colonies, and the Savages or Natives.* London. J. Johnson. 1804.

John Woods. *Two Years Residence in the Settlement on the English Prairie in the Illinois Country, United States. With an Account of Its Animal and Vegetable Productions, Agriculture, &c. &c. A Description of the Principal Towns, Villages, &c., &c. with the Habits and Customs of the Back-Woodsmen.* London. Longman, Hurst, Rees, Orme, and Brown. 1822.

GAZETTEERS AND EMIGRANT GUIDES

Lewis C. Beck. *A Gazetteer of the States of Illinois and Missouri Containing a General View of Each State—a General View of Their Counties—and a Particular Description of Their Towns, Villages, Rivers, &c. &c.* Albany, N.Y. C. R. and G. Webster. 1823.

[E. Chamberlain]. *The Indiana Gazetteer or Topographical Dictionary of the State of Indiana.* Indianapolis. E. Chamberlain. 1849.

Daniel S. Curtiss. *Western Portraiture, and Emigrants Guide: A Description of Wisconsin, Illinois, and Iowa; with Remarks on Minnesota and Other Territories.* New York. J. H. Holton. 1852.

Henry William Ellsworth. *Valley of the Upper Wabash, Indiana, with Hints on Its Agricultural Advantages: Plan of a Dwelling, Estimates of Cultivation, and Notices of Labor-Saving Machines.* New York. Pratt, Robinson, and Co. 1838.

Frederick Gerhard. *Illinois as It Is; Its History, Geography, Statistics, Agriculture.* Chicago. Keen & Lee. 1857.

John Gregory. *Industrial Resources of Wisconsin.* Milwaukee. Starr's Book and Job Printing Office. 1855.

John Knight. *The Emigrant's Best Instructor, or The Most Recent and Important Information Respecting the United States of America.* 2nd ed. London. M. Wilson. 1818.

Lippincott's New and Complete Gazetteer of the United States. Philadelphia. 1854.

[Samuel Augustus Mitchell]. *Illinois in 1837; a Sketch Descriptive of the Situation, Boundaries, Face of the Country. Prominent Districts, Prairies, Rivers, Minerals, Animals, Agricultural Products, Public Lands, Plans of Internal Improvement, Manufactures, &c. of the State of Illinois.* Philadelphia. S. Augustus Mitchell and Grigg & Elliot. 1837.

J. M. Peck. *A Gazetteer of Illinois in Three Parts: Containing a General View of the State; a General View of Each County; and a Particular Description of Each Town, Settlement, Stream, Prairie, Bottom, Bluff, etc.* Jacksonville, Illinois. J. M. Peck. 1834.

John Scott. *The Indiana Gazetteer or Topographical Dictionary* (1826). (Indiana Historical Society Publications, XVIII). Indianapolis. Indiana Historical Society. 1954.

URBAN LITERATURE

William Brass. *The Railroads, History, and Commerce of Chicago.* Chicago. 1854.

Charles Cist. *Cincinnati in 1841: Its Early Annals and Future Prospects.* Cincinnati. 1841.

Charles Cist. *The Cincinnati Miscellany, or Antiquities of the West: And*

Pioneer History and General Local Statistics Compiled for the Western General Advertiser from October 1, 1844 to April 1, 1846. 2 vols. Cincinnati. Robinson and Jones. 1845-46.

Neville B. Craig. *The History of Pittsburgh.* Pittsburgh. J. H. Mellor. 1851.

Benjamin Drake and E. D. Mansfield. *Cincinnati in 1826.* Cincinnati. 1827.

Daniel Drake. *Natural and Statistical View or Picture of Cincinnati and the Miami Country.* Cincinnati. Looker and Wallace. 1815.

Thomas S. Feron. *Philadelphia and Her Western Railroad Connections.* n.p. 1852.

John Hogan. *Thoughts About the City of St. Louis, Her Commerce and Manufactures, Railroads, &c.* St. Louis. Republican Steam Press Print. 1854.

E. D. Holton. "Commercial History of Milwaukee." *Collections of the State Historical Society of Wisconsin,* IV (1857-58), 258-289.

Julius P. Bolivar MacCabe. *Directory. Cleveland and Ohio City. For the Years 1837-1838.* Cleveland. Sandford & Lott Book and Job Printers. 1837.

George H. Thurston. *Pittsburgh as It Is; or, Facts and Figures, Exhibiting the Past and Present of Pittsburgh, Its Advantages, Resources, Manufactures, and Commerce.* Pittsburgh. W. S. Haven. 1857.

John S. Wright. *Chicago: Past, Present, Future. Relations to the Great Interior, and to the Continent.* 2nd ed. Chicago. Horton & Leonard. 1870.

GENERAL AND STATISTICAL

J. S. Buckingham. *America, Historical, Statistical, and Descriptive.* 3 vols. London. Fisher, Son & Co. 1841.

M[athew] Carey. *A View of the Ruinous Consequences of a Dependence on Foreign Markets for the Sale of the Great Staples of This Nation, Flour, Cotton, and Tobacco.* Philadelphia. M. Carey & Son. 1820.

Tench Coxe. *A View of the United States of America, in a Series of Papers, Written at Various Times Between the Years 1787 and 1794.* Philadelphia. William Hall. 1794.

James Hall. *Notes on the Western States: Containing Descriptive Sketches of Their Soil, Climate, Resources, and Scenery.* Philadelphia. Harrison Hall. 1838.

James Hall. *The West: Its Commerce and Navigation.* Cincinnati. H. W. Derby & Co. 1848.

David Macpherson. *Annals of Commerce, Manufactures, Fisheries, and Navigation with Brief Notices of the Arts and Sciences Connected with Them. Containing the Commercial Transactions of the British Empire and Other Countries from the Earliest Accounts to the Meet-*

ing of the Union Parliament in January, 1801. 4 vols. London. Nichols and Son. 1805.

J. R. M'Culloch. *A Dictionary, Practical, Theoretical, and Historical, of Commerce and Commercial Navigation.* Henry Vethake, ed. 2 vols. Philadelphia. Hart, Carey and Hart. 1852.

Jedidiah Morse. *The American Universal Geography; or A View of the Present State of all the Kingdoms, States, and Colonies in the Known World.* 2 vols. 7th ed. Charleston, S.C. Lincoln & Edmonds. 1819.

Timothy Pitkin. *A Statistical View of the Commerce of the United States of America: Its Connection with Agriculture and Manufactures and an Account of the Public Debt, Revenues, and Expenditures of the United States.* 2nd ed. New York. James Eastburn. 1817.

Solon Robinson, ed. *Facts for Farmers; also for the Family Circle. A Compost of Rich Materials for All Land-Owners. About Domestic Animals and Domestic Economy; Farm Buildings; Gardens, Orchards, and Vineyards; and All Farm Crops, Tools, Fences, Fertilization, Draining, and Irrigation.* 2 vols. New York. Johnson and Ward. 1865.

Ezra C. Seaman. *Essays on the Progress of Nations, in Civilization, Productive Industry, Wealth, and Population.* New York. Charles Scribner. 1852.

Thomas Tooke. *A History of Prices and of the State of the Circulation, from 1793 to 1837; Preceded by a Brief Sketch of the State of the Corn Trade in the Last Two Centuries.* 2 vols. London. Longman, Orme, Brown, Green, and Longmans. 1838.

D. B. Warden. *Statistical, Political, and Historical Account of the United States of North America: From the Period of Their First Colonization to the Present Day.* 3 vols. Edinburgh. Archibald Constable and Co. 1819.

Secondary Sources

GENERAL

Henry Adams. *History of the United States of America During the Administration of Thomas Jefferson.* 2 vols. in 1. New York. Albert and Charles Boné. 1930.

J. Leander Bishop. *A History of American Manufactures from 1608 to 1860: Exhibiting the Origin and Growth of the Principal Mechanic Arts and Manufactures, from the Earliest Colonial Period to the Adoption of the Constitution and Comprising Annals of the Industry of the United States in Machinery, Manufacturing and Useful Arts, with a Notice of the Important Inventions, Tariffs, and the Results of Each Decennial Census.* 2 vols. Philadelphia. Edward Young & Co. 1864.

Paul W. Gates. *The Farmer's Age: Agriculture 1815-1860* (The Economic History of the United States, III). New York. Holt, Rinehart and Winston. 1960.

Lewis Cecil Gray. *History of Agriculture in the Southern United States to 1860* (Carnegie Institution of Washington, *Publication 430*). 2 vols. New York. 1941.

Fred Mitchell Jones. *Middlemen in the Domestic Trade of the United States, 1800-1860* (Illinois Studies in the Social Sciences, XXI). Urbana. University of Illinois Press. 1937.

Edward C. Kirkland. *A History of American Economic Life*. 3rd ed. New York. Appleton-Century-Crofts, Inc. 1951.

Isaac Lippincott. *Internal Trade of the United States, 1700-1860* (Washington University Studies, IV, St. Louis). Chicago. University of Chicago Press. 1916.

Ulrich B. Phillips. *American Negro Slavery. A Survey of the Supply, Employment and Control of Negro Labor as Determined by the Plantation Regime*. New York. D. Appleton and Co. 1929.

Kenneth M. Stampp. *The Peculiar Institution. Slavery in the Ante-Bellum South*. New York. Alfred A. Knopf. 1956.

Arthur P. Whitaker. *The Spanish-American Frontier: 1783-1795. The Westward Movement and the Spanish Retreat in the Mississippi Valley*. Boston. Houghton Mifflin Co. 1927.

Arthur P. Whitaker. *The Mississippi Question, 1795-1803. A Study in Trade, Politics, and Diplomacy*. New York. D. Appleton-Century Co. 1934.

REGIONAL, STATE, AND LOCAL

Robert G. Albion. *The Rise of New York Port, 1815-1860*. New York. Charles Scribner's Sons. 1939.

Russell H. Anderson. "Advancing Across the Eastern Mississippi Valley." *Agricultural History*, XVII (April, 1943), 97-114.

Lewis E. Atherton. *The Pioneer Merchant in Mid-America* (University of Missouri Studies, XIV). Columbia. University of Missouri Press. 1939.

Wyatt W. Belcher. *The Economic Rivalry Between St. Louis and Chicago, 1850-1880* (Columbia University Studies in History, Economics, and Public Law, DXXIX). New York. Columbia University Press. 1947.

Thomas S. Berry. *Western Prices Before 1861. A Study of the Cincinnati Market* (Harvard Economic Studies, LXXIV). Cambridge, Mass. Harvard University Press. 1943.

Arthur C. Boggess. *The Settlement of Illinois, 1778-1830* (Chicago Historical Society Collections, V). Chicago. Chicago Historical Society. 1908.

James E. Boyle. *Speculation and the Chicago Board of Trade*. New York. The Macmillan Co. 1921.

R. Carlyle Buley. *The Old Northwest. Pioneer Period. 1815-1840*. 2 vols. Indianapolis. Indiana Historical Society. 1950.

Theodore L. Carlson. *The Illinois Military Tract. A Study of Land Occupation, Utilization and Tenure* (Illinois Studies in the Social Sciences, XXXII). Urbana. University of Illinois Press. 1951.

Logan Esarey. *A History of Indiana from Its Exploration to 1850.* Indianapolis. W. K. Stewart. 1915.

George N. Fuller. *Economic and Social Beginnings of Michigan. A Study of the Settlement of the Lower Peninsula During the Territorial Period, 1805-1837.* Lansing. Michigan Historical Commission. 1916.

W. Freeman Galpin. "The American Grain Trade to the Spanish Peninsula, 1810-1814." *American Historical Review,* XXVIII (October, 1922), 24-44.

W. Freeman Galpin. "The Grain Trade of New Orleans, 1804-1814." *Mississippi Valley Historical Review,* XIV (March, 1928), 496-507.

Henry Clyde Hubbart. *The Older Middle West. 1840-1880. Its Social, Economic, and Political Life and Sectional Tendencies Before, During, and After the Civil War.* New York. D. Appleton-Century Co. 1936.

A. L. Kohlmeier. *The Old Northwest as the Keystone of the Arch of the American Federal Union. A Study in Commerce and Politics.* Bloomington, Ind. The Principia Press, Inc. 1938.

Isaac Lippincott. *A History of Manufactures in the Ohio Valley to the Year 1860.* Chicago. University of Chicago Press. 1914.

Almon E. Parkins. *The Historical Geography of Detroit.* Lansing. Michigan Historical Commission. 1918.

Bessie Louise Pierce. *A History of Chicago.* 2 vols. New York. Alfred A. Knopf. 1937-40.

William V. Pooley. *The Settlement of Illinois from 1830 to 1850* (Bulletin of the University of Wisconsin History Series, I). Madison. University of Wisconsin Press. 1908.

Richard Lyle Power. *Planting Corn Belt Culture. The Impress of the Upland Southerner and Yankee in the Old Northwest* (Indiana Historical Society Publications, XVII). Indianapolis. Indiana Historical Society. 1953.

Harold Sinclair. *The Port of New Orleans.* New York. Doubleday, Doran & Co., Inc. 1942.

Richard C. Wade. *The Urban Frontier: The Rise of Western Cities, 1790-1830* (Harvard Historical Monographs, XLI). Cambridge, Mass. Harvard University Press. 1959.

R. B. Way. "The Commerce of the Lower Mississippi in the Period 1830-1860." *Mississippi Valley Historical Association Proceedings* (1918-19), 57-68.

Francis P. Weisenburger. *The Passing of the Frontier, 1825-1850* (History of the State of Ohio, III). Columbus. Ohio State Archeological and Historical Society. 1941.

FOREIGN COMMERCE

Donald G. Barnes. *A History of the English Corn Laws from 1660 to 1846.* New York. F. S. Crofts & Co. 1930.

Norman S. Buck. *The Development of the Organisation of the Anglo-American Trade, 1800-1850.* New Haven, Conn. Yale University Press. 1925.

D. G. Creighton. *The Commercial Empire of the St. Lawrence, 1760-1850.* Toronto. The Ryerson Press. 1937.

Chauncey M. Depew, ed. *One Hundred Years of American Commerce, 1795-1895.* 2 vols. New York. D. O. Haynes & Co. 1895.

Ralph H. Hidy. *The House of Baring in American Trade and Finance. English Merchants Bankers at Work, 1763-1861* (Harvard Studies in Business History, XIV). Cambridge, Mass. Harvard University Press. 1949.

H. A. Innis and A. R. M. Lower, eds. *Select Documents in Canadian Economic History, 1783-1885.* Toronto. University of Toronto Press. 1933.

Emory R. Johnson, T. W. Van Metre, G. G. Huebner, and D. S. Hanchett. *History of Domestic and Foreign Commerce of the United States.* 2 vols. Washington, D.C. Carnegie Institution of Washington. 1915.

Thomas P. Martin. "The Staff of Life in Diplomacy and Politics During the Early Eighteen Fifties." *Agricultural History,* XVIII (January, 1944), 1-15.

J. Fred Rippy. *Rivalry of the United States and Great Britain over Latin America (1818-1830).* Baltimore. The Johns Hopkins Press. 1929.

Henri Sée. "Commerce Between France and the United States, 1783-1784." *American Historical Review,* XXXI (July, 1926), 732-752.

Herbert J. Wunderlich. "Foreign Grain Trade of the United States, 1835-1860." *The Iowa Journal of History and Politics,* XXXIII (January, 1935), 27-76.

TRANSPORTATION

Hugh G. J. Aitken. *The Welland Canal Company. A Study in Canadian Enterprise.* Cambridge, Mass. Harvard University Press. 1954.

Leland D. Baldwin. *The Keelboat Age on Western Waters.* Pittsburgh. University of Pittsburgh Press. 1941.

Elbert Jay Benton. *The Wabash Trade Route in the Development of the Old Northwest* (Johns Hopkins University Studies in Historical and Political Science, Series XXI). Baltimore. The Johns Hopkins Press. 1903.

Rudolph A. Clemen. "Waterways in Livestock and Meat Trade." *American Economic Review,* XVI (December, 1926), 640-652.

James Croil. *Steam Navigation and Its Relation to the Commerce of Canada and the United States.* Toronto. William Briggs. 1898.

Frank H. Dixon. *A Traffic History of the Mississippi River System* (National Waterways Commission, *Document 11*). Washington, D.C. Government Printing Office. 1909.

Logan Esarey. *Internal Improvements in Early Indiana* (Indiana Historical Society Publications, V). Indianapolis. Indiana Historical Society. 1912.

Paul W. Gates. *The Illinois Central Railroad and Its Colonization Work.* Cambridge, Mass. Harvard University Press. 1934.

William F. Gephart. *Transportation and Industrial Development in the Middle West* (Columbia University Studies in History, Economics and Public Law, XXXIV). New York. Columbia University Press. 1909.

Carter Goodrich. *Government Promotion of American Canals and Railroads, 1800-1890.* New York. Columbia University Press. 1960.

E. W. Gould. *Fifty Years on the Mississippi; or Gould's History of River Navigation.* St. Louis. Nixon-Jones Printing Co. 1889.

Mildred L. Hartsough. *From Canoe to Steel Barge on the Upper Mississippi.* Minneapolis. University of Minnesota Press. 1934.

Harlan Hatcher. *Lake Erie.* Indianapolis. Bobbs-Merrill Co. 1945.

Walter Havighurst. *The Long Ships Passing. The Story of the Great Lakes.* New York. The Macmillan Co. 1942.

Arthur B. Hirsch. "The Construction of the Miami and Erie Canal." *Mississippi Valley Historical Association Proceedings* (1919-20), 349-362.

Archer B. Hulbert. *The Paths of Inland Commerce. A Chronicle of Trail, Road, and Waterway.* New Haven, Conn. Yale University Press. 1920.

Louis C. Hunter. *Steamboats on the Western Rivers. An Economic and Technological History.* Cambridge, Mass. Harvard University Press. 1949.

John H. Krenkel. *Illinois Internal Improvements, 1818-1848.* Cedar Rapids, Iowa. The Torch Press. 1958.

Charles T. Leavitt. "Transportation and the Livestock Industry of the Middle West to 1860." *Agricultural History,* VIII (January, 1934), 20-33.

Judson Fiske Lee. *Transportation as a Factor in the Development of Northern Illinois Previous to 1860* (University of Chicago Libraries reprint from the *Illinois State Historical Society Journal,* X). Chicago. 1917.

C. P. McClelland and C. C. Huntington. *History of the Ohio Canals. Their Construction, Cost, Use and Partial Abandonment.* Columbus. Ohio State Archeological and Historical Society. 1905.

B. Henry Meyer *et al. History of Transportation in the United States Before 1860.* Washington, D.C. Peter Smith. 1948.

Thomas D. Odle. "The American Grain Trade of the Great Lakes, 1825-1873." *Inland Seas*, VII (Winter, 1951), 237-245; IX (Spring, 1953), 52-58, 105-109, 162-168, 256-262.

Ralph G. Plumb. "Lake Michigan Navigation in the 1850's." *Inland Seas*, VII (Winter, 1951).

Henry V. Poor. *Sketch of the Rise and Progress of the Internal Improvements and of the Internal Commerce of the United States with a Review of the Charges of Monopoly and Oppression Made Against Railroad Corporations*. New York. H. V. and H. W. Poor. 1881.

James W. Putnam. *The Illinois and Michigan Canal. A Study in Economic History* (Chicago Historical Society Collections, X). Chicago. Chicago Historical Society. 1918.

Abraham H. Sadove. *Transport Improvement and the Appalachian Barrier. A Case Study in Economic Innovation*. Harvard University. Unpublished doctoral dissertation. 1950.

Paul B. Trescott. "The Louisville and Portland Canal Company, 1825-1874." *Mississippi Valley Historical Review*, XLIV (March, 1958), 686-708.

Noble E. Whitford. *History of the Canal Systems of the State of New York, Together with Brief Histories of the Canals of the United States and Canada* (*Supplement* to the *Annual Report of the State Engineer and Surveyor of the State of New York for 1905*). 2 vols. Albany. State Printer. 1906.

AGRICULTURE

C. R. Ball, C. E. Leighty, O. C. Strive, and O. E. Baker. "Wheat Production and Marketing." *United States Department of Agriculture Yearbook, 1921*. Washington, D.C. Government Printing Office. 1922.

Ernest Ludlow Bogart. *Economic History of American Agriculture*. New York. Longman, Green and Co. 1923.

Margaret B. Bogue. *Patterns from the Sod. Land Use and Tenure in the Grand Prairie, 1850-1900* (Illinois State Historical Society Collections, XXXIV). Springfield. Illinois State Historical Society. 1959.

Clarence H. Danhoff. "The Fencing Problem in the Eighteen-Fifties." *Agricultural History*, XVIII (October, 1944), 168-186.

Peter Tracy Dondlinger. *The Book of Wheat. An Economic History and Practical Manual of the Wheat Industry*. New York. Orange, Judd and Co. 1908.

W. C. Flagg. "The Agriculture of Illinois, 1683-1876." *Transactions of the Department of Agriculture of the State of Illinois, 1875*, new series, V (1876).

Herbert A. Kellar. "The Reaper as a Factor in the Development of Agriculture of Illinois, 1834-1865." Illinois State Historical Society *Transactions*, XXXIV (1927), 105-114.

Charles B. Kuhlman. *The Development of the Flour-Milling Industry in the United States with Special Reference to the Industry in Minneapolis*. Boston and New York. Houghton Mifflin Co. 1929.

W. A. Lloyd, J. I. Falconer, and C. E. Thorne. *The Agriculture of Ohio* (Ohio Agricultural Experiment Station, *Bulletin 326*). Wooster. 1918.

Arthur G. Peterson. "Futures Trading with Particular Reference to Agricultural Commodities." *Agricultural History*, VII (April, 1933), 68-80.

Leo Rogin. *The Introduction of Farm Machinery in Its Relation to the Productivity of Labor in the Agriculture of the United States During the Nineteenth Century* (University of California Publications in Economics, IX). Berkeley. University of California Press. 1931.

John Storck and Walter D. Teague. *Flour for Man's Bread. A History of Milling*. Minneapolis. University of Minnesota Press. 1952.

Earl S. Sparks. *History and Theory of Agricultural Credit in the United States*. New York. Thomas Y. Crowell Co. 1932.

John G. Thompson. *The Rise and Decline of the Wheat Growing Industry in Wisconsin* (Bulletin of the University of Wisconsin Economic and Political Science Series, V). Madison. University of Wisconsin Press. 1908.

INDEX

Acreage: in Ohio, in wheat and corn, 198-99, 240; in Ill., improved, 1850's, 202, in wheat, 1860, 203, effect of Ill. Central R.R. on wheat and corn, 259, improved in 12 Galena R.R. counties, 1850's, 261; in Wis., improved, 1850's, 206, 208, in wheat, 1856-60, 207; in Mich., 240

Agriculture: in economy of U.S., 172-73

Akron, Ohio: mentioned, 21; grain trade, 1830's-40's, 61, 62, 63

Alabama: grain deficiency, 215

Albany, N.Y.: rail connections, 54, 103

Alexandria, Va.: in West Indian grain trade, 181, 182

Alton, Ill.: in St. Louis grain trade, 27, 28, 158n28; packing industry, 145

Animal products. See Pork; Provisions

Arkansas, 47

Ashtabula, Ohio: mentioned, 54; trade undercut by Cleveland, 66, 67

Assumption, Ill.: effect of Ill. Central R.R., 258-59

305